THE SOUTH YORKSHIRE MOORS

THE SOUTH YORKSHIRE MOORS

by Christopher Goddard

commemorative plaque on Sheffield Town Hall

For the men and women who fought
for our right to enjoy these moors

Published by Gritstone Publishing Co-operative
Birchcliffe Centre, Hebden Bridge, West Yorkshire, HX7 8DG

www.gritstonepublishing.co.uk

Reprint of First Edition – 2019

Printed in Huddersfield by Had-Print

Text and images © Christopher Goddard 2019

The moral right of Christopher Goddard to be identified as
the author of this work has been asserted in accordance with
the Copyright Design and Patents Act of 1988.

ISBN 978-0-9955609-6-3

ACKNOWLEDGEMENTS

With thanks to everyone who helped make this book possible:

Rob Blake, Richard Carr, Terry Howard, Gill Corteen, Nick
Goddard, Roger Goddard, Bill Gordon, Paul Besley, Ian
Winterburn, my colleagues at Gritstone Publishing Co-
operative (Andrew Bibby, Andrew McCloy, Chiz Dakin and
Colin Speakman) as well as all the friendly and invaluable staff
at Sheffield Local Studies Library and Archives.

And most of all my wonderfully supportive partner, editor,
proof-reader and general sounding-board Caroline. x

THE SOUTH YORKSHIRE MOORS

CONTENTS

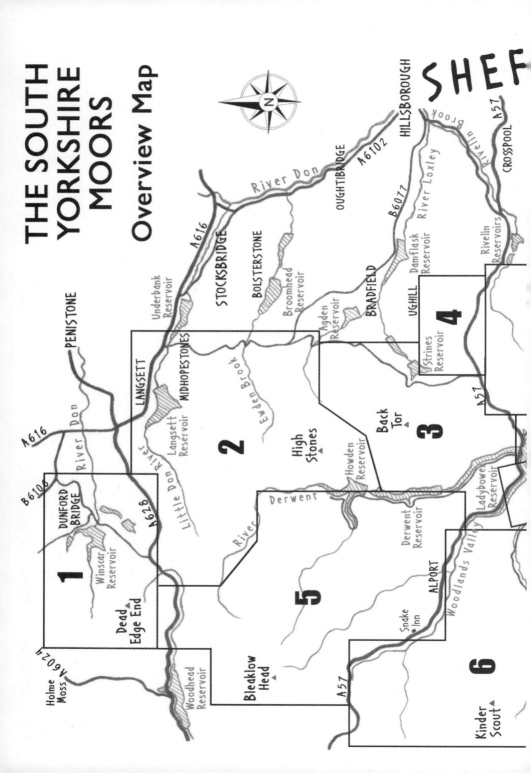

THE SOUTH YORKSHIRE MOORS

Overview Map

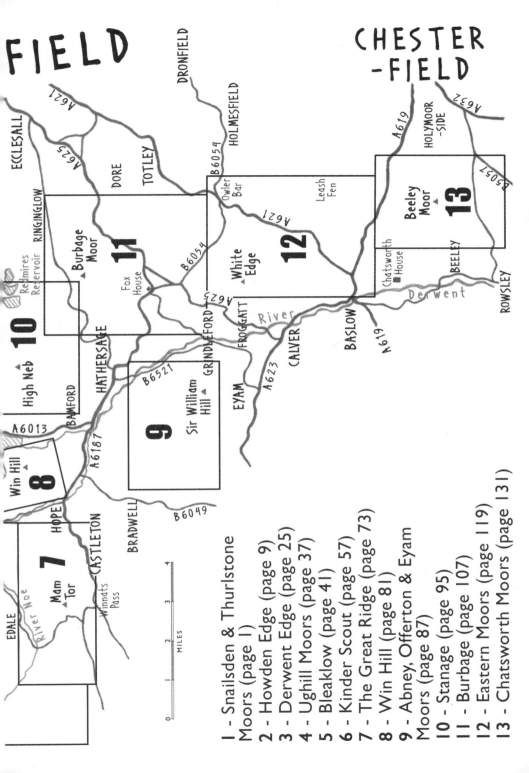

FIELD

CHESTER
-FIELD

THE SOUTH YORKSHIRE MOORS

*'Come to a place like this, shut your mouth and shut your mind and walk
on the moor, walk in the wind and the sun, and you will understand soon
enough that this world is a great animal, alive and breathing, that we walk
through it, we breathe with it, we are its breath'*
(Paul Kingsnorth, *Beast*)

I grew up on the edge of a city, but always thought that I had a very healthy
outdoor childhood. During the long summer holidays my brother and I made dens
in the woods, rode bikes in the plantation, made up names for the weaselling holes
of Wharncliffe Crags, and roamed across the hills towards Bradfield. On Sundays
Dad would drive us out to Strines, Langsett, Ladybower or Redmires and we'd hike
up onto the open moors for half the day, then come back for Sunday lunch. He told
us about the nesting birds we saw squawking angrily as we passed and about all the
trees we saw, and we'd forget it all by the following week. In summer we swam in
the streams and in winter we jumped in bunises (a term we made up for deep
pockets of snow that stayed long after the rest had melted). In late summer we
picked bilberries as Dad had done in his youth on Totley Moss – they had no car
then and relied on the train through Totley Tunnel and the bus to Fox House to
take them out for weekend jaunts on the moors.

I still can't stand urban places for long, but somehow Sheffield is different, for it
is fused onto the moors in a way no other major UK city is. It is a city built on
rough terrain – the name Hallam means 'bouldery ground' – and its moors once
stretched right down towards the centre of town. The Anglo-Saxon word *mor*
relates to a low-lying, uncultivated, and often peaty bog of the sort found in the
Low Countries, but came to be used more widely in Britain to describe the
similarly uncultivable upland landscape of the Pennines and the South West. It was
initially used for rough areas of common pasture on the edge of a settlement, from
which we get local names like Shalesmoor, Crookesmoor, Pitsmoor and The Moor
(originally an uncultivated pasture between Sheffield and Little Sheffield). But as the
city grew and this was steadily enclosed, it came to be used for the barren wastes
that lay beyond the walls. It is still there, right on the doorstep of the western
suburbs, so that you can walk straight out of Totley, Ringinglow, Lodge Moor and
Stocksbridge onto open moorland.

Even as it belched out black smoke and suffocated itself throughout the 19th
century, industrial Sheffield was described by John Ruskin as 'the dirty picture in
the golden frame'. The landscape may have been just as dirty – it is estimated that
at the height of the industrial era up to three tonnes of soot fell on every square
mile of northern England each day – yet the soot blended seamlessly with the black
peat that oozed thickly beneath the heather and cottongrass. As the gritstone
outcrops were darkened, so they gained stature as brooding walls that mirrored
the slate grey skies. On a winter day, you can be walking on the Dark Peak plateaus
at midday and be sure night is about to fall. Your step quickens as if something
primal is closing in and you need to get out before it is too late.

The Peak District National Park was created in 1951, confirming what locals
already knew about the area – that it is a special landscape worth protecting. The
boundary grazed the edge of the city and ran just a couple of miles from my
childhood home, sanctifying this playground and meaning we had to share it with

increasing numbers of visitors from further afield. But the moors' presence as a backdrop to the city is a source of its great pride to this day.

While we should be grateful for this beautiful wild landscape on our doorstep, we should be under no illusion about it. This landscape is not 'natural'. It has been managed by humans for centuries, even millennia, altered since Bronze Age man began cutting down trees on the high ground, cultivating the thin soil and accelerating the formation of the peat that dominates the landscape today. Since the 18th century the moors have become an artificial landscape, whose natural plant succession has been deliberately arrested to create favourable conditions for grouse shooting. Even the apparently unusable wastelands of Bleaklow and Kinder Scout have been subject to peat cutting on such a vast scale that it has changed the shape and vegetation of the hills. People often get het up about the eyesore of the huge cement works in the Hope Valley, not appreciating that the Peak District has long been more an industrial landscape than a rural one. It had the world's most profitable lead industry in the 17th century, a well-established reputation for quarried millstones until the 20th century, and places like Hathersage, Matlock and Cromford (home of Arkwright's famous cotton mill) were every bit as sooty during the Industrial Revolution as towns on the Yorkshire side of the hills. It turns out these apparently empty moors are anything but. While we may often be alone on the moors, the landscape all around us is etched with the lines of history and its many ghosts.

the Cakes of Bread on Derwent Edge

MY SOUTH YORKSHIRE MOORS

'Along the ridge ran a faint foot-track... those who knew it well called it a path'
(Thomas Hardy, *Return of the Native*)

I appreciate that at first glance the notion of the South Yorkshire Moors doesn't make obvious sense as the parameters for a moorland guide. It probably makes even less sense if you look closely at the map; while there is a fair hunk of moors at the north-west corner of the county around Dunford Bridge, Langsett and Bradfield, this quite quickly tapers to a narrow strip east of Stanage Edge and then is abruptly cut off beyond Burbage and Fox House. The county boundary with Derbyshire descends to Totley Brook and hems Sheffield in tightly to the south-west. It made even greater incursions into the city before the boundary was moved in the 1930s, before which Dore was the gateway to Derbyshire, with Burbage and Totley Moors on the other side of the county line. This boundary dates back to the ancient kingdoms of Mercia and Northumberland and was established only after several battles, raids and counter raids before England was united at the Dore Stone in 829. Like all boundaries, it could easily have ended up very differently.

For the purposes of this book, however, I am ignoring the county boundary and dealing only with the part of the Pennine gritstone moors on the east side of the nation's great watershed. The Derwent and its tributaries (the Noe, Ashop and Alport) flow east into the Trent and the North Sea, thus I see them as a natural extension of the Yorkshire side of the hills, while the River Etherow flowing down Longdendale and the River Goyt end up in the Mersey and the Irish Sea and so do not form part of this book. The boundary lines that are drawn on the map don't always reflect the psychological boundaries that one subtly creates, and this is what I imagined to be the South Yorkshire Moors. Family weekend walks in Derbyshire around Ladybower, Alport Castles, Froggatt Edge and Big Moor were as much a part of living in the city as parts of the local landscape that did happen to be in South Yorkshire, like Winscar and Langsett Reservoirs. It always made sense to me that Yorkshire continued as far as the Pennines did, and that the Pennine watershed was the natural border, with Lancashire on the other side. Thus it was that I never explored the Hayfield side of Kinder, never visited Glossop except to queue to get on the M67 on the way to North Wales and still have never walked around Dovestone Reservoir. My South Yorkshire Moors stretched to the point where I looked out at Manchester from the edge of the hills before turning towards home. In very much the same way, I always thought of Chesterfield as being part of South Yorkshire because it was covered by Radio Sheffield and the local papers wrote about their football games like any local team. Though I'm sure this doesn't sound wholly respectful, it is not meant to disparage Derbyshire or treat part of the county as an annexe of Yorkshire. It is a wonderful and varied county with a fascinating history that just happens to form part of the Pennine chain between Sheffield and Manchester. So, for the rest of this book, read South Yorkshire as South Yorkshire and parts of north Derbyshire.

I have divided the moors not by individual peaks but rather by natural land-masses as so much of the area is composed

Bleaklow Head summit cairn

of great plateaus whose high points are not their defining features. The highest ground in the book, Kinder Scout and Bleaklow, rear up impressively but have ill-defined tops where it is impossible to tell if any one peat hag is higher than another. I include a list of high points *(see page xiv)* solely for the peak-bagger. Only the moorland lump west of the Derwent that comprises Abney, Offerton and Eyam Moors stands apart from the others. The rest of the moors form a continuous arc around the head of the Derwent watershed that slopes down to the outskirts of South Yorkshire's towns and cities. The Great Ridge and Win Hill are outlying limbs of Kinder Scout, which blends into Bleaklow, which blends into Howden Edge, which blends into Derwent Edge, all without dropping much below 500m. Similarly the Eastern Moors form one gently subsiding moorland mass from Stanage down to Chatsworth Moors, where the gritstone finally peters out around Matlock. There is little that divides these masses other than rivers and roads, so I have separated them into natural hunks divided by main roads, but there are always areas like Totley Moor which, it may be argued, could be linked to the moorland either side.

The chapters are arranged generally north to south, with detailed maps of all the moorland designated as 'open access land'. The idea is that people can explore these moors and discover their features for themselves, whether walking, running or riding. For those who prefer a guided route, there are round routes to each of these moors that are seven to fifteen miles long, though sadly I have been unable to link them all with public transport. The demise of the 222 Dambuster bus route up past Derwent and Howden Reservoirs, and the end of services over the Snake Pass, mean it is no longer possible to access the more remote parts of Bleaklow, Kinder and Howden without a car, a bike or some very fit legs. Combined with the closure of the road beyond Fairholmes on summer weekends and Bank Holidays, this means that it is now very hard for those working during the week to do the routes from the top of this road. However, out of season it remains a lovely place to visit and there are plenty of other places to go during the summer.

What I try to do with the routes is provide something different from the usual walks on these well-trodden hills. I seek out the faint sheeptrack that may be difficult to follow but yields a seldom-seen corner of the moor, or I try to take in a remote prehistoric site which our modern paths have long by-passed. This stubborn conceit means that there is some rough ground to cross and undoubtedly occasional cursing of the author. To help with this, the routes are graded with varying degrees of difficulty; Easy, Moderate and Strenuous refer more to the roughness of the terrain than the distance. My Easy routes are never totally straightforward but will tend to have a reasonably clear path throughout, whereas a Strenuous route is likely to have some pathless sections crossing tussocks or groughlands and require more careful navigation. You should always carry an OS map and compass, but this is particularly important on the Strenuous routes as, with the mist down, the featureless plateaus of the Dark Peak are notoriously disorientating. As a teenager I remember heading up one of the Peat Cloughs onto Bleaklow and imagining it would be simple to turn right on the ridge at the top. When I emerged from the grough the cloud was thick and nothing was clear, so I took the compass out and followed the high ground to my right heading what I thought was west. The compass appeared to agree, sort of. I thought the red arrow was north, but it seemed it must be the white arrow. Either that or I had somehow turned 180° approaching the ridge. So I ploughed on for a couple of miles until I was descending out of the mist. I could see some strange rocks ahead and it took me some time to realise that I'd been going entirely the wrong way and, instead of coming down into Longdendale, was dropping into the Derwent Valley. I recount this as a cautionary tale, secretly hoping that I am not alone in this idiocy.

A GUIDE TO OPEN ACCESS LAND

Most of us should be familiar with the notion of 'access land', or more correctly 'open access land', which was defined by the Countryside and Rights of Way Act 2000. It includes all registered common land and all land considered 'open country' (mountain, moor, heath or down), areas that can now be easily identified on all new 1:25,000 Ordnance Survey maps by pale yellow shading. However, it is not always clear how to access these areas, even though the act states that 'means of access' (i.e. gaps, stiles, gates, bridges) should be provided both onto and within areas of access land where 'necessary for giving the public reasonable access to that land in exercise of the right conferred above'. In practice this is not always the case; with new fences springing up all the time and local authorities' resources stretched, it is very hard for them to ensure reasonable easement across this open country. New fences on the National Trust's estates tend to have regular stiles, but those on private grouse-shooting estates can leave you with no choice but to climb a fence or wall. For example, the fenceline along the county boundary over Dead Edge End stretches most of the six miles from Salter's Brook to Holme Moss without a single stile, and large parts of Beeley Moor above Chatsworth are inaccessible from the adjacent roads without climbing a combination of walls and fences. Obviously, where a stile or gate exists, it should be used; even if it is locked, this is usually the best place to climb over. The law makes it difficult though, as you are considered a trespasser if you cause any damage to walls or fences on access land.

Even within the land that has been mapped as open country there are exclusions; any land covered by buildings (including those under construction) or their immediate curtilage; land within 20m of a dwelling or building used for housing livestock; land used as a garden or golf course; ploughed or cropped land; land used for active quarrying. In an interesting quirk, Snailsden Lodge above Dunford Bridge is entirely surrounded by open country but the track through its yard is excluded, meaning you have to skirt the rough moorland around its walls to rejoin the track the other side. In addition, landowners are allowed to restrict access to open access land for up to twenty-eight days in a year by prior application (though this is not permitted on Christmas Day, Good Friday, or any Bank Holiday or summer weekend day).

The CRoW Act states that we can use access land for the 'purposes of open-air recreation', but not the following; driving a vehicle, riding a bike, using a boat, bathing, lighting fires, shooting, fishing, camping, para-gliding, playing organised games, intentionally damaging wildlife (including foraging), using a metal detector, or disrupting any legal activity. Thus, if you swim in a mountain stream or collect edible wild plants for dinner, you can legally be considered a trespasser. However, the landowner can only pursue costs and only where damage can be proven, and on the whole common sense prevails as long as you respect the owners and users of the land.

The main issue one is likely to encounter is with those involved in grouse shooting, which dominates many of the moors. Red grouse may be shot between August 12th and December 10th, during which time you may come across a shoot in progress or being prepared. While it is the responsibility of those shooting to keep an eye on any users of Public Rights of Way, you may surprise them by appearing from elsewhere. It is usually worth seeking their advice, certainly making them aware of your presence, and often they will wave you through or suggest a slight detour to avoid the shoot. If they ask you to wait, it is worth noting that most shoots are very brief. In my experience, encounters with shooting parties have been very civilised, but if challenged you should assert your right to be there. The landowner does have the right to 'restrict access at their discretion in certain circumstances' for up to twenty-eight days a year, but this should be clearly signed.

One of the great frustrations with the South Yorkshire Moors is how much of it is out of bounds to dogs. While dogs are always permitted on Public Rights of Way, it is at the landowner's discretion on open access land. Though we may live in 'Dog's Own Country', nearly all of the grouse-shooting estates on the South Yorkshire side of the hills from Snailsden to Stanage have chosen to exclude dogs. I have included information at the start of every chapter and mentioned where individual routes are unsuitable for dogs, but you should also follow local guidance. Dogs fare rather better on the National Trust areas of Kinder, Bleaklow, the Upper Derwent Valley and the Eastern Moors, though you should keep them on a short lead (meaning of fixed length and not more than 2m) during the ground nesting bird season (March 1st to July 31st) or in the vicinity of livestock. The same should be respectfully applied on Public Rights of Way, though the law states only that a dog should be 'on a lead or otherwise under close control' when in an enclosure with sheep. It is an offence to allow a dog to chase livestock, but the landowner may shoot the dog only if it is the only reasonable way to prevent it from worrying or harming livestock.

All of my routes on the open moors are on access land, sometimes skirting awkwardly around the perimeter to reach an onward path; so as long as you are on the route you should assert your right to be there. My other maps do include some paths or tracks that cross private land, usually as reference points rather than recommended access routes. Where they are clearly signed as private I have tried to mark them as such, but in some cases their status is unclear. As a general rule, follow local signage and if in doubt refer to the Ordnance Survey 1:25,000 map.

ACCESS SUMMARY

• Open access land is not always legally accessible – restrictions and exclusions may be in place. Follow local signage as long as it is clear and dated.

• Unless a specific diversion is in force, Public Rights of Way are always legally accessible, even when access land restrictions and exclusions are in place.

• Dogs are excluded from large areas of the South Yorkshire Moors, especially between March 1st – July 31st. Check before setting off and follow local signage.

• However, dogs are always allowed on Public Rights of Way and are not required to be on leads, just under close control, but it is advisable to keep dogs on leads in the vicinity of livestock and during the ground-nesting bird season.

• Respect all other users of the moor, especially those with guns(!), but don't be intimidated.

THE GEOLOGY OF THE SOUTH YORKSHIRE & NORTH DERBYSHIRE MOORS

'Into this wild abyss, the womb of nature, and perhaps her grave.'
(John Milton, *Paradise Lost*)

The rocks of South Yorkshire and the Peak District were all formed in the Carboniferous period that began 360 million years ago, with all the beds tilting slightly from north to south. Limestone was formed first, composed of the shells of marine animals, laid down when the area lay beneath a tropical sea. Gritstone, a type of hard sandstone, was formed subsequently from loose sediment deposited on an enormous river delta draining from what is now the Scottish Highlands. However, there is not just one layer of gritstone, but rather a whole series of sedimentary layers of grit and loose shale. Some of the layers are harder than others due to the way they were laid down in different delta formations over millions of years. The Chatsworth Grit and Rivelin Grit can be seen in Stanage and the Eastern Edges, as well as Chinley Churn, Cown Edge and Ramshaw Rocks to the west, while the Kinderscoutian Grit can be seen further north on the highest plateaus. Subsequent movement of the Earth's crust led to the whole Pennine region subsiding, with the coal measures (coal-bearing marine shales) laid on top while it was at the bottom of an ocean. The original Kinderscoutian Grit was soon buried 2km underground, allowing it to become greatly compacted and heated, forming the defined sandstone we see today.

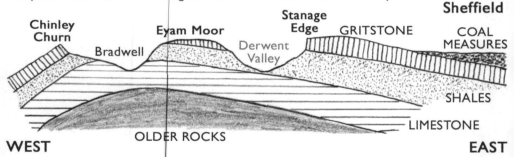

At the end of the Carboniferous period (around 300 million years ago), further movements in the Earth's crust uplifted the whole Pennine range to form a distinct anticline (the broad shape in the image above). The beds of these rocks are flat on top of the Pennines (i.e. Kinder Scout and Bleaklow) but inclined by 5° as the beds dip towards Sheffield to the east and 15° towards Manchester in the west; thus Stanage Edge and the Eastern Edges are far steeper than the angled crags of Ramshaw Rocks and the Roaches. Erosion has since removed most of the higher parts, revealing many of the older rocks below and exposing different rocks in different areas.

Coal measures remain overlain on the grit to the immediate west of Sheffield, but these are the lower, less valued coal seams, yielding pot clay, coking coal and ganister (or crow stone) and interspersed with further sandstone layers that form the Loxley and Wharncliffe Edges. Where the coal outcropped locally, these seams were worked around Hollow Meadows, Ringinglow, Ughill and across the Eastern Moors, but it was not rich enough to justify digging deep shafts. Although some shafts and trial holes were sunk, usually worked only by a hand windlass (or winch), the quality of the coal was poor. It was largely used in local lead smelting, lime burning and for domestic use. You have to continue to the other side of Sheffield to reach the more valuable upper coal seams which form the South Yorkshire Coalfield.

The carboniferous limestone is exposed only west of the River Derwent and south of Castleton, due to the angle of the beds and the uplift of this part of Derbyshire. Yet elsewhere it is not far beneath the surface, so oil was drilled in Edale and Alport in the 1930s when it was thought it might be discovered within the limestone. The gritstone-limestone boundary is well seen above Bradwell and Eyam, where the steep edges rise from the northern limit of the limestone plateau to gritstone peat moors.

The High Peak has been covered several times by ice up to a kilometre thick, but the movement of these sheets was restricted by flowing glaciers either side of the Pennines and, as a result, few obviously glacial valleys developed. The last time this area was covered by ice was 100,000 years ago as there was no ice cover here during the last Ice Age 12,000 years ago, but ice melt at the end of this and other Ice Ages did create the valleys of South Yorkshire and North Derbyshire, as well as the beginnings of the gritstone edges. These were further heightened by a long freeze-thaw and chemical weathering process. Weaknesses in the joints and beds of the rock allowed wind, rain and frost to penetrate the rock and create its unique slabs, cracks and buttresses, as well as causing large blocks to break off the edges and leave scattered blockfields below the edges. Various tors in the Peak were formed by acid rainwater eroding joints in the rock, helped by ice freezing in the cracks, and finally rounded smooth by wind carrying tiny rock particles. At the end of the last Ice Age there would have been very little vegetation and these uplands would have been like a moonscape, so plenty of material would have been blown around by the wind.

Where rivers have cut down through the sandstone to underlying shale, landslips are common. Shale is weak and impervious to water, so percolating rainwater is trapped in fissures in the rock, eventually forming an unstable soggy mudstone that cannot support the heavier strata above. Though this occurs over a period of thousands of years, the landslips themselves can be sudden; those in Alport Dale and at Mam Nick date from around 8,000 years ago, whereas the Mam Tor and Edale landslips didn't begin until 3,600 years ago.

Many of these features can be clearly seen in Edale and the hills either side, though it should be noted that the geology of each area is slightly different. The Kinderscoutian Grit is the upper layer of gritstone, formed of the coarsest sandstone and pebbles, and is found in the tors around the edge of the Kinder Scout plateau. Quartz is eroded from the gritstone and its grains form the sand that is seen in places on the plateau. The Grindslow Shales form a thin layer of sandy flags below the plateau edge and are associated with landslips along their base. The Shale Grit is made up of a series of layers of dark shale and coarse sandstone that were formed by strong currents on the Pennine Delta. It forms a defined bench on the steep slopes above the valley and is best seen on Back Tor and the upper parts of Broadlee Bank Tor. The Mam Tor Beds form the unstable landslipped parts of Mam Tor, Broadlee Bank Tor and Cold Side, and are comprised of a fine mix of sandstone, silt and shale. The Edale shales, forming the floor of the valley, are comprised of black mudstone. On the south side of the Great Ridge, the underlying limestone is exposed around Castleton.

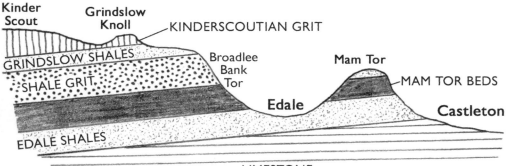

List of High Points in South Yorkshire & parts of north Derbyshire covered in this book

(over 300m and with a prominence of at least 20m)

1	Kinder Scout	636m	SK 085875	Chapter 7, p62
2	Bleaklow Head	633m	SK 092960	Chapter 2, p50
3	Brown Knoll	569m	SK 083851	Chapter 7, p68
4	Lord's Seat	550m	SK 112834	Chapter 8, p74
5	High Stones	548m	SK 188943	Chapter 3, p19
6	Margery Hill	546m	SK 189957	Chapter 3, p18
7	Featherbed Top	544m	SK 090921	Chapter 7, p58
	Mill Hill	544m	SK 061904	Chapter 7, p58
9	Outer Edge	541m	SK 177970	Chapter 3, p11
10	Back Tor	538m	SK 198910	Chapter 4, p26
11	Alport Moor	535m	SK 120946	Chapter 2, p44
12	Horse Stone Naze	527m	SK 158975	Chapter 3, p10
13	Mam Tor	517m	SK 128836	Chapter 8, p75
14	Dead Edge End	499m	SE 124017	Chapter 1, p2
15	Lose Hill	476m	SK 153854	Chapter 8, p77
16	Snailsden Pike	475m	SE 132033	Chapter 1, p2
17	Win Hill Pike	463m	SK 187851	Chapter 6, p83
18	The Tower (Alport Castles)	461m	SK 141914	Chapter 2, p42
19	High Neb	458m	SK 228853	Chapter 10, p97
20	Stanage Edge South	457m	SK 251830	Chapter 10, p101
21	Cook's Study Hill	451m	SK 131041	Chapter 1, p2
22	Upper Hey	446m	SK 178943	Chapter 3, p19
23	Burbage Moor	438m	SK 271825	Chapter 11, p110
24	Thornseat Moor	432m	SK 230927	Chapter 4, p28
25	Sir William Hill	429m	SK 215779	Chapter 9, p91
26	Bamford Moor	426m	SK 211847	Chapter 10, p97
	Barker Bank	426m	SK 139846	Chapter 8, p76
28	Burton Bole	417m	SK 194807	Chapter 9, p88
29	Nether Hey	416m	SK 179932	Chapter 3, p19
	Abney Moor	416m	SK 180794	Chapter 9, p88
31	Lodge Moor	409m	SK 237898	Chapter 5, p38
32	*Onesmoor*	*398m*	*SK 277929*	*Not in book*
33	Windlow Hill	388m	SK 266783	Chapter 12, p120
34	Cattis-side Moor	384m	SK 241828	Chapter 8, px
35	*Crook Hill*	*382m*	*SK 183868*	*Not in book*
36	Beeley Moor	371m	SK 293687	Chapter 13, p133
37	*Wood Royd Hill*	*370m*	*SE 182058*	*Not in book*
38	*Upper Whitley Edge*	*367m*	*SE 192049*	*Not in book*
39	Black Tor (White Edge)	366m	SK 261763	Chapter 12, p121
40	*Hartcliff Hill*	*364m*	*SE 221018*	*Not in book*
41	*Salter Hills*	*359m*	*SK 250972*	*Not in book*
42	*Abney Low*	*347m*	*SK 203794*	*Not in book*
43	*Gibraltar Rocks*	*340m*	*SK 249909*	*Not in book*
44	*Browns Edge*	*318m*	*SE 206009*	*Not in book*
45	*Wharncliffe Chase*	*317m*	*SK 314963*	*Not in book*
46	*Hunshelf Bank*	*311m*	*SK 267995*	*Not in book*
47	Birchen Edge	310m	SK 279731	Chapter 12, p125
	Allman Well Hill	*310m*	*SK 283968*	*Not in book*
49	*Greno Knoll*	*306m*	*SK 323956*	*Not in book*

THE HISTORY OF THE SOUTH YORKSHIRE & NORTH DERBYSHIRE MOORS

'The Moors – all hail! Ye changeless, ye sublime,
That seldom hear a voice, save that of Heaven!'
(Ebenezer Elliott, *Village Patriarch*)

THE MARCH OF THE PEAT

The moors were not always covered in peat. In the beginning there were trees, lots of them. The warm climate that followed the last Ice Age around 8000BCE encouraged the development of the wildwood that reached the tops of the hills in this part of the country. Alder dominated in the wet valleys, becoming oak, pine and elm further up the slopes, culminating with birch and hazel on the higher ground. Evidence of this former forest was unearthed when boundary ditches, roads and drains were dug on the Dark Peak moors. In 16th-century texts there are references to prehistoric fir trees being buried only half a yard deep in the peat. The remains of Hordron Forest were discovered beneath Boardhill Moors when drains were dug in the 19th century, and tree stumps the size of torsos were found on Stanage and Moscar Moors when drains were cut. Even now, ancient tree trunks are sometimes washed out in heavy storms.

There was no peat when our earliest ancestors made their summer camps on these hills in the Mesolithic era (the middle Stone Age from 8000-4500BCE). These nomadic hunter-gatherers left only the remains of flint and chert tools and weapons, which probably came from the Yorkshire Wolds. These microliths have been discovered across the Pennine moors in the sandy soil that lies beneath the layers of peat, and can still be found occasionally beneath natural rock shelters, or where the peat has recently been exposed. There is a Flint Hill on Broomhead Moor near where a Mesolithic hunter-gatherers' camp has been excavated, and flints from the early Mesolithic period have been found on Mickleden Edge and across the Eastern Moors.

The peat only began to be formed on the uplands when the climate deteriorated, rainfall increased and fire (manmade or otherwise) cleared areas of trees. Slowly the soils in the uplands turned acidic and the trees changed to scrub, with peat forming where water sat on the moorland plateau. Peat formation was at its height during a lush, warmer phase around 6000-4500BCE, making the Dark Peak's moors among the oldest peatlands in the UK. Peat forms where plant matter sits in water and does not rot, but simply becomes piled upon itself. Most of the minerals are washed out of it by the water so it is not fertile and further inhibits the growth of trees. The blanket bog that was formed by this process continued to spread across the moors until after the Iron Age, forming a six to ten foot deep layer of peat on the highest plateaus. However, in the woods below 500m there was limited peat cover until a succession of vegetation burnings took place during subsequent millennia.

During the Neolithic era (4500-2200BCE), people first began farming and building permanent residences in Britain, requiring clearance of the forest, generally on higher, drier ground. The lighter sandy soils and flat expanses of the Eastern Moors were among the most fertile in the area and Neolithic rock shelters have been discovered on both Gardom's Edge and Carl Wark. However, the bulk of settlement and clearance here took place during the Bronze Age (2200-800BCE), the Eastern Moors providing some of the finest examples of Middle Bronze Age settlements in the country. Cultivation of cereals and the grazing of livestock were possible due to a slightly warmer climate and a lack of peat on these lower moors. Walls and earth banks were constructed as field boundaries and the stones cleared from these enclosures were piled into large cairns that litter the landscape. At Swine Sty and Stoke Flat on Big Moor, Birchen Edge and Chatsworth Moors to the south, Wet Withens on Eyam Moor, and at Ash Cabin Flat on Hallam Moors, there are substantial remains of these field systems, cairns and hut circles. The settlements of separate family groups at Toad's Mouth and Winyard's Nick, barely half a mile apart on Burbage, suggest clearly defined areas of settlement existed on a small scale. These sites have been preserved on the moors in a way they haven't been where land was farmed in later periods, so it is very difficult to know how much land was settled before the introduction of the iron plough changed the face of land in the Iron Age.

Ritual and funerary parts of the landscape, usually separated from the main settlements, are often found nearby; burial cairns and barrows, as well as small stone circles and ring cairns. Barrows (large heaps of earth and stone covering a prehistoric burial place) were usually in prominent positions on the high moors as they served an important purpose in affirming the link between a community and the land. Grand ceremonies took place occasionally for the burial of important figures, while smaller burial cairns were built on the edge of settlements to remind the living of the dead and assert a family's ancestral rights to the land. However, most cairns from this period were formed of stones cleared from the surrounding area so that the land could be farmed. Many of the stones from these cairns and barrows were subsequently stolen to build roads and walls, meaning large imposing features like the Apronful of Stones and the original Ringing Lowe have completely disappeared.

Ring cairns and stone circles are similar Bronze Age features, the former being earthen circles that may or may not have had a ring of stones within them (i.e. Cicely Low, Offerton Moor and Hob Hurst's House). Stone circles, of varied size and usually comprising a series of small stones (2-3 feet high), are dotted around the Eastern Moors and include the Seven Stones of Hordron, Wet Withens, Offerton Moor, and the various Barbrook circles. Undoubtedly there is a relationship between all the different stone circles in the area and there are many striking alignments; on a local scale, the circles at Brown Edge, Barbrook III and Barbrook I are all in a direct line; on a regional scale, the Seven Stones of Hordron, Cicely Low and Wet Withens all line up with the important sites at Arbor Low and the Bull Ring further south in Derbyshire. Various stones were erected around Barbrook I circle to study alignments of the sun and moon, as they were at the Old Woman on Bamford Moor.

Soil and grass development over the last three millennia has obscured many sites on the moors, so most of the standing stones at circles like Barbrook III and Smelting Hill on Offerton Moor are almost completely buried by historic soil and peat – only the tops of a few stones protrude from the peat now. One of the few benefits of moorland fires is that they tend to expose many of the historic remains that had previously been lost. A 1959 fire on Big Moor revealed many new finds around the Swine Sty settlement site, which were exposed again in the summer of 2018.

Bamford Moor stone circle

There is far less evidence of settlement on the high moors of Bleaklow, Kinder and Howden. However, the existence of large Bronze Age barrows on high ridges, such as those on Lord's Seat, Mam Tor, Margery Hill, Nether Moor (Kinder) and the two Pike Lowes, as well as the stone circle at Ewden Beck, suggests that peat formation may have obscured settlement sites in these areas. These barrows are usually associated with important figures like chieftains or high status families, but there is much we don't understand. Though stories of a settlement of small wooden huts on the raised bog of Leash Fen prior to the Roman invasion are generally thought fanciful, when the Duke of Rutland ordered its drainage in the 19th century, , cut pieces of black oak were discovered in the channels. Many of these sites are also likely to have been used and reused from the early Bronze Age to the Iron Age and so are hard to date exactly.

The climate became cooler and wetter in the late Bronze Age and, by the beginning of the Iron Age (800-43BCE), peat had begun to develop on the lower moorlands of the Eastern Moors as well as the higher plateaus. What were sustainable farming practices in the lowlands resulted in the nutrients being washed away and the soil becoming waterlogged on the high ground. Once denuded of trees, the Eastern Moors began to resemble the higher Dark Peak plateaus – it is likely that, had people not settled these areas, they would have retained their tree cover to this day. Though the moors were still used for summer grazing in the Iron Age, settlement retreated further down the hillsides and south from the peat to the limestone White Peak.

Derbyshire was home to the Iron Age Brigantes people, who covered much of northern England. This was a loose collection of autonomous tribes, one of which was based around Carl Wark and another around Mam Tor. There is little evidence from this era on the moors beyond the vast rampart ditch around the summit of Mam Tor, although the natural defences of Carl Wark were probably also used during this period. Both of these features had previously been used in the Bronze Age, the latter perhaps as a ceremonial gathering ground like that on top of Gardom's Edge.

Farming was abandoned on these moorland areas by the late Iron Age and, when the Romans arrived in Britain, they encountered a landscape that had already lost much of its tree cover. Although peat formation continued until the Middle Ages, it slowed greatly as the climate cooled and had a final depth that varies from 20cm to 4m. Over the past 2,000 years, it has been steadily eroded and cut into due to higher rainfall and human activity.

INVASION AND EXPLOITATION

When the Romans arrived in the 1st century BCE they encountered little resistance in Derbyshire and South Yorkshire, unlike that offered by the Brigantes tribes further north. They built a fort at Brough (Navio) to serve the same purpose as the earlier fort on Mam Tor, which guarded the entrance to the important trans-Pennine pass of Winnats, as well as allowing exploitation of the area's lead resources. The Roman road between Navio and Templeborough (near the junction of the Rother and Don) ran through Redmires Reservoirs and close to the line of Stanedge Lodge Drive as it went over the top of Stanage. This was a military road, but it is thought that the Romans constructed another commercial road to the south, which ran past Carl Wark, Houndkirk Moor and Ringinglow. On the other side of the hills there was a fort now known as Melandra that stood by the River Etherow near Glossop, and a Roman road crossed the moors between here and Navio via the Snake Pass. After crossing the shoulders of Win Hill and Cowms Moor, it is generally said that Doctor's Gate followed the line of the Roman Road, but the line actually ran across the less steep mosses to the south. Longdendale was the other great Pennine crossing into

South Yorkshire used by the Romans, and there has been a suggestion of a Portway running north-south across the moors of the Dark Peak, providing a root for the name Alport both in the Woodlands Valley and further south near Youlgreave. There are certainly many supernatural tales of ghostly legionnaires marching across the moors of Bleaklow.

Throughout the Roman occupation, the moors continued to be used solely as summer grazing by the locals in much the same way as before. This prevented any regeneration of woodland on the hills, so trees tended to survive only in the steep cloughs. People would have continued to speak with a Brythonic tongue in this area until the end of the Dark Ages. Although relatively few Celtic place names survive, those that do tend to relate to rivers (Derwent, Don and Noe) and mountains (Kinder, Mam Tor, Higger Tor, Carl Wark and Dinas Sitch Tor). Hathersage, Grindleford, Bamford, Eyam and Bradwell may also be of Celtic origin.

The Angles arrived in Britain in the 5th century, soon after the Romans departed in 410AD, leaving a greater impact on the area's place names than anyone else; these include any places ending in -field (Chesterfield, Bradfield, Ecclesfield, Dronfield and Sheffield), -worth (Dungworth, Sugworth, Cartworth, Dodworth and Hawksworth) -ton (Stannington, Norton, Thurlstone and Penistone), -borough (Mosborough, Worsbrough, Mexborough and Conisborough), -ley (Totley, Loxley, Wadsley, Walkley and Barnsley) and -ham (Rotherham). South Yorkshire and Derbyshire lay on opposite sides of the often-disputed border between the kingdoms of Mercia and Northumbria. The first boundary marker at Stanage Pole dates from this post-Roman period, as does the legendary battle fought near Hope that was said to have led to the names Win Hill and Lose Hill[1]. The Pecsaetan ('settlers of the Peak')[2] were an ancient hill tribe recorded in the 7th century who formed one of the semi-autonomous people who made up Mercia. Meanwhile Hallamshire was one of sixteen shires in the kingdom of Northumbria, its name relating to halgh, signifying its position at the edge of the territory. The boundary between them followed the Sheaf and the Don, the name Sheaf (a corruption of sheath) referring to a divider. Dore was an important gateway between the two kingdoms and played a role in uniting the kingdoms for the first time. The Dore Stone marked the place where in 829 King Eanred of Northumbria surrendered and King Ecgbert became the first King of England.

the Dore Stone

The Vikings arrived in Yorkshire in 867 and set out the counties as we know them. Both Derbyshire and Yorkshire's ridings were created in the late 9th/early 10th century, with the boundary little changed since. It originally followed the Sheaf downstream from Dore, then joined Meers Brook, only moving outwards slightly with the development of Sheffield's suburbs in the 1930s, bringing Totley, Bradway, Greenhill, Woodseats, Meersbrook and Norton into the city. The Vikings gave us names like Ughill, Onesacre, Holmesfield, Grimes-thorpe, Jordanthorpe, Hackenthorpe, Maltby and Storrs.

---

[1] Here, it is said the Northumbrians defeated the Saxons by rolling boulders downhill towards the advancing army (see p81 for more information). Though this story is generally treated as pure fantasy, it may be based on a real battle that took place nearby, possible at Carl Wark, where it is easier to imagine some of the many boulders being rolled down on a Saxon horde.
[2] 'Peac lond' was referred to in 924, thus Peakland might have been a more appropriate name for the National Park than the Peak District name that was concocted at the time. Peac is an Old English word for pointy, though some have suggested the area's name originally comes from Peaks Hole (the old name for Peak Cavern), whose name derives from puca, a Gaelic name for a spirit (hence its alternative name of Peak's or Devil's Arse).

xviii

The Lordship of Hallamshire was an ancient territory holding all land south of the Little Don and equating quite closely to the Sheffield metropolitan area. It was originally served by Ecclesfield Church, an early Christian site, with Sheffield simply a chapel-of-ease on the way there. As late as 1642, these and Bradfield were the only churches in the manor. Penistone parish formed the southwestern extremity of the Honour of Pontefract, the De Lacys' land that extended to Langsett and Thurlstone parishes on the edge of the moors. Within this, manors were granted in return for military service, though many of these arrangements were wiped away by the Normans in 1066. One of these was the Manor of Penisale, whose court and market was located somewhere near Langsett and is long lost to history.

After the Norman Conquest, Hallamshire was administered by the de Furnivals from Sheffield Castle, originally a motte-and-bailey and, from the 13th century, a stone edifice[3]. They created various sub-manors, but central manorial courts oversaw everything, including the already important cutlery trade. A large deer park was created south of the Sheaf and Don, centred around Manor Lodge, and vast areas of commons were set aside for hunting. Rivelin (which included most of Stanage), Hawksworth (which covered the area around Strines) and Loxley formed chases (or firths) for the hunting of deer. Hunting parties on the Duke of Norfolk's Rivelin Chase set out from Rivelin Lodge at Lodge Moor, with its deer-keepers based at Redmires. In the adjacent Lordship of Wortley, Wharncliffe Chase was used as a deer chase by the Wortley family from 1252. Red, roe and fallow deer were all hunted, as well as hares, pheasants and moor game (which included grouse). Wolves, which were previously common in the wooded valleys of Bleaklow and Kinder, were hunted out of existence in Henry II's reign as a game predator. The chases were not always in use, though, so the moors would also have been grazed by commoners between hunts, as well as those passing through seasonally. The lords also operated large cattle ranches, or vaccaries, at Fulwood Booth, Old Booth near Bradfield, Windleden on Thurlstone Moors, and the various booths of Edale. The name Booth here relates to the herdsman's summer shelter and has the same meaning as bothy, referring to a temporary seasonal shelter.

The Royal Forest of the Peak was established in 1151 and covered most of the High Peak west of the River Derwent from Longdendale to Buxton. It belonged to the Crown and was administered from Peveril Castle, with a foresters' hall near its centre at the village of Peak Forest. It was subject to the draconian Forest Laws until they were relaxed in the mid-13th century, and then became part of the Duchy of Lancaster in 1351. The Eastern Moors and Hallamshire Moors were also designated as a Royal Forest in the 12th century, but did not become as established and the designation was abandoned by 1225.

During this period, various lands were given to abbeys by landowners who left part of their estate in exchange for burial at the monastery and sometimes the title of an honorary canon. This land was then rented out to lay farmers and yeomen on long leases by the canons, who also erected crosses on the boundaries of their land, many of which still remain; Edale Cross, Whibbersley Cross, Godfrey's Cross, Shillito Cross and both Lady Crosses. In the 12th century the Manor of Glossop, including Longdendale and large parts of Bleaklow, was granted to the monks of Basingwerk Abbey in North Wales by Henry II. Later King John granted Crook Hill to the canons of Welbeck Abbey, who founded another grange in the Upper Derwent Valley in the 1250s. Their pasture included most of Howden and Derwent Edges, which were well grazed with cattle and sheep at a time when the climate was slightly warmer and

---

[3] Sheffield Castle was demolished following the English Civil War, its memory preserved in the names of Castle Market and Castlegate, beneath which its remains are now being excavated.

drier than present. Large areas of land were granted to the monks of Beauchief Abbey in the 13th century, including Totley Moor, Burbage Moor, Beeley Moor, Harewood Grange, Rivelin and Fulwood Moors, and parts of Stanage. Names like Abbey Brook, Nungrain Brink, Friar's Ridge, and Friar's Walk Wood reflect this history.

Where they didn't follow natural features, the remote moorland boundaries between manors were occasionally marked by stone crosses, but there were few man-made boundary markers, so certain rocks, wells and other features became established as parish and property boundaries. Beatings of the bounds by villagers took place every few years to establish the exact lines and prevent disagreement. A confrontation between farmers of Thurlstone and Holmfirth parishes in the 16th century resulted in the death of one of the former. In places, ditches were cut through the peat to demarcate boundaries, form defined tracks, for drainage, and to stop fire spreading. The broad ditches of Broomhead Dyke, Sewards Lode on Howden Edge, and Cartledge Stones Ridge on Derwent Edge are all medieval boundary divisions, and the deep trench of Broad Rake from Stanage End to Moscar is part of the ancient boundary between the manors of Hallamshire and Hathersage. Many place names on the moors relate to boundaries; mere (i.e. Meersbrook or Thurlstone Mere), limb (i.e. Limb Valley), shire (i.e. Shirebrook or Shirecliffe), hoar or hare (i.e. Horse Stone, Harden Moor, Harewood Moor or Hordron), tree (i.e. the Wigan Tree) and wain (i.e. Wain Stones) can all mean a boundary place.

Attempts to cultivate the moors in the 12th and 13th centuries were necessitated by population growth, which continued steadily until the mid-14th century. Intakes on the edge of the moor were granted by the Lord of the Manor for an entry fee and usually represented piecemeal ad hoc incursions into the wastes. The medieval enclosure at Lawrence Field near Padley Gorge dates from this period; most others were destroyed by later cultivation, but here enclosure walls and hut outlines were left deserted on the barren rocky waste. With the arrival of the Black Death in 1348-9, the country's population was reduced by more than a third and so less fertile sites like these were quickly abandoned. This retreat from the moorland edges was usually only temporary, though, with most sites resettled in the Middle Ages.

After the Dissolution of the Monasteries in the 1530s, the abbey lands were seized by the Crown and often sold on. Beauchief Abbey's estate was bought by Sir Nicholas Shelley and stayed in his family until its purchase by the Duke of Rutland around 1900. The Earl of Shrewsbury bought Basingwerk Abbey's estate in Glossop and that of Welbeck Abbey in the Upper Derwent Valley. William Cavendish was a Suffolk landowner and government servant who was one of Henry VIII's lackeys for overseeing the surrender of the monasteries. In 1554 he swapped his land for many of the monastic granges of Derbyshire and married Bess of Hardwick, part of the local gentry, with whom he built the first Chatsworth House in 1552. The Cavendishes were created the Earls of Devonshire in 1618, paying £10,000 for the title.

The fashion for deer hunting declined in the late 16th century as the value of grazing land increased with the price of wool and meat. Sheep was big business on some of the larger Peak District estates in the 16th century and the Royal Forest of the Peak title, though still in use, was entirely irrelevant by the late 17th century. The Dukes of Norfolk inherited the Lordship of Hallamshire by marriage in the 17th century, but as it wasn't their main residence they let the manor, deer park and chases run down, eventually culling the deer and putting tenant farmers on the land. Rivelin was used later than the other Hallamshire chases but, after the chase here was abandoned, many of its woods were cut down as land was turned over to sheep and cattle. Much of Rivelin's great oak woods were removed by the early 18th century, and Ewden's great yews were cut down to make into handles for knives by Sheffield cutlers.

The moors, though, were still viewed as waste land, useless if they could not be brought under cultivation. Daniel Defoe, in his *Tour Through the Whole Island of Great Britain* in 1724, summed up a lot of his contemporaries' views when he called the Dark Peak 'the most desolate, wild, and abandoned country in all England'. Thomas Hobbes, a philosopher who would later be known for Leviathon, tutored the Cavendish family at Chatsworth and wrote widely about the Derbyshire Hills. His book *De Mirabilibus Pecci*, published in 1636, was the first about the Seven Wonders of the Peak, which were all on or close to the limestone of the White Peak, Mam Tor being the furthest north. Few travellers were interested in exploring the gritstone moors, whose features were also on private land and largely out of bounds to visitors – in some cases rock features were even blown up or destroyed to prevent interest. The tour of the Seven Wonders of the Peak became fashionable with early travellers in the 17th and 18th centuries, but like most things they didn't impress Defoe.

He would have been more impressed by the industry of the Peak District, which had been worked for its resources since the Bronze Age settlers first started producing buttons and bracelets from shale. Charcoal was made in the woods of the Upper Derwent Valley, where over two hundred charcoal-burning hearths have been identified, and medieval iron-smelting furnaces used charcoal from the woods of Padley Gorge to heat the iron ore that was present in the coal measures to produce malleable pig iron. However, lead mining had been the most important industry in Derbyshire since the Romans and was at its height in the 17th and 18th centuries. Early lead smelting sites (known as boles) can be found across the area; these were hollow depressions dug into well-ventilated west-facing hillsides, into which layers of wood and ore were piled. Molten lead flowed out the bottom to solidify in moulds or was ladled into them. There are Bole Hills on Eyam Moor and near Padley, Burton Bole and Smelting Hill on Abney Moor, and Smeltingmill Wood near Beeley Moor.

By the end of the 16th century open-air boles were replaced by smelting mills, like that on Bar Brook above Baslow, where small dams allowed water-powered bellows to heat whitecoal *(see page xxiii in The West Yorkshire Woods: Part 1 for more information)*. The fringe of Sheffield and Chesterfield had water power and coppiced woods where white coal was produced, so lead from the White Peak was often smelted here. By this time Derbyshire's lead industry was the most productive in Europe, with the finished product exported via the inland port at Bawtry before the opening of the Chesterfield Canal in 1777. By the 18th century, coal-fired cupola furnaces replaced this method; lower-grade lead could be used as the intense heat of the furnace expelled sulphur and arsenic impurities. There was one at Ringinglow, where there was a ready source of coal on the doorstep. Most slag heaps from the earlier boles were taken away for resmelting in cupola hearths, though occasionally some were left untouched (like that on Lodge Moor near Moscar, and on Lead Hill near Ashopton, the slag identifiable now only by bright green grassy mounds in otherwise dour grass and heather). The Derbyshire lead industry declined in the 1820s as it became hard to source cheap local coal, and most cupolas had closed by the 1860s.

Bawtry port and the Chesterfield Canal were also used for exporting millstones from the northern Peak, particularly around Hathersage. A Millstone Gate led from Millstone Edge across Owler Tor and Big Moor towards the port. It was a profitable industry from the 15th century and its marks dominate the Eastern Edges. The last millstones were sold to a Swedish paper mill in 1939, but the industry had largely collapsed in the 1920s, leaving hundreds of stones abandoned in situ *(see p130 for more information on the millstone industry).*

abandoned millstone

TRANS-PENNINE TRANSPORT

Many of the earliest routes across the Pennines were salters' ways from Cheshire's famous saltfields of Northwich, Middlewich and Nantwich. Salt was needed to preserve food over the winter and formed the primary trade of these arterial routes during the Middle Ages, though Sheffield's knives were transported in the other direction, with quarried stone, lead and wool leaving Derbyshire in both directions. The main routes crossed the hills through Longdendale, heading for Wakefield, Barnsley, Doncaster and Rotherham via Salter's Brook at Woodhead; via Winnats Pass and the Long Causeway over Stanage (part of whose surface dates from the 1560s), passing Saltergate Lane near Bamford Station and heading into Sheffield via Psalter Lane[4]; and via Sir William Hill and Curbar Gap, crossing the Bar Brook at Salter's Ford and arriving in Chesterfield via Saltergate.

However, these saltways formed just part of the network of packhorse tracks, which were the main form of travel until the late 18th century. Their route was often unclear across the moorland and, though there might be a deep holloway (a sunken groove) or laid causey (a stone causeway) on the steep climb up the edge, most routes across the moors were braided and ill defined, often requiring local knowledge for safe passage. There were relatively few routes across Kinder, Bleaklow and Howden due to the hazardous nature of the terrain, but Stanage, Burbage and the Eastern Moors are riddled with old tracks and holloways. Cut Gate across Howden Edge is named for its deep peat-cut line (see p22 for more details), but the route still needed marking by a line of stakes and was maintained by the Duke of Norfolk until the late 19th century. There were also many more localised routes by which commoners drove their sheep and cattle to the wastes, or brought turf down for burning in their homes. These holloways often end abruptly on the moorland edge, at a quarry, turbary (peat-cutting) ground or grazing pasture.

Guide stoops[5] and waymarkers were standing stones erected to aid travellers across remote featureless moors, the only difference between the two being that waymarkers didn't contain any lettering or directions. The earliest examples are boundary crosses of the types found at Edale Cross, Shillito Cross, Whibbersley Cross and both Lady Crosses. At these wayside crosses, weary travellers could offer a prayer, though many crosses were destroyed in the Puritanical days of Cromwell, or later by gamekeepers, to prevent people from being tempted to trespass to get to them. Lady's Cross (near White Edge) had its shaft broken so it was less obvious from the road and New Cross (near Strines) had its cross removed. Maps at this time were expensive and exclusive, used only for legal purposes or by literate, well-heeled travellers – the first affordable one-inch Ordnance Survey map was not drawn until the early 19th century.

Edale Cross

After 1697, Parliament required local Justices of the Peace to mark out roads in moorland areas and put up guide stoops at junctions. In 1709, Derbyshire law required the placement of guide stoops along all packhorse roads and many stones are dated from this year or 1737, when another order was made.

---

[4] Psalter Lane was originally Salters Way and was only rebranded in the 19th century in an effort to attract more wealthy residents to the area by giving it an ecclesiastical connection (the psalter refers to the Book of Psalms).

[5] The word stoop is from the Viking language and was used in the north to refer to any stone post.

Many crudely carved stones sprung up with phonetic spellings of placenames. The later ones had hands or arrow directions, whereas the earlier ones relied only on the convention that, when facing the inscription of the place you wanted to go, you'd turn right for the direction. Many guide stoops were probably painted white with black lettering, and this was certainly standard around Bradfield. They were rendered redundant by the advent of turnpikes, when the stones were used as gate stoops or broken up for other uses, like roads. When some were re-erected after the war, many were put back in the wrong places or facing the wrong direction. Even today, many of these are rediscovered half buried; a stone on Beeley Moor that was buried during the war was found and re-erected in the 1990s.

a guide stoop on Beeley Moor

Public and private roads traditionally related not to their use but to their maintenance, whether by the local parish or landowner. After 1555, each parish was responsible for road repairs within its bounds, so all villagers were required to give either labour or tools each year. The result was a lot of very amateur bodging of roads and very basic surfacing, as well as great variation in standard between different parishes. Turnpikes developed from the 17th century as a way to improve the standard of long-distance travel in terms of navigation, surfacing and safety.

The first turnpike was constructed across the Dark Peak in the 1730s, with the old saltway up Londgendale being improved by the Manchester and Saltersbrook Turnpike. The early turnpikes were built by gangs of labourers with only manual tools like spades and picks, and the Snake Road was still made this way around 1820. They were approximately twenty feet wide and surfaced with small stones. Houndkirk Road is a well-preserved example as it was quickly abandoned due to newer routes being constructed nearby. Early turnpikes tended to follow the line of existing routes, simply improving the surface, though many of these were suited more to packhorses than carriages as they descended steeply straight across valleys and rarely avoided steep hills. A famous example was Mortimer Road, built in 1771 following the line of Halifax Gate, a packhorse route between the Hope Valley and Penistone (and beyond to Halifax); it required extra horses to be added to the usual train to pull the carriages up the hills at Ewden, Agden and Strines, where the 'take-off' stones can still be seen.

Tolls were taken at numerous toll bars along these routes, some of whose footings can still be found, while others are preserved in names like Owler Bar and Hunter's Bar[6]. Tolls varied depending on what transport was being used and what was being carried, higher tolls being paid by carriages and carts, particularly those carrying heavy wares like millstones. Cattle-droving remained popular until the 1870s, with drovers between Rotherham and Glossop making use of the new Snake Pass route in the 19th century and often resting overnight at the Snake Inn.

By the end of the 18th century the first new routes were forged by the turnpikes, making use of easier gradients and sometimes cutting terraces into existing hillsides; the Surprise View route down Millstone Edge, the A625 route down Froggatt Edge, the doomed switchback road across the face of Mam Tor, and finally the famous Snake Road.

---

[6] Older names like Baslow Bar, Rowsley Bar and Curbar relate not to toll bars, though, but instead the steep hills climbed by early roads.

The route across Boardhill Moor – a notoriously treacherous boggy route that regularly took travellers to their grave in the winter months, even after it became the Doncaster and Saltersbrook Turnpike – was only really improved when the route was moved to the line of the current A628 in 1828. The later turnpike roads are mirrored almost exactly by today's network of main roads, including the Wadsley to Langsett Turnpike (now the A616) and the Baslow to Sheffield Turnpike via Owler Bar and Totley (now the A621).

This turnpike network, along with the subsequent development of the railways, enabled Sheffield to grow from a modest population of 12,000 in 1750 to 240,000 by 1871. For example, the Sheffield to Glossop Turnpike helped to develop the western suburbs of Sheffield at Broomhill, Ranmoor and Crosspool. However, the railways quickly replaced coach travel and meant most toll roads never became profitable for their investors; in 1830, the Liverpool and Manchester Railway became the first modern steam railway, and by 1838 Sheffield was linked to Rotherham by rail. The turnpike tolls were set by Acts of Parliament and only renewed every twenty-one years, so profits gradually declined anyway; plus the landowning gentry were exempted from paying tolls. By the 1840s, the Snake Road cost nearly ten times as much to repair as it took in tolls. Turnpike licences were not renewed from 1867 onwards and the last toll was taken at Hunter's Bar in 1884, when the toll booth was overturned by a mob shortly after midnight on its last day. By then Highways Boards had been established to oversee the maintenance of roads and most former turnpikes became the responsibility of local government rather than private shareholders.

There was a great demand for lime from the Peak District in the growing city of Sheffield for use in building mortar. Much of it was transported to Ladybower, where it was burnt to produce quicklime in the large quarry behind the inn, before being taken over the moor to Sheffield. So great was the trade at one time that a tramway was planned beneath Mam Tor and Win Hill to bring in larger quantities of limestone. Tramways were used for transporting building stone from Bole Hill Quarry to the Derwent and Howden Reservoirs at the turn of the 20th century.

PARLIAMENTARY ENCLOSURE AND THE GROUSE AGE

'The enclosure system has been one of unexampled absurdity and injustice. It has been conducted on the principle of "Unto him that hath shall be given, and from him that hath not shall be taken away even that which he hath".'
(William Howitt, *Rural Life of England*, 1838)

Many of the moorland wastes were considered common land (the King's Land) from the early medieval period, with commoners' rights to pasture livestock, quarry stone, cut peat and gather bracken and moss. The number of animals that could be grazed by each farmer on the commons was closely controlled by the manorial courts and, when the herd was driven onto the moor each spring, it was counted at the lydgate that marked the beginning of common land (thus Lidgate above Holmesfield, Lydgate Lane in Crosspool, and Lidgett Lane in Dinnington).

Peat was widely collected on the Peak District's moors, primarily as fuel, but also for roofing and animal bedding. Paupers cut and dried peat on the moors during the summer months, with common rights of turbary well established on Totley Moss, around Edale, and in the Derwent and Woodlands Valleys. Large areas of grass within the heather are generally where peat was dug over many years. Despite cheaper coal arriving by turnpike, peat continued to be the major source of fuel for poorer households until the late 19th century (see p86 for about peat gathering).

Commoners also had rights to quarry stone for buildings or walls and to gather fallen wood in the woods. Bracken was also widely cut for use as litter and thatch and burnt to produce potash in the making of soap. It and moss were also gathered for winter bedding for animals, and its harvesting was carefully controlled. Now that it is not cut, bracken coverage is difficult to inhibit, tending to spread particularly quickly when heather areas are overgrazed by sheep.

Not all the moors were commons, though; large parts of Howden, Derwent and Hope Woodlands were manorial pastures with rent paid for grazing livestock, providing the lords with rent for otherwise unused land. In the Upper Derwent Valley there were cattle heys lower down for summer pasturing (the names Upper Hey, Nether Hey, Cow Hey, Ox Hey and Calf Hey survive) and sheepwalks higher up the moors. Sheep pastures were well defined on the high moors without the need for boundary walls because the sheep were hefted, but some pastures were surrounded by earthen banks, an example of which can be seen at John Field Howden below Back Tor. Derbyshire Gritstone and Woodlands Whiteface (aka the Penistone) sheep were the hardy hill flocks most associated with the area.

Enclosure of the commons began in the 15th century, when walls and hedges increasingly parcelled up the land for grazing, and continued after the Dissolution of the Monasteries. The landowners who created by this increased the entry rates, tried to enclose former sheepwalks and grazed their own herds on the common land. The Duchy of Lancaster was an example, having taken ownership of large parts of the Royal Forest of the Peak in the 17th century when the Crown suffered financial problems. These landowners were met with great opposition from local peasants, who rioted and even took them to court. There were also many illegal piecemeal enclosures by tenants on the edge of the moors; these were often overlooked by landlords as their rental value was minimal, but greatly resented by those whose common grazing land was being steadily diminished. In 1723 the Black Act created offences relating to trespass, some punishable by death – the name related to 'blacks' who painted their faces with soot and hunted on private land – but it was not until the late 18th century that the most profound changes occurred to the ownership and use of the moorland landscape.

A Board of Agriculture report in 1793 entitled General View of the Agriculture of the West Riding of Yorkshire recommended the enclosure of the common moors, their drainage and the building of walls on a vast scale to improve the acreage of land that could be cropped and its overall productivity. The Napoleonic Wars necessitated this increase in agricultural production and led to land that was previously uncultivated being enclosed through a series of Acts of Parliament that had begun in this area in 1779 with the enclosure of Ecclesall parish. Large straight-walled enclosures that can still be readily identified were laid out, along with the straight roads and byways of the kind that can be seen across the Eastern Moors. The Ecclesfield Enclosure Act alone made 18,000 acres of previously common moorland into private land.

Parliamentary Enclosure took place in different years in each parish, depending on how long it took to sort out the various claims to land there; Bolsterstone (1782), Hallam and Stannington (1791-1805), Ecclesfield (1811), Langsett (1811-14), Thurlstone (1812-16), Hathersage (1808-30), Bradfield (1811-26), Baslow (1819-26), Midhope (1818-23), Dore (1809-22) and Totley (1839-42). Generally if the owners of more than three-quarters of the land within a parish approved, enclosure was imposed on the other landowners. Land was then divided up by commissioners of the parish or township, but many of the poorer residents' claims were dismissed – their previous use of the commons for grazing ponies or gathering bracken and peat was deemed illegal. The larger landowners received the most but often opted for what seemed the worst land, the vast moorland wastes, which they invariably received in their entirety. They already had a vision of the sort of vast shooting estate that the Duke of Rutland would go on to establish at Longshaw and the Duke of Norfolk would acquire on Stanage. A small allotment on Strines Moor for use by the poor of Bradfield parish was an exception to the rule. There were enclosure riots in July 1791 when 6000 acres of common land disappeared in Stannington, Hallam, Fulwood, Stoors and Dungworth, including many village greens and the Hallam Moors. The rioting lasted three days, during which windows were smashed, prisoners were set free from the prison and attempts were made to burn down the Vicar of Sheffield's residence in Broom Hall, while cries of 'No King' were shouted (inspired by the spirit of the French Revolution). The dragoons had to be called in from Nottingham to restore order and one supposed instigator was hanged in York.

By the end of the enclosures in the mid-19th century, almost all of the moorland wastes were in private hands and managed primarily for their grouse-shooting potential. Estates included Snailsden (the Spencer-Stanhopes), Boardhill (Sir Thomas Pilkington), Midhope (the Bosvilles), Broomhead (the Rimington-Wilsons), Howden and Derwent (the Duke of Norfolk), Bleaklow and Kinder (the Duke of Devonshire) and Longshaw (the Duke of Rutland), many of which remain intact to this day. After the enclosure of the commons, the farmers paid rent for grazing on the moorland and were required to keep their sheep within the enclosed heaths between April and September so as not to interfere with the grouse.

Though heather burning had taken place on the moors from the 14th century to provide sheep with more palatable young heather, its scale greatly increased in the 19th century. Young heather is more digestible, while that more than ten years old is no use for feed, providing only cover and shelter for the birds to nest. Grips were dug across the moors to improve drainage and encourage heather growth, the most dramatic of which are the Duke of Devonshire's broad scars across the ridges of Bleaklow. Birds of prey were often hunted to extinction locally to protect the valuable but vulnerable red grouse[7]. Quartz grit, which helped the grouse grind the heather, was laid out on the moors at intervals (these can now be seen on plastic trays marked by short stakes). Small walled enclosures on the moors were built to grow black oats that also fed the grouse and these can still be seen on Big Moor, Burbage and Broomhead.

Before they began to be shot on the wing in the late 17th century, grouse shooting began as a form of hawking, with the birds caught in nets. In the 18th century, during which the game laws and hunting season were established, the sport involved a long walk with a guide and a dog. Although popular, it did not burgeon until the development of driven grouse shooting in the mid-19th century. Boardhill and Snailsden were among the first estates in the UK to practice this, with birds being driven towards a line of stationary butts. This enabled far larger bags to be shot in a day – on a single famous day in 1893, a record 1,324 brace were shot on Broomhead Moor – and required increasingly intensive management of the moors to keep them stocked with birds.

a grouse butt

---

[7] Red grouse is a sub-species of the willow grouse that is found only in the British Isles and has a diet almost exclusively of heather. Although black grouse were at one time common on the Dark Peak moors, its numbers dwindled and it was hunted to extinction during the 19th century. Attempts to reintroduce it in the Upper Derwent Valley in 2003 failed due to attacks by raptors and foxes.

In 1832 the game laws had changed to give game rights to the owner of the land rather than the Lord of the Manor, with rents increasing greatly as a result. The shooting rights on many moors were let to game associations, clubs whose members paid for tickets, though Stanage was among those let to private individuals. One of these, B. P. Broomhead, built Stanedge Lodge in 1869, while William Wilson later had carved over a hundred numbered grouse drinking troughs across the moor to prevent his birds going elsewhere for water. These individuals also erected lines of boundary stones carved with their initials to mark their domain; these can be found low in the heather on most of South Yorkshire's moorland.

Gamekeepers were employed to manage these estates and remote lodges built for them to live in. They also made use of cabins that had been used by shepherds in the 17th and 18th centuries to watch over the moors by night during the nesting season and particularly dry periods when fires were more likely. They were also used by shooting parties for resting and lunching, elaborate spreads laid on at the more upmarket estates. These crumbled stone structures or the

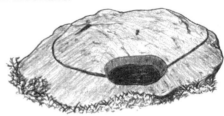

one of William Wilson's grouse drinking troughs on Hallam Moors

footings of temporary wooden cabins represent some of the only obvious features on the upper wastes of Bleaklow, Howden, Derwent and Kinder and were often built beside springs *(see p8 for more information on grouse shooting)*.

Though it is easy to condemn grouse shooting as a rich man's folly, a great deal has been preserved on our moors because they have been used for deer hunting and grouse shooting for most of the past thousand years. Only a short period in the 17th and 18th centuries saw intense grazing on the moors, so prehistoric sites have lain almost untouched here, where they have disappeared in more agricultural landscapes. Historian David Hey has also suggested that much of the moorland fringe of Sheffield would have been covered in conifers in the early 20th century had it not been so bountiful for grouse. The first plantations around the moor edges were established in the early 19th century, including those around Dunford Bridge, while the reservoirs of the Derwent Valley were planted with 20th-century forests. However, when one considers the scale of plantations on similar land in Scotland and South Wales it is hard not to agree with him.

The grazing of sheep on the moors declined greatly by the early 20th century, with many of the old sheep and cattle farms that once thrived becoming run down and abandoned after the establishment of the grouse monoculture. It was widely thought that sheep had an adverse impact on grouse numbers and they were banished from Broomhead Moor in 1879, while the Duke of Rutland banned them between 1901-11 and again between 1924-7. It is now generally agreed that sheep aid the grouse population by creating sheep tracks and sheltering places in winter, digging out food and leaving scraps, and by eating the moor grasses that could otherwise choke out the heather, but there was far more money to be made from grouse shooting than grazing land.

The only respite for the birds was during the World Wars, when grouse shooting was abandoned and the moors used for military training. During World War I, troops were camped at Totley Rifle Range, which had opened in 1900, and at Redmires, where the Sheffield Pals Battalion trained for trench warfare on Hill 60. Longshaw Lodge served as a hospital and sphagnum moss was collected from the moors for use as dressings; those who were encouraged to go out and harvest it were known to joke "so now we're allowed to go on the moors?"

During World War II most of South Yorkshire's moorland was used extensively for army training. The 57 Anti-Aircraft Brigade had 5,000 troops at Langsett and Derwent, while other troops trained for the Normandy Landings on Midhope Moor, Burbage, Big Moor and Chatsworth Moors, where earthworks, tank targets and gun platforms were built and many of the rocks were peppered with gunshot. Wooden lookout structures were built on strategic high points – Rod Moor, Crook Hill and Strines Moor – and starfish decoy sites were laid out on Derwent Edge, Houndkirk Moor, Curbar Gap, Rother Valley, Bradfield Moors (near Emlin) and close to the former Flouch Inn to draw German bombers away from important sites in Sheffield. Some guide stoops on the moors were buried by the Home Guard to prevent them aiding downed enemy parachutists. When New Zealand pilot Paul Rabone and his Scottish companion crashed their Defiant fighter plane on Rowlee Pasture in 1941, a local farmer mistook them for Germans.

Despite all the disruption, the grouse and their overlords are still there, but the gulls that used to nest on Leash and Lucas Fens between the wars were scared away for good when the area was used to detonate the unexploded bombs that had been dropped during the Sheffield Blitz in 1941.

FROM TRESPASS-LAND TO ACCESS LAND

'This stretch of Derbyshire reminds one more of the Highlands of Scotland, where the peasants have been hunted out of certain glens to make room first for sheep and then for deer... The High Peak is similarly sacred to grouse.'
(J.B. Firth, *Highways and Byways in Derbyshire*, 1908)

The growth of grouse shooting's importance during the 19th century and the obsession with maximising the number of grouse on the moors essentially closed the Dark Peak moorland off to the common person. Though affordable passenger trains and coaches started to make the moors of the Peak District accessible for day trips from the rapidly growing cities of Sheffield and Manchester, there were very few places that could be legally explored. It became what G.H.B. Ward and others referred to as 'trespass-land', with eagle-eyed gamekeepers and their hands looking out for intruders. Even bilberry picking, which had been practised for centuries and saw ingenious picking machines invented in the 19th century, was no longer allowed.

Some long-established rights of way were enshrined in the Enclosure Acts, such as Duke's Road, included in the Ecclesfield Enclosure Act, but many others were lost forever, like Emlin Dike Road, New Cross Road and Mitchell Gate on Bradfield Moors. Previous gates and drives were walled up and, as the grouse pastures became more fiercely protected, ancient paths were increasingly being blocked off. The law seemed happy to allow ancient routes across the moors like Doctor's Gate on Bleaklow, Derwent Road across Derwent Edge, and the Snake Path to disappear until people began to stand up to these impositions around the turn of the 20th century.

The first rambling clubs were formed in the late 19th century and the Climbers' Club was founded in 1898. Climbers had begun setting routes on Upper and Nether Tors in the 1890s and Wharncliffe Crags predated Stanage as the most popular gritstone edge in the country. The Kyndwr Club was founded in 1900 by a group of Sheffield and Derby climbers and walkers, including J.W. Puttrell and Ernest Baker, pioneers of access rights in the Peak District. One of the most influential ramblers' groups was the Sheffield Clarion Ramblers' Club, founded in 1900 after a ramble around Kinder Scout organised by G.H.B. (or Bert) Ward via an advertisement in the pages of the weekly Socialist paper *The Clarion*. The club grew steadily through the early part of the 20th century and, though the initial rambles were always on public footpaths, other trespasses were soon arranged. These Midnight or Rakes' Rambles set off under the cover of darkness for forbidden places like Bleaklow and Howden to avoid alerting the gamekeepers. Ward would cry Walt Whitman's line 'Pioneers, oh pioneers!' as they walked, and many from the club were directly involved in the fight for access to the moorlands that continued throughout the next century.

The Snake Path was reopened in 1897 after protracted talks between landowners and the Peak District and Northern Counties Footpaths Preservation Society[8], formed in Manchester in 1894 to fight this long-running battle for access across Kinder Scout. There was to be another route offered across Kinder Downfall to link up with the Jacob's Ladder route, but the landowners backtracked due to the amount of trespassing people were doing off the Snake Path. Vandalism of stone walling or remote cabins, rolling stones down hillsides and setting fires (whether deliberately or accidentally) also counted against the ramblers. Informal agreements were reached between established ramblers groups and gamekeepers, some of the earliest of which were on the Eastern Moors. In 1909, a campaign by John Derry, Bert Ward and others persuaded the Duke of Rutland to open up the path along Froggatt Edge to groups of up to six people, although this was rescinded in 1924 and access would not be established here until after World War II.

It wasn't just private landowners who restricted access to the moors. As well as clearing farms within the watersheds to prevent contamination of the water, the water boards were vehemently opposed to public access. Reservoirs had been built to provide drinking water for the growing urban population of Sheffield since dams were constructed at Crookesmoor in 1782. Dale Dyke Reservoir was among the more famous early failures, when its embankment collapsed in 1864, killing 240 people in the Great Sheffield Flood. It was rebuilt in the 1870s, when Agden and Strines Reservoirs were also built in the River Loxley's catchment. Work on the huge Derwent Valley dams began at the turn of the century (see p36 for more information on this project), but the Derwent Valley Water Board tried to block off routes out of the valley and the planting of conifers around the reservoirs took no account of these existing routes. Bert Ward thought reservoir-building served as a good excuse for the authorities to close off existing rights of way, including the ancient bridleway from Westend to Alport that was closed off in 1922. After a protest by the Peak District and Northern Counties Footpaths Preservation Society, an offer was made to allow access only on the first weekend of the month during daylight hours. It took until 1940 to establish it as a right of way, and even now it is still only a footpath rather than a bridleway. The Miller's Arms pub at Saltersbrook House was pulled down by Manchester Corporation to prevent contamination of the Longdendale reservoirs in the 1920s, when other reservoirs were also being built at Broomhead, Morehall, Langsett, Midhope and Underbank.

The interwar period saw a huge growth of rambling as a way for people to get out of the towns and cities where they lived and worked. Weekend trains were filled with ramblers and it was considered a craze in the 1920s, with an estimated ten thousand ramblers in the Peak District each weekend. Places on the edge of the moor took advantage by providing refreshments, like the Round House in Ringinglow and Higger Lodge above Hathersage. However, access to the moors was still very limited and watchers were employed alongside gamekeepers at the weekends to prevent

---

[8] Its precursors were the Hayfield and Kinder Scout Ancient Footpaths Association and the Manchester Association for the Preservation of Ancient Public Footpaths, which had begun its work in 1826.

trespassing. The Duke of Rutland even ordered places on his land that served refreshments to stop doing so.

Access to Kinder Scout had to be sought from James Watts, a Manchester businessman who owned much of the moor for sporting purposes. Although initially permission was often granted, its increasing popularity made him more reticent. When two men died trespassing on Kinder in the winter of 1922, Watts refused access to the summit thereafter. He had an injunction taken out against G.H.B. Ward, having seen an article in the local press in which Ward spoke about a memorial service for one of the men held at Kinder Downfall. However, trespassing increased subsequently on Kinder, particularly among the working class who found themselves excluded from many of the gentleman's agreements that the ramblers' federations had arranged. It was one of these groups, the British Workers' Sports Federation, whose secretary Benny Rothman organised the notorious mass trespass on Kinder Scout on April 24th 1932. Though little trespassing occurred on this day compared to events like public searches on the plateau for missing persons, the fact that five of the young ringleaders were imprisoned for up to six months drew great attention to the movement *(see p72 for more information on this event)*.

Since the 1920s, ramblers had gathered in June every year at Winnats Pass for an access rally to support the proposed Access to the Mountains Bill. In 1928 Labour MP C.P. Trevelyan spoke to the large crowd, but it was nothing compared to the crowd that arrived on 26th June 1932, which was around five thousand strong and partially co-opted by the militant left wing, who sang 'The Internazionale'. There was another rally at Jacob's Ladder and a second mass trespass in September 1932, when a large number of ramblers from Sheffield followed the disputed Duke's Road across Broomhead Moors. They were met by up to a hundred gamekeepers near Abbey Brook and in violent clashed the ramblers were struck with pit props, but the police were reluctant to make arrests on this occasion. Another trespass on Stanage Edge on 16th October was prevented by mounted police and patrols with dogs.

The Duke of Rutland, who was known as 'the fox-hunting Duke' and was responsible for the many Duke's Drives around the Eastern Moors, was forced to sell the Longshaw Estate in 1927 to pay death duties. At 12,300 acres it was the largest grouse estate in Derbyshire and South Yorkshire, and was broken up for sale. By 1933 money was raised by public appeal from various industrialists and activists in Sheffield to purchase Longshaw Park for £14,000 under the guide of the Longshaw Committee[9], before being given to the National Trust. Burbage Moor was bought by the Sheffield Corporation, who intended to construct a large reservoir in the Burbage Valley. After this plan was shelved following local opposition, the moor was opened to the public. The rest of the Duke's moors were sold to the Chesterfield Corporation and the Rural Development Council, the latter simply renting out the shooting rights and keeping the rest of the moors closed to the public, including all of Big Moor. After World War II, this area was also proposed as a large military training area (like those on the Wiltshire Downs and Mynydd Epynt), but this plan was rejected.

Some access concessions were made in the 1930s by the Chatsworth Estate and Sheffield Water Board. Derwent Road was an ancient cut gate (packhorse route) across the moor between Moscar Cross and Derwent village; its existence had been denied by the landowner, but it was established as a right of way in 1933. However, though some landowners were increasingly sympathetic to public access. they did not act for fear of reducing the value of their estate and most moorland remained exclusive ground at the outbreak of World War II.

---

[9] The National Council of Ramblers' Federations, the first national body representing the interests of ramblers and precursor of the Ramblers' Association, was formed at Longshaw Lodge in 1931.

In 1939, the Access to Mountains Act was finally passed, an access bill first presented in 1884 by MP James Bryce initially seeking a right to roam on the Scottish mountains. Having originally aimed to secure unrestricted access to all mountains, it was presented unsuccessfully 18 times and was so watered downpost when it came in that it had little or no effect. By then, the Standing Committee for National Parks had been formed and there were meetings to discuss proposals for a Peak District National Park at Edale in 1938 and 1939. The idea had first been drawn up in the early 20th century by the founder of the Friends of the Peak District, Ethel Gallimore (later Haythornthwaite). By the 1930s there were suggestions of a separate national park for Dovedale, where much of the land had been granted to the National Trust and countryside wardens were already in place. These were eventually united as a single entity, originally termed The Peak District and Dovedale.

As soon as the war was over, the National Parks Commission was set up and the National Park and Access to the Countryside Act of 1949 repealed the earlier bill. National Parks were supported by Labour's new post-war government, with ten promised and the Peak District becoming the UK's first National Park in 1951. This paved the way for the negotiation of various access agreements, with financial compensation offered to landowners in exchange for public access. The first access agreement was on Kinder Scout, with freedom to roam granted on large parts of the plateau in 1954 and extended to Bleaklow in 1957. The Derwent and Howden Moors Estate was acquired by the National Trust in 1952 with the assistance of the National Land Fund, which had been set up in 1946 to buy and preserve beautiful places as a lasting memorial to those who had fought in the war[10]. The Hope Woodlands Estate was added in 1959, including further swathes of Bleaklow. Part of Langsett Moors was opened up in 1961 and public access to all of Stanage Edge was granted in the 1960s. The Pennine Way was designated as the first long distance path in 1951, though it did not officially open until 1965. Although much of this publicly accessible moorland was closed for shooting on August 12th and subsequent Saturdays in the shooting season, many of the early activists assumed that the hard work had been done.

In fact the main problem now seemed to be managing the huge numbers of visitors who wanted to take advantage of the new National Park. The Threat to the Peak had been published in 1932 by the Council for the Protection of Rural England, highlighting the disfiguration of the countryside taking place and stressing our duty to look after it. Consequently, the Warden Guide Service was set up in 1954, staffed by volunteers and coordinated by Tom Tomlinson, the first National Park Warden in the country. They were a go-between with landowners and farmers, and advised visitors (the first information centre was set up in the Old Nags Head in Edale), rescued those in distress and ensured the country code was being followed. Visitors were admonished for starting fires, dropping litter, breaking branches, carving initials in rocks and toppling boulders, the latter two being particular problems. Many were prosecuted and fined for rolling boulders down hillsides onto targets like cabins, or heading out into the Peak with chisels and hammers. Two men were caught chopping up the timber of Ashop Clough Cabin to use as firewood in the 1950s and Wood Moor Cabin was vandalised in the 1960s.

---

[6] £50 million was originally promised to this fund, though this was reduced to £10 million in 1957 and the fund was eventually abolished in 1980.

Like rambling, climbing was booming after World War II. Before then it had tended to be confined to those with connections to the landowners as most of the crags were on private land. There were relatively few working-class climbers in the 1930s, but this quickly changed after the war and the standard of climbing leapt as a result, with Joe Brown and Dan Whillans notable names among the early working-class climbers. Climbing gear developed too; from gardening gloves and a rope around your waist to modern belays that allowed harder routes to be tried with less risk. An access agreement for climbers on Stanage Edge was quickly reached after the formation of the National Park with then owner, Army Officer Colonel Beach.

However, a glance at the map in the early 1980s reveals how much moorland in private hands was still fiercely guarded, particularly on the South Yorkshire side of the hills. Snailsden Moor, Thurlstone Moor, Midhope Moor, Broomhead Moor, Bradfield Moors, parts of Stanage and most of the Eastern Moors[11] were still no-go areas. In the run up to celebrations for the 50th anniversary of the original Kinder Trespass, a mass trespass was organised on Bamford Moor in March 1982. Two hundred people took part but there was no repeat of the earlier clashes and it led to the formation of the Sheffield Campaign for Access to Moorland (SCAM). While the Ramblers' Association was busy lobbying the Labour Party, then in opposition, to include a Right to Roam Act in its manifesto, SCAM led the way with direct action. They actively trespassed on the moors of the Peak District to highlight the still prevalent attitude to public access in the UK's most popular National Park.

*old sign on
Snailsden Moors*

By the end of 1982, much of Kinder Scout was bought by the National Trust and became open access in perpetuity, since when there has been no grouse shooting on any but a few of its northern slopes. Following the purchase of Kinder Scout, the Kinder and High Peak Advisory Committee was set up with Benny Rothman as its first chairman and continues to promote the Spirit of Kinder events. SCAM continued to organise dozens of mass trespasses until the late 1990s, including an event on Boardhill and Thurlstone Moors in September 1991 that attracted hundreds of ramblers and with Benny Rothman in attendance. In 2000 the Countryside and Rights of Way Act was passed by the Labour government, finally enshrining public access to the moors. Sheffield City Council and the Peak District National Park Authority were the only councils in the UK to support the act, and a plaque was unveiled on Sheffield Town Hall to remember those who had campaigned for access rights. Though the fight for access to the moors appeared to have been won, this same bill declared that the definitive map will be closed in 1st January 2026. Thereafter no new public highways or rights of way can be claimed, though many discussed historical routes in this book remain unrecognised. Hence there are still plenty of local battles to be won before this deadline.

---

[11] The Eastern Moors did not become part of the Peak District until 1984 due to a reluctance by the water authorities to give up the control of their catchments around Barbrook and Ramsley Reservoirs, which supplied Chesterfield's water.

THE FUTURE

With access established, the priority now must surely be to reinstate and promote a healthy moorland environment. The moors that were won were discovered to be in very bad condition due to a wide range of factors. Peat formation had declined since the Middle Ages, with peat-forming bog mosses known as sphagnum increasingly replaced by cottongrass, and these problems have accelerated over the last two hundred years. Atmospheric pollution, overgrazing, footpath erosion, peat harvesting, drainage and moorland fires (whether accidental or intentional as a form of heather management) have greatly damaged the delicate balance of the peat plateaus. In the late 20th century, Kinder and Bleaklow were characterised by great black peat scars and huge bowls of exposed peat, across which you slopped uncomfortably when trying to explore.

Moors for the Future, a partnership between the National Trust, the RSPB, Natural England, the National Park Authority and local water boards, has set about large scale damming and reseeding projects across the blanket bogs of Kinder, Bleaklow, Howden and Snailsden. The Pennine Way and other paths have been laid with flagstones, fences have been erected to restrict livestock grazing, and many of the drains that were dug to drain the moors for grouse have been blocked. The heather, bilberry, crowberry and bracken that are found on the better-drained areas of moorland are giving way to moorland grasses, alpine species and eventually sphagnum that hold the soggy peat sponge together on the high plateaus.

The conifer plantations of the 1930s that surround the upper Derwent, Alport and Woodlands Valleys are being gradually replanted with native deciduous species like oak, birch and hazel. Few are of much value as timber as it costs so much to extract from the steep valley sides. Felling at Alport and Westend should see native broadleaves return to these remote valleys, taking us back to how the landscape would have looked for much of the last two millennia.

The next great threat is likely to be climate change, which we're witnessing as wet winters and hot, dry summers – the fires of 2018 on Saddleworth Moor being a clear threat to the precarious moorland environment. The Eastern Moors represent the very base of the Pennine chain and change is usually seen here first. Though usually associated with heathlands further south, birds like the nightjar and Dartford warbler have been nesting here recently. The grouse-shooting season has also been affected by climate change, with falling stock and new diseases blamed on it. We might have to get used to more changes in bird migration and weather patterns, and somehow cope with this without the EU money that has supported so much of the recent work. But on a more positive note the Dark Peak moors look healthier than they have done for centuries and many conflicting interests are being successfully balanced at least for the time being.

a dunlin

A MOORLAND GLOSSARY

bar = steep hillside trackway
bents = ground covered in bent grass
biggin = building
bole = iron smelting site
booth (or **butt**) = temporary herdsman's shelter on summer grazing ground
bur (or **burgh**) = fortification
cairn = pile of stones (either waymarker, field clearance or ancient burial site)
carr = bog or wooded marshland
cote = cottage
cowm = deep hollow or valley
dene (or **dean**) = valley
dun = hill
field = clearing
firth = wood or chase
glead = kite or other hawk
grain = fork of stream
grange = land belonging to a monastery
greaves = woodland grove
grough = deep peat channel
hag = peat bank
hagg = place cleared of trees
ham = homestead
hanging = land on steep slope
hare (or **hoar**) = boundary place
hey = hedged enclosure
hollin = holly trees grown for winter food
holme = island
hope = enclosed valley
hurst = wooded hill
ing = meadow
intake = land enclosed from moor
jagger = leader of packhorse train
laund = a narrow tongue of ground
ley (or **lea**) = woodland glade or clearing
low = hill or burial mound
mere = boundary place
owler = alder
rake = narrow hill path
reddle (or **ruddle**) = red-coloured, usually relating to ochre
rocher = steep rocky bank
rod = clearing
shaw = copse
sick (or **sike**) = small ditch or stream
slack = a shallow valley or wet area below a slope
stoop = a stone post
storrs (or **storthes**) = plantation or coppice wood
strines = stream or junction of streams
thorp = outlying farmstead
ton = farmstead or village
wash = a watery place, or where sheep were washed
worth = enclosure or dwelling

CHAPTER 1 – SNAILSDEN & THURLSTONE MOORS

High Point: Dead Edge End, 499m

Grid Ref: SE124017

Map Sheet: OL1 (Dark Peak)

Access: No access for dogs on any of these moors other than very limited Public Rights of Way.

Public Transport: Bus 29 runs infrequently from Sheffield and Penistone to Carlecotes/ Dunford Bridge.

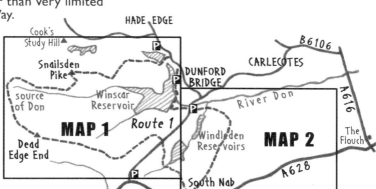

In the far north-western corner of South Yorkshire, these quiet moors butt up against the edge of West Yorkshire. Their heathery expanses are almost entirely given over to grouse shooting, and it is rare to meet another walker away from Dunford Bridge and the Trans-Pennine Trail. They do, however, throw up three satisfying summits and cradle a series of charming reservoirs and the line of the Woodhead Tunnel.

Snailsden Moors comprise a renowned shooting estate above Winscar Reservoir and its owners long resisted any public access. It is here the River Don has its source high on the Pennine watershed. Thurlstone Moors have previously been known as Boardhill Moors, another popular shooting estate surrounding the Dog & Partidge Inn. Thurlstone is derived from an old Danish name, Thurulf, and the sooty village that gives the moor its name feels more like part of West Yorkshire, with its lines of textile mills and weavers' cottages. The moors are best explored from Dunford Bridge, which nestles between the two moorland areas.

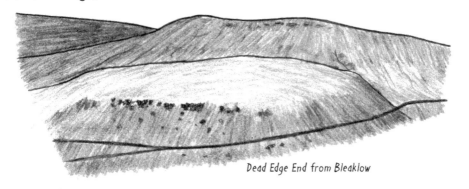

Dead Edge End from Bleaklow

MAP 1: SNAILSDEN MOORS

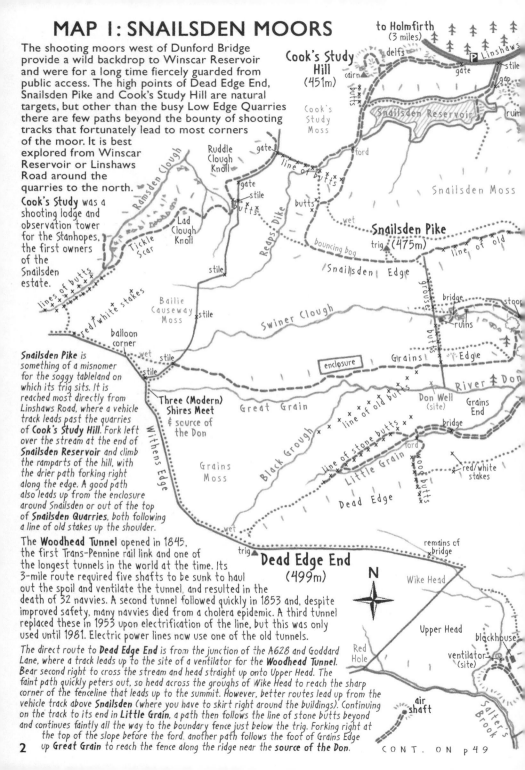

The shooting moors west of Dunford Bridge provide a wild backdrop to Winscar Reservoir and were for a long time fiercely guarded from public access. The high points of Dead Edge End, Snailsden Pike and Cook's Study Hill are natural targets, but other than the busy Low Edge Quarries there are few paths beyond the bounty of shooting tracks that fortunately lead to most corners of the moor. It is best explored from Winscar Reservoir or Linshaws Road around the quarries to the north.

Cook's Study was a shooting lodge and observation tower for the Stanhopes, the first owners of the Snailsden estate.

Snailsden Pike is something of a misnomer for the soggy tableland on which its trig sits. It is reached most directly from Linshaws Road, where a vehicle track leads past the quarries of **Cook's Study Hill**. Fork left over the stream at the end of **Snailsden Reservoir** and climb the ramparts of the hill, with the drier path forking right along the edge. A good path also leads up from the enclosure around Snailsden or out of the top of **Snailsden Quarries**, both following a line of old stakes up the shoulder.

The **Woodhead Tunnel** opened in 1845, the first Trans-Pennine rail link and one of the longest tunnels in the world at the time. Its 3-mile route required five shafts to be sunk to haul out the spoil and ventilate the tunnel, and resulted in the death of 32 navvies. A second tunnel followed quickly in 1853 and, despite improved safety, many navvies died from a cholera epidemic. A third tunnel replaced these in 1953 upon electrification of the line, but this was only used until 1981. Electric power lines now use one of the old tunnels.

The direct route to **Dead Edge End** is from the junction of the A628 and Goddard Lane, where a track leads up to the site of a ventilator for the **Woodhead Tunnel**. Bear second right to cross the stream and head straight up onto Upper Head. The faint path quickly peters out, so head across the groughs of Wike Head to reach the sharp corner of the fenceline that leads up to the summit. However, better routes lead up from the vehicle track above **Snailsden** (where you have to skirt right around the buildings). Continuing on the track to its end in **Little Grain**, a path then follows the line of stone butts beyond and continues faintly all the way to the boundary fence just below the trig. Forking right at the top of the slope before the ford, another path follows the foot of Grains Edge up **Great Grain** to reach the fence along the ridge near the **source of the Don**.

2

CONT. ON p49

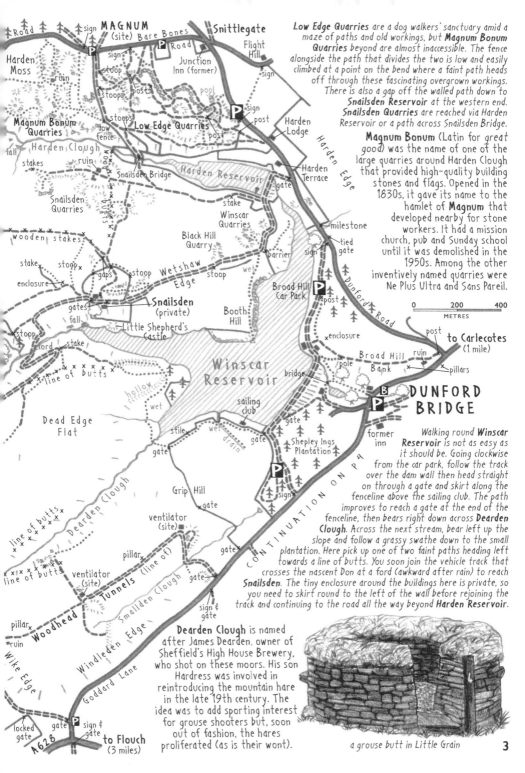

Low Edge Quarries are a dog walkers' sanctuary amid a maze of paths and old workings, but **Magnum Bonum Quarries** beyond are almost inaccessible. The fence alongside the path that divides the two is low and easily climbed at a point on the bend where a faint path heads off through these fascinating overgrown workings. There is also a gap off the walled path down to **Snailsden Reservoir** at the western end. **Snailsden Quarries** are reached via Harden Reservoir or a path across Snailsden Bridge.

Magnum Bonum (Latin for great good) was the name of one of the large quarries around Harden Clough that provided high-quality building stones and flags. Opened in the 1830s, it gave its name to the hamlet of **Magnum** that developed nearby for stone workers. It had a mission church, pub and Sunday school until it was demolished in the 1950s. Among the other inventively named quarries were Ne Plus Ultra and Sans Pareil.

Walking round **Winscar Reservoir** is not as easy as it should be. Going clockwise from the car park, follow the track over the dam wall then head straight on through a gate and skirt along the fenceline above the sailing club. The path improves to reach a gate at the end of the fenceline, then bears right down across **Dearden Clough**. Across the next stream, bear left up the slope and follow a grassy swathe down to the small plantation. Here pick up one of two faint paths heading left towards a line of butts. You soon join the vehicle track that crosses the nascent Don at a ford (awkward after rain) to reach **Snailsden**. The tiny enclosure around the buildings here is private, so you need to skirt round to the left of the wall before rejoining the track and continuing to the road all the way beyond **Harden Reservoir**.

Dearden Clough is named after James Dearden, owner of Sheffield's High House Brewery, who shot on these moors. His son Hardress was involved in reintroducing the mountain hare in the late 19th century. The idea was to add sporting interest for grouse shooters but, soon out of fashion, the hares proliferated (as is their wont).

a grouse butt in Little Grain

Map labels:

Road · sign · MAGNUM (site) Bare Bones · Snittlegate · Flight Hill · Road · Harden Moss · ruin · sign · stoop · Junction Inn (former) · Road · sign · posts · stoops · pool · sign · Harden Lodge · stoops · sign · post · Magnum Bonum Quarries · low fence · Low Edge Quarries · post · Harden Terrace · Harden Clough · fall · stakes · ruin · Snailsden Bridge · Harden Reservoir · gate · Harden Edge · Snailsden Quarries · stake · Winscar Quarries · milestone · wooden stakes · Black Hill Quarry · tied gate · sign · stake · stoop · enclosure · gaps · stoop · Wetshaw Edge · stoop · wet · barrier · Broad Hill Car Park · post · Dunford Road · gates · fall · Snailsden (private) · Booth Hill · enclosure · to Carlecotes (1 mile) · stoop · ford · stake · Little Shepherd's Castle · post · ruin · pillars · line of butts · Broad Hill Bank · pole · bridge · DUNFORD BRIDGE · Dead Edge Flat · hollow · Winscar Reservoir · sailing club · gate · former inn · wet · stile · wet · gate · drain · gate · Shepley Ings Plantation · sign · gate · line of butts · Dearden Clough · Grip Hill · gate · ventilator (site) · pillar (line of) · ventilator (site) · Tunnels (line of) · Smallden Clough · gate · sign & gate · line of butts · Woodhead · Windleden Edge · Goddard Lane · pillar · ruin · Wike Edge · locked gate · gate · sign & gate · A628 · to Flouch (3 miles)

0   200   400
METRES

CONTINUATION ON P4

3

MAP 2: THURLSTONE MOORS

Thurlstone Moors form a long strip of largely untrodden moorland on the north side of the A628 Woodhead Road. There are few focal points beyond the trigpoint on South Nab and the Windleden Reservoirs, and most of the moor is path-free. Well-defined bridleways skirt the moor edge, but only a few tracks up Long Grain and Short Grain offer a way into its heart. Dunford Bridge offers an obvious starting point though it is hard not to find yourself on the uneventful Trans-Pennine Trail cycleway.

In the 1970s, the construction of Winscar Dam brought up to 700 workers to Dunford Bridge and the village grew to have its own picture house. The station closed in 1970 and even the **Stanhope Arms** is now a private residence.

In the 15th century, the Lord of Thurlstone Manor had a cattle-rearing vaccary at **Windleden** and a dwelling is recorded there from the early 14th century.

While the *Trans-Pennine Trail* along the former railway line is the obvious route east out of **Dunford Bridge**, it runs adjacent to the moor itself. Instead, where you meet the trail at a signpost, you can double back right and join a track running up onto **Black Bank**. The track divides, with the right fork climbing steadily to follow lines of grouse butts up **Long Grain**. The stream can be followed all the way up to South Nab though there is no path at the top end. The left fork leads across Long Grain and Short Grain, keeping left below the quarries and water works building to return to the moor edge. The track runs out near the enclosures of **Rolly Holme** though sheeptracks can be picked up to continue across or above the enclosures to **Wogden End**.

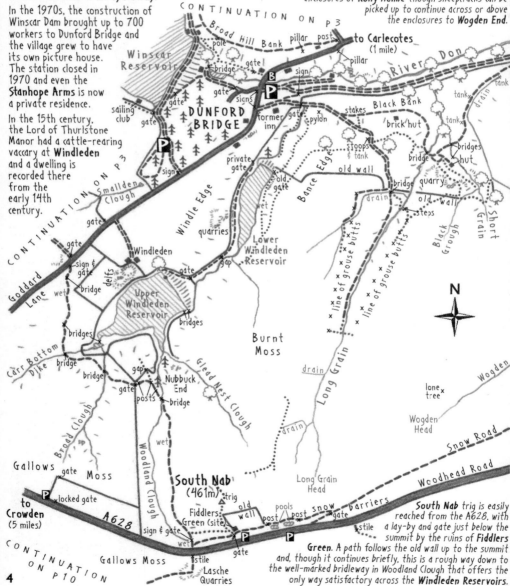

South Nab trig is easily reached from the A628, with a lay-by and gate just below the summit by the ruins of **Fiddlers Green**. A path follows the old wall up to the summit and, though it continues briefly, this is a rough way down to the well-marked bridleway in Woodland Clough that offers the only way satisfactory across the **Windleden Reservoirs**.

4

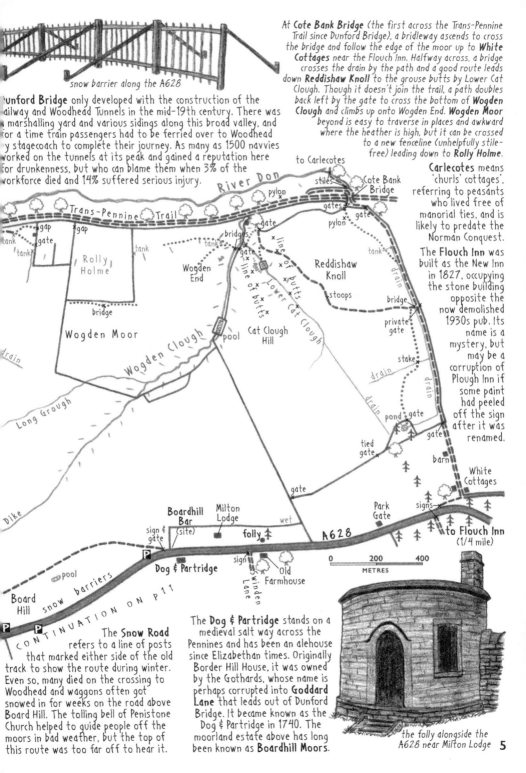

snow barrier along the A628

At **Cote Bank Bridge** (the first across the Trans-Pennine Trail since Dunford Bridge), a bridleway ascends to cross the bridge and follow the edge of the moor up to **White Cottages** near the Flouch Inn. Halfway across, a bridge crosses the drain by the path and a good route leads down **Reddishaw Knoll** to the grouse butts by Lower Cat Clough. Though it doesn't join the trail, a path doubles back left by the gate to cross the bottom of **Wogden Clough** and climbs up onto Wogden End. **Wogden Moor** beyond is easy to traverse in places and awkward where the heather is high, but it can be crossed to a new fenceline (unhelpfully stile-free) leading down to **Rolly Holme**.

Dunford Bridge only developed with the construction of the railway and Woodhead Tunnels in the mid-19th century. There was a marshalling yard and various sidings along this broad valley, and for a time train passengers had to be ferried over to Woodhead by stagecoach to complete their journey. As many as 1500 navvies worked on the tunnels at its peak and gained a reputation here for drunkenness, but who can blame them when 3% of the workforce died and 14% suffered serious injury.

Carlecotes means 'churls' cottages', referring to peasants who lived free of manorial ties, and is likely to predate the Norman Conquest.

The **Flouch Inn** was built as the New Inn in 1827, occupying the stone building opposite the now demolished 1930s pub. Its name is a mystery, but may be a corruption of Plough Inn if some paint had peeled off the sign after it was renamed.

(map labels)
to Carlecotes · River Don · stiles · Cote Bank Bridge · pylon · gates · gate · pylon · Trans-Pennine Trail · bridges · gate · gap · gap · tank · gate · tank · tank · line of butts · tank · tank · drain · Rolly Holme · Wogden End · line of butts · Reddishaw Knoll · bridge · private gate · bridge · Lower Cat Clough · stoops · Wogden Moor · Wogden Clough · pool · Cat Clough Hill · drain · stake · drain · drain · Long Grough · drain · pond · gate · gate · tied gate · barn · White Cottages · Dike · gate · Park Gate · signs · Boardhill Bar (site) · Milton Lodge · wet · folly · A628 · to Flouch Inn (1/4 mile) · sign & gate · pool · snow barriers · sign · Dog & Partridge · Swinden Lane · Old Farmhouse · Board Hill · CONTINUATION ON P11

0   200   400
METRES

The **Snow Road** refers to a line of posts that marked either side of the old track to show the route during winter. Even so, many died on the crossing to Woodhead and waggons often got snowed in for weeks on the road above Board Hill. The tolling bell of Penistone Church helped to guide people off the moors in bad weather, but the top of this route was too far off to hear it.

The **Dog & Partridge** stands on a medieval salt way across the Pennines and has been an alehouse since Elizabethan times. Originally Border Hill House, it was owned by the Gothards, whose name is perhaps corrupted into **Goddard Lane** that leads out of Dunford Bridge. It became known as the Dog & Partridge in 1740. The moorland estate above has long been known as **Boardhill Moors**.

the folly alongside the A628 near Milton Lodge

ROUTE 1: THREE TRIGS FROM DUNFORD

6 Retrace your steps from **Snailsden Pike** trig and follow the path back along the top of Snailsden Edge with a line of old wooden stakes for company. Descending to a junction above the lodge at Snailsden, turn left, then keep right around **Snailsden Quarries**. Follow the track down to **Harden Reservoir** and cross the dam wall to reach Dunford Road.

ruined building at Snailsden Quarry

Snailsden Quarries

ruin

butts

Snailsden Pike

6 (475m)

trig

line of old stakes

gaps

Snailsden Edge

Snailsden

Swiner Clough

grouse butts

ruins

The water from **Don Well** was said by 19th century grouse shooters to be the finest to mix with brandy, but its 20" opening is nowhere to be seen on the bank from which it used to flow.

stile

stile

Three (Modern) Shires Meet & source of the Don

enclosure

Grains Edge

Great Grain (River Don)

butts

Don Well (site)

Grains Moss

5 From **Dead Edge End**, continue along the boundary fence all the way along Withens Edge. There are rough paths both sides but unhelpfully no stiles across. Just beyond the true **source of the River Don** (which is also the boundary of South Yorkshire, West Yorkshire and Derbyshire), another fenceline is met. Follow this right to the next stile, from which a path descends right into Great Grain alongside the nascent Don. Continue past an old enclosure to a line of old grouse butts, beyond which you should follow the line of an old wall climbing steeply left up and over **Grains Edge**. Continue down into **Swiner Clough**, crossing the stream by some old workings before doubling back left to rejoin the old wall as it climbs straight up Snailsden Edge. Bear left near the top and join the path along the edge for 100m, before forking right on a faint path up to the trig point on **Snailsden Pike**.

Withens Edge

Dead Edge End

wet

5 (499m)

trig

remains of bridge

Pathless

Wike Head

pillar

ventilator (site)

pillar

Tunnels (of)

Wike Edge

Woodhead (line

N

pool

blockhouse

0   250   500   750
METRES

Distance: 10 miles (16.2km)

Ascent: 390m

Difficulty: Strenuous

Parking: Free car parks in the centre of Dunford Bridge and alongside Winscar Reservoir.

Public Transport: Dunford Bridge is served by the infrequent 29 bus route from Sheffield & Penistone.

Character: A fine circuit of the moors above Dunford Bridge, taking in the three summits of South Nab, Dead Edge End and Snailsden Pike, as well as Winscar, Harden and Upper Windleden Reservoirs. There are necessarily a couple of rough pathless sections, so careful navigation is needed on these less-trodden grouse shooting moors, but solitude is almost guaranteed. *Note: no dogs are allowed on nearly all of this route.*

4 Continue up the vehicle track as it follows the line of the **Woodhead Tunnels**, heading straight on at the next ventilator site. Soon after passing a triangulation pillar on the right, the path descends **Wike Edge**. Branch off right here along the top of the slope, following a faint path below the peat shelf. Following the line of the right fork of the stream should bring you to the fence corner at **Wike Head**. Stay on the right side of the fenceline all the way up to the trig point on **Dead Edge End**.

Upper Windleden, **Harden** and **Snailsden Reservoirs** were constructed in the 1890s to provide water for Dewsbury and Heckmondwike. In May 1914, a bomb was discovered below the valve tower of Upper Windleden Reservoir, thought to have been laid by the suffragettes of the Women's Social and Political Union during a particularly militant phase just before the outbreak of World War 1. It would have resulted in water flooding down into the lower reservoir and a potential burst that could have inundated the upper Don Valley.

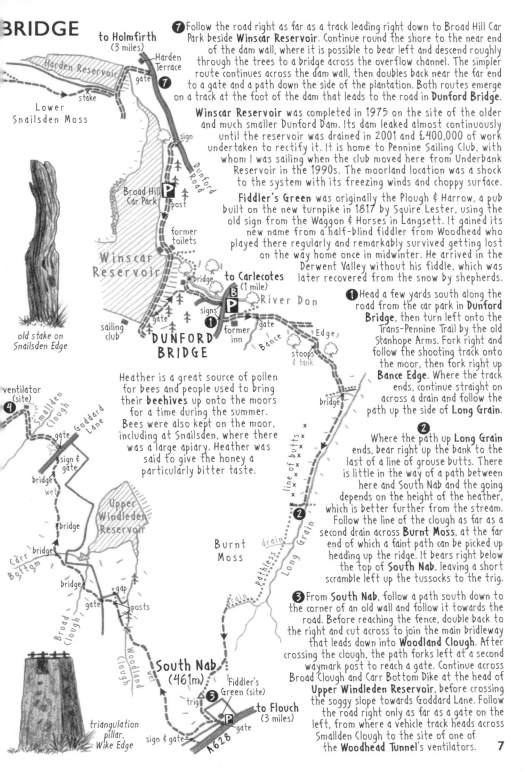

7 Follow the road right as far as a track leading right down to Broad Hill Car Park beside **Winscar Reservoir**. Continue round the shore to the near end of the dam wall, where it is possible to bear left and descend roughly through the trees to a bridge across the overflow channel. The simpler route continues across the dam wall, then doubles back near the far end to a gate and a path down the side of the plantation. Both routes emerge on a track at the foot of the dam that leads to the road in **Dunford Bridge**.

Winscar Reservoir was completed in 1975 on the site of the older and much smaller Dunford Dam. Its dam leaked almost continuously until the reservoir was drained in 2001 and £400,000 of work undertaken to rectify it. It is home to Pennine Sailing Club, with whom I was sailing when the club moved here from Underbank Reservoir in the 1990s. The moorland location was a shock to the system with its freezing winds and choppy surface.

Fiddler's Green was originally the Plough & Harrow, a pub built on the new turnpike in 1817 by Squire Lester, using the old sign from the Waggon & Horses in Langsett. It gained its new name from a half-blind fiddler from Woodhead who played there regularly and remarkably survived getting lost on the way home once in midwinter. He arrived in the Derwent Valley without his fiddle, which was later recovered from the snow by shepherds.

1 Head a few yards south along the road from the car park in **Dunford Bridge**, then turn left onto the Trans-Pennine Trail by the old Stanhope Arms. Fork right and follow the shooting track onto the moor, then fork right up **Bance Edge**. Where the track ends, continue straight on across a drain and follow the path up the side of **Long Grain**.

2 Where the path up **Long Grain** ends, bear right up the bank to the last of a line of grouse butts. There is little in the way of a path between here and South Nab and the going depends on the height of the heather, which is better further from the stream. Follow the line of the clough as far as a second drain across **Burnt Moss**, at the far end of which a faint path can be picked up heading up the ridge. It bears right below the top of **South Nab**, leaving a short scramble left up the tussocks to the trig.

3 From **South Nab**, follow a path south down to the corner of an old wall and follow it towards the road. Before reaching the fence, double back to the right and cut across to join the main bridleway that leads down into **Woodland Clough**. After crossing the clough, the path forks left at a second waymark post to reach a gate. Continue across Broad Clough and Carr Bottom Dike at the head of **Upper Windleden Reservoir**, before crossing the soggy slope towards Goddard Lane. Follow the road right only as far as a gate on the left, from where a vehicle track heads across Smallden Clough to the site of one of the **Woodhead Tunnel**'s ventilators.

Heather is a great source of pollen for bees and people used to bring their **beehives** up onto the moors for a time during the summer. Bees were also kept on the moor, including at Snailsden, where there was a large apiary. Heather was said to give the honey a particularly bitter taste.

Map labels:
to Holmfirth (3 miles)
Harden Reservoir
Harden Terrace
gate
Lower Snailsden Moss
stake
sign
old stake on Snailsden Edge
Dunford Road
Broad Hill Car Park
P
post
former toilets
Winscar Reservoir
bridge
to Carlecotes (1 mile)
River Don
sailing club
gate
signs
P
former inn
gate
DUNFORD BRIDGE
Bance Edge
stoops & tank
bridge
line of butts
Long Grain
drain
Pathless
Burnt Moss
ventilator (site)
4
Smallden Clough
gate
Goddard Lane
sign & gate
bridge
wet
Upper Windleden Reservoir
bridge
Carr Bottom
bridge
bridge
gate
gap
posts
Broad Clough
Woodland Clough
wet
South Nab (461m)
Fiddler's Green (site)
trig
3
triangulation pillar, Wike Edge
sign & gate
to Flouch (3 miles)
P
gate
A628

7

GROUSE SHOOTING

Grouse have been hunted on the Dark Peak moors since the medieval chases, when they were known as moor fowl, but it wasn't until after Parliamentary Enclosure and the removal of the moorland commons that the sort of vast moorland estate with which we are now familiar began to be managed almost exclusively for grouse. Hunting had been governed since the Middle Ages, but a 1671 act of parliament restricted the hunting of moor fowl, hares and pheasants to those who owned land worth more than £100 per year. It led to gamekeepers being appointed by the Lords of the Manor with powers to seize guns and dogs. By 1772, the hunting season was established, with grouse allowed to be shot only between August 12th and December 10th.

Hawking and netting were the traditional hunting methods until the late 17th century, when the Wilsons of Broomhead claimed they were the first to shoot grouse on the Pennine moors. Even then, grouse shooting involved a long walk with a heavy 12" bore muzzle-loading gun that was used to shoot birds as they flew away. Each shooter was accompanied by a moor guide, who would load the gun with shot and black powder and carry birds, and they would both end the day with a black face from the powder.

By the 1860s the breech-loading shotgun was invented and the grouse were driven towards a line of stationary stone butts, a method imported from the continent but first practised in the UK on Boardhill Moor by Walter Spencer-Stanhope, who hid in a grough while the birds were driven towards him. Early butts were made by piling up turf sods; Oxstone Dale Road on Burbage Moor was known as T'Sod Walk for this reason. Huge bags could now be shot and on one day in 1893 1,324 brace of birds were shot on Broomhead Moor by just nine guns, more than on any Scottish estate to that point. Shot birds were gathered while the shooters were lunching, then shipped off in crates by rail for delivery to London hotels.

Gangs from Sheffield regularly poached on the moors and it reached a head on August 12th 1840, when an annual pilgrimage on Midhope Moors saw violent clashes with gamekeepers, one of whom died from his injuries. Similar events occurred on the Duke of Norfolk's land until a slew of prosecutions put an end to this organised activity.

Tracks were constructed across the moors to the butts, cabins were built for storage and for lunchtime shelters (the Duke of Rutland's staff would prepare lavish picnics in his lodges around Longshaw) and drains were dug on the wetter ground to encourage heather to grow rather than cotton-grass and sphagnum. As the moors were managed more intensively, the heather was burned on careful 12-15 year cycles and the moors' ecology was profoundly altered. Sheep were still grazed on some grouse moors out of season, but others like the Duke of Rutland and William Wilson of Beauchief Hall (who created the grouse drinking troughs on Stanage) banned them to try to maximise the number of grouse, despite plenty of evidence to the contrary.

the red grouse

Buzzards, merlins, herons, kites, falcons, ravens and eagles were all exterminated by grouse interests throughout the 19th and 20th centuries, and birds like peregrine falcons, crows, goshawks and hen harriers still are. They were only interested in the red grouse, a sub-species of the European willow grouse that was known as the 'king of game birds'.

Despite a decline in the industry since its Edwardian heyday and the fact that disease and heatwaves have restricted shooting in recent years, half a million grouse are still shot in Britain each year. Though many of the Peak District's more popular moors are now free of shooting, South Yorkshire's moorland fringe remains a stronghold, which is why dogs are still excluded from almost all the open access land there.

CHAPTER 2 – HOWDEN EDGE

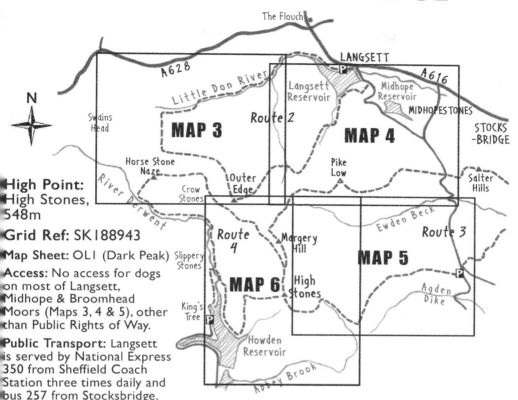

High Point: High Stones, 548m

Grid Ref: SK188943

Map Sheet: OL1 (Dark Peak)

Access: No access for dogs on most of Langsett, Midhope & Broomhead Moors (Maps 3, 4 & 5), other than Public Rights of Way.

Public Transport: Langsett is served by National Express 350 from Sheffield Coach Station three times daily and bus 257 from Stocksbridge.

This great expanse of moorland is South Yorkshire's wilderness, stretching from Langsett, Midhope and the edge of Stocksbridge to the remote head of the Derwent Valley. Howden Edge itself runs northwest from Abbey Brook to Swains Head over the trio of similarly high tops at High Stones, Margery Hill and Outer Edge. Howden is a corruption of Holden, which is how the area was referred to until the 19th century, and refers to a wood in the valley.

All of Howden's northern and eastern flanks are dominated by grouse shooting, while the southwest corner above Howden Reservoir is owned by the National Trust. Road access to Howden is restricted on summer weekends but, along with the shore of Langsett Reservoir, this is the most popular part of the moor. Yet the whole area provides many different and fascinating aspects; from the barren wastes of Broomhead (that most exclusive of hunting grounds) to the intricate shapes of Crow Stones and the ancient stony heap of Pike Low.

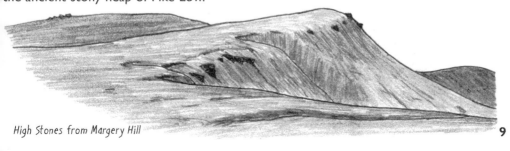

High Stones from Margery Hill

MAP 3: HOWDEN EDGE NORTH-WEST

The most remote corner of Howden Edge stands above the heads of the Derwent and Little Don Valleys. It is a broad boggy ridge at this point with a foul reputation for swallowing boots and more, with its finest edges on spurs to the south at Horse Stone Naze and Crow Stones, the latter a particularly wonderful array of weathered rocks. Though it is only a stone's throw from the desolate Woodhead Road, it is most commonly accessed from King's Tree or Langsett and then only by the keenest bog-trotters.

The quickest but least satisfying way onto Howden Edge is from the busy A628 Woodhead Road. The old turnpike road can be followed to Lady Cross, from where a faint line heads south across the soggy watershed over Round Hill to the main path on Featherbed Moss. Alternatively a stile half a mile to the east yields a fainter path dropping down towards Loftshaw Clough and then following a line of grouse butts on Long Moor to reach the barn at Upper Hordron.

Horse Stone

At the **Shepherds Meeting Stones** farmers from the Derwent Valley, Longdendale and Langsett met twice yearly in July and November to exchange stray sheep in the days before moorland fences. Two stoops that marked the spot are no longer to be found.

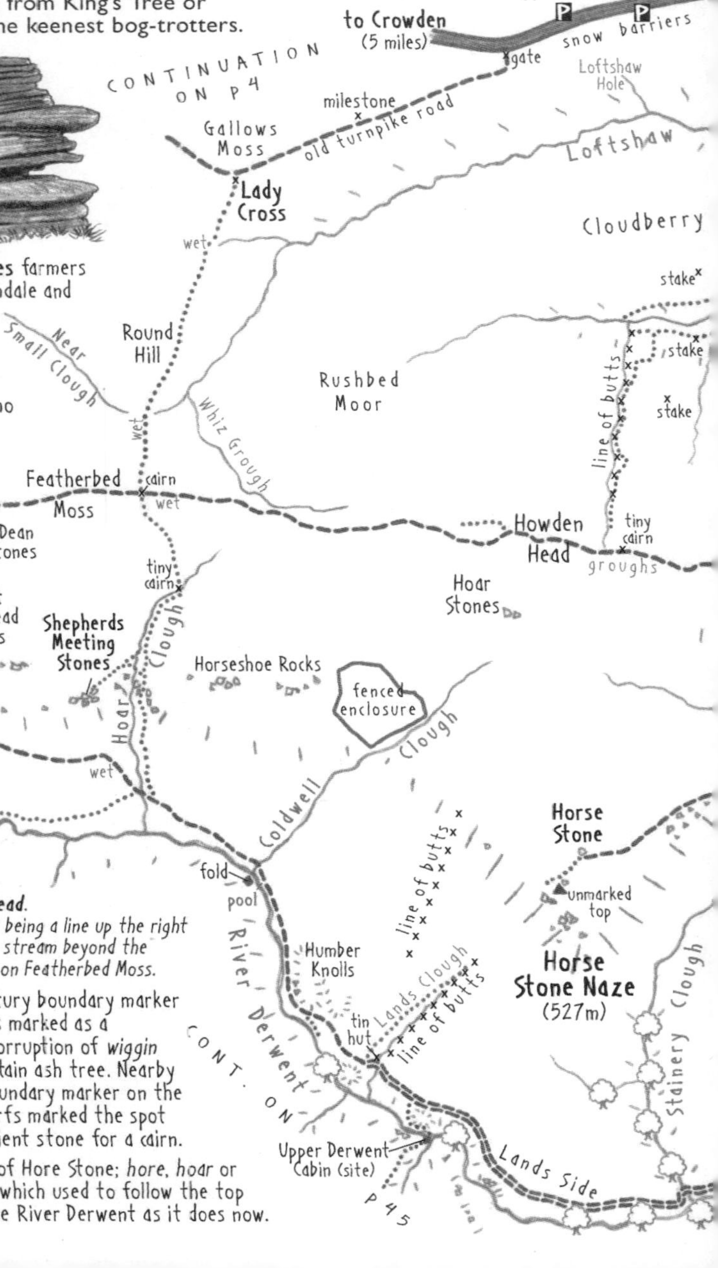

to Crowden (5 miles)

CONTINUATION ON P4

CONTINUATION ON P2

Gallows Moss

milestone

old turnpike road

snow barriers

gate

Loftshaw Hole

Loftshaw

Lady Cross

wet

Cloudberry

stake x

Near Small Clough

Round Hill

Whiz Grough

Rushbed Moor

line of butts

stake

stake

1894 Stone

Featherbed Moss

cairn

wet

Little Dean Head Stones

Howden Head

tiny cairn

groughs

stile

tiny cairn

Great Dean Head Stones

Shepherds Meeting Stones

Hoar Clough

Hoar Stones

Swains Head

stile

Horseshoe Rocks

fenced enclosure

CONTINUATION ON P49

Wigan Tree (site)

wet

Coldwell Clough

line of butts

Horse Stone

The main path up the **River Derwent** is delightful, particularly where it narrows beyond Lands Clough. It eventually ascends across the hillside to reach the watershed at **Swains Head**. There are few paths off it, the best being a line up the right side of **Hoar Clough** - it crosses the stream beyond the stones to reach the watershed path on Featherbed Moss.

The **Wigan Tree** was a 19th-century boundary marker of which nothing remains and was marked as a tree stump by 1955. Wigan is a corruption of wiggin or wicken, referring to the mountain ash tree. Nearby **Swains Head** was a significant boundary marker on the ridge above and a large pile of turfs marked the spot at one time, there being insufficient stone for a cairn.

The **Horse Stone** is a corruption of Hore Stone; hore, hoar or hare relate to a boundary, which used to follow the top of the edge rather than the River Derwent as it does now.

fold

pool

River Derwent

Humber Knolls

Lands Clough

line of butts

tin hut

unmarked top

Horse Stone Naze (527m)

Stainery Clough

CONT. ON P45

Upper Derwent Cabin (site)

Lands Side

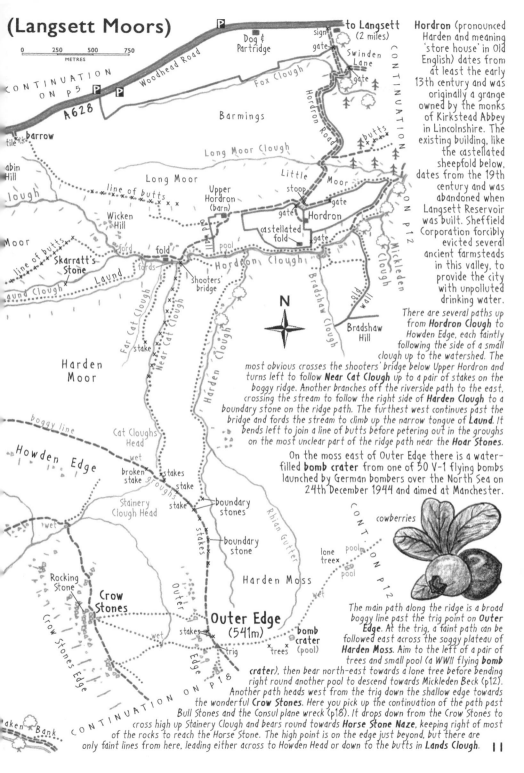

(Langsett Moors)

0   250   500   750
METRES

to Langsett
(2 miles)

Map labels:

P — Dog & Partridge
sign
gate
Swinden Lane
gate
Fox Clough
Hordron Road
CONTINUATION ON P5
Woodhead Road
A628
P   P
Barmings
barrow
tile
abin Hill
lough
Long Moor Clough
Little Moor
stoop
butts
CONTINUATION ON P12
Long Moor
line of butts
Upper Hordron (barn)
gate
gate
Hordron
Wicken Hill
Mickleden Clough
Moor
line of butts
Skarratt's Stone
Laund
ford
fold
fords
shooters' bridge
pool
castellated fold
gate
wall
Hordron Clough
Bradshaw Clough
Bradshaw Hill
Laund Clough
Far Cat Clough
Near Cat Clough
Harden Clough
N
Harden Moor
stake
Cat Cloughs Head
wet
broken stake
stakes
stake
groughs
stake
boundary stones
Stainery Clough Head
stake
boundary stone
Howden Edge
wet
stakes
Rhian Gutter
lone tree
pool
pool
cowberries
CONTINUATION ON P12
Rocking Stone
Crow Stones
Outer Edge
Harden Moss
wet
Crow Stones Edge
wet
stakes
trig
Outer Edge
(541m)
trees
bomb crater (pool)
bomb crater (pool)
aken Bank
CONTINUATION ON P18

Hordron (pronounced Harden and meaning 'store house' in Old English) dates from at least the early 13th century and was originally a grange owned by the monks of Kirkstead Abbey in Lincolnshire. The existing building, like the castellated sheepfold below, dates from the 19th century and was abandoned when Langsett Reservoir was built. Sheffield Corporation forcibly evicted several ancient farmsteads in this valley, to provide the city with unpolluted drinking water.

There are several paths up from **Hordron Clough** to Howden Edge, each faintly following the side of a small clough up to the watershed. The most obvious crosses the shooters' bridge below Upper Hordron and turns left to follow **Near Cat Clough** up to a pair of stakes on the boggy ridge. Another branches off the riverside path to the east, crossing the stream to follow the right side of **Harden Clough** to a boundary stone on the ridge path. The furthest west continues past the bridge and fords the stream to climb up the narrow tongue of **Laund**. It bends left to join a line of butts before petering out in the groughs on the most unclear part of the ridge path near the **Hoar Stones**.

On the moss east of Outer Edge there is a water-filled **bomb crater** from one of 50 V-1 flying bombs launched by German bombers over the North Sea on 24th December 1944 and aimed at Manchester.

The main path along the ridge is a broad boggy line past the trig point on **Outer Edge**. At the trig, a faint path can be followed east across the soggy plateau of **Harden Moss**. Aim to the left of a pair of trees and small pool (a WWII flying **bomb crater**), then bear north-east towards a lone tree before bending right round another pool to descend towards Mickleden Beck (p12). Another path heads west from the trig down the shallow edge towards the wonderful **Crow Stones**. Here you pick up the continuation of the path past Bull Stones and the Consul plane wreck (p18). It drops down from the Crow Stones to cross high up Stainery Clough and bears round towards **Horse Stone Naze**, keeping right of most of the rocks to reach the Horse Stone. The high point is on the edge just beyond, but there are only faint lines from here, leading either across to Howden Head or down to the butts in **Lands Clough**.

11

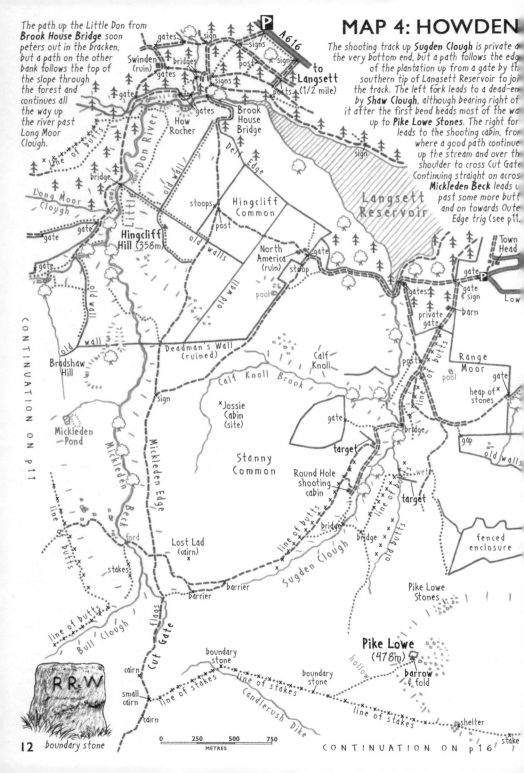

MAP 4: HOWDEN

The path up the Little Don from **Brook House Bridge** soon peters out in the bracken, but a path on the other bank follows the top of the slope through the forest and continues all the way up the river past Long Moor Clough.

The shooting track up **Sugden Clough** is private at the very bottom end, but a path follows the edge of the plantation up from a gate by the southern tip of Langsett Reservoir to join the track. The left fork leads to a dead-end after the first bend heads most of the way up to **Pike Lowe Stones**. The right fork leads to the shooting cabin, from where a good path continues up the stream and over the shoulder to cross Cut Gate. Continuing straight on across **Mickleden Beck** leads up past some more butts and on towards Outer Edge trig (see p.11).

to **Langsett** (1/2 mile)

CONTINUATION ON p11

CONTINUATION ON p16

12 boundary stone

EDGE NORTH-EAST (Midhope Moors)

Midhope Moors rise above Langsett and Midhope Reservoirs and are well seen from the A616 above Langsett. Langsett Reservoir and Hingcliff Common are well frequented but the rest of the moor is left to sheep and shooting. Grouse butts abound, providing plenty of ways up from Upper Midhope and Ewden. The focus of the moor is the rock-scattered knoll and burial cairn of Pike Lowe, but Ewden Height and the remains of its tank range also provide plenty of interest.

Midhope is so named as it lies halfway up the valley of the Little Don. Its enclosure in 1823 led to the creation of the long, straight walls on the edges of the moor, including **Deadman's Wall**, which was built by John Beaver and was said to have crossed a local burial ground. The moorland estate became owned by the Bosville-MacDonald family, a notable Penistone family after whom Bosville's Piece was named.

The slopes of **Midhope Moors** were widely used by troops as a training area during World War II, particularly in the lead up to the Normandy Landings. Upper Midhope became an army camp and was known as Little Congo. There was a tank range on the side of Ewden Height, with brick winch houses used to move targets known as hornets across the moor, as well as a tank wash to remove peat from the tanks at the end of the day. On Range Moor there are the remains of several artillery targets, bunkers and gun emplacements. North America was also used for target practice by tanks and the ruins today bear the scars of shell and artillery fire. Midhope and Langsett Reservoirs were seen as obvious targets for German bombers, so vast **catenary defences** were constructed across them – 100-foot high cables from which hung girders to prevent bombers flying close to the dams. The concrete base of one of the pylons that held these can be seen on Bosville's Piece and live artillery shells keep being unearthed on the moors above, so tread carefully (leave alone and report grid ref. of anything found).

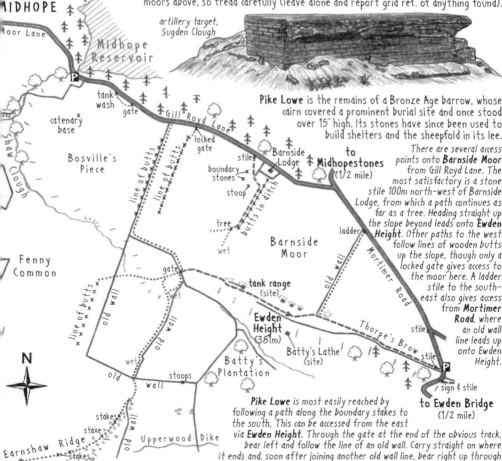

artillery target,
Sugden Clough

Pike Lowe is the remains of a Bronze Age barrow, whose cairn covered a prominent burial site and once stood over 15' high. Its stones have since been used to build shelters and the sheepfold in its lee.

There are several access points onto **Barnside Moor** from Gill Royd Lane. The most satisfactory is a stone stile 100m north-west of Barnside Lodge, from which a path continues as far as a tree. Heading straight up the slope beyond leads onto **Ewden Height**. Other paths to the west follow lines of wooden butts up the slope, though only a locked gate gives access to the moor here. A ladder stile to the south-east also gives access from **Mortimer Road**, where an old wall line leads up onto Ewden Height.

Pike Lowe is most easily reached by following a path along the boundary stakes to the south. This can be accessed from the east via **Ewden Height**. Through the gate at the end of the obvious track, bear left and follow the line of an old wall. Carry straight on where it ends and, soon after joining another old wall line, bear right up through the stones of **Earnshaw Ridge**, soon joining the line of stakes. A faint path doubles back to reach the prominent cairn, but it may be easier to cut across sooner from a shelter in a cluster of rocks.

Map labels:
to Langsett (1/2 mile)
UPPER MIDHOPE
Moor Lane
Midhope Reservoir
tank wash
catenary base
Bosville's Piece
Shaw Clough
Fenny Common
line of butts
old wall
Gill Royd Lane
gate
locked gate
stile
boundary stones
stoop
tree
butts in ditch
wet
gate
wet
tank range (site)
Barnside Lodge
Barnside Moor
ladder
Ewden Height (381m)
Batty's Lathe (site)
Batty's Plantation
Thorpe's Brow
stile
stile
Mortimer Road
to Midhopestones (1/2 mile)
old wall
wet
stoops
wall
stakes
stake
stakes
stake
tree
Earnshaw Ridge
Upperwood Dike
sign & stile
to Ewden Bridge (1/2 mile)
N

Distance: 10½ miles (17km)

Ascent: 430m

Difficulty: Moderate

Parking: Free parking at Langsett Barn off the A616 in Langsett.

Public Transport: Langsett is best served by the National Express 350 from Sheffield Coach Station three times daily.

Character: An exploration of the less frequented end of Howden Edge, combining a long walk up to the head of the Little Don River with some serious bog-trotting over Outer Edge. Some of the paths are faint shooting tracks or liable to be overgrown with bracken in summer, and navigational care is needed on the tops.

Note: no dogs are allowed on most of this route.

ROUTE 2: OUTER

Skarratt's Stone honours a regular member of George Howson's shooting parties who is said to have regularly rested here for a shot of whisky on the way up to the butts as he was scared of the fo...

2 The path drops down at the end of **Crookland Wood** and stays along the right side of the stream. At a footbridge, bear right up the bank before crossing **Lon... Moor Clough**. Fork left of the walled enclosure on Little Moor beyond; in summer the path can be thick with bracken, but persists to return to the river bank. A fenceline soon hems you in as you pass a castellated sheepfold, but the path continues along the stream until forced up the rough bank to join the main track heading down **Hordron Bank** to a shooters' footbridge.

Alternative Route: If the Little Don is high and hard to cross or you fancy a shortcut, an alternative route crosses the shooters' bridge and heads up the butts along the side of **Near Cat Clough**. A faint path leads all the way to some stakes on the watershed path at the top.

3

The main route continues up **Hordron Clough** beyond the shooters' footbridge and forks left across a ford about 250m further upstream. A well-worn quad track leads all the way up the narrow tongue of Laund (to the right of which can be found **Skarratt's Stone**). At the top bend left up a line of grouse butts and continue on a faint path beyond, following the grough in the same direction to reach a lone cairn in a sea of peaty lumps at **Howden Head**. Even though there is higher ground ahead, this marks the line of the main path along the watershed – if you near the **Hoar Stones** you've gone too far. Turn left at the cairn (a bearing of 95°) and, though it is not immediately obvious, you soon pick up a wide boggy line along the barren top of this part of **Howden Edge**.

Prior to their establishment as grouse-shooting moors, the higher parts of **Langsett Moors** were divided into sheepwalks, areas of common pasture linked to particular farms, including Sheephouse, Aldermanshead, Upper and Lower Hordron. It is interesting to note how far the first two farms on the list are from this moor, being a couple of miles the other side of Langsett.

4 From the top of **Near Cat Clough**, th... watershed path is more clearly marked by... line of stakes and boundary stones, bendin... round to the south to ascend the sog... ramparts of **Outer Edge**. Its shallow roc... edge stands to the west of the trig poin... but the route heads east on a faint lin... heading left from the trig. Aim to the lef... of a couple of lonely trees and, passing a sma... pool (the bomb crater of a V-1 flying bom... see p11), bear round to the northeast acros... the boggy moss. There are myriad quad line... but you should aim towards another lon... tree. Bend right before this to pa... another pool and begin t... descend towards **Micklede... Beck**, heading straigh... across a line of butt...

EDGE & THE LITTLE DON FROM LANGSETT

1 From **Langsett Barn** car park descend to join the well-surfaced path heading right around the forested shore of Langsett Reservoir. Stay on the main path to its end at a road track above **Brook House Bridge**. Turn right here, then immediately left, crossing the left of two bridges. Fork left down the stream to a gate, then follow a path above the bank of the **Little Don River**.

Langsett was originally Langkeside, referring to the long side of the ridge on the north side of the Little Don. It developed as a village only when the A616 was constructed as the Wadsley-Langsett Turnpike in 1805. The **Waggon & Horses**, simply known as The Inn until 1924, followed in 1809.

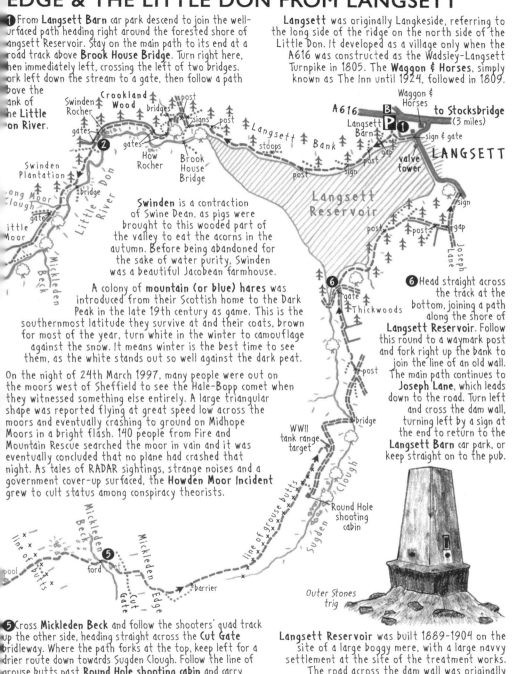

Swinden is a contraction of Swine Dean, as pigs were brought to this wooded part of the valley to eat the acorns in the autumn. Before being abandoned for the sake of water purity, Swinden was a beautiful Jacobean farmhouse.

A colony of **mountain (or blue) hares** was introduced from their Scottish home to the Dark Peak in the late 19th century as game. This is the southernmost latitude they survive at and their coats, brown for most of the year, turn white in the winter to camouflage against the snow. It means winter is the best time to see them, as the white stands out so well against the dark peat.

On the night of 24th March 1997, many people were out on the moors west of Sheffield to see the Hale-Bopp comet when they witnessed something else entirely. A large triangular shape was reported flying at great speed low across the moors and eventually crashing to ground on Midhope Moors in a bright flash. 140 people from Fire and Mountain Rescue searched the moor in vain and it was eventually concluded that no plane had crashed that night. As tales of RADAR sightings, strange noises and a government cover-up surfaced, the **Howden Moor Incident** grew to cult status among conspiracy theorists.

4 Head straight across the track at the bottom, joining a path along the shore of **Langsett Reservoir**. Follow this round to a waymark post and fork right up the bank to join the line of an old wall. The main path continues to **Joseph Lane**, which leads down to the road. Turn left and cross the dam wall, turning left by a sign at the end to return to the **Langsett Barn** car park, or keep straight on to the pub.

3 Cross **Mickleden Beck** and follow the shooters' quad track up the other side, heading straight across the **Cut Gate** bridleway. Where the path forks at the top, keep left for a drier route down towards Sugden Clough. Follow the line of grouse butts past **Round Hole shooting cabin** and carry straight on to join the vehicle track by the remains of a brick target on the **WWII tank range**. Cross Sugden Clough and at the top of the bank fork left by a waymark post to follow a fence down past the plantation towards **Langsett Reservoir**.

Langsett Reservoir was built 1889-1904 on the site of a large boggy mere, with a large navvy settlement at the site of the treatment works. The road across the dam wall was originally going to cut straight through the Waggon & Horses, but now has a kink after the landlord objected. The castellated **valve tower** is modelled on Lancaster Castle's gatehouse.

The north side of **Ewden Beck** is hard to reach as the track up to it past Ewden Lodge Farm is private and there is no satisfactory crossing point over the wooded stream, especially with a new fenceline on its north side. It is possible to drop down to it from the path along **Earnshaw Ridge** and Pike Lowe (see p12-13) and there is a lovely pool and falls by the old washfold beneath **Fox Stones**. When the bracken is down, it is not hard to follow the stream up from here, while quad tracks wind across **White Carr Ridge** above.

CONTINUATION ON p12

CONTINUATION ON p18

Earnshaw Ridge

White Carr

line of

boundary stone
line of stakes
boundary stone
line of stakes
shelter line of stakes
tree
line of stakes

White Carr Ridge
cairn
small cairn
cairn
Candlerush Dike
tree
Raddle Pits
pool

Cut Gate
wet

Spring Gutter

Hawthorn Ridge
Hawthorn Clough
falls
washfold
new fence
Fox Stones
line of old wall
Gallows Rocher

a boundary stone on Dukes Road carrying the initials of Mr R. Rimington Wilson, who owned Broomhead Moor in the late 19th century

RRW

Long Pole Ridge
Stirling plane wreck
Stainery Clough
Oaken Clough

N

The barren mosses between Cut Gate and Duke's Road are largely untrodden away from the grouse butts, with the only path following Cartledge Brook north-west towards the back of Howden Edge. This path branches off **Duke's Road** between a pair of cairns where it turns south towards Cartledge Stones (p28). One line follows the boundary stones down towards the top of Abbey Clough. The other turns right across the heather, soon joining the line of **Cartledge Brook**. At the first major grough on the left, you can turn left by a tiny cairn and follow this up to join a line of grouse butts and a good path on towards **Wet Stones** (p19). Alternatively, you can continue up Cartledge Brook and fork left where the stream divides; when the path peters out on the moss, look for a faint line heading west towards the summit of **High Stones** (p19).

Middle Moss
tree
line of grouse butts
stake
stakes
bridge
bridge
Flint Hi
cairn

CONTINUATION ON p19

0   250   500   750
METRES

wet
tiny cairn
line of butts
picnic tables
Cartledge Brook
Round Hill
pool
Brushen Croft Ridge
cairns
cairns
gate
stile
cairn
stiles
boundary stone
cairn & stone
cairn
fallen boundary stone
boundary stone
cairn
pool
cairn
former butts
Duke's Road
cairn
Hobson Moss
fenced enclosure
gate
Blackhole
Hobson Moss Dike

Robin Hood's Chair is said to have stood near the head of Agden Clough in the 16th century, 'a large stone with a semi-circular hollow place in the side' and a low table in front.
I've been unable to locate this landmark, though there is a Robin Hood's Spring on Hurkling Edge.

16

HOWDEN EDGE SOUTH-EAST (Broomhead Moor)

Broomhead Moor was renowned for the finest grouse shooting in South Yorkshire and remains dominated by shooting interests. It is a wild and largely featureless expanse of heather between the inaccessible wooded valleys of Agden and Ewden, usually crossed only via Duke's Road. However, regular burning means it is not hard to venture off piste and discover remote rocky outcrops and charming moorland streams, usually in blissful solitude.

Gallows and **Raven Rocher** are fine rocky outcrops where legend has it men were hung or flung in sacrifice to Odin, whose sacred bird was the raven.

A pair of paths branch off the shooting track after its first bend. The right path peters out near the Ewden Beck Stone Circle, the left forges a line down through the rhododendron to the remains of an old bridge on Ewden Beck.

*A vehicle track runs parallel to **Broomhead Dike** to the shooting lodge, where a path forks right to a line of remote butts in Oaken Clough. The main path continues south past the closest butts; at the end you can bear right on quad tracks up onto Flint Hill or follow the deep grough of Rushy Dike down to Duke's Road.*

The **cairn** on Hurkling Edge was built from the ruins of a hut called Nancy Tent. Previously a tent was erected here to serve beer to those shooting on the Glorious 12th.

Broomhead Hall has been the site of 3 halls and home to the prominent Wilson family, who rose to prominence under Elizabeth I. The last was a vast Gothic pile that was demolished in 1976.

Bar Dike is an ancient British defensive ditch across an important ridge, while **Broomhead Dike** is a striking medieval boundary ditch on the commons of Wigtwizzle parish, similar to that on Cartledge Stones Ridge.

Duke's Road was built by the Duke of Norfolk for grouse shooting on his estate, following the line of an old cart gate used by those in Bradfield for quarrying stone and summering cattle above Howden. Though it was established as a public road in the 1811 Ecclesfield Enclosure Act, it was closed off by the landowners and the site of a second mass trespass of 1932.

The low stones of **Ewden Beck Stone Circle** are embedded in an earth bank that was exposed after a moorland fire. Two burial cairns have been found inside the circle and there are 17 barrows scattered across the moor to the south-west. There were doubtless more to the east but this land has been farmed.

Map labels

Upperwood Dike · old wall · grouse butts · private track · gate · Holt Rocher · Ewden Coppice · Ewden Bridge · Ewden Beck Stone Circle · bridge (site) · post · idge · Park Cote · stoops · gap · Ewden Beck · Raven Rocher · barrows · gate · Broomhead Dike · Cat Clough · sign · gas marker · P · Broomhead Hall Farm · Side Head Beck · old wall · sign & gate · gas marker · line of butts · Black Brook · Mortimer Road · fold · shooting lodge · stake · lines of butts · take · x · gas marker · boundary stone · gas marker · Hall House (site) · Nancy Tent cairn · boundary stones · line of boundary stones · sign & gate · Rushy Dike · pool · boundary stone · old walls · Duke's Road · Apronful of Stones (site) · Hanson Cross · boundary stone · Robin Hood's Spring · Hurkling · Hurkling Stones (inc. Devil's Spectacles) · Edge · P · P · gate · Bar Dike · ruin · line of butts · Flinthill Dike · Nixon House (site) · Mortimer House · Hollin's Ground · boundary stone · Agden Dike · to Strines (3.5 miles)

CONTINUATION ON P28

17

MAP 6: HOWDEN EDGE SOUTH-WEST (Howden Edge)

Howden Edge itself overlooks Howden Reservoir and the head of the River Derwent and is crested by a series of rocky clusters. It is a remote but beautiful area reached only from the top of the road past the reservoirs or a long walk in from Fairholmes, yet remains justly popular and full of paths.

The watershed can be followed from the top of Cut Gate to **Outer Edge** trig, but it is a soggy trudge. A better path leaves by a huge cairn at Cut Gate End and skirts round the heathery edge to **Bull Stones** and on to **Crow Stones**. Nearing a second line of butts between the two, you need to bear right to reach the onward path at the wreckage of a post-war **Consul plane**. Fainter paths also head up through the heather to Outer Edge from here, Bull Stones and Cut Gate End.

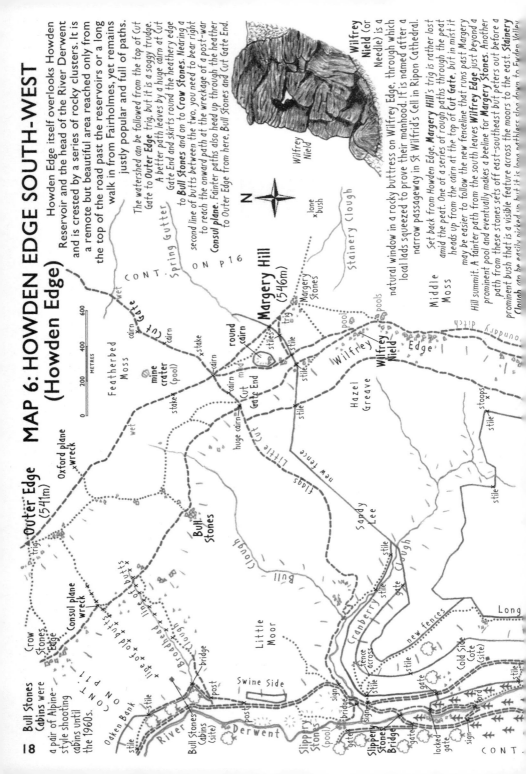

Wilfrey Nield

Wilfrey Nield (or Needle) is a natural window in a rocky buttress on Wilfrey Edge, through which local lads squeezed to prove their manhood. It is named after a narrow passageway in St Wilfrid's Cell in Ripon Cathedral.

Set back from Howden Edge, **Margery Hill's** trig is rather lost amid the peat. One of a series of rough paths through the peat heads up from the cairn at the top of Cut **Gate**, but in mist it may be easier to follow the new fenceline that runs past Margery Hill summit. A fainter path from the south leaves **Wilfrey Edge** just beyond a prominent pool and eventually makes a beeline for **Margery Stones**. Another path from these stones sets off east-southeast but peters out before a prominent bush that is a visible feature across the moors to the east. **Stainery Clough** can be easily picked up but it is long pathless slog down to Ewden Valley.

N

× lone bush

Outer Edge (541m) trig

Crow Stones Edge

Bull Stones Cabins were a pair of Alpine-style shooting cabins until the 1960s.

Consul plane wreck

Oxford plane wreck

line of old butts

Broadhead Clough

butts

Cut Gate

CONT. ON P11

Oaken Bank

stile

River Derwent

Bull Stones Cabins (Site)

Bull Stones

Little Moor

bridge

post

post

Swine Side

Slippery Stones (pool)

Slippery Stones Bridge

sign

bridge

gate

gate

sign

locked gate

gate

sign

ford

CONT.

Featherbed Moss

wet

cairn

Cut Gate

cairn

stake

mine crater (pool)

cairn

Cut Gate End

stake

cairn

round cairn

huge cairn

Cut mud

new fence

Little flags

Cut

Spring Gutter

CONT. ON P.16

wet

cairn

cairn

stake

Margery Hill (546m) trig

stiles

stile

Margery Stones

Wilfrey Nield

Wilfrey Edge

pool

pool

pools

Hazel Greave

Sandy Lee

Middle Moss

Stainery Clough

boundary ditch

stoops ×

stile

stile

stile

stile

Cranberry Clough

fence across

stile

gate

new fences

Cold Side Cote (site)

stile

stile

gate

sign

sign

sign

Long

METRES: 0 200 400 600

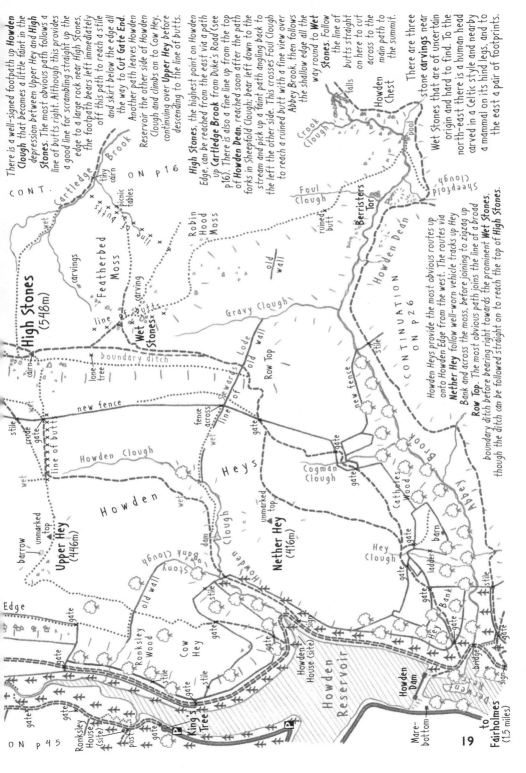

There is a well-signed footpath up **Howden Clough** that becomes a little faint in the depression between **Upper Hey** and **High Stones**. The most obvious path follows a line of butts right. Although this provides a good line for scrambling straight up the edge to a large rock near High Stones, the footpath bears left immediately off this path to reach a stile and skirt below the edge all the way to **Cut Gate End**. Another path leaves Howden Reservoir on the other side of Howden Clough and climbs on to Cow Hey, continuing over **Upper Hey** before descending to the line of butts.

High Stones, the highest point on Howden Edge, can be reached from the east via a path up **Cartledge Brook** from Duke's Road (see p16). There is also a fine line up from the top of **Howden Dean**, reached soon after the path forks in Sheepfold Clough: bear left down to the stream and pick up a faint path angling back to the left the other side. This crosses Foul Clough to reach a ruined butt with a fine view over Abbey Brook, then follows the shallow edge all the way round to **Wet Stones**. Follow the line of butts straight on here to cut across to the main path to the summit.

There are three stone **carvings** near **Wet Stones** that are of uncertain origin and hard to find. To the north-east there is a human head carved in a Celtic style and nearby a mammal on its hind legs, and to the east a pair of footprints.

Howden Heys provide the most obvious routes up onto Howden Edge from the west. The routes via **Nether Hey** follow well-worn vehicle tracks up Hey Bank and across the moss, before joining to zigzag up **Row Top**. The most obvious path joins the line of **High Stones** before bearing right towards the prominent **Wet Stones**, though the ditch can be followed straight on to reach the top of **High Stones**.

Distance: 15 miles (24.4km)
Ascent: 480m
Difficulty: Strenuous

Parking: Limited street parking by the church in Bolsterstone and a small lay-by along Heads Lane.

Public Transport: The closest bus stop is less than half a mile from Bolsterstone at Coal Pit Lane, where the SL1/SL1A Supertram Link buses from Middlewood stop every 20 minutes.

Character: A grand yomp up the long ridge that leads all the way from Bolsterstone to the top of Pike Lowe. After continuing over the high tops of Margery Hill and High Stones, the route returns via Duke's Road and Broomhead Reservoir. Though some of the paths are faint, it is generally good walking that is perfect for striding out.

Note: No dogs allowed on parts of this route.

ROUTE 3: HIGH

❷ Follow **Mortimer Road** briefly up to the top of the hill, then turn left over a stile and follow the obvious track along the top of **Ewden Height**, on top of which are the remains of a WWII tank range. Reaching a gateway, turn left along the fence and pick up the line of an old wall. Follow this to its end, where a faint path continues straight on and crosses the line of an even more run-down old wall.
Follow this left only briefly; as it bends left carry straight on up the shoulder of the moor towards some stones and the first of a series of stakes marking a fine path up **Earnshaw Ridge**.

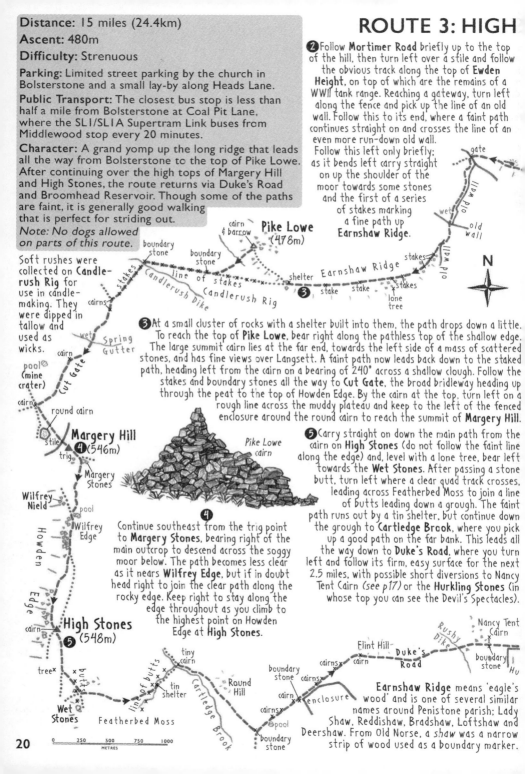

Soft rushes were collected on **Candlerush Rig** for use in candle-making. They were dipped in tallow and used as wicks.

❸ At a small cluster of rocks with a shelter built into them, the path drops down a little. To reach the top of **Pike Lowe**, bear right along the pathless top of the shallow edge. The large summit cairn lies at the far end, towards the left side of a mass of scattered stones, and has fine views over Langsett. A faint path now leads back down to the staked path, heading left from the cairn on a bearing of 240° across a shallow clough. Follow the stakes and boundary stones all the way to **Cut Gate**, the broad bridleway heading up through the peat to the top of Howden Edge. By the cairn at the top, turn left on a rough line across the muddy plateau and keep to the left of the fenced enclosure around the round cairn to reach the summit of **Margery Hill**.

❺ Carry straight on down the main path from the cairn on **High Stones** (do not follow the faint line along the edge) and, level with a lone tree, bear left towards the **Wet Stones**. After passing a stone butt, turn left where a clear quad track crosses, leading across Featherbed Moss to join a line of butts leading down a grough. The faint path runs out by a tin shelter, but continue down the grough to **Cartledge Brook**, where you pick up a good path on the far bank. This leads all the way down to **Duke's Road**, where you turn left and follow its firm, easy surface for the next 2.5 miles, with possible short diversions to Nancy Tent Cairn (see p17) or the **Hurkling Stones** (in whose top you can see the Devil's Spectacles).

❹ Continue southeast from the trig point to **Margery Stones**, bearing right of the main outcrop to descend across the soggy moor below. The path becomes less clear as it nears **Wilfrey Edge**, but if in doubt head right to join the clear path along the rocky edge. Keep right to stay along the edge throughout as you climb to the highest point on Howden Edge at **High Stones**.

Earnshaw Ridge means 'eagle's wood' and is one of several similar names around Penistone parish; Lady Shaw, Reddishaw, Bradshaw, Loftshaw and Deershaw. From Old Norse, a *shaw* was a narrow strip of wood used as a boundary marker.

20

STONES & PIKE LOWE FROM BOLSTERSTONE

n 1768 Hans Winthrop Mortimer, a London property dealer, sank all his money into **Mortimer Road**, an ambitious turnpike project. It ran between Grindleford and Penistone but proved too steep for carriages, with additional horses being required on several sections. Stones marked 'take off' by the Strines Inn and on Ewden Height related to these. Unlike the horses, the road never took off and Mortimer died penniless in 1907.

❶ In **Bolsterstone**, go through the lychgate into St Mary's Churchyard and turn left to pass the eponymous **Bolster Stones**. Follow the path to the far end of the graveyard and join Heads Lane leading out of the village. At the end of the road, go through the gate and follow the track onto **Whitwell Moor**. Where this bends left at a waymark post, head straight up to the trig point on the highest of the **Salter Hills**. Continue along the high ground into a pine wood and follow the path down the slope. After 200m, head a short way down to the left off the path to where a gate leads out into the fields. Follow a path along the wall as it bends round to the right to reach **Mortimer Road**.

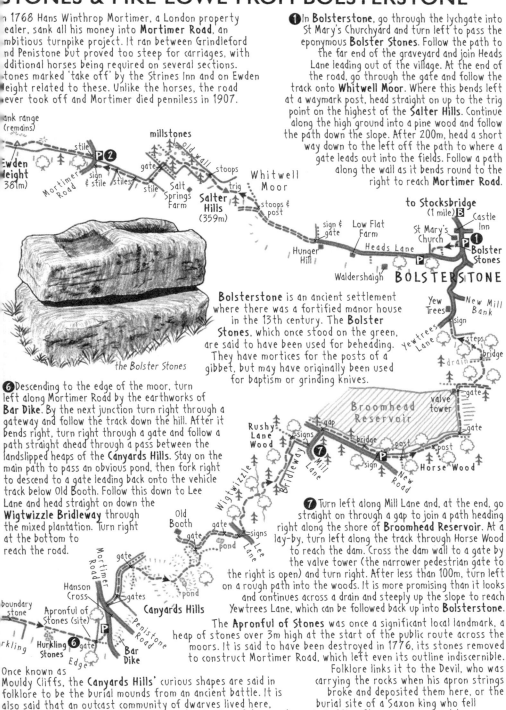

the Bolster Stones

Bolsterstone is an ancient settlement where there was a fortified manor house in the 13th century. The **Bolster Stones**, which once stood on the green, are said to have been used for beheading. They have mortices for the posts of a gibbet, but may have originally been used for baptism or grinding knives.

❻ Descending to the edge of the moor, turn left along Mortimer Road by the earthworks of **Bar Dike**. By the next junction turn right through a gateway and follow the track down the hill. After it bends right, turn right through a gate and follow a path straight ahead through a pass between the landslipped heaps of the **Canyards Hills**. Stay on the main path to pass an obvious pond, then fork right to descend to a gate leading back onto the vehicle track below Old Booth. Follow this down to Lee Lane and head straight on down the **Wigtwizzle Bridleway** through the mixed plantation. Turn right at the bottom to reach the road.

❼ Turn left along Mill Lane and, at the end, go straight on through a gap to join a path heading right along the shore of **Broomhead Reservoir**. At a lay-by, turn left along the track through Horse Wood to reach the dam. Cross the dam wall to a gate by the valve tower (the narrower pedestrian gate to the right is open) and turn right. After less than 100m, turn left on a rough path into the woods. It is more promising than it looks and continues across a drain and steeply up the slope to reach Yewtrees Lane, which can be followed back up into **Bolsterstone**.

The **Apronful of Stones** was once a significant local landmark, a heap of stones over 3m high at the start of the public route across the moors. It is said to have been destroyed in 1776, its stones removed to construct Mortimer Road, which left even its outline indiscernible. Folklore links it to the Devil, who was carrying the rocks when his apron strings broke and deposited them here, or the burial site of a Saxon king who fell in battle after an encampment here.

Once known as Mouldy Cliffs, the **Canyards Hills'** curious shapes are said in folklore to be the burial mounds from an ancient battle. It is also said that an outcast community of dwarves lived here, giving rise to the name of nearby Dwariden (valley of dwarves).

ROUTE 4: HOWDEN EDGE FROM HOWDEN RESERVOIR

Distance: 11 miles (17.5km)

Ascent: 520m

Difficulty: Moderate

Parking: Free parking at King's Tree by Howden Reservoir (road closed Sundays, summer Saturdays and Bank Holidays).

Public Transport: None at present beyond Fairholmes car park, 5 miles back down the valley.

Character: A grand circuit of Howden Edge and the Upper Derwent from the remote road end at the very top of the Derwent Valley. After climbing its highest point at High Stones, the route sticks to the most striking rocky outcrops of Howden Edge and avoids the boggy morass above. There are short rough sections up and down the edge, but reasonable paths are followed in the main and the route has the added bonus of a swimming hole to round off the walk.

6 There is no satisfactory path off **Horse Stone Naze** and it is a steep and rough grassy descent to the top of **Lands Clough**. Bearing diagonally right makes the slope marginally easier, but you should still bend back round towards the first of a line of wooden grouse butts leading down into **Lands Clough**. Keep to the right side of the stream to pick up a gradually improving path down into the **Upper Derwent Valley**. Turn left at the bottom on a broad track that leads a merry stroll back down this beautiful remote valley.

5 From **Crow Stones**, a good path descends steadily towards the top of **Stainery Clough**. In a deep grough head left slightly to pick up the continuation of the path, which crosses the stream at a large rock. Continue left, climbing steadily up onto **Horse Stone Naze** and keeping to the right of most of the scattered rocks on its slopes. At the top, the path rises to the **Horse Stone** itself, perched in the middle of a boggy plateau. The path continues faintly southwest towards the unmarked high point of Horse Stone Naze and stops abruptly on the edge.

4 From the **Bull Stones**, continue across the slope on a narrowing path that crosses a line of butts at the top of **Broadhead Clough**. Nearing a second line of butts, fork right up to an open area of black peat that is scattered with the wreckage of an Airspeed **Consul plane**. The path is clearer beyond, continuing across the slope as it climbs steadily to the rocks of **Crow Stones Edge**. Continue to the **Crow Stones** at the far end of the edge, some of the finest formations in South Yorkshire.

Cut Gate is a corruption of Cart Gate and was an early packhorse route used by the inhabitants of the Derwent and Woodlands Valleys to take livestock to Penistone Market. It was originally a trench-cut boundary, like the broad ditch that can be seen running along the edge past **High Stones**.

green hairstreak butterfly

An Airspeed **Consul plane** crashed into Crow Stones Edge on 12th April 1951 and parts of it are scattered near the top of a peaty gully. Having been surplus to requirements during the war, it was purchased by an Icelandic airline. As it was being taken home from Croydon, pilot Páll Magnusson lost his way in bad weather, killing all three on board. The RAF lost two aircraft in the Dark Peak on the same ill-fated day.

Margery Hill (546m) / High Stones (548m)

Map labels: trig, new stiles, Wilfrey Nield, Margery Hill (546m), pools, Wilfrey Edge, High Stones (548m), cairn, prominent rock, fence, crude gate, line of butts, unmarked top, Upper Hey (446m), Howden (Clough), Cow Hey, Hindholes Clough, old wall, Long Edge, gate, sign, locked gate, stile, ford, bridge sign, sign, bridge, Slippery Stones (pool), Derwent, Howden Reservoir, gates, posts, King's gate, Tree, B, P, Linch Clough, to Fairholmes (4.5 miles)

Slippery Stones is said to be named after the moss-covered black stones in the stream, but it more likely refers to the landslips that have defined the shape of the valley floor.

3 You can follow either of the paths north from **High Stones**, but the finest bears left and skirts along the top of the edge. They rejoin by the rugged rocks of **Wilfrey Edge**, where you should keep left along the bank, passing above the natural window of Wilfrey Nield (see p.18). Reaching a fenceline, a short diversion right leads to the trig point on **Margery Hill**, but the route continues along the edge. Turn left at the main Cut Gate path only as far as a huge cairn, from which a path branches off right and follows the slope round to the stately **Bull Stones**.

2 Turn right below the crags of **Long Edge** and follow the track along the eastern side of Howden Reservoir. After a mile, it bends round to the left to skirt around the **Howden Clough** inlet and an unsigned path leads steeply up the bank to the left. It continues onto the open moor of Cow Hey, becoming a grassy quad track that winds its way up onto the unmarked eminence of **Upper Hey**. The path becomes fainter as it drops down to join a line of grouse butts heading straight for the rocky face of **High Stones**. Go through or over the crude gate at the end, then pick up a faint line heading straight up the edge. Do not veer off left but keep up the slope, aiming slightly to the left of the most prominent rock. It is a rough grassy scramble towards the top before you emerge near the small cairn that marks the highest point on **Howden Edge**.

In an enclosure close to the summit of **Margery Hill** is a Bronze Age round cairn, which is thought to comprise of a burial cairn surrounded by huge mound of peat 50m in diameter. Though no remains have yet been unearthed in limited excavations, it is likely to have been an important burial place. The site is now covered in peat and heather so it is hard to make out the shape or the stones.

7 After crossing both Stainery and Broadhead Cloughs, the valley widens slightly with a series of landslipped mounds alongside the **River Derwent**. A small path turns right over one of these to follow the river down to the Peak District's finest natural swimming pool at **Slippery Stones**, where you'll have earned your dip. Rejoin the main path soon after and keep right to cross the large stone bridge and follow the vehicle track back down to **King's Tree** the way you headed out.

The ancient **packhorse bridge** near Slippery Stones, which once had a cross on its south side, has always seemed oversized for its remote location. This is because it originally stood near Derwent Hall on a busy packhorse route between Sheffield and Glossop. Having been restored in 1682, it was dismantled upon the construction of Ladybower Reservoir in the 1940s. It was stored in a barn for the rest of the war and its numbered stones were re-assembled here by public subscription in 1959 as a memorial to guidebook writer and access campaigner John Derry.

A lower rocking stone at the **Crow Stones** has collapsed, but the distinctive **Rocking Stone** still remains, though it would be very unwise and difficult to try it out.

the rocking stone by Crow Stones

1 From the end of the public road at **King's Tree**, continue along the track through the plantation above **Howden Reservoir**. After half a mile, fork right to reach a ford over the **River Derwent**. Immediately beyond, turn right onto a faint path through the trees and along the river bank. Scrambling up a low rocky bank, aim for a stile in the fence above, from where a path leads up to the main track.

Alternative route: In summer it's simple to cross the stones by the ford, but if the river is high it's worth continuing up the track to the main bridge and turning right at the sign beyond to follow the main track down the opposite bank.

23

LAPWING

The lapwing, also known as the peewit or green plover, is a migratory bird that winters on lowland marshes and breeds on the uplands in spring. It nests variously on hay meadows, rough pastures and moorland heather, though its nests are very basic and the chicks leave hours after hatching. It can be identified by its white undercarriage, black wings and the male's distinctive forked crest, but it also has a green hue to its darker back. The name lapwing refers to its irregular way of flying and literally means 'leaping with a wink in'. It is renowned for its screeching hoop of a call, the *pee-wit* of its nickname that is part of its display flight and is liable to startle you. Its population has suffered greatly in recent years due to changes in farming methods and it is now on the Red List of Threatened Species in the UK.

a male lapwing

SKYLARK

a wary skylark

The skylark is a small mottled brown bird with a pale undercarriage that is heard more than seen on the moors. The skylark's song is the sound of spring and early summer, as it hovers imperceptibly overhead with a constant twittering burble. It is part of the male's territorial display, during which you often find yourself squinting into the bright sky as the birds rise to a height of up to 100m. Both male and female have the distinctive crest, which is raised only in alarm or anticipation. The lark part of its name means 'of the field' and refers to its laying eggs in shallow nests on grassland. As a result it has suffered even greater population decline due to intensive farming methods and, though still common, is also now on the Red List.

CHAPTER 3 – DERWENT EDGE

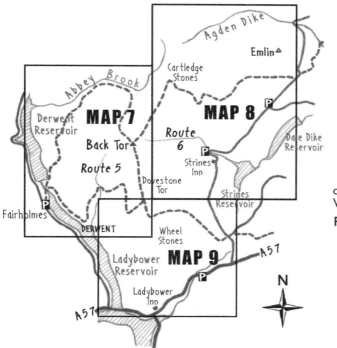

High Point: Back Tor, 538m

Grid Ref: SK198910

Map Sheet: OL1 (Dark Peak)

Access: No access for dogs on the eastern slopes of Derwent Edge, other than Public Rights of Way (most of Maps 8 & 9).

Public Transport: Bus 273 runs from Sheffield to Fairholmes, with a better service at weekends. Ladybower Inn is also served by the more frequent 274 service.

'The wind is always blowing as you sit on the cairn on the topmost slanting rock of Back Tor, and a more empty, homeless scene you cannot find' (John Derry, 1934)

Derwent Edge runs north from the Ladybower Inn to Abbey Brook, and is crested by a series of fabulous castellations; the Wheel Stones, Salt Cellar, Dovestone Tor, Cakes of Bread and Back Tor. The latter forms one of the most satisfying high points in this book, its trig clinging to one of the great rocks at the heart of this moorland expanse. Its two sides are very different; the steep western flank is owned by the National Trust, easily accessed from the busy Fairholmes car park and covered in paths; the gentler eastern flanks are given to grouse shooting and harder to access, though they contain several fascinating old stones and ancient trackways.

Derwent, like the Welsh *derw*, is derived from a Celtic word meaning 'abounding in oaks' and beautiful woods once lined the Derwent Valley. These days there are pockets of ancient woodland amid the great plantations that were planted around the reservoirs, which so dominate the scene and famously drowned the villages of Derwent and Ashopton in the 1930s.

Back Tor and Lost Lad from Cartledge Stones

MAP 7: DERWENT EDGE NORTH-WEST (Back Tor & Dovestone Tor)

The northern half of Derwent Edge forms a beautiful hillside overlooking Derwent and Ladybower Reservoirs and is dominated by the fine summit of Back Tor. It is deservedly busy, even though its only real access point is the giant Fairholmes car park, from which there are any number of routes out of the forest towards the rock-crested skyline above, each distinctive outcrop individually named.

Abbey Bank is a confusing shoulder leading from Derwent Reservoir up to **Back Tor** as many different paths and faint lines can be followed. The most direct route forks left off the main path in the forest near Abbey Grange and climbs steadily above Hey Clough. Near the top, turn left over a stile and cross Greystones Moss on a beeline for Lost Lad Hillend. I prefer following Abbey Brook up **Howden Dean**, a dramatic valley from which you can cut up to the summit via Sheepfold Clough or join the ridge at **Cartledge Stones**.

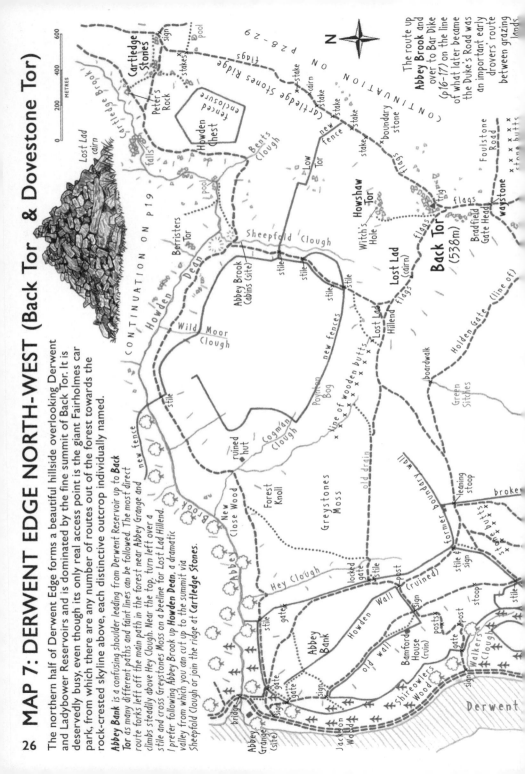

The route up **Abbey Brook** and over to Bar Dike (p16-17) on the line of what later became the Duke's Road was an important early drovers' route between grazing lands.

CONTINUATION ON P28-29

N

600
400
200
0
METRES

Cartledge Stones

Lost Lad cairn

Cartledge Brook

sign
pool

Peter's Rock

falls
pool

Howden Chest

fenced enclosure

Bents Clough

stakes
stake
cairn
stake
new stake
fence
boundary stone

Berristers Tor

Sheepfold Clough

Low Tor

Howshaw Tor

Foulstone Road
stone butts

CONTINUATION ON P19

Howden Dean

Witch's Hole

Lost Lad (cairn)

flags
trig
Bradfield Gate Head
waystone

Back Tor
(538m)

stile
stile
stile

Lost Lad Hillend

flags
flags

Wild Moor Clough

stile

new fences

Holden Gate (line of)

boardwalk

Green Sitches

Abbey Brook (Cabins site)

Poynton Bog

line of wooden butts

Cogman Clough

ruined hut

old drain

leaning stoop

broker

former boundary wall

Greystones Moss

Forest Knoll

stone butts

New Close Wood

Abbey Brook

Hey Clough

locked gate

stile

post

stile
sign

stile
sign

stile

stone butts

Howden Wall

post (ruined)

posts

Bamford House (ruin)

Walkers Clough

Abbey Bank

old wall

gate
post

stoop

gate
sign

bridge

Abbey Grange (site)

sign
gate
gate
gate
sign
sign

Shireowlers Wood

Jackson Wood

Derwent

Lost Lad marks a slight but distinctive rise on the shoulder of Back Tor. The large cairn is said to commemorate Abraham Lowe, a 13-year old shepherd boy who got lost in a blizzard and froze to death with his dog Bob. He scratched the words 'Lost Lad' into a nearby rock and the ghost of the lad and his sheepdog have since been reported. Actually Lost Lad is a corruption of Landlord's Seat Hill, seat being a Saxon word for a projecting piece of land.

John Field Howden was a medieval field whose shallow earth banks are followed by a faint path around the hillside below Dovestone Tor.

Cakes of Bread

grough

mini bread cakes

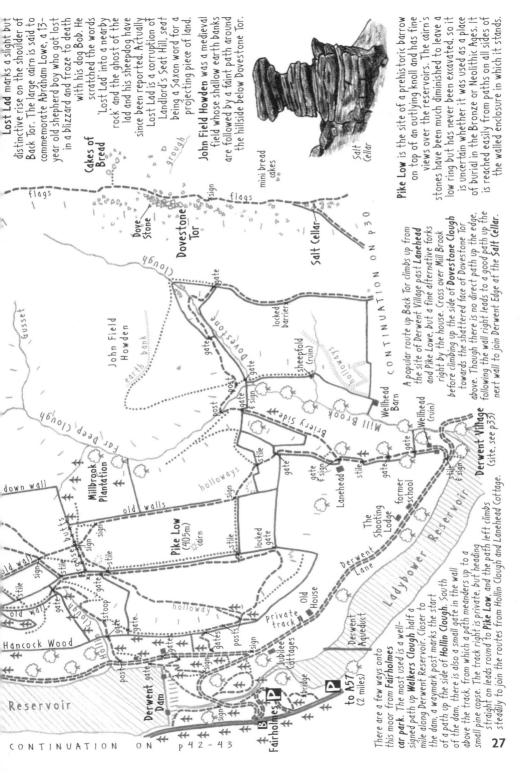

Salt Cellar

Pike Low is the site of a prehistoric barrow on top of an outlying knoll and has fine views over the reservoirs. The cairn's stones have been much diminished to leave a low ring but has never been excavated, so it is uncertain whether it was used as a place of burial in the Bronze or Neolithic Ages. It is reached easily from paths on all sides of the walled enclosure in which it stands.

A popular route up Back Tor climbs up from the site of Derwent Village past **Lanehead** and **Pike Lowe**, but a fine alternative forks right by the house. Cross over Mill Brook before climbing up the side of **Dovestone Clough** towards the shattered face of Dovestone Tor above. Though there is no direct path up the edge, following the wall right leads to a good path up the next wall to join **Derwent Edge** at the **Salt Cellar**.

There are a few ways onto this moor from **Fairholmes** car park. The most used is a well-signed path up **Walkers Clough** half a mile along Derwent Reservoir. Closer to the dam, a waymark post marks the start of a path up the side of **Hollin Clough**. South of the dam, there is also a small gate in the wall above the track, from which a path meanders up to a small pine copse. The track right is private, but heading straight on leads round to **Pike Low**, and the path left climbs steadily to join the routes from Hollin Clough and Lanehead Cottage.

---

flags

Dove Stone

Dovestone Tor

sign

flags

Salt Cellar

CONTINUATION ON P30

Dovestone Clough

gate

gate

John Field Howden

earth bank

Far Deep Clough

locked barrier

Sheepfold (ruin)

holloways

post

gate

sign

gate

Gusset

down wall

Millbrook Plantation

old walls

sign

sign

stile

Briery Side

Mill Brook

Wellhead Barn

Wellhead (ruin)

stile

gate

gate & sign

sign

holloways

Pike Low (405m) cairn

stile

locked gate

sign

gate & sign

Lanehead

former school

stile

gate

stile & sign

Derwent Village (site, see p33)

old walls

stile

Gusset butts

gate

sign

sign

stile

Ladybower Reservoir

old wall

sign

stile

holloway

The Shooting Lodge

old wall

gate

gate

Clough

stoop

gate

posts

sign

Old House

Private track

Derwent Lane

Derwent Aqueduct

Hancock Wood

Hollin Clough

post

gate

gates

gates

posts

sign

Jubilee Cottages

bridge

Reservoir

Derwent Dam

B

P **Fairholmes**

P

to A57 (2 miles)

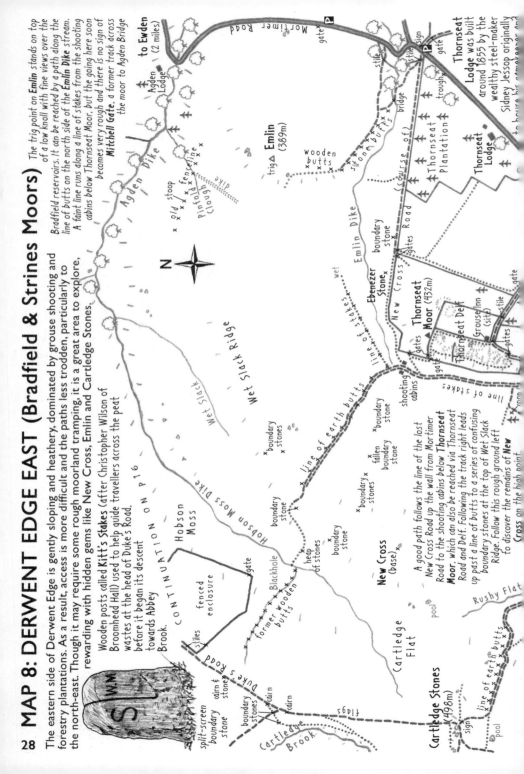

MAP 8: DERWENT EDGE EAST (Bradfield & Strines Moors)

The eastern side of Derwent Edge is gently sloping and heathery, dominated by grouse shooting and the forestry plantations. As a result, access is more difficult and the paths less trodden, particularly to the north-east. Though it may require some rough moorland tramping, it is a great area to explore, rewarding with hidden gems like New Cross, Emlin and Cartledge Stones.

The trig point on **Emlin** stands on top of a low knoll with fine views over the Bradfield reservoirs. It can be reached by a path along the line of butts on the north side of the **Emlin Dike** stream. A faint line runs along a line of stakes from the shooting cabins below Thornseat Moor, but the going here soon becomes very rough and there is no sign of **Mitchell Gate**, a former track across the moor to Agden Bridge.

Wooden posts called **Kitt's Stakes** (after Christopher Wilson of Broomhead Hall) used to help guide travellers across the peat wastes at the head of Duke's Road, before it began its descent towards Abbey Brook.

A good path follows the line of the lost New Cross Road up the wall from Mortimer Road to the shooting cabins below **Thornseat Moor**, which can also be reached via Thornseat Road and Delf. Following the track right leads up past a line of butts to a series of confusing boundary stones at the top of Wet Slack Ridge. Follow this rough ground left to discover the remains of **New Cross** on the high point.

Thornseat Lodge was built around 1855 by the wealthy steel-maker Sidney Jessop originally to house his gamekeeper and lodge. Its rooms were panelled with cedar and the grounds held a swimming pool; by the 1930s it had become a children's home. Since the 1980s it has been derelict and crumbling steadily into ruin.

to Low Bradfield (1.5 miles)

Even though large areas have been cut down and abandoned to become moorland, *Holling Dale* and *Bole Edge Plantations* remain private but for the charming permissive path running parallel to Mortimer Road. To avoid trespassing, you can follow Foulstone Road up to the top of the forest, then turn right below Foulstone Cottage on a faint path alongside the wall. This reaches the shooting track up *Rushy Flat Dike* that leads almost all the way to the ridge near the fine *Cartledge Stones*. From the north you can follow the vehicle track downhill from the shooting cabins, then turn right to pass a coop. The path becomes fainter until it appears to peter out on the wet ground, but persevere towards an old gap in the wall ahead, from which you can follow the wall right all the way round to the shooting track.

The **Strines Inn** (which has also been known as the Taylors Arms) was built in 1275 as a farmhouse, only later becoming an inn. It is haunted by the ghost of the grey lady, who is said to have been shot accidentally by the landlord (one of the Worrall family) in the 16th century. The name comes from *strind*, a dialect word for a stream.

New Cross was a medieval wayside cross on New Cross Road (previously Emlin Dike Road), which may have been a sheep and cattle drovers' route or a corpse road by which bodies were taken from the Upper Derwent Valley to the church at Bradfield. Once a substantial feature, only the cross base remains, carved with the outline of a sword. The cross was broken up by game-keepers but the shaft stood until the 1990s before disappearing. The adjacent moor is covered in more recent boundary stones, though it is hard to make sense of the boundaries they are demarcating; many are engraved with BJY and RWW, while another has a distinctive split-screen (see sketch).

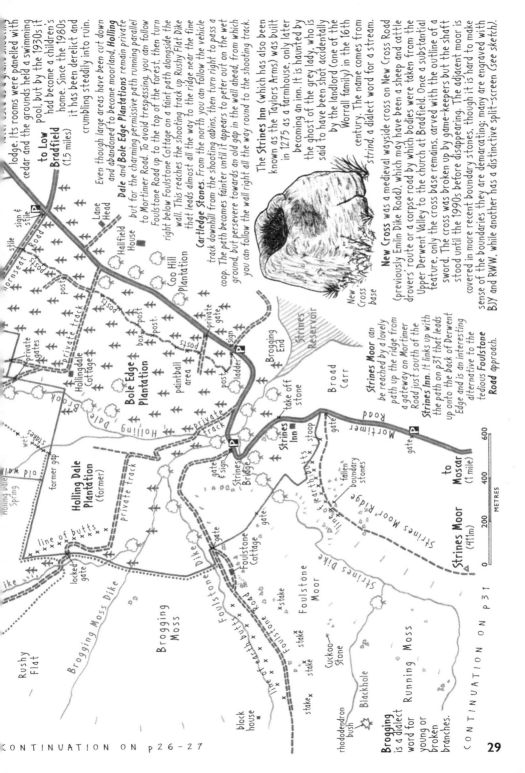

New Cross base

Strines Moor can be reached by a lovely path up the ridge from a gateway on Mortimer Road just south of the *Strines Inn*. It links up with the path on p31 that leads up onto the back of Derwent Edge and is an interesting alternative to the tedious *Foulstone Road* approach.

Lane Head

Halfield House

Coo Hill Plantation

Bole Edge Plantation

Hollingdale Cottage

paintball area

Strines Reservoir

Brogging End

Broad Carr

Strines Inn

Strines Bridge

take off stone

stoop

gate

to Mosar (1 mile)

fallen boundary stones

Holling Dale Plantation (former)

Holling Dale Dike

Holling Dale Spring

former gap

line of butts

locked gate

Brogging Moss Dike

Foulstone Cottage

Foulstone Dike

Strines Dike

Strines Moor (411m)

Strines Moor Ridge

line of (earth) butts

Mortimer Road

| 0 | 200 | 400 | 600 |

METRES

Rushy Flat

Brogging Moss

Foulstone Road

Foulstone Moor

line of earth butts

Cuckoo Stone

Running Moss

block house

rhododendron bush

Blackhole

Brogging is a dialect word for young or broken branches.

CONTINUATION ON p26-27

CONTINUATION ON p31

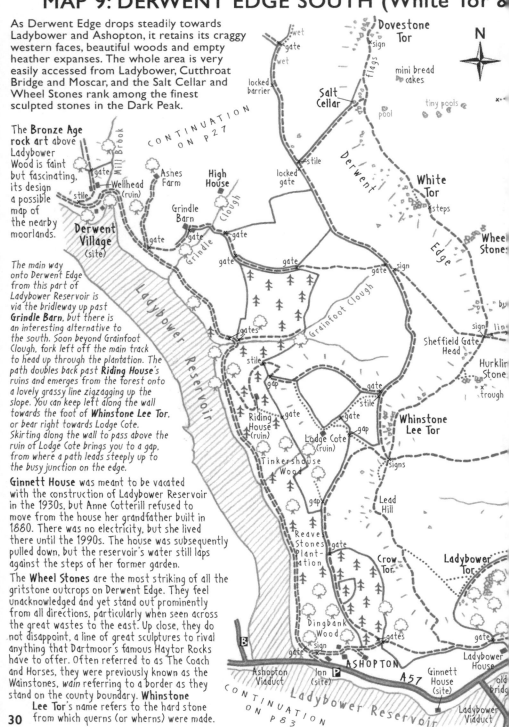

As Derwent Edge drops steadily towards Ladybower and Ashopton, it retains its craggy western faces, beautiful woods and empty heather expanses. The whole area is very easily accessed from Ladybower, Cutthroat Bridge and Moscar, and the Salt Cellar and Wheel Stones rank among the finest sculpted stones in the Dark Peak.

The **Bronze Age** rock art above Ladybower Wood is faint but fascinating, its design a possible map of the nearby moorlands.

The main way onto Derwent Edge from this part of Ladybower Reservoir is via the bridleway up past **Grindle Barn**, *but there is an interesting alternative to the south. Soon beyond Grainfoot Clough, fork left off the main track to head up through the plantation. The path doubles back past* **Riding House**'s *ruins and emerges from the forest onto a lovely grassy line zigzagging up the slope. You can keep left along the wall towards the foot of* **Whinstone Lee Tor**, *or bear right towards Lodge Cote. Skirting along the wall to pass above the ruin of Lodge Cote brings you to a gap, from where a path leads steeply up to the busy junction on the edge.*

Ginnett House was meant to be vacated with the construction of Ladybower Reservoir in the 1930s, but Anne Cotterill refused to move from the house her grandfather built in 1880. There was no electricity, but she lived there until the 1990s. The house was subsequently pulled down, but the reservoir's water still laps against the steps of her former garden.

The **Wheel Stones** are the most striking of all the gritstone outcrops on Derwent Edge. They feel unacknowledged and yet stand out prominently from all directions, particularly when seen across the great wastes to the east. Up close, they do not disappoint, a line of great sculptures to rival anything that Dartmoor's famous Haytor Rocks have to offer. Often referred to as The Coach and Horses, they were previously known as the Wainstones, *wain* referring to a border as they stand on the county boundary. **Whinstone Lee Tor**'s name refers to the hard stone from which querns (or wherns) were made.

30

CONTINUATION ON p29

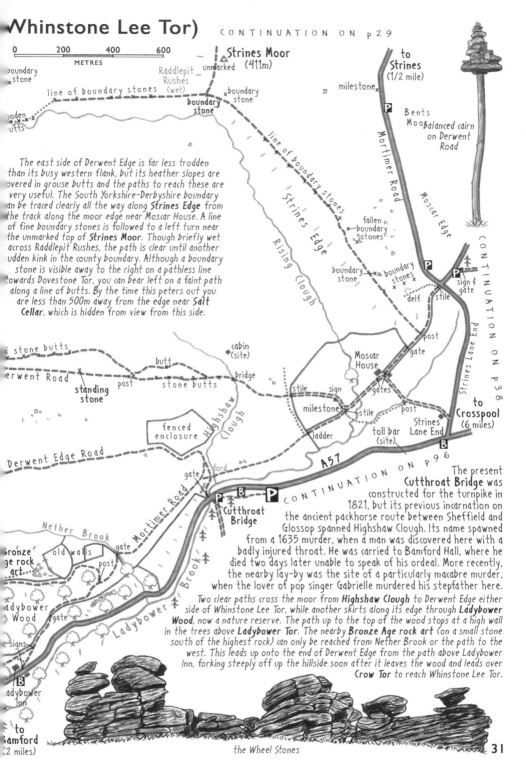

Strines Moor
(411m)

to
Strines
(1/2 mile)

boundary
stone

Raddlepit
Rushes
(wet)

unmarked

line of boundary stones

boundary
stone

boundary
stone

milestone

Bents
Moo balanced cairn
on Derwent
Road

ooden
utts

The east side of Derwent Edge is far less trodden
than its busy western flank, but its heather slopes are
covered in grouse butts and the paths to reach these are
very useful. The South Yorkshire-Derbyshire boundary
can be traced clearly all the way along **Strines Edge** from
the track along the moor edge near Moscar House. A line
of fine boundary stones is followed to a left turn near
the unmarked top of **Strines Moor**. Though briefly wet
across Raddlepit Rushes, the path is clear until another
sudden kink in the county boundary. Although a boundary
stone is visible away to the right on a pathless line
towards Dovestone Tor, you can bear left on a faint path
along a line of butts. By the time this peters out you
are less than 500m away from the edge near **Salt
Cellar**, which is hidden from view from this side.

line of boundary stones

Strines Edge

Mortimer Road

Moscar Edge

Rising Clough

fallen
boundary
stones

boundary
stone

boundary
stones

sign &
gate

delf

stile

CONTINUATION ON p38

stone butts

butt

cabin
(site)

post

Moscar
House

gate

post

Strines Lane End

erwent Road

standing
stone

post

stone butts

bridge

stile

sign

gates

to
Crosspool
(6 miles)

fenced
enclosure

Highshaw Clough

stile

milestone

stile

post

Strines
Lane End

Derwent Edge Road

gate

ford

ladder

toll bar
(site)

A57

B

CONTINUATION ON p96

P B P

**Cutthroat
Bridge**

Mortimer Road

Nether Brook

old walls

gate

post

Ladybower Brook

ronze
ge rock
art

adybower
Wood

gate

signs

B

adybower
Inn

to
Bamford
(2 miles)

The present
Cutthroat Bridge was
constructed for the turnpike in
1821, but its previous incarnation on
the ancient packhorse route between Sheffield and
Glossop spanned Highshaw Clough. Its name spawned
from a 1635 murder, when a man was discovered here with a
badly injured throat. He was carried to Bamford Hall, where he
died two days later unable to speak of his ordeal. More recently,
the nearby lay-by was the site of a particularly macabre murder,
when the lover of pop singer Gabrielle murdered his stepfather here.

Two clear paths cross the moor from **Highshaw Clough** to Derwent Edge either
side of Whinstone Lee Tor, while another skirts along its edge through **Ladybower
Wood**, now a nature reserve. The path up to the top of the wood stops at a high wall
in the trees above **Ladybower Tor**. The nearby **Bronze Age rock art** (on a small stone
south of the highest rock) can only be reached from Nether Brook or the path to the
west. This leads up onto the end of Derwent Edge from the path above Ladybower
Inn, forking steeply off up the hillside soon after it leaves the wood and leads over
Crow Tor to reach Whinstone Lee Tor.

the Wheel Stones

31

32

ROUTE 5: DERWENT EDGE FROM FAIRHOLMES

Distance: 9 miles (14.5km)

Ascent: 550m

Difficulty: Moderate

Character: A slightly different take on a popular route up Back Tor, combining the beautiful valleys of Dovestone Clough and Howden Dean with the gritstone sculptures of Derwent Edge. The route is on paths throughout and relatively straightforward to follow.

Parking: Pay car park at Fairholmes. Some limited free parking in lay-bys along the road towards the A57.

Public Transport: Bus 273 runs intermittently from Sheffield to Fairholmes car park, with a better service at weekends.

The name **Abbey Brook** relates to a monastic grange established in the mid 13th century under what is now Derwent Reservoir by the White Canons of Welbeck Abbey. **Abbey Grange** was established at One Man's House, a name that relates to the former hermitage here, but all that remains is the tiled floor of what was the grange's dairy. Previously part of the royal hunting grounds, the monks were granted parts of the Upper Derwent Valley by King John, first establishing a large community at Crookhill Grange between the Ashop and Derwent Valleys in the late 12th century. This large site included a bakehouse, brewery, tannery and a number of forges. The grange system was widespread, involving laymen who farmed land for the monks on large tracts of ground, often in remote places near parish boundaries. The rearing of horses was banned on granges, but **Marebottom Farm** (now the waterworks house by Howden Dam, *p19*) may relate to this activity, for which many monks were fined.

A **cogman** is an old dialect term for an itinerant pedlar.

Shireowlers Wood (see *p26*) below Bamford House refers to boundary alders, planted to demarcate the land, as does **Ollerbrook** in Edale.

Back Tor is so-called as it stands back from the rest of Derwent Edge. It has been suggested **Berristers Tor** is a corruption of Bear's Tooth, which would fit the profile of this striking prow.

5 Soon after **Lost Lad** cairn, fork right off the main flagged path and descend gently off the shoulder towards **Sheepfold Clough**. Cross a number of fencelines before dropping into beautiful **Howden Dean**. Follow the clear path left down the clough that separates Derwent and Howden Edges.

5 **Lost Lad** (cairn)

Lost Lad Hillend

6 After a mile the path crosses **Cogman Clough** near the ruin of an old sheepfold. At the crest of the hill the other side, bear left onto a faint path angling up the slope below **Forest Knoll**. This continues above a shallow clough to reach a clearer path, which you follow right over the stream and up to a stile. Turn left beyond, then right at the next junction, heading down to a sign above the ruin of **Bamford House**, where you turn left after admiring the fine view

4 Beyond **Dovestone Tor** you can deviate right briefly towards the impressive outcrops of the **Cakes of Bread**, but the main path continues all the way up to the large gritstone hunks on the summit of **Back Tor**. The onward flagged path leads left shortly before the trig, heading down to the large cairn at Lost Lad

Back Tor (538m)

trig   flags   waystone

Bradfield Gate Head

Back Tor summit

Bamford House (ruin)

old waymill sign

post

stile

old wall

stile

stile

7

METRES

0   200   400   600

Climb steadily to a stile on the skyline, then turn right along the fenceline. After the next stile, turn left to a gate by an older pine plantation. Fork right immediately beyond to drop down into the head of **Hollin Clough**, where a good path winds steeply down to emerge on the shore of **Derwent Reservoir**. Follow the track briefly left, then fork right off it and keep right to descend by the foot of **Derwent Dam**. Rejoin Derwent Lane at the bottom to return to Fairholmes car park.

Among Dovestone Tor's many turrets, the **Dove Stone** itself is a large boulder beneath the main rock-face. Above the edge there are several striking rocks mimicking the shape of a bird, including one with a hole right through it. The name relates not to the bird though, but rather to dow or dew, the latter a corruption of the Gaelic *dubh*, meaning black.

Ladybower may be named after the Derbyshire De Bower family, who owned land in the valley.

Derwent village was a much smaller hamlet than Ashopton, best known for the grand buildings that were drowned there. Of four chapels built by the canons of Welbeck Abbey, only that in Derwent remained in use beyond the Dissolution of the Monasteries. The last incarnation of **Derwent Church** was built on this site in the 1860s and held its last service on March 17th 1943. Despite having been moved to the church in Chelmorton, its bells are still said to toll beneath the waters of Ladybower. Its tower and steeple were left standing when the reservoir was built, but later demolished for safety reasons. **Derwent Hall** was also lost; built by Henry Balguy in 1672, it was replete with oak panels, tapestries and terraced gardens, and was later used as a country seat and shooting lodge by the Duke of Norfolk.

The **Cakes of Bread** are fascinating gritstone outcrops that stand out clearly across Strines Moor, but their form is most apparent from Dovestone Tor, where they stand out as three clear loaves. However, the baker will be disappointed, as the most easterly has clearly not risen at all well.

3 After crossing **Dovestone Clough** near the top, bear right across the slope and follow a fence up to a gate, then turn right along the wall at the foot of Derwent Edge. Though wet in places, this soon crosses another wall, after which you turn left up its side on a beeline for the distinctive **Salt Cellar**. Just beyond this outcrop lies the main path along Derwent Edge, which you follow left up onto **Dovestone Tor**.

2 Follow the path left between the ruins of **Wellhead** and up a holloway heading through the trees. At a gate by Lanehead, fork right on a permissive path across Briery Side. Reaching the open moor, this crosses **Far Deep Clough** and doubles back through the bracken. Fork left before the gate and climb steeply up the side of **Dovestone Clough** with Dovestone Tor towering above.

1 From **Fairholmes car park** follow the private road of Derwent Lane across the river below Derwent Dam – a path by the café leads along the river to it. Stay on the road for a mile along the shore of **Ladybower Reservoir**, before forking left at a sign just before the submerged site of **Derwent Village**. If the water is low, it is worth bearing right down to the shore to take a closer look at what remains beneath the reservoir.

Map labels: Cakes of Bread · Dove Stone · flags · sign · Salt Cellar · Dovestone Tor · Derwent Edge · flags · wet · gate · stile · Dovestone Clough · gate · post · gate · gate · Far Deep Clough · post · gate · Briery Side · N · Mill Brook · Wellhead (ruin) · gate · Lanehead · gate & sign · stile · gate · The Shooting Lodge · Derwent Village (site) · stile & sign · a ring ouzel · Derwent Lane · Old House · Ladybower Reservoir · Hollin Clough · stoop · gate · post · gate · Derwent Reservoir · Steps · sign · café · Jubilee Cottages · Derwent Dam · Fairholmes · to A57 (2 miles)

33

Derwent Edge is a particularly good place to see the area's **mountain hares** – sometimes it seems that the place is positively jumping with them. Originally from Scotland, their white winter coats are less than advantageous in the milder Peak District.

a mountain hare

7 Turn right at a larger path, then left up a vehicle track below **Thornseat Moor**. At th shooting cabins, turn right to climb to the wall corner above. A fair path leads along the fence then wall all the way down to **Mortimer Road**. Turn left for 100m then right down the quieter lane of Windy Bank.

shooting cabins

stakes

Thornseat Mo

Cartledge Stones

sign

6

stakes

line of butts

pool

flags

Cartledge Stones Ridge

Rushy Flat Dike

N

Rushy Flat

old wall

stakes *wet*

old gap

Holling Dale Plantation (former)

6 At **Cartledge Stone** you look west across th top of Abbey Brook to Howden Edge; keep right before descending off the stone and double back to join a vehicle track along a line of substantial butts. A possibl shortcut heads right at a stake on the climb up to Cartledge Stones to reach th same point. After Butt 4 bear right onto a gentler path cutting the corner down t **Rushy Flat Dike**. After rejoining the track to cross the stream, bear immediately lef up through the pine trees to pick up a faint path following the fence then wall aroun the former plantation. It gets rougher beyond the line of an old wall and, soon afte there is an obvious former gap on the right. Turn left here and follow a line of stake through the thick heather and across a small stream. Beyond a brief wet area, yo start to pick up a path again, soon aiming to the right of some stunted conifer.

cairn

flags

boundary stone

trig

Back Tor (538m)

waystone

Foulstone Road

flags

Cakes of Bread

Dove Stone

Dovestone Tor

sign

flags

Derwent Edge

Salt Cellar

5

tiny pools

In 1940 a **Starfish decoy site** was laid out on the back of Derwent Edge, its lights and fires successfully luring German bombers away from Sheffield an delaying the Sheffield Blitz by a couple of months. It was controlled from concrete blockhouse that can still be seen east of Back Tor on Broggin Moss (p29). The moor is covered in bom craters, now covered with heather o filled with water, and there are likel unexploded bombs buried in the peat

5 It is a delightful and straightforward walk along Derwent Edge from the **Salt Cellar** to Back Tor via **Dovestone Tor** and the **Cakes of Bread**, both of which are worth a short detour. The trig point on **Back Tor** stands on one of its many fine gritstone sculptures. Keep right past it to rejoin the flags along the shallow ridge of empty moor leading for a further mile to **Cartledge Stones**.

boundary stone

Raddlepit Rushes (wet)

Strines Moor (411m)

boundary stones

wooden butts

boundary stones

4

Rising Clough

boundary stones

Strines Edge

boundary stones

3 Follow the track right past Mosca Cross Farm and bend right before the 18t century guide stoop (the likely inspiratio for Whitcross in Charlotte Brontë's *Jan Eyre*). The track becomes muddier as i descends to join **Sugworth Road**. G left, then straight on over a stile at th junction beyond. Rather than follow th obvious path, bear right and pick up fainter line through the heather. Thoug it peters out near a small quarry, yo soon reach the clear path heading u **Strines Edge** along a fine line o stones marking the county boundary

Mortimer Road

Sugworth Road

P

gate

sign & gate

gate

delf

stile

Moscar Cross (site)

guide stoop

4 Shortly before the unmarked high point of **Strines Moor**, the path drops down to cross **Raddlepit Rushes**. It is briefly wet but a path continues west along the boundary stones; where the boundary bends right, a faint path heads left to a line of wooden butts along the grough at the top of **Rising Clough**. Any semblance of a path finally peters out, leaving a quarter of a mile of boggy tussocks to the flagged path along Derwent Edge. Keep west past a series of small bog pools to reach the edge near the distinctive weathered cap of the **Salt Cellar**, which is hidden from view from this side beneath a slight edge.

34

0   250   500   750
METRES

BRADFIELD

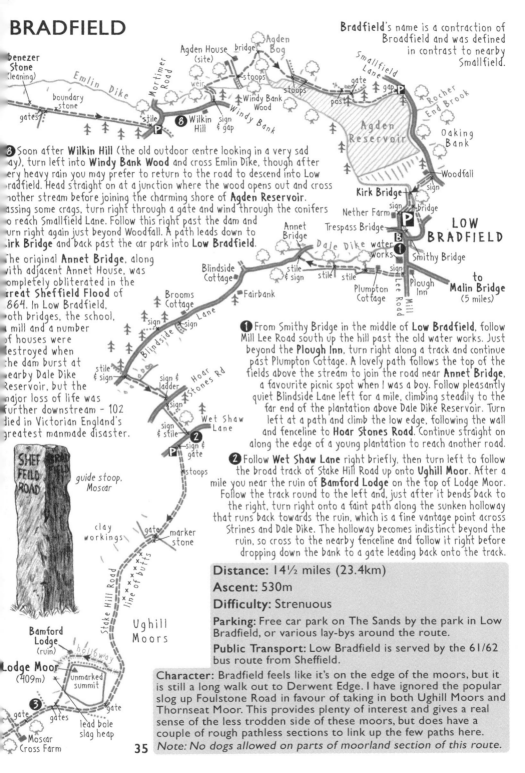

Bradfield's name is a contraction of Broadfield and was defined in contrast to nearby Smallfield.

❽ Soon after **Wilkin Hill** (the old outdoor centre looking in a very sad way), turn left into **Windy Bank Wood** and cross Emlin Dike, though after very heavy rain you may prefer to return to the road to descend into Low Bradfield. Head straight on at a junction where the wood opens out and cross another stream before joining the charming shore of **Agden Reservoir**. Passing some crags, turn right through a gate and wind through the conifers to reach Smallfield Lane. Follow this right past the dam and turn right again just beyond Woodfall. A path leads down to Kirk Bridge and back past the car park into **Low Bradfield**.

The original **Annet Bridge**, along with adjacent Annet House, was completely obliterated in the Great Sheffield Flood of 1864. In Low Bradfield, both bridges, the school, a mill and a number of houses were destroyed when the dam burst at nearby Dale Dike Reservoir, but the major loss of life was further downstream – 102 died in Victorian England's greatest manmade disaster.

❶ From Smithy Bridge in the middle of **Low Bradfield**, follow Mill Lee Road south up the hill past the old water works. Just beyond the **Plough Inn**, turn right along a track and continue past Plumpton Cottage. A lovely path follows the top of the fields above the stream to join the road near **Annet Bridge**, a favourite picnic spot when I was a boy. Follow pleasantly quiet Blindside Lane left for a mile, climbing steadily to the far end of the plantation above Dale Dike Reservoir. Turn left at a path and climb the low edge, following the wall and fenceline to **Hoar Stones Road**. Continue straight on along the edge of a young plantation to reach another road.

❷ Follow **Wet Shaw Lane** right briefly, then turn left to follow the broad track of Stake Hill Road up onto **Ughill Moor**. After a mile you near the ruin of **Bamford Lodge** on the top of Lodge Moor. Follow the track round to the left and, just after it bends back to the right, turn right onto a faint path along the sunken holloway that runs back towards the ruin, which is a fine vantage point across Strines and Dale Dike. The holloway becomes indistinct beyond the ruin, so cross to the nearby fenceline and follow it right before dropping down the bank to a gate leading back onto the track.

Distance: 14½ miles (23.4km)

Ascent: 530m

Difficulty: Strenuous

Parking: Free car park on The Sands by the park in Low Bradfield, or various lay-bys around the route.

Public Transport: Low Bradfield is served by the 61/62 bus route from Sheffield.

Character: Bradfield feels like it's on the edge of the moors, but it is still a long walk out to Derwent Edge. I have ignored the popular slog up Foulstone Road in favour of taking in both Ughill Moors and Thornseat Moor. This provides plenty of interest and gives a real sense of the less trodden side of these moors, but does have a couple of rough pathless sections to link up the few paths here.

Note: No dogs allowed on parts of moorland section of this route.

35

DERWENT VALLEY RESERVOIRS

With an increasing demand for drinking water, the expanding cities of Sheffield, Derby, Leicester and Nottingham put forward several different proposals for damming the Derwent and Ashop valleys in the 1890s. The parliamentary committee recommended they seek a single joint bill, and this formed the basis of the Derwent Valley Water Act in 1899. Six reservoirs were approved, including Ronksley, Ashopton and Hagglee Reservoirs (the latter stretching all the way up the Woodlands Valley to Alport Bridge). Sheffield was originally going to be excluded as it was not part of the Derwent watershed, but it was considered that there was enough water to supply all the cities. The water was to be split unevenly four ways with the costs shared accordingly.

The first phase was the construction of the Howden and Derwent Reservoirs, with an aqueduct all the way from Derwent Dam to Derby, Nottingham and Leicester. A separate tunnel branched off this to the new waterworks at Rivelin, which would supply much of Sheffield. After initial surveys, the Derwent Dam was moved a quarter of a mile upstream and built 25' higher. This removed the need for the costly and remote Ronksley Reservoir, which was planned to flood the valley beyond Howden (around Stepping Stones). Though most dams until this point were built of earth banks with a puddle clay core, the recent collapses of Bilberry and Dale Dyke dams and the propensity for landslips in the area meant that stone masonry was used. Similar structures had recently been built at Llyn Efyrnwy and Nant Elan in mid-Wales and many Welsh workers were involved, their descendants still living in the area today.

Stone for Howden and Derwent Dams was originally to be dug from a huge quarry in Ladybower Gorge, with waste materials dumped along Nether Brook, but protests led by George Wightman obstructed this. Instead a site at Bole Hill *(see p109)* was used, with stone taken by incline to Grindleford and then by rail to the dams. Around 400 people were employed at Bole Hill Quarry and 1.2 million tons of stone removed in 7½ years of activity. The dams were not completed until 1914, with the labour force peaking at 2,753 in 1908. Many of the navvies lived at the temporary settlement of Birchinlee *(see p42 for more information on Tin Town)*, but living and working conditions were far better than they had been in the mid-19th century, when the tunnels at Woodhead and Totley were notoriously dangerous places to work.

In 1924, the Duke of Norfolk agreed to sell Derwent Hall to the water board in 1924, the only thing preventing the flooding of the whole Derwent valley. Thus, the three dams planned as the second phase of the original act were superseded by Ladybower Dam, a 140'-high earth embankment with a clay and concrete core. Work began in 1935 and continued through the war despite obvious difficulties with labour and materials, so it was not finished until 1943, with George VI opening it officially in 1945. Derwent and Ashopton villages were flooded and their residents rehoused in an estate built by the water board at Yorkshire Bridge.

During World War II, the Derwent Reservoirs (like Langsett Reservoir) were taken over by the 57 Anti-Aircraft Brigade, with over 5,000 troops training between the two sites. The Dambusters practised throughout 1943 for bombing the Mohne and Edersee Dams in the Ruhr Valley; Lancaster bombers famously flying low over the dams to drop bouncing bombs. After the success of Operation Chastise in May 1943, a fear of reprisal by the Germans led to smoke canisters being laid all around the Derwent

Valley Reservoirs. At Strines, Midhope and Langsett, great steel columns up to 325ft high were erected to hang lattice grids across the reservoirs and prevent low-flying aircraft.

Demand for water continued to rise and, as well as the 1920s conduit through the hillside from the River Ashop to Derwent Reservoir, a further conduit was constructed beneath Win Hill from the River Noe near Nether Booth. In 1949, a dam across Edale was again given consideration, but the valley's unstable shale meant it was ultimately deemed unsuitable. There was also talk of raising Howden Dam by a further 45', but by 1985 the magnificent Gothic dam structures had been Grade II listed.

Derwent dam

CHAPTER 4 – UGHILL MOORS

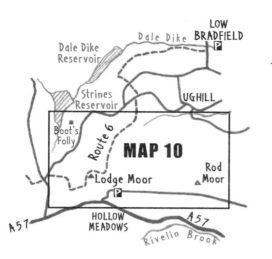

High Point:
Lodge Moor, 409m

Grid Ref: SK237898

Map Sheet: OL1 (Dark Peak)

Access: No restrictions.

Public Transport: Buses 273/274 run fairly regularly from Sheffield to Hollow Meadows. Buses 61/62 run regularly between Sheffield and Low Bradfield.

Ughill Moors form an outlying moorland area between Strines and the Rivelin Valley that it is tempting to ignore entirely. There are only small parcels of largely unremarkable access land on Rod Moor, Lodge Moor and around Boot's Folly, but it is a remnant of the medieval Black Moors. These lay within Stannington parish and covered most of the land around the head of the Rivelin Valley, before being gradually diminished by Parliamentary Enclosure acts, particularly around Hollow Meadows. Ughill Moors, along with part of Hallam Moors on the back of Stanage, are all that remain.

The name Ughill derives from Uhgil, referring to Uha's Valley, an Old Norse name probably dating from the first settlement of the nearby village's around the 10th century. Lady's Seat was an earlier name for the summit of Ughill Moor, probably before the lodge was constructed on it in the early 19th century, since when it has been known as Lodge Moor. Rod Moor is little more than a slight eminence on the long ridge that slopes all the way down to Stannington and Malin Bridge.

It is hard to spend a day on this small moorland area, but it's good for an evening's exploring from Moscar Heights or Sugworth Edge. The familiar tower of Boot's Tower is its best-known landmark, but the ruined lodge is also worth a closer look.

Ughill Moors and Boot's Folly from Strines

Boot's Folly (sometimes known as Strines Tower) stands prominently above Strines Reservoir and was built in 1927 by Charles Boot, the civil engineer who owned **Sugworth Hall**. It is often said that he wanted to be able to view his wife's grave at the church in High Bradfield, but the project was largely conceived to keep his estate workers busy during the Great Depression. The tower was originally panelled inside and the steps were removed when a cow became stuck on the viewing platform at the top in the 1970s. Nowadays it is more likely to be full of sheep. In the heaps of stone nearby are ornamental columns from Brunswick Chapel in the centre of Sheffield; these were removed for safekeeping after it was bombed during the war, but the chapel was never rebuilt.

The 19th-century **marker stone** by Stake Hill Road is thought to mark the boundary between the Ughill and Sugworth estates.

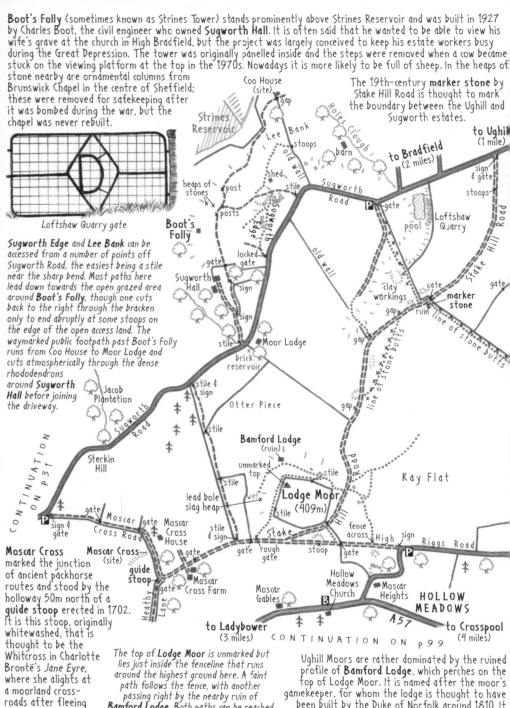

Loftshaw Quarry gate

Sugworth Edge and **Lee Bank** can be accessed from a number of points off Sugworth Road, the easiest being a stile near the sharp bend. Most paths here lead down towards the open grazed area around **Boot's Folly**, though one cuts back to the right through the bracken only to end abruptly at some stoops on the edge of the open access land. The waymarked public footpath past Boot's Folly runs from Coo House to Moor Lodge and cuts atmospherically through the dense rhododendrons around **Sugworth Hall** before joining the driveway.

Moscar Cross marked the junction of ancient packhorse routes and stood by the holloway 50m north of a **guide stoop** erected in 1702. It is this stoop, originally whitewashed, that is thought to be the Whitcross in Charlotte Brontë's *Jane Eyre*, where she alights at a moorland cross-roads after fleeing Mr Rochester in the middle of the night.

38

The top of **Lodge Moor** is unmarked but lies just inside the fenceline that runs around the highest ground here. A faint path follows the fence, with another passing right by the nearby ruin of **Bamford Lodge**. Both paths can be reached from **Stake Hill Road**, either through a rough gate through the wall to the south or across some reedy ground to the east.

Ughill Moors are rather dominated by the ruined profile of **Bamford Lodge**, which perches on the top of Lodge Moor. It is named after the moor's gamekeeper, for whom the lodge is thought to have been built by the Duke of Norfolk around 1810. It was built as a tall lookout tower, but Bamford is said to have been unreservedly poor at his job and so it has been in ruins for about 150 years.

MAP 10: UGHILL MOORS

Ughill Moors are made up of two separate chunks of open access moorland; Lodge Moor and Rod Moor. The former is the true top, though only the latter is marked by a trig point. Though here are relatively few paths across this moorland it remains worth exploring, with short rewarding walks to the ruins of Bamford Lodge or Boot's Folly, the latter being the most prominent and recognisable landmark in the area.

The whole area around Ughill is marked by mines and quarries. The large pool in **Loftshaw Quarry** marks the site of one of the area's last pot clay and ganister mines. Ganister is a heavy yellow-grey form of clay that can withstand very high temperatures, so it was highly sought after in the 19th century for making refractory bricks that lined Sheffield's steel furnaces. The D on the gate relates to its owners, the Dysons of Stannington. There are also numerous former shafts and trial holes around the basin in which **Crawshaw** shelters, with most of the area's small pools marking their sites. The hillside in between is also interestingly known as **Furnace Hill**.

As recently as the 1850s, **Crawshaw Wood** ('crow's wood') covered the whole moorland enclosure between Crawshaw and Crawshaw Lodge, though it is hard to believe it now, as nothing remains other than a few trees around the edge of the moor. However, the name **Rod Moor** itself is from an Old English word rod for cleared land, suggesting a much earlier felling. Nearby **Beeton Rod** is a corruption of Beacon Rod, referring to a beacon fire that would have been lit on this prominent hillside in the Middle Ages.

Boot's Folly

There are a couple of public footpaths across **Rod Moor**, but otherwise little in the way of paths. The trig point is most easily reached by following a faint line along the crest from the main vehicle track to a gate above the trees of the **Jew's Burial Ground**. The rest of this eastern enclosure is rough and pathless, while the hillside around Hall Broom Quarry is strangely omitted from the open access agreement.

At one time here were **Five Blades Farm** five stone mausoleums behind **Moscar stables**. The first was built in 1891 by jeweller Horatio Bright for his late wife. He had an organ installed which he would play to her. In 1983 the mausoleums were vandalised and robbed. The bodies were reinterred at the Jew's Burial Ground and the buildings demolished.

At the heart of Ughill Moors, **Kay Flat** is a featureless expanse of heather with only a few grouse butts for company. There is no sign of the line of boundary stones that once crossed it and little in the way of paths. The eastern boundary can be followed from a stile off Rod Side to Stake Hill Road; though rough across a bracken-covered section in the middle, it becomes clear as you pass passing a line of old butts. The open access enclosure around **Furnace Hill** consists of rough tussocks and can be accessed only off Stake Hill Road.

Bamford Lodge ruins

THE RAVEN

There are few more awe-inspiring sights than the soaring raven, an imposing black creature that has inspired much mythology across the world. Raven is a broad term for a number of the larger species of the *corvus* family and is distinct from the smaller crow. They are the most intelligent of all birds, their intelligence said to rival that of primates, with many different vocalisations in their calls – human mimicry forms a core element of Edgar Allen Poe's epic poem *The Raven*. They were also known to help people and wolves hunt, revealing the location of deer so that they could feast on what was left over. There is a deep respect and fear of these unique birds, portrayed in many of these cultures as tricksters, playing games with us.

Due to their colour and taste for carrion, the raven has long been associated with death, with tombstones also known as ravenstones. In Greek mythology ravens are associated with prophecy and symbols of bad luck, in Swedish folklore they represent the ghosts of murdered people, and in German tradition they are the souls of the damned. In Native American mythology they are symbols of transformation and metamorphosis, and in many shamanic cultures the raven is an important spirit and key figure in creation. Ravens famously guard the Tower of London and are still looked after by a yeoman warder for, if they disappear, England is said to fall.

The common (or northern) raven is the only raven found in the UK; it has a large bill, which it uses to pull apart the flesh of the dead animals it scavenges on, and a wingspan of up to 1.5m, larger than that of the buzzard. It can be distinguished from a large crow due to its wedge-shaped tail, shaggy throat feathers and deep, throaty 'croar' call. There are now over ten thousand breeding pairs in the UK and the raven is an occasional resident in the Dark Peak. If you're very lucky, the male can be seen performing impressive acrobatic displays in late winter/early spring before breeding. Nests are usually laid on cliffs and crags, with the young leaving after about a month, and breeding pairs often return to previous nesting sites. It is a rare success story as there were once only a thousand pairs in the UK, mainly because they were persecuted by farmers as they posed a threat to livestock. Their recent recovery and spread across lowland Britain has seen renewed calls again for them to be considered fair game for shooting, as they also feed on small mammals and other birds' eggs.

CHAPTER 5 – BLEAKLOW

High Point:
Bleaklow Head, 633m

Grid Ref: SK092960

Map Sheet:
OL1 (Dark Peak)

Access: No restrictions.

Public Transport: Bus 273 runs from Sheffield to Fairholmes, with a better service at weekends. No service up Woodlands Valley.

Bleaklow was described by poet Edward Boaden Thomas as 'more a monster than a mountain'. There is certainly nothing mountainous about it, yet it represents one of England's few great untamed wildernesses, a 35-square-mile morass of peat between Longdendale and the Derwent and Woodlands Valleys. The name Bleaklow is, aptly, from the Old English *blaec hlaw* for a 'dark hill'.

   Bleaklow shows little of itself from the main roads to the north and south, instead rising quietly from the valleys and stretching long sinewy limbs out from its black, peaty heart. Only at Alport Castles does it easily give up its secrets to the visitor; otherwise its most enchanting outcrops are hidden deep in the Alport Valley or high above the head of the River Derwent. The summit ridge (if it can be called that) between Bleaklow Head and Bleaklow Stones is a barely discernable warren of deep groughs, magical at times but totally disorientating, so that you never feel you have mastered Bleaklow.

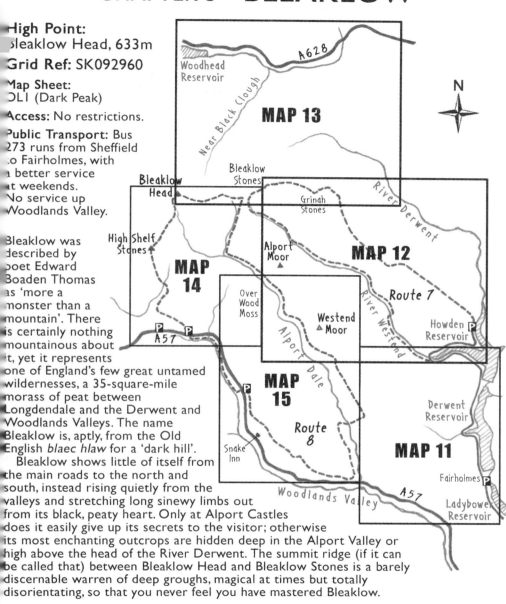

Bleaklow Head, Bleaklow Stones and Grinah Stones from Ridgwalk Moor

MAP 11: BLEAKLOW SOUTH-EAST (Birchinlee & Alport Castles)

The most popular and accessible corner of Bleaklow reaches out a long limb of forested land down the west side of the Derwent Valley reservoirs. It is usually accessed from Fairholmes, though the focal point is undoubtedly the dramatic landslips of Alport Castles, overlooking Alport Dale. In truth there is little else to see above the reservoirs, but these empty pastures provide a way into the wilder heart of Bleaklow.

The track up through **Fagney Plantation** ends near a stile

onto the moor, from where a faint line winds all the way to the ridge path just south of Westend Moor trig.

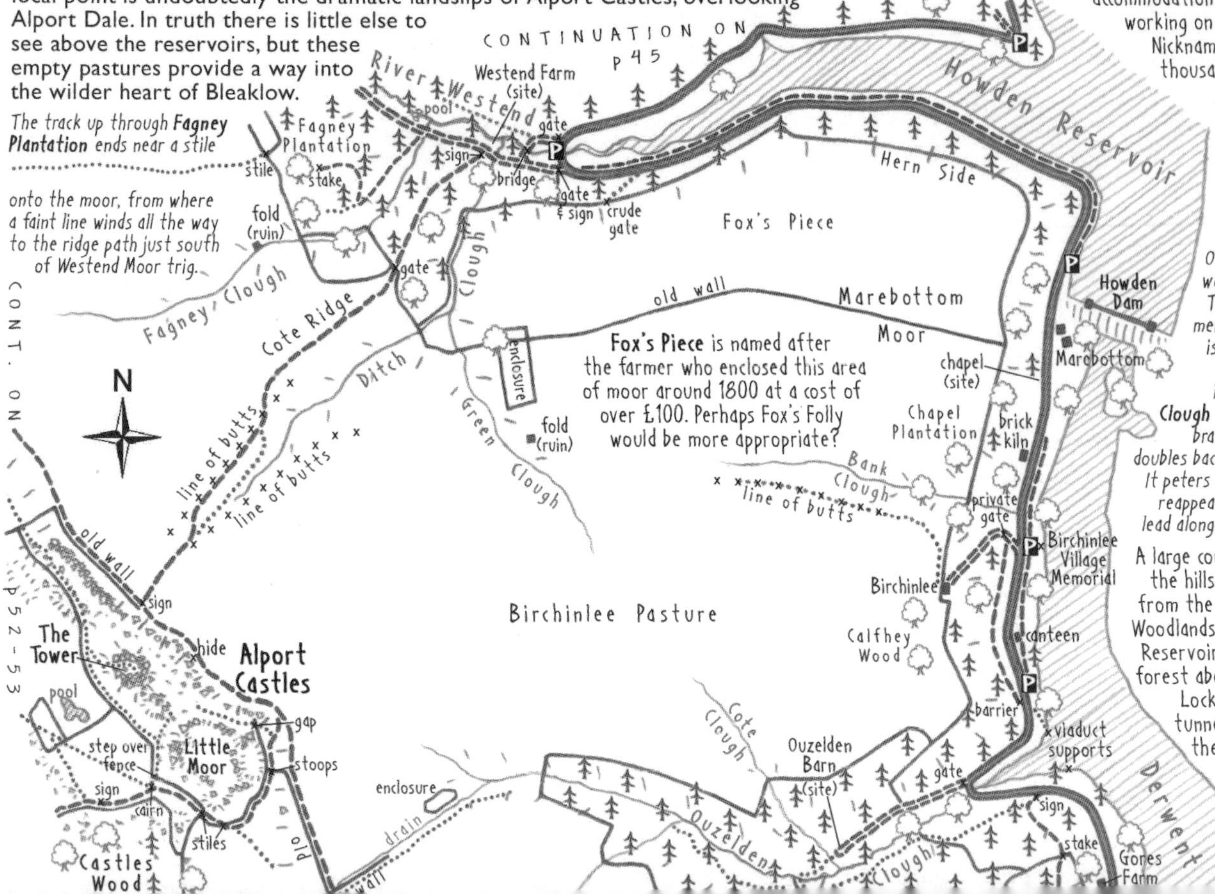

Birchinlee Farm was demolished to make way for the village that took its name, which provided temporary accommodation for the families of the navvies working on the Derwent and Howden Dams. Nicknamed **Tin Town**, it housed up to a thousand people and included a church, hospital, recreation hall, shops, school, library, police station, canteen and all-important refreshment house.

The main path from Howden to Alport Castles heads up **Cote Ridge** on a good shooters' track. Otherwise there is very little in the way of paths on **Birchinlee Pasture.**
The track up to Birchinlee from the memorial alongside Derwent Reservoir is private so the path along the line of butts by Bank Clough is almost inaccessible. The track up **Ouzelden Clough** leads onto a faint line through the bracken that crosses the stream then doubles back to the right through the forest. It peters out as the clough steepens, before reappearing the other side of the fence to lead alongside the drain up to the path along the ridge.

A large conduit leads beneath the hillside to feed water from the River Ashop in the Woodlands Valley into Derwent Reservoir. It emerges in the forest above Fairholmes near Locker Brook. A similar tunnel takes water from the River Noe beneath Win Hill and into Ladybower Reservoir.

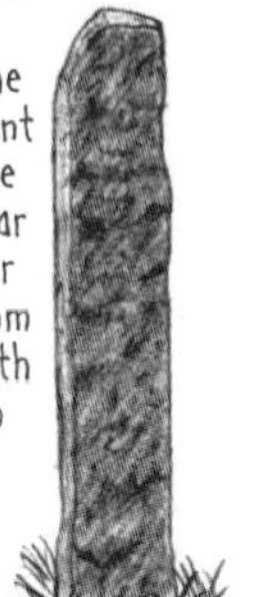

Fox's Piece is named after the farmer who enclosed this area of moor around 1800 at a cost of over £100. Perhaps Fox's Folly would be more appropriate?

CONTINUATION ON P45

CONT. ON p52-53

Howden Reservoir

Hern Side

Marebottom Moor

Fox's Piece

Howden Dam

Marebottom

chapel (site)

brick kiln

private gate

Chapel Plantation

Birchinlee Village Memorial

canteen

viaduct supports

barrier

gate

sign

Grove Farm

Derwent

Bank Clough

line of butts

Birchinlee

Calfhey Wood

Ouzelden Barn (site)

Cote Clough

Ouzelden Clough

Birchinlee Pasture

old wall

fold (ruin)

enclosure

Green Clough

Westend Farm (site)

bridge

pool

gate

crude gate

sign

Fagney Plantation

stile

stake

fold (ruin)

Fagney (Clough)

Cote Ridge

Ditch Clough

line of butts

line of butts

old wall

sign

Alport Castles

gap

stoops

Little Moor

stiles

slide

The Tower

pool

step over fence

cairn

sign

Castles Wood

enclosure

drain

Hagg Guide Stoop

N

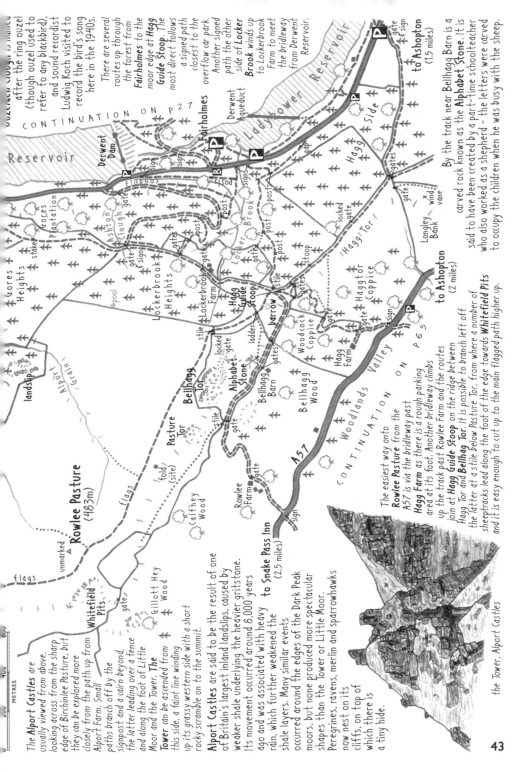

...after the ring ouzel (though ouzel used to refer to any blackbird), and sound recordist Ludwig Koch visited to record the bird's song here in the 1940s.

There are several routes up through the forest from *Fairholmes* to the moor edge at *Hagg Guide Stoop*. The most direct follows a signed path closest to the overflow car park. Another signed path the other side of *Locker Brook* winds up to Lockerbrook Farm to meet the bridleway from Derwent Reservoir.

By the track near Bellhagg Barn is a carved rock known as the *Alphabet Stone*. It is said to have been created by a part-time schoolteacher who also worked as a shepherd – the letters were carved to occupy the children when he was busy with the sheep.

CONTINUATION ON P 27

CONTINUATION ON P 65

Reservoir

Derwent Dam

Fairholmes

Ladybower Reservoir

to Ashopton (1.5 miles)

Gores Heights

Gores Plantation

Ashton Clough

Derwent Aqueduct

Locker Brook

Lockerbrook Farm

Lockerbrook Heights

Hagg Side

Longley Bank — wind vane

gate & sign

Hagg Guide Stoop

barrow

Woodcock Coppice

Hagg Tor

Haggtor Coppice

to Ashopton (2 miles)

Hagg Farm

Bellhagg Barn

Alphabet Stone

Bellhagg Tor

Bellhagg Wood

Woodlands Valley

A57

Bellhagg Tor

Pasture Tor

fold (site)

Calfhey Wood

Rowlee Farm

Rowlee Pasture (483m)

landslip

Alport Grain

flags

unmarked

Whitefield Pits

Gillott Hey Wood

to Snake Pass Inn (2.5 miles)

The *Alport Castles* are usually viewed from above, looking across from the sharp edge of Birchinlee Pasture, but they can be explored more closely from the path up from Alport Farm. Small paths branch off by the signpost and a cairn beyond, the latter leading over a fence and along the foot of Little Moor and the Tower. The *Tower* can be ascended from this side, a faint line winding up its grassy western side with a short rocky scramble on to the summit.

Alport Castles are said to be the result of one of Britain's largest inland landslips, caused by weaker shale underlying the heavier gritstone. Its movement occurred around 8,000 years ago and was associated with heavy rain, which further weakened the shale layers. Many similar events occurred around the edges of the Dark Peak moors, but none produced more spectacular shapes than the Tower or Little Moor. Peregrines, ravens, merlin and sparrowhawks now nest on its cliffs, on top of which there is a tiny hide.

The easiest way onto *Rowlee Pasture* from the A57 is via the bridleway past *Hagg Farm* as there is a rough parking area at its foot. Another bridleway climbs up the track past Rowlee Farm and the routes join at *Hagg Guide Stoop* on the ridge between *Hagg Tor* and *Bellhag Tor*. It is possible to branch left off the latter at a stile below Pasture Tor, from where a number of sheeptracks lead along the foot of the edge towards *Whitefield Pits* and it is easy enough to cut up to the main flagged path higher up.

the Tower, Alport Castles

MAP 12: BLEAKLOW EAST
(Westend Valley & Ronksley Moor)

The most remote and seemingly empty corner of all the Dark Peak moors, this is a rewarding place to visit, whether for its quiet cloughs or the striking Grinah and Barrow Stones. It is most easily reached from Howden Reservoir, but there are a surprising number of paths tentatively following the streams and ridges into the bleak interior.

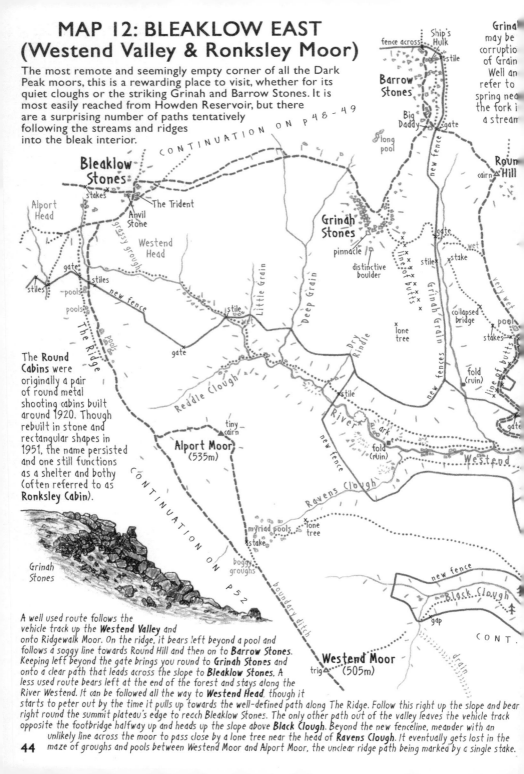

CONTINUATION ON P 48-49

Grina may be corruptio of Grain Well an refer to spring nea the fork i a stream

fence across
Ship's Hulk
stile

Barrow Stones

Big Daddy
gate
long pool

Bleaklow Stones

Roun Hill
cairn

stakes
The Trident
Anvil Stone

Alport Head

Westend Head

grassy grough

gate
stiles
stiles
pools
pools
new fence

The Ridge
pools

Grinah Stones

pinnacle
distinctive boulder

line of butts
stile
stake
wet

very wet

Grinah Grain

collapsed bridge
pool
stakes

lone tree

line of butts

gate

fold (ruin)

Little Grain
Deep Grain
stile

gate

Dry Rindle

new fences

stile

The **Round Cabins** were originally a pair of round metal shooting cabins built around 1920. Though rebuilt in stone and rectangular shapes in 1951, the name persisted and one still functions as a shelter and bothy (often referred to as **Ronksley Cabin**).

Reddle Clough

tiny cairn

Alport Moor (535m)

River Wark
fold (ruin)

Westend

new fence

Ravens Clough

CONTINUATION ON P 52

myriad pools
lone tree
stake

boggy groughs

boundary ditch

new fence

Black Clough

gap

CONT.

drain

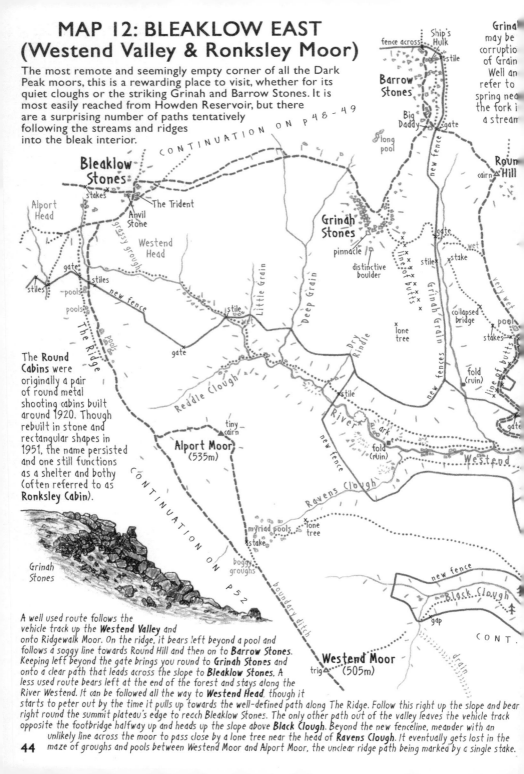

Grinah Stones

Westend Moor (505m)
trig

A well used route follows the vehicle track up the **Westend Valley** and onto Ridgewalk Moor. On the ridge, it bears left beyond a pool and follows a soggy line towards Round Hill and then on to **Barrow Stones**. Keeping left beyond the gate brings you round to **Grinah Stones** and onto a clear path that leads across the slope to **Bleaklow Stones**. A less used route bears left at the end of the forest and stays along the River Westend. It can be followed all the way to **Westend Head**, though it starts to peter out by the time it pulls up towards the well-defined path along The Ridge. Follow this right up the slope and bear right round the summit plateau's edge to reach Bleaklow Stones. The only other path out of the valley leaves the vehicle track opposite the footbridge halfway up and heads up the slope above **Black Clough**. Beyond the new fenceline, meander with an unlikely line across the moor to pass close by a lone tree near the head of **Ravens Clough**. It eventually gets lost in the maze of groughs and pools between Westend Moor and Alport Moor, the unclear ridge path being marked by a single stake.

44

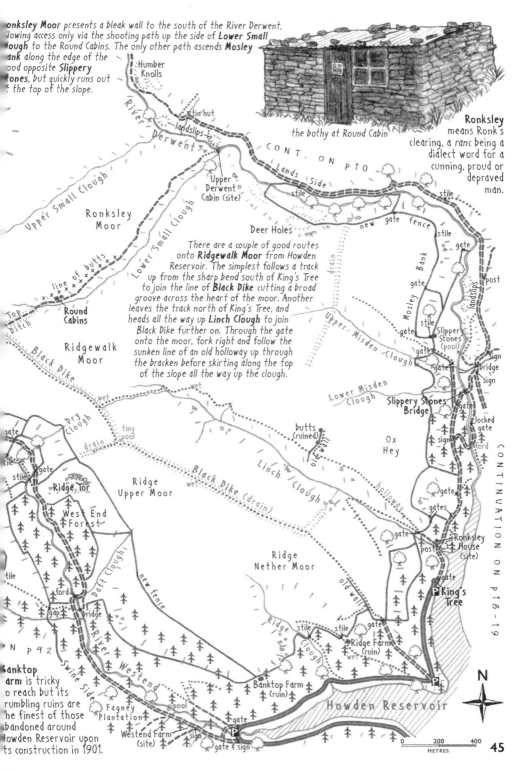

onksley Moor presents a bleak wall to the south of the River Derwent, llowing access only via the shooting path up the side of **Lower Small ough** to the Round Cabins. The only other path ascends **Mosley ank** along the edge of the ood opposite **Slippery tones**, but quickly runs out the top of the slope.

the bothy at Round Cabin

Ronksley means Ronk's clearing, a *ranc* being a dialect word for a cunning, proud or depraved man.

Humber Knolls

tin hut

landslips

River Derwent

CONT. ON P10

Upper Derwent (cabin (site))

Lands Side

stile

stile

Upper Small Clough

Ronksley Moor

new gate fence

stile

Deer Holes

gate

Lower Small Clough

Mosley Bank

gate

post

landslips

line of butts

There are a couple of good routes onto **Ridgewalk Moor** from Howden Reservoir. The simplest follows a track up from the sharp bend south of King's Tree to join the line of **Black Dike** cutting a broad groove across the heart of the moor. Another leaves the track north of King's Tree, and heads all the way up **Linch Clough** to join Black Dike further on. Through the gate onto the moor, fork right and follow the sunken line of an old holloway up through the bracken before skirting along the top of the slope all the way up the clough.

stile

gate

Upper Misden Clough

Slippery Stones (pool)

Round Cabins

gate

sign

Top Ditch

Ridgewalk Moor

Black Dike

wet

wet

Lower Misden Clough

bridge

sign

Slippery Stones Bridge

gate

Dry Clough

drain

tiny pool

butts (ruined)

old wall

Ox Hey

locked gate

ford

sign

gate

stile

gate

Black Dike (drain)

Linch Clough

holloway

gate

Ridge Tor

Ridge Upper Moor

wet

gates

West End Forest

gate

Ridge Nether Moor

post

Ronksley House (site)

C O N T I N U A T I O N   O N   p 1 8 - 1 9

gate

ford

gap

bridge

new fence

Daft Clough

old wall

gate

King's Tree

N p42

River Westend

Swine Side

Ridge Clough

stile

stile

gate

Ridge Farm (ruin)

wet

anktop arm is tricky o reach but its rumbling ruins are he finest of those bandoned around owden Reservoir upon ts construction in 1901.

Fagney Plantation

pool

Banktop Farm (ruin)

Howden Reservoir

Westend Farm (site)

sign

gate

gate & sign

0   200   400
METRES

N

45

ROUTE 7: BLEAKLOW AND GRINAH

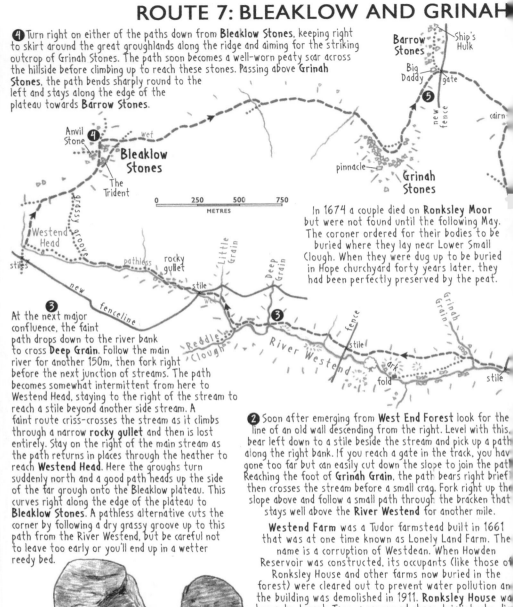

4 Turn right on either of the paths down from **Bleaklow Stones**, keeping right to skirt around the great groughlands along the ridge and aiming for the striking outcrop of **Grinah Stones**. The path soon becomes a well-worn peaty scar across the hillside before climbing up to reach these stones. Passing above **Grinah Stones**, the path bends sharply round to the left and stays along the edge of the plateau towards **Barrow Stones**.

Anvil Stone

4

wet

Bleaklow Stones

The Trident

grassy groove

Westend Head

stiles

pathless

rocky gullet

Little Grain

Deep Grain

stile

wet

new fenceline

Reddle Clough

River Westend

fence

stile

ark

fold

Grinah Grain

stile

Barrow Stones

Ship's Hulk

Big Daddy

gate

5

new fence

cairn

Grinah Stones

pinnacle

0   250   500   750
METRES

In 1674 a couple died on **Ronksley Moor** but were not found until the following May. The coroner ordered for their bodies to be buried where they lay near Lower Small Clough. When they were dug up to be buried in Hope churchyard forty years later, they had been perfectly preserved by the peat.

3 At the next major confluence, the faint path drops down to the river bank to cross **Deep Grain**. Follow the main river for another 150m, then fork right before the next junction of streams. The path becomes somewhat intermittent from here to Westend Head, staying to the right of the stream to reach a stile beyond another side stream. A faint route criss-crosses the stream as it climbs through a narrow **rocky gullet** and then is lost entirely. Stay on the right of the main stream as the path returns in places through the heather to reach **Westend Head**. Here the groughs turn suddenly north and a good path heads up the side of the far grough onto the Bleaklow plateau. This curves right along the edge of the plateau to **Bleaklow Stones**. A pathless alternative cuts the corner by following a dry grassy groove up to this path from the River Westend, but be careful not to leave too early or you'll end up in a wetter reedy bed.

2 Soon after emerging from **West End Forest** look for the line of an old wall descending from the right. Level with this, bear left down to a stile beside the stream and pick up a path along the right bank. If you reach a gate in the track, you hav gone too far but can easily cut down the slope to join the path Reaching the foot of **Grinah Grain**, the path bears right brief then crosses the stream before a small crag. Fork right up the slope above and follow a small path through the bracken that stays well above the **River Westend** for another mile.

Westend Farm was a Tudor farmstead built in 1661 that was at one time known as Lonely Land Farm. The name is a corruption of Westdean. When Howden Reservoir was constructed, its occupants (like those of Ronksley House and other farms now buried in the forest) were cleared out to prevent water pollution an the building was demolished in 1911. **Ronksley House wa** home to Joseph Tagg, a renowned sheep trialist who die in 1953 at the age of 86 on top of Ridgewalk Moor. Hi loyal collie Tip stayed with her master's body until it was discovered four months later. She lived another two years and her memorial stand by Derwent Dam.

There are descriptions of there being as many as a dozen rocking stones in the **Barrow Stones**, but most are likely to have been destroyed in the 19th century by grouse-shooting interests. The name originally referred to the clough below and is named for the birch or alder trees that grew there.

46 *the eye-catching Big Daddy boulder at Barrow Stones*

STONES FROM HOWDEN RESERVOIR

5 **Barrow Stones** are reached by the arresting Big Daddy boulder, below which a path leads through the gate and across to Round Hill. If you want to explore the stones, continue along the edge but you'll need to retrace your steps to this gate. At the cairn on **Round Hill**, turn right and descend to the soggy shoulder of **Ridgewalk Moor**. The wet line leads along the crest to a pool and a junction with the shooting track just beyond. Continue straight across, then bear right out of the deep groove of **Black Dike** to pick up a path running along its south side.

Black Dike is one of a number of broad drains cut across Ronksley and Ridgewalk Moors by the Duke of Devonshire in the early 19th century. Its aim was to dry out the bog and make it more suitable for breeding grouse, but it was also used to cut peat along its length, hence its substantial width.

Distance: 10 miles (16.1km)

Ascent: 430m

Difficulty: Moderate

Parking: Lay-bys alongside Howden Reservoir between King's Tree and the Westend Valley. Road closed Sundays, Bank Holidays and summer Saturdays.

Public Transport: None at present beyond Fairholmes.

Character: A fine venture into the remote country around the Westend Valley. The route follows the River Westend all the way to its source near Bleaklow Stones before returning along the ridge above, crested by the impressive Grinah and Barrow Stones. Parts of the route are rough and pathless, but it is a relatively simple route through this terrain, the main problem being accessing the start at weekends now the bus service up to King's Tree no longer runs.

6 Follow **Black Dike** until the groove turns sharply left. Cross the drain here and pick up a path along its left side that descends into the top of **Linch Clough**. Cross the stream and follow a faint path along the edge of the slope as it winds down the north side of the clough. Some way beyond the line of an old wall the path bears right down an old holloway through the bracken to emerge at a gate into the forest. Continue down the stream to pick up the main track around Howden Reservoir, following it right to **King's Tree**. The road leads round the shore to the Westend Valley.

cairn on Round Hill, constructed from the remains of a lookout hut used by gamekeepers for catching poachers

King's Tree refers to a Hungarian oak tree planted by King George VI on 25th September 1945 to commemorate the end of World War II, the same day he officially opened Ladybower Reservoir. It stands in the middle of the mini roundabout at the end of the road.

1 From the bridge over the River Westend at the end of **Howden Reservoir**'s long western limb, follow the track either side of the wood. They join to follow the left bank of the river through the forestry plantations. After a mile cross a bridge to the right and rejoin the track beyond a ford to continue up past **West End Forest**.

The roads round the reservoirs were built by a group of men from Chapel-en-le-Frith who returned home only at weekends.

Ronksley Moor

pool

Black Dike

Ridgewalk Moor

wet

wet

tiny stake

old wall

fence

gate

stile

old wall

Ridge Tor

2

West End Forest

Daft Clough

ford

bridge

River Westend

Fagney Plantation

P **1**

sign

sign & gate

Westend Farm (site)

gate

Linch Clough

holloway

old wall

Ronksley House (site)

gate

post

gate

King's Tree

P

Ridge Clough

P

Howden Reservoir

to Fairholmes (2 1/2 miles)

N

The northern slopes of Bleaklow climb up from the busy A628 Woodhead Road and its line of reservoirs. Though most of it is the Lancashire side of the Pennine watershed, I have mapped this north-eastern corner that links Bleaklow to Howden Edge around the head of the River Derwent. The disorientating groughlands here are easily accessed by the long Black Cloughs that lead up from the A628, but may also form part of a longer round from Howden Reservoir.

*The main access point from the north-east is the car park below the A628 by the former **Woodhead Station**. A shooting track leads along the other side of the river and up the rocky side of **Far Black Clough** after fording the stream (be aware this can be awkward to cross in spate). Stay on the east bank of the stream as it continues far beyond the butts to a fork near White Stones, where you cross the stream and follow a faint line into the groughs. Continue up the maze of channels to reach **Bleaklow Stones** on the edge of the summit plateau; if you're very lucky you may find the path that leads straight to them. Another path follows **Near Black Clough**, keeping right before the ford to climb up to the top of the woods and follow the west side of the clough all the way to the heart of the plateau. After crossing an old fenceline, the path becomes fainter; look to turn right up one of the groughs to pick up a path leading directly to the summit cairn on **Bleaklow Head**. Halfway up Near Black Clough, a faint quad track crosses the path, leading left across a bridge and up into the wasteland of Bleaklow Meadows. While it may seem uninviting, following the left edge of the groughs leads close to the **Botha plane wreckage** on a barren shoulder overlooking Middle Black Clough. A rough traipse back across the groughs leads up onto the ramparts of **Near Bleaklow Stones**, a fine collection of rocks among which you'll find the lesser wreckage of a **Defiant**.*

the Anvil Stone, Bleaklow Stones

There is little reason to wander across the groughs of Bleaklow Meadows unless searching for two nearby **plane wrecks**. The **Botha** W5103 was brand new when it crashed in December 1941. It was being delivered to RAF Hawarden from the factory in Leeds and a section of its wing remains. Less is seen of the **Defiant** N3378 fighter plane that crashed in August 1941. Both its crew members died and the wreck was only discovered by shepherds a month later as it had been so far off course.

to Tintwistle (6 miles)

Ironbower Rocks

Woodhead Station (former)   stile

flow station

sign

Birchen Bank

ford

quar

cabins (site)

line of butts

waterfall

falls

Birchen Bank Moss

Black Moss

Featherbed Moss

to Stable Clough

bridge

Near Black Clough

Middle Black Clough

Botha plane wreckage

bridge

pools

Bleaklow Meadows (deep groughs)   pools

White Stones

pools   stake

pool   pool

striking rocks

Defiant plane wreckage

deep groughs

pool

Near Bleaklow Stones

lone tree

old stile

old fence

grassy grough

deep grough

Pennine Way

Bleaklow Stones

Anvil Stone

pole & cairn

Bleaklow Head (633m)

Bleaklow Hill

pools

stakes

stake

stake

stake   stake

stake   stake

mud   stake

The Trident

to Grina Stones

Alport Head

CONT. ON p 51

0   250   500   750   100

METRES

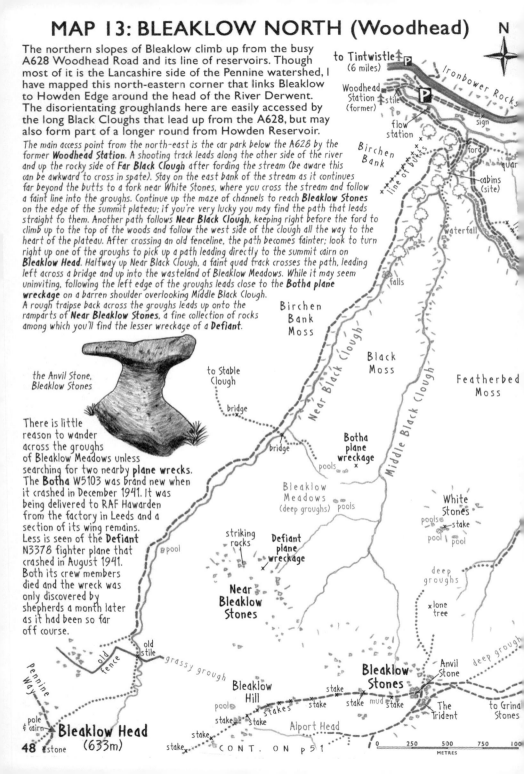

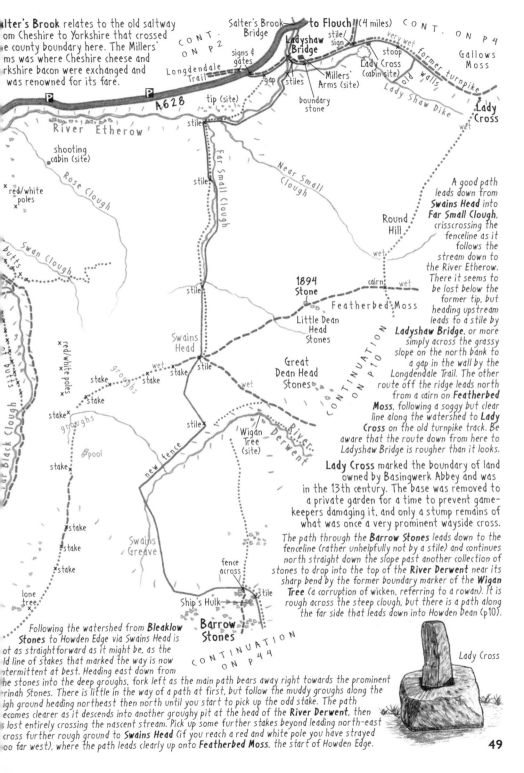

Map labels:

lter's Brook relates to the old saltway om Cheshire to Yorkshire that crossed e county boundary here. The Millers' ms was where Cheshire cheese and rkshire bacon were exchanged and was renowned for its fare.

to Flouch (4 miles) CONT. ON P4

Salter's Brook Bridge

CONT. ON P2

Ladyshaw Bridge

stile/sign

very wet

former turnpike

Gallows Moss

signs & gates

Longdendale Trail

stoop

Lady Cross (cabin site)

gap

stiles

Millers' Arms (site)

old walls

Lady Shaw Dike

Lady Cross

A628

tip (site)

boundary stone

wet

River Etherow

stile

shooting cabin (site)

stile

Far Small Clough

Near Small Clough

Round Hill

x red/white poles
x

Rose Clough

wet

cairn   wet

Swan Clough

butts

stile

1894 Stone

Featherbed Moss

Little Dean Head Stones

Swains Head

Great Dean Head Stones

red/white poles
x
x

stake   groughs   wet
stake
stake   stake   stile

wet

CONTINUATION ON P10

far Black Clough

butts

stake

groughs

stake

pool

stile

Wigan Tree (site)

River Derwent

new fence

stake

Swains Greave

fence across

stake

stake

lone tree
x

Ship's Hulk

stile

Barrow Stones

CONTINUATION ON P44

A good path leads down from **Swains Head** into **Far Small Clough**, crisscrossing the fenceline as it follows the stream down to the River Etherow. There it seems to be lost below the former tip, but heading upstream leads to a stile by **Ladyshaw Bridge**, or more simply across the grassy slope on the north bank to a gap in the wall by the Longdendale Trail. The other route off the ridge leads north from a cairn on **Featherbed Moss**, following a soggy but clear line along the watershed to **Lady Cross** on the old turnpike track. Be aware that the route down from here to Ladyshaw Bridge is rougher than it looks.

Lady Cross marked the boundary of land owned by Basingwerk Abbey and was in the 13th century. The base was removed to a private garden for a time to prevent game-keepers damaging it, and only a stump remains of what was once a very prominent wayside cross.

The path through the **Barrow Stones** leads down to the fenceline (rather unhelpfully not by a stile) and continues north straight down the slope past another collection of stones to drop into the top of the **River Derwent** near its sharp bend by the former boundary marker of the **Wigan Tree** (a corruption of wicken, referring to a rowan). It is rough across the steep clough, but there is a path along the far side that leads down into Howden Dean (p10).

Lady Cross

Following the watershed from **Bleaklow Stones** to Howden Edge via Swains Head is ot as straightforward as it might be, as the ld line of stakes that marked the way is now ntermittent at best. Heading east down from he stones into the deep groughs, fork left as the main path bears away right towards the prominent rinah Stones. There is little in the way of a path at first, but follow the muddy groughs along the igh ground heading northeast then north until you start to pick up the odd stake. The path ecomes clearer as it descends into another groughy pit at the head of the **River Derwent**, then s lost entirely crossing the nascent stream. Pick up some further stakes beyond leading north-east cross further rough ground to **Swains Head** (if you reach a red and white pole you have strayed oo far west), where the path leads clearly up onto **Featherbed Moss**, the start of Howden Edge.

MAP 14: BLEAKLOW WEST
(Shelf Moor & Snake Summit)

The Pennine ridge stretches from the top of the Snake Road to Bleaklow Head, making this the most easily accessed part of the Bleaklow plateau. It is well trodden, particularly around Higher Shelf Stones and its famous plane wreck, yet most of the paths are hard to trace through the deep groughs of the ridge. To the east the land drops steeply into the head of Alport Dale around remote Grains in the Water.

There are numerous paths on the plateau around the B29 plane wreckage, but none leads satisfactorily to Bleaklow Head. Faint lines set off but become lost in the deep groughs at the head of Hern Clough. Only the Hern Stones break up the peat morass; if you can reach them, faint paths lead across to the Pennine Way, which follows the deepest grough up to the summit.

Devil's Dike (also known as Shelf Dike) is a broad drainage ditch whose line is followed by the Pennine Way. It was originally dug for the monks of Basingwerk Abbey in the 13th century as a boundary ditch for their wood pasture on Shelf Moor. According to legend, the Devil gouged it in rage after losing a wager with Doctor Talbot for his soul.

The Pennine Way winds its way unevenfully through the peat hags from the Snake Summit to Bleaklow Head. There are various smaller paths off it towards Higher Shelf Stones, the most obvious following a broad drain near Alport Low or forking left at a marker stone in Hern Clough. However, the most satisfying route follows Crooked Clough, branching off Doctor's Gate to follow the fenceline up the valley. The path splits several ways as it crosses the streams above the waterfall, but keeping left brings you up the flank to the rocky edge south of the trig. The B29 plane wreck is easily found to the north-east, with many of these paths leading directly to it.

Doctor's Gate is named after Doctor Talbot, an illegitimate son of the Earl of Shrewsbury. After becoming the Vicar of Glossop in 1491, he helped pave the road over the moors, as he used it to visit his family seat in Sheffield. The well-defined packhorse route in parts follows the line of a Roman Road (see p53) that ran between the forts at Navio (Brough) and Melandra (near Glossop). Some of the original medieval surface can still be seen in its upper reaches, near where a guide stoop called the Old Woman likely once stood. It is said T'owd Lad (also referred to as T'owd Woman) haunts Bleaklow and is seen as a horned creature, the Celtic God Cernunnos or Herne (after which Hern Stones/Clough may be named).

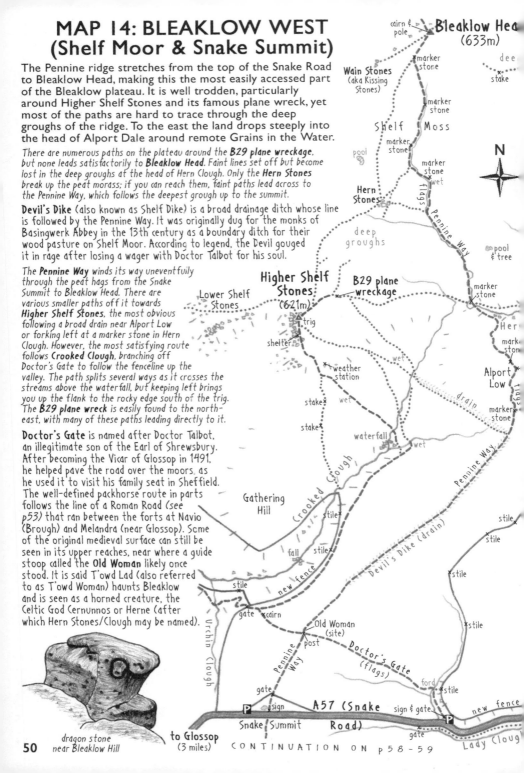

cairn & pole

Bleaklow Hea (633m)

marker stone

dee

stake

Wain Stones (aka Kissing Stones)

marker stone

Shelf Moss

marker stone

pool

marker stone

wet

Hern Stones

flags

Pennine Way

deep groughs

pool & tree

Higher Shelf Stones (621m)

Lower Shelf Stones

B29 plane wreckage

marker stone

trig

Her

mark ston

shelter

wet

Alport Low

weather station

wet

drain

marker stone

stake

wet

stake

waterfall

wet

Pennine Way

Gathering Hill

Crooked Clough

stile

stile

stile

Devil's Dike (drain)

stile

fall

stile

stile

new fence

stile

stile

stile

Urchin Clough

gate

cairn

Old Woman (site)

post

Doctor's Gate (flags)

Pennine Way

stile

gate

ford

sign & gate

P

sign

new fence

Snake Summit

A57 (Snake Road)

P

gate

Lady Cloug

to Glossop (3 miles)

dragon stone near Bleaklow Hill

50

CONTINUATION ON p58-59

Bleaklow Hill
stake
stake stake
stake
on mound

Alport Head

to Bleaklow
Stones

↑ P 44

Westend
Head

dragon
stone

stile
stile gate stile

pools

Near Fork
Grain

new fence

Far Fork
Grain

stile

stile

The
Swamp

wet

stile

The Ridge

pools

C O N T I N U A T I O N   O N

stile

stile

Grains in
the Water

wet

Clough

stile

cairn

stile

River Alport

wet

pools

pool

stile

pool

falls

stile

new fence

Over Wood
Moss
(538m)

pool
tiny
cairn

stake

C O N T I N U A T I O N   O N   P 5 2

stake

pool

stake

Upper North
Grain Cabin

Upper North Grain

pool

line of grouse butts
x x x x

pool

stile
P
P
fall

stile

enclosure

Nether North
Grain

to Snake Inn (1 1/2 miles)

0   200   400   600
METRES

Grains in the Water marks the junction of Hern Clough and the River Alport and stands in a broad bowl surrounded by barren moors. It is the only place where the **River Alport** opens out and its steep rocky precipices abate. The main path up the east side of Alport Dale continues left here and follows **Hern Clough** west to the Pennine Way. It is also possible to follow the right fork north; though indistinct at first, the path becomes clearer as it climbs towards **Alport Head**. Beyond the fenceline, the obvious path bears right to skirt around the plateau to reach **Bleaklow Stones**, joining paths up from Westend Head. Turning left brings you back to the stream, which can be followed through the groughs all the way to the stakes along the ridge on **Bleaklow Hill**.

The Peak District's most famous plane wreck is the **B29 Superfortress Over-Exposed** that lies scattered across the bare peat northeast of Higher Shelf Stones trig. It crashed in 1948 on a routine flight soon after having been involved in the Berlin Airlift during the Cold War. All 13 crew were killed and, although the RAF tried to bury the wreckage, much remains, including allegedly Captain Langdon P. Tanner's gold wedding ring.

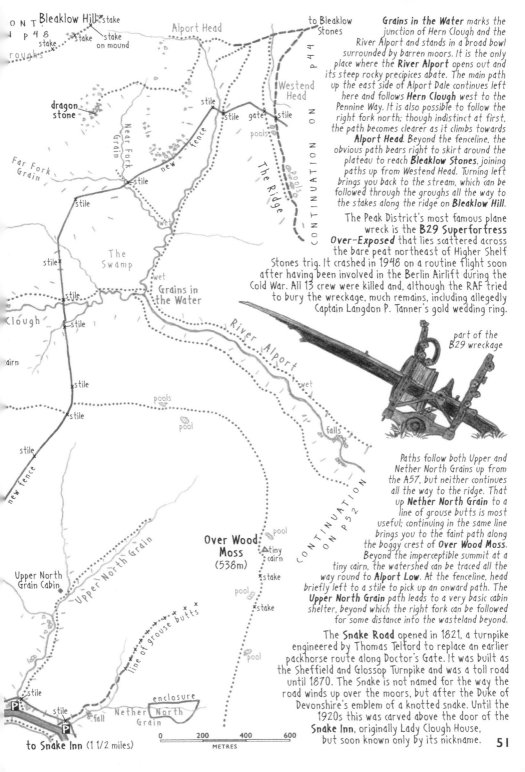

part of the
B29 wreckage

Paths follow both Upper and Nether North Grains up from the A57, but neither continues all the way to the ridge. That up **Nether North Grain** to a line of grouse butts is most useful; continuing in the same line brings you to the faint path along the boggy crest of **Over Wood Moss**. Beyond the imperceptible summit at a tiny cairn, the watershed can be traced all the way round to **Alport Low**. At the fenceline, head briefly left to a stile to pick up an onward path. The **Upper North Grain** path leads to a very basic cabin shelter, beyond which the right fork can be followed for some distance into the wasteland beyond.

The **Snake Road** opened in 1821, a turnpike engineered by Thomas Telford to replace an earlier packhorse route along Doctor's Gate. It was built as the Sheffield and Glossop Turnpike and was a toll road until 1870. The Snake is not named for the way the road winds up over the moors, but after the Duke of Devonshire's emblem of a knotted snake. Until the 1920s this was carved above the door of the **Snake Inn**, originally Lady Clough House, but soon known only by its nickname.

51

MAP 15: BLEAKLOW SOUTH (Alport Dale & Cowms Moor)

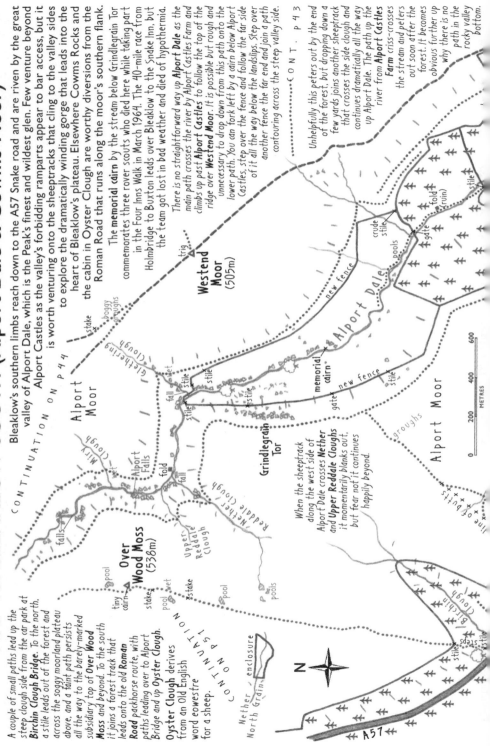

Bleaklow's southern limbs reach down to the A57 Snake road and are riven by the great valley of Alport Dale, which is the Peak's finest and wildest glen. Few venture beyond Alport Castles as the valley's forbidding ramparts appear to bar access, but it is worth venturing onto the sheeptracks that cling to the valley sides to explore the dramatically winding gorge that leads into the heart of Bleaklow's plateau. Elsewhere Cowms Rocks and the cabin in Oyster Clough are worthy diversions from the Roman Road that runs along the moor's southern flank.

The **memorial cairn** by the stream below Grindlegrain Tor commemorates three river scouts who died here while taking part in the Four Inns Walk in March 1964. The 40-mile race from Holmbridge to Buxton leads over Bleaklow to the Snake Inn, but the team got lost in bad weather and died of hypothermia.

There is no straightforward way up **Alport Dale** as the main path crosses the river by **Alport Castles Farm** and climbs up past **Alport Castles** to follow the top of the ridge over **Westend Moor**. It is possible but rough and unnecessary to drop down from this path onto the lower path. You can fork left by a cairn below Alport Castles, step over the fence and follow the far side of it all the way below the landslips. Step over another fence the far end and join a path contouring across the steep valley side.

~CONT. P43~

Unhelpfully this peters out by the end of the forest, but dropping down a few yards joins another sheeptrack that crosses the side clough and continues dramatically all the way up Alport Dale. The path up the river from **Alport Castles Farm** criss-crosses the stream and peters out soon after the forest. It becomes obvious further up why there is no path in the rocky valley bottom.

When the sheeptrack along the west side of Alport Dale crosses **Nether** and **Upper Reddale Cloughs** it momentarily blanks out, but fear not it continues happily beyond.

A couple of small paths lead up the steep clough side from the car park at **Birchin Clough Bridge**. To the north, a stile leads out of the forest and across the soggy moorland plateau above, and a faint path persists all the way to the barely-marked subsidiary top of **Over Wood Moss** and beyond. To the south it joins a forest track that leads onto the old **Roman Road** packhorse route, with paths leading over to Alport Bridge and up **Oyster Clough**.

Oyster Clough derives from an Old English word eowestre for a sheep.

Westend Moor (505m)

Alport Moor

Grindlegrain Tor

Alport Dale

Alport Moor

Glethering Clough

Miry Clough

Alport Falls

Nether Reddale Clough

Over Wood Moss (538m)

Upper Reddale Clough

memorial cairn

new fence

groughs

stake

trig

stile

stile

stile

stiles

stile

gate

new fence

stile

gate (ruin)

fold

crude stile

pools

stile

falls

fall

fold

fall

boggy groughs

tiny cairn

stake

pool wet

stakes

pool

pool

pools

line of butts

Blichin Clough

stile

stile

slabs

stile

N

Nether enclosure

North Grain

A57

0   200   400   600
METRES

CONTINUATION ON P.44

CONTINUATION

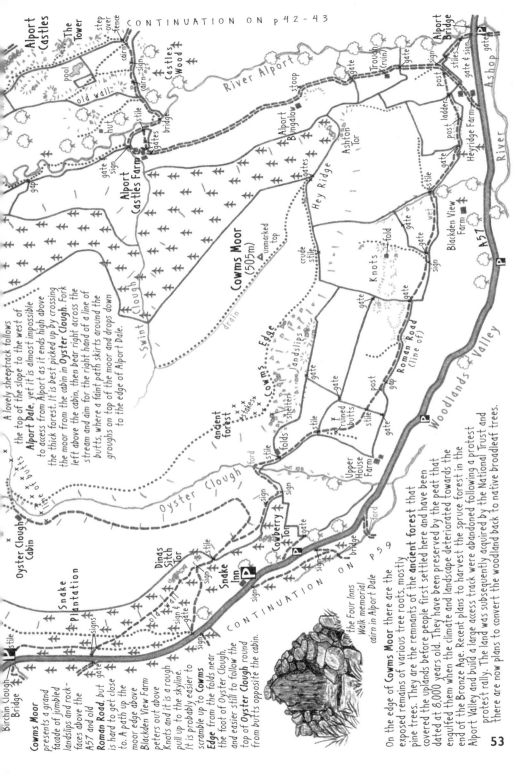

CONTINUATION ON p 42-43

Alport Castles

The Tower

step over fence

cairn

old wall

pool

Castles Wood

cairn sign

hut

stile

bridge

gate sign

gates

Alport Castles Farm

gap

River Alport

stoop

Alport Bungalow

Ashton Tor

gate

Trough (ruin)

post ladder

Heyridge Farm

Alport Bridge

stiles

gate & sign

gate

post sign

Ashop

gate

River

Hey Ridge

gates

stile

gate

wet

gate

Blackden View Farm

A57

Cowms Moor (505m)

Unmarked top

crude stile

fold

Knots

sign

gate

Swint Clough

drain

Cowms Edge

landslips

gate

gate

Roman Road (line of)

gap

post

Woodlands Valley

ancient forest

gates

stile

folds

shelter

gate

ruined butts

stile

gate

P

ford

Upper House Farm

stile

sign

Oyster Clough

sign

ford

P

Oyster Clough Cabin

x butts x

x x

Dinas Sitch Tor

sign

stile

Cowberry Tor

gate

bridge

Snake Plantation

stile

signs

old wall

sign & gate

Snake Inn

P

sign

CONTINUATION ON P 59

Birchin Clough Bridge

stile

Cowms Moor
presents a grand facade of jumbled landslips and rockfaces above the A57 and old **Roman Road**, but is hard to get close to. A path up the moor edge above Blackden View Farm peters out above Knots and it is a rough pull up to the skyline. It is probably easier to scramble up to **Cowms Edge** from the foot of Oyster Clough, and easier still to follow the top of Oyster Clough round from butts opposite the cabin.

A lovely sheeptrack follows the top of the slope to the west of **Alport Dale**, yet it is almost impossible to access from Alport as it ends high above the thick forest. It is best picked up by crossing the moor from the cabin in **Oyster Clough**. Fork left above the cabin, then bear right across the stream and aim for the right hand of a line of butts, where a faint path skirts around the groughs on top of the moor and drops down to the edge of Alport Dale.

the Four Inns Walk memorial cairn in Alport Dale

On the edge of **Cowms Moor** there are the exposed remnants of various tree roots, mostly pine trees. They are the remnants of the **ancient forest** that covered the uplands before people first settled here and have been dated at 8,000 years old. They have been preserved by the peat that engulfed them when the climate and landscape deteriorated towards the end of the Bronze Age. Recent plans to harvest the spruce forest in the Alport Valley and build a large access track were abandoned following a protest protest rally. The land was subsequently acquired by the National Trust and there are now plans to convert the woodland back to native broadleaf trees.

53

ROUTE 8: BLEAKLOW HEAD FROM BIRCHIN CLOUGH/ALPORT BRIDGE

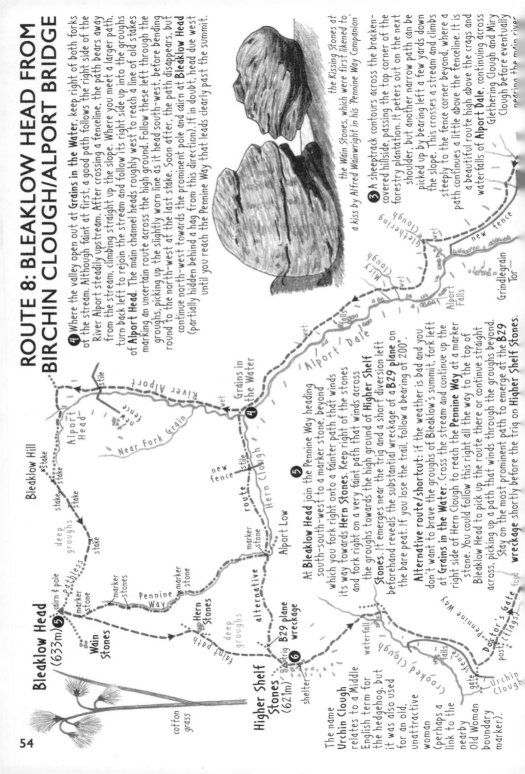

④ Where the valley open out at **Grains in the Water**, keep right of both forks of the stream. Although faint at first, a good path follows the right side of the River Alport steadily upstream. After crossing a fenceline, the path bears away from the stream, climbing straight up the slope. Where you meet a larger path, turn back left to rejoin the stream and follow its right side up into the groughs of **Alport Head**. The main channel heads roughly west to reach a line of old stakes marking an uncertain route across the high ground. Follow these left through the groughs, picking up the slightly worn line as it head south-west, before bending round to the north-west at the last stake. Soon after, the path disappears, but continue north-west towards the prominent pole and cairn at **Bleaklow Head** (partially hidden behind a hag from this direction). If in doubt, head due west until you reach the Pennine Way that leads clearly past the summit.

③ A sheeptrack contours across the bracken-covered hillside, passing the top corner of the forestry plantation. It peters out on the next shoulder, but another narrow path can be picked up by bearing left a few yards down the slope. This crosses a stream and climbs steeply to the fence corner beyond, where a path continues a little above the fenceline. It is a beautiful route high above the crags and waterfalls of **Alport Dale**, continuing across Glethering Clough and Miry Clough before eventually nearing the main river.

the Kissing Stones at the **Wain Stones**, which were first likened to a kiss by Alfred Wainwright in his *Pennine Way Companion*.

⑤ At **Bleaklow Head** join the Pennine Way heading south-south-west to a marker stone, beyond which you fork right onto a fainter path that winds its way towards **Hern Stones**. Keep right of the stones and fork right on a very faint path that winds across the groughs towards the high ground of **Higher Shelf Stones**. It emerges near the trig and a short diversion left beforehand reveals the substantial wreckage of a **B29 plane** on the bare peat. If you lose the trail, follow a bearing of 200°.

Alternative route/shortcut: if the weather is bad and you don't want to brave the groughs of Bleaklow's summit, fork left at **Grains in the Water**. Cross the stream and continue up the right side of Hern Clough to reach the **Pennine Way** at a marker stone. You could follow this right all the way to the top of Bleaklow Head to pick up the route there or continue straight across, picking up a path that winds through the groughs beyond. Stay on the most prominent path to emerge at the **B29 wreckage** shortly before the trig on Higher Shelf Stones.

The name **Urchin Clough** relates to a Middle English term for the hedgehog, but it was also used for an old, unattractive woman (perhaps a link to the nearby Old Woman boundary marker).

Bleaklow Head (633m)

Wain Stones

cotton grass

Bleaklow Hill

Alport Head

Near Fork Grain

River Alport

new fence

stile

deep groughs

stake

cairn & pole

marker stone

marker stones

Pennine Way

Hern Stones

faint path

deep groughs

B29 plane wreckage

Hern Clough

marker stone

alternative route

Alport Low

Grains in the Water

new fence

stile

wet

Alport Dale

Falls

wet

Glethering Clough

Miry Clough

wet

Alport Falls

new fence

Grindlegrain Tor

Higher Shelf Stones (621m)

trig

shelter

Crooked Clough

waterfall

Falls

gate

fence

Urchin Clough

Doctor's Gate post (flags)

ford

Pennine Way

6 At the trig point pick up a path heading south along the top of the rocks. This bears left and descends into **Crooked Clough**, crossing a little above a waterfall where the stream forks. After crossing a second stream join a path leading right along the slope above the clough. This joins a fenceline to reach **Doctor's Gate**, where you turn left to head back over the Pennine Way. Carry straight on down into the clough and emerge on the A57 opposite **Thomason's Hollow**.

7 Though the A57 could be followed left back to Birchin Clough, there is no way off this busy road and a preferable route follows the **Lady Clough** stream. To reach the faint path alongside the road you can either head 100m right up the road to a gate or clamber over the wall at one of its lower points. The path becomes clearer once it drops down to the stream and is well defined through the **Snake Plantation**. After a mile turn left at a junction just before a bridge and head up to the road opposite **Birchin Clough** car park.

2 Follow the track for a mile up to **Alport Castles Farm**, turning right over a ladder just before the buildings. Cross the River Alport at the bridge and climb steeply up the fence towards the dramatic outline of **Alport Castles**. Reaching a second cairn, bear left off the main path and step over the low fence where rocks are piled up in the corner. Follow a faint line left along the fence beneath the **Tower**. It is possible to climb up this rocky tor from this side via a faint path up the far shoulder but it is a bit of a scramble at the top. Keep along the fence until a fenceline crosses at the far end of the cliffs and it is simple to step over the fence again in the corner.

Alport Castles Farm was the original site of the annual **Woodlands Love Feast**, a unique Methodist festival that predates the Methodist Church. It commemorates 46 non-conformist ministers who were evicted from their parishes after the 1662 Act of Uniformity and forced to conduct illegal services in remote and secret places like this. It still takes place at the austere chapel near the A57 built by the Duke of Devonshire in 1866 for his tenant farmers. On the first Sunday in July, revival hymns are sung, bread broken, and testimonies made. Later the feast includes beef, ham and pies.

The notable suffragette **Hannah Mitchell** was born at Alport Castles Farm in 1872, before leaving home at 14. She became a socialist, going on to write for the **Manchester Guardian** and becoming a magistrate.

1 From **Birchin Clough** car park, head south over a stile, following a path through the plantation parallel to the A57. At the next sign bear left up the slope to emerge beneath **Dinas Sitch Tor**. Carry straight on out of the forest, forking right halfway up the slope to join a fence along the edge of the plantation. Descend steeply to cross **Oyster Clough** and keep right up the wall. Follow the left fork across the open pasture before rejoining the wall and a clearer path (the line of a Roman Road) as it descends steadily towards **Heyridge Farm**. Bear left around the farm and join the vehicle track soon after.

To join the route from Alport Bridge, cross the A57 from the rough lay-by and follow the well-defined path up the field edge to the vehicle track near Heyridge Farm.

Distance: 13½ miles (21.8km)

Ascent: 650m

Difficulty: Strenuous

Parking: Free car park on A57 at Birchin Clough (½ mile north of the Snake Inn). Limited parking at Alport Bridge and Thomason's Hollow.

Public Transport: There is currently no public transport up the Woodlands Valley.

Character: An adventurous route following dramatic Alport Dale onto the wild Bleaklow plateau and returning via Higher Shelf Stones and the famous B29 plane wreck. The paths are often narrow and ill defined, particularly on the disorientating summit plateau, so good navigational skills, an OS map and a compass are a must in any weather.

MOORS FOR THE FUTURE

My image of the Dark Peak's moorland plateaus from my childhood is of a desert-like moonscape composed of oozing black channels and towering peat hags. Very little then grew on Bleaklow and Kinder Scout, but I loved this bewildering, alien landscape, especially when the mist left me in complete solitude. It was as wild a place as I knew growing up, yet just a few miles from home.

It is a very different place now, just thirty years later. Though you can still find places where the black peat is exposed in barren bowls, much of the moorland plateaus are covered with short grass and the groughs are filled with water behind plastic, wooden or Hessian dams. This is the work of the Moors for the Future Partnership, a £2.5-million project to restore the South Pennine moorland, supported by the Peak District National Park, the National Trust, RSPB and the water companies.

The UK has 15% of the Earth's peat stores and this is thought to store more carbon than all of Britain and France's forests, so its preservation is vital for slowing climate change. As the peat dries out, it leaks carbon dioxide at a rapid rate – in its current condition, 700m^2 of peat in the Pennines causes more greenhouse gas pollution than a town of 50,000 people. The state of the moorland landscape is the result of overgrazing, burning, draining and acid erosion, particularly over the past two centuries. Since the early 19th century, sphagnum moss, which is fundamental to the formation of peat but particularly affected by sulphur dioxide levels, has been greatly diminished by air pollution. Farming subsidies after World War II encouraged farmers to graze more sheep on the hills and resulted in overgrazing. Combined with the growth in rambling's popularity, the upland landscape became denuded, with grass dominating over heather and large areas of bare peat being created. Once exposed, the peat surface becomes unstable and is easily eroded and lost into rivers.

When the National Trust acquired the Kinder Scout plateau in 1982, they had to deal with upland erosion from the outset. Sheep were excluded, walls and fences rebuilt, firm path surfaces constructed and limestone dust applied to encourage indigenous seeds to grow. However, by the end of the 20th century most of the peat moors of the Dark Peak were so badly damaged that as SSSIs they were in 'adverse condition' and in danger of being unrecoverable.

Work began on a far larger scale in 2003 and teams of Moors for the Future staff and volunteers are often seen on the high moors, along with heaps of materials flown in by helicopter. The grips (short man-made drains) that were dug in the 20th century have been blocked or removed, and natural peat gullies dammed with hundreds of small barriers. Brash has been spread across areas of exposed peat, which have been re-sown with quick-growing grasses. These allow shrubs like heather, bilberry and crowberry to establish, and eventually sphagnum moss to develop and hold the whole peat surface together. New fences have been put up around large parts of Bleaklow and Kinder Scout as part of these restoration projects. The exclusion of sheep prevents the vegetation being grazed while it is trying to establish a foothold on the peat. It is estimated that these fences will be in place for fifteen years.

Work has been successfully undertaken on Kinder Scout, Bleaklow and Howden, and is now underway on Snailsden and Thurlstone Moors. The result is an increase in biodiversity and the restoration of many moorland bird habitats, an improvement in water quality (high peat sediment in the water is a problem the water companies are having to spend a lot of money treating), and a reduction in the likelihood of flooding downstream. It is still early days, but the landscape on Bleaklow and Kinder Scout is now classified as being in 'unfavourable recovering' condition.

a newly-blocked grough on Bleaklow

CHAPTER 6 – KINDER SCOUT

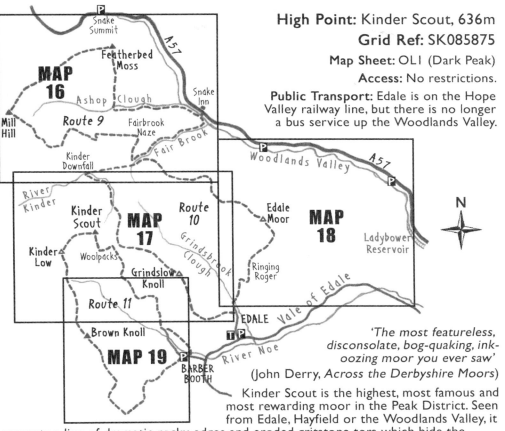

High Point: Kinder Scout, 636m

Grid Ref: SK085875

Map Sheet: OL1 (Dark Peak)

Access: No restrictions.

Public Transport: Edale is on the Hope Valley railway line, but there is no longer a bus service up the Woodlands Valley.

'The most featureless, disconsolate, bog-quaking, ink-oozing moor you ever saw'
(John Derry, *Across the Derbyshire Moors*)

Kinder Scout is the highest, most famous and most rewarding moor in the Peak District. Seen from Edale, Hayfield or the Woodlands Valley, it presents a line of dramatic rocky edges and eroded gritstone tors which hide the central plateau that John Derry describes. Though Kinder's black heart is far greener these days thanks to the work of the National Trust and Moors for the Future, it is still a bewildering grough landscape whose true high point is almost impossible to fathom. Though the point marked by a small cairn is usually taken to be the summit, Ordnance Survey claim that two other points on the plateau reach the same height of 636m.

The name Kinder Scout, a curious blend of Celtic and Norse, is of uncertain origin, having been translated variously as 'craggy hill', 'place with wide views' and 'projecting hill with beacon fires'. The closest meaning is probably 'water falling over the edge', originally referring specifically to the edge by the Downfall. The Edale side of the hill was called Edale Moor and Noe Stoole Hill on early maps, with the summit itself largely ignored. Later it became a famous battleground in the fight for access to the moors; owned by the National Trust since 1982, it is now completely free from grouse shooting and more endangered by its own popularity.

Kinder Scout's Northern Edges from Mill Hill

MAP 16: KINDER SCOUT NORTH

The northern edge of the Kinder plateau looks out across the top of the Snake Pass towards Bleaklow. Beyond Black Ashop Edge's dramatic ramparts, home to some of the finest rock sculptures on the plateau, the moorland changes abruptly to the gentle mossy slopes of Featherbed Top and Mill Hill. Though the Pennine Way carves a route through here, there are few paths. All routes lead down to the A57 Snake Road at the head of the Woodlands Valley, the only way to access this moorland from the east

Featherbed Top is a featureless grassy summit rising gently above the Pennine Way. It can be reached by a faint line running across the soggy moor from the lay-by at the Snake Summit, or by heading east across pathless ground from the sharp bend in the Pennine Way by the groughs of Featherbed Moss. Alternatively tracks lead up past the butts either side of Upper Gate Clough, a faint path following a line of stakes up from the western butts.

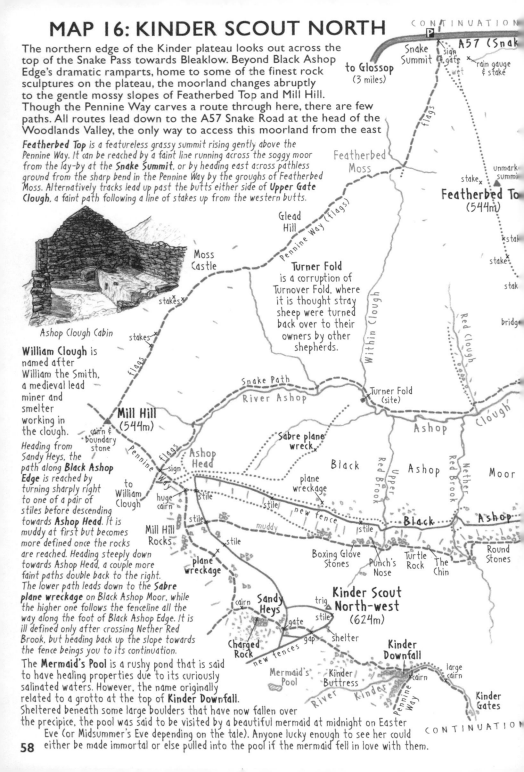

Ashop Clough Cabin

William Clough is named after William the Smith, a medieval lead miner and smelter working in the clough.

*Heading from Sandy Heys, the path along **Black Ashop Edge** is reached by turning sharply right to one of a pair of stiles before descending towards **Ashop Head**. It is muddy at first but becomes more defined once the rocks are reached. Heading steeply down towards Ashop Head, a couple more faint paths double back to the right. The lower path leads down to the **Sabre plane wreckage** on Black Ashop Moor, while the higher one follows the fenceline all the way along the foot of Black Ashop Edge. It is ill defined only after crossing Nether Red Brook, but heading back up the slope towards the fence beings you to its continuation.*

The **Mermaid's Pool** is a rushy pond that is said to have healing properties due to its curiously salinated waters. However, the name originally related to a grotto at the top of **Kinder Downfall**. Sheltered beneath some large boulders that have now fallen over the precipice, the pool was said to be visited by a beautiful mermaid at midnight on Easter Eve (or Midsummer's Eve depending on the tale). Anyone lucky enough to see her could either be made immortal or else pulled into the pool if the mermaid fell in love with them.

Turner Fold is a corruption of Turnover Fold, where it is thought stray sheep were turned back over to their owners by other shepherds.

Snake Summit

to Glossop (3 miles)

A57 (Snak

sign & gate — rain gauge & stake — wet

flags

Featherbed Moss

Featherbed To (544m)

unmark summi

stake

stak

stake

bridge

Red Clough

Glead Hill

Moss Castle

Pennine Way (flags)

stakes

flags

Within Clough

Snake Path

River Ashop

Turner Fold (site)

Ashop — Clough

Mill Hill (544m)

cairn & boundary stone

Pennine Way

flags

sign

Ashop Head

to William Clough

huge cairn

Stile

stile

Sabre plane wreck

plane wreckage

stile

muddy

new fence

Black

Ashop

Red Brook

Upper

Nether

Red Brook

Moor

Black — Ashop

Mill Hill Rocks

plane wreckage

stile

stile

Boxing Glove Stones

Punch's Nose

Turtle Rock

The Chin

Round Stones

cairn

Sandy Heys

trig

Kinder Scout North-west (624m)

stile

gate

gap

shelter

Kinder Downfall

large cairn

cairn

Charged Rock

new fences

Mermaid's Pool

Kinder Buttress

River Kinder

Pennine Way

Kinder Gates

(The Northern Edges)

The **Snake Path** begins just up the road from the Snake Inn, following the north bank of the River Ashop all the way to Ashop Head. It is joined by paths through the **Snake Plantation**, which is best accessed opposite Birchin Clough car park. A good path follows the Lady Clough stream all the way from the Snake Path to the end of the trees. There is no easy way onto the **Snake Road** here, though the path continues more roughly along the stream then roadside until a gate gives access beyond **Thomason's Hollow**.

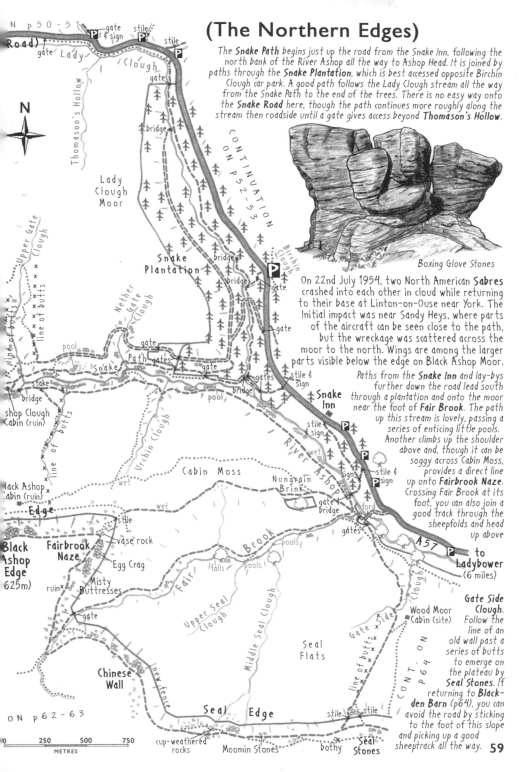

Boxing Glove Stones

On 22nd July 1954, two North American **Sabres** crashed into each other in cloud while returning to their base at Linton-on-Ouse near York. The initial impact was near Sandy Heys, where parts of the aircraft can be seen close to the path, but the wreckage was scattered across the moor to the north. Wings are among the larger parts visible below the edge on Black Ashop Moor.

Paths from the **Snake Inn** and lay-bys further down the road lead south through a plantation and onto the moor near the foot of **Fair Brook**. The path up this stream is lovely, passing a series of enticing little pools. Another climbs up the shoulder above and, though it can be soggy across Cabin Moss, provides a direct line up onto **Fairbrook Naze**. Crossing Fair Brook at its foot, you can also join a good track through the sheepfolds and head up above

to **Ladybower** (6 miles)

Gate Side Clough. Follow the line of an old wall past a series of butts to emerge on the plateau by **Seal Stones.** If returning to **Blackden Barn** (p64), you can avoid the road by sticking to the foot of this slope and picking up a good sheeptrack all the way. **59**

ROUTE 9: BLACK ASHOP EDGE, MILL HILL &

Distance: 10½ miles (17km)
Ascent: 550m
Difficulty: Moderate
Parking: Free parking in lay-bys near the Snake Inn.
Public Transport: Unfortunately there is currently no public transport up the Snake Pass.

Character: A tour of Kinder Scout's northern edges and the bleak moorland tops of Mill Hill and Featherbed Top. The route takes in a series of fine weathered rocks and beautiful cloughs, but does include a couple of rough pathless sections where route-finding requires car and the use of a compass in the mist.

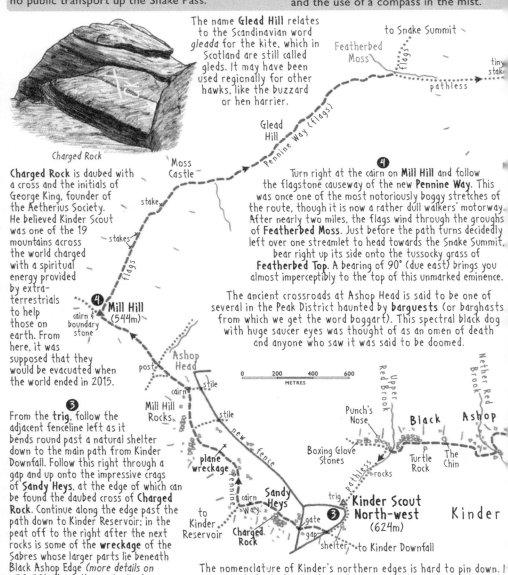

The name **Glead Hill** relates to the Scandinavian word *gleada* for the kite, which in Scotland are still called gleds. It may have been used regionally for other hawks, like the buzzard or hen harrier.

Charged Rock

Charged Rock is daubed with a cross and the initials of George King, founder of the Aetherius Society. He believed Kinder Scout was one of the 19 mountains across the world charged with a spiritual energy provided by extra-terrestrials to help those on earth. From here, it was supposed that they would be evacuated when the world ended in 2015.

❸
From the **trig**, follow the adjacent fenceline left as it bends round past a natural shelter down to the main path from Kinder Downfall. Follow this right through a gap and up onto the impressive crags of **Sandy Heys**, at the edge of which can be found the daubed cross of **Charged Rock**. Continue along the edge past the path down to Kinder Reservoir; in the peat off to the right after the next rocks is some of the **wreckage** of the Sabres whose larger parts lie beneath Black Ashop Edge (*more details on p58-59*). The path eventually drops down to Ashop Head, where you carry straight on up the Pennine Way to **Mill Hill**.

❹
Turn right at the cairn on **Mill Hill** and follow the flagstone causeway of the new **Pennine Way**. This was once one of the most notoriously boggy stretches of the route, though it is now a rather dull walkers' motorway. After nearly two miles, the flags wind through the groughs of **Featherbed Moss**. Just before the path turns decidedly left over one streamlet to head towards the Snake Summit, bear right up its side onto the tussocky grass of **Featherbed Top**. A bearing of 90° (due east) brings you almost imperceptibly to the top of this unmarked eminence.

The ancient crossroads at Ashop Head is said to be one of several in the Peak District haunted by **barguests** (or barghests from which we get the word boggart). This spectral black dog with huge saucer eyes was thought of as an omen of death and anyone who saw it was said to be doomed.

The nomenclature of Kinder's northern edges is hard to pin down. I was separated into Black Edge and Fairbrook Edge in 1627, then late referred to as Ashop or **Black Ashop Edge**, black due to its dar northerly outlook. Often now simply referred to as The Edge or Norther Edges, I have reinstated what I think is its most appropriate older name

60

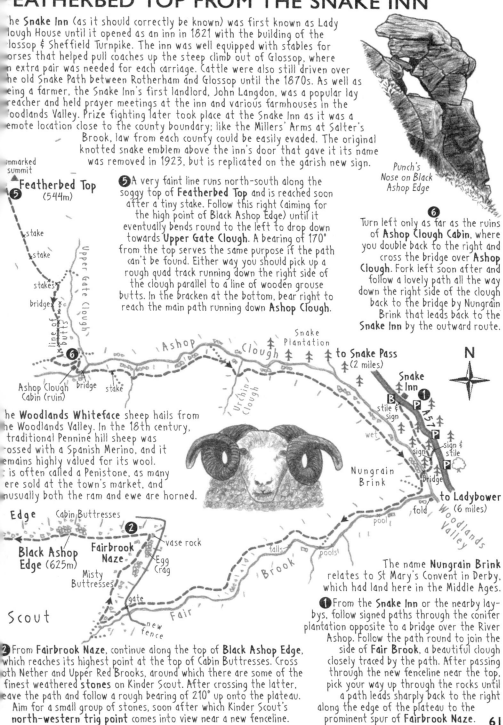

he **Snake Inn** (as it should correctly be known) was first known as Lady lough House until it opened as an inn in 1821 with the building of the lossop & Sheffield Turnpike. The inn was well equipped with stables for orses that helped pull coaches up the steep climb out of Glossop, where n extra pair was needed for each carriage. Cattle were also still driven over he old Snake Path between Rotherham and Glossop until the 1870s. As well as eing a farmer, the Snake Inn's first landlord, John Langdon, was a popular lay reacher and held prayer meetings at the inn and various farmhouses in the oodlands Valley. Prize fighting later took place at the Snake Inn as it was a emote location close to the county boundary; like the Millers' Arms at Salter's Brook, law from each county could be easily evaded. The original knotted snake emblem above the inn's door that gave it its name was removed in 1923, but is replicated on the garish new sign.

Punch's Nose on Black Ashop Edge

Unmarked summit

Featherbed Top
(544m)

stake

stake

stakes

bridge

Upper Gate Clough

line of butts

5 A very faint line runs north-south along the soggy top of **Featherbed Top** and is reached soon after a tiny stake. Follow this right (aiming for the high point of Black Ashop Edge) until it eventually bends round to the left to drop down towards **Upper Gate Clough**. A bearing of 170° from the top serves the same purpose if the path can't be found. Either way you should pick up a rough quad track running down the right side of the clough parallel to a line of wooden grouse butts. In the bracken at the bottom, bear right to reach the main path running down **Ashop Clough**.

6 Turn left only as far as the ruins of **Ashop Clough Cabin**, where you double back to the right and cross the bridge over **Ashop Clough**. Fork left soon after and follow a lovely path all the way down the right side of the clough back to the bridge by Nungrain Brink that leads back to the **Snake Inn** by the outward route.

6

bridge stake

Ashop ... Clough

Snake Plantation

to Snake Pass (2 miles)

Ashop Clough Cabin (ruin)

Urchin Clough

Snake Inn **1**

B stile & sign

P A57

sign & stile

P

he **Woodlands Whiteface** sheep hails from he Woodlands Valley. In the 18th century, traditional Pennine hill sheep was rossed with a Spanish Merino, and it emains highly valued for its wool. : is often called a Penistone, as many ere sold at the town's market, and nusually both the ram and ewe are horned.

N

wet

sign

Nungrain Brink

Bridge

P

fold

to Ladybower (6 miles)

Woodlands Valley

Edge   Cabin Buttresses

2

vase rock

Black Ashop Edge (625m)

Fairbrook Naze

Egg Crag

Misty Buttresses

gate

new fence

Fair

Brook

falls

pool

pools

The name **Nungrain Brink** relates to St Mary's Convent in Derby, which had land here in the Middle Ages.

1 From the **Snake Inn** or the nearby lay-bys, follow signed paths through the conifer plantation opposite to a bridge over the River Ashop. Follow the path round to join the side of **Fair Brook**, a beautiful clough closely traced by the path. After passing through the new fenceline near the top, pick your way up through the rocks until a path leads sharply back to the right along the edge of the plateau to the prominent spur of **Fairbrook Naze**.

Scout

2 From **Fairbrook Naze**, continue along the top of **Black Ashop Edge**, which reaches its highest point at the top of Cabin Buttresses. Cross oth Nether and Upper Red Brooks, around which there are some of the finest weathered **stones** on Kinder Scout. After crossing the latter, eave the path and follow a rough bearing of 210° up onto the plateau. Aim for a small group of stones, soon after which Kinder Scout's **north-western trig point** comes into view near a new fenceline.

61

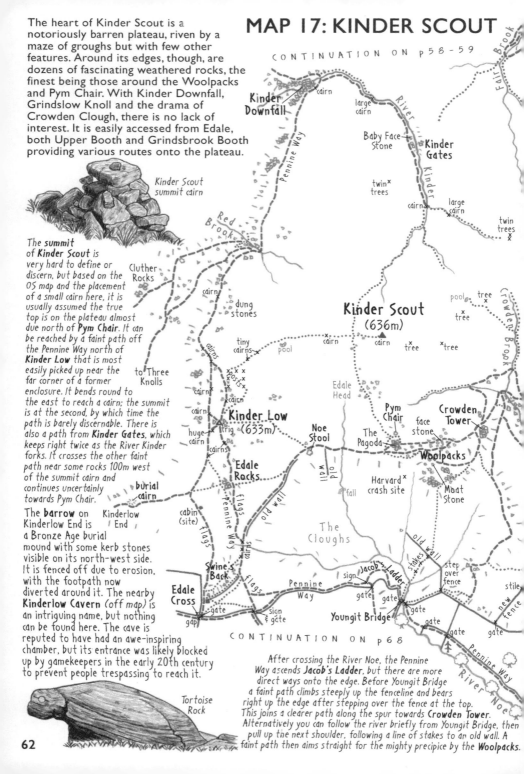

MAP 17: KINDER SCOUT

The heart of Kinder Scout is a notoriously barren plateau, riven by a maze of groughs but with few other features. Around its edges, though, are dozens of fascinating weathered rocks, the finest being those around the Woolpacks and Pym Chair. With Kinder Downfall, Grindslow Knoll and the drama of Crowden Clough, there is no lack of interest. It is easily accessed from Edale, both Upper Booth and Grindsbrook Booth providing various routes onto the plateau.

Kinder Scout summit cairn

The **summit** of **Kinder Scout** is very hard to define or discern, but based on the OS map and the placement of a small cairn here, it is usually assumed the true top is on the plateau almost due north of **Pym Chair**. It can be reached by a faint path off the Pennine Way north of **Kinder Low** that is most easily picked up near the far corner of a former enclosure. It bends round to the east to reach a cairn; the summit is at the second, by which time the path is barely discernable. There is also a path from **Kinder Gates**, which keeps right twice as the River Kinder forks. It crosses the other faint path near some rocks 100m west of the summit cairn and continues uncertainly towards Pym Chair.

The **barrow** on Kinderlow End is a Bronze Age burial mound with some kerb stones visible on its north-west side. It is fenced off due to erosion, with the footpath now diverted around it. The nearby **Kinderlow Cavern** (off map) is an intriguing name, but nothing can be found here. The cave is reputed to have had an awe-inspiring chamber, but its entrance was likely blocked up by gamekeepers in the early 20th century to prevent people trespassing to reach it.

Tortoise Rock

After crossing the River Noe, the Pennine Way ascends **Jacob's Ladder**, but there are more direct ways onto the edge. Before Youngit Bridge a faint path climbs steeply up the fenceline and bears right up the edge after stepping over the fence at the top. This joins a clearer path along the spur towards **Crowden Tower**. Alternatively you can follow the river briefly from Youngit Bridge, then pull up the next shoulder, following a line of stakes to an old wall. A faint path then aims straight for the mighty precipice by the **Woolpacks**.

Map labels: CONTINUATION ON p58-59; Fair Brook; Kinder Downfall; cairn; large cairn; River Kinder; Baby Face Stone; Kinder Gates; twin trees; cairns; large cairn; twin trees; Pennine Way; Red Brook; Cluther Rocks; cairn; dung stones; Kinder Scout (636m); pool; tree; Crowden Brook; tiny cairns; cairn; cairn; tree; tree; to Three Knolls; posts; cairn; Edale Head; Pym Chair; The Pagoda; face stone; Crowden Tower; cairn; Kinder Low (633m); trig; Noe Stool; Woolpacks; huge cairn; cairns; Edale Rocks; Harvard crash site; Moat Stone; burial cairn; cabin (site); flags; Pennine Way; old wall; The Cloughs; fall; P I O W I I; old wall; stakes; step over fence; stile; new fence; Kinderlow End; Swine's Back; flags; sign; Jacob's Ladder; gate; gate; gate; gate; gate; Edale Cross; gap; gate; sign & gate; Youngit Bridge; Pennine Way; River Noe; CONTINUATION ON p68

CENTRAL (The Plateau)

Various bald areas on the plateau, like those around Kinder Low, Red Brook, Sandy Heys, Ringing Roger and Upper Moor, have been caused by fires within the last century.

Four Jacks Cabin in Grindsbrook Clough was repaired by four men named Jack in the 1930s, though by the 40s it was badly vandalised. It was originally constructed by Micah Tym around 1870 and known as Mike's Church.

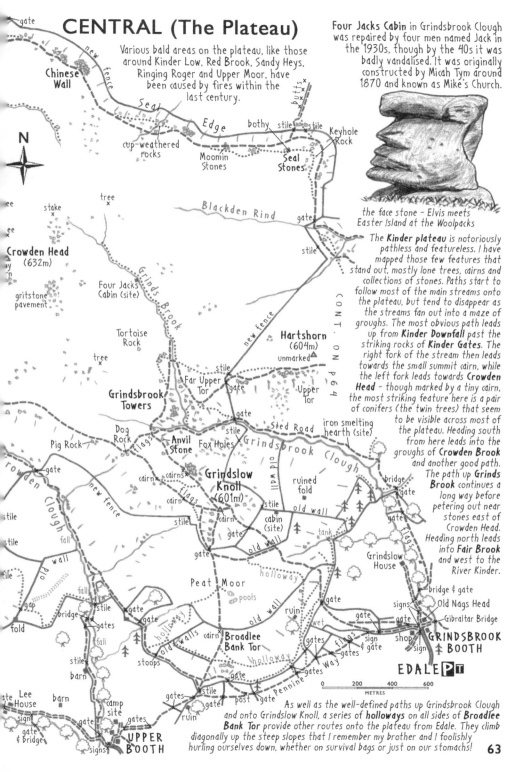

the face stone - Elvis meets Easter Island at the Woolpacks

Chinese Wall

Seal Edge

new fence

gate

N

cup-weathered rocks

Moomin Stones

butts

bothy   stile   stile   Keyhole Rock

Seal Stones

tree stake

Crowden Head (632m)

gritstone pavement

Blackden Rind

gate

stile

Four Jacks Cabin (site)

Grinds Brook

Hartshorn (604m)
unmarked

new fence

Tortoise Rock

tree

stile

Far Upper Tor
gate

Upper Tor

Grindsbrook Towers

gate

Dog Rock

stile

Sted Road

iron smelting hearth (site)

Pig Rock

Anvil Stone

Fox Holes

flags

Grindsbrook Clough

old wall

bridge
gate

cairn cairns

Grindslow Knoll (601m)

ruined fold

old wall

gate

flags

cairn

cairn

stile

cabin (site)

tank

old wall

gate

Grindslow House

new fence

fall

wall

gate

old wall

Peat Moor

pools

holloway

bridge & gate

Old Nags Head

gap
bridge

stile   gate
gates

fall

holloway

cairn

Broadlee Bank Tor

old walls

ruin   wet

gate

gate
gate

signs
Gibraltar Bridge

shop
sign

GRINDSBROOK BOOTH

stile

barn

stoops

holloway

gates

flags sign & gate

Pennine Way

EDALE P T

Lee House

barn

camp site

gates

gate

stile

post gate

ruin

gates
gate
signs

UPPER BOOTH

0   200   400   600
METRES

gate & bridge

signs

The **Kinder plateau** is notoriously pathless and featureless. I have mapped those few features that stand out, mostly lone trees, cairns and collections of stones. Paths start to follow most of the main streams onto the plateau, but tend to disappear as the streams fan out into a maze of groughs. The most obvious path leads up from **Kinder Downfall** past the striking rocks of **Kinder Gates**. The right fork of the stream then leads towards the small summit cairn, while the left fork leads towards **Crowden Head** - though marked by a tiny cairn, the most striking feature here is a pair of conifers (the twin trees) that seem to be visible across most of the plateau. Heading south from here leads into the groughs of **Crowden Brook** and another good path. The path up **Grinds Brook** continues a long way before petering out near stones east of Crowden Head. Heading north leads into **Fair Brook** and west to the River Kinder.

As well as the well-defined paths up Grindsbrook Clough and onto Grindslow Knoll, a series of **holloways** on all sides of **Broadlee Bank Tor** provide other routes onto the plateau from Edale. They climb diagonally up the steep slopes that I remember my brother and I foolishly hurling ourselves down, whether on survival bags or just on our stomachs!

63

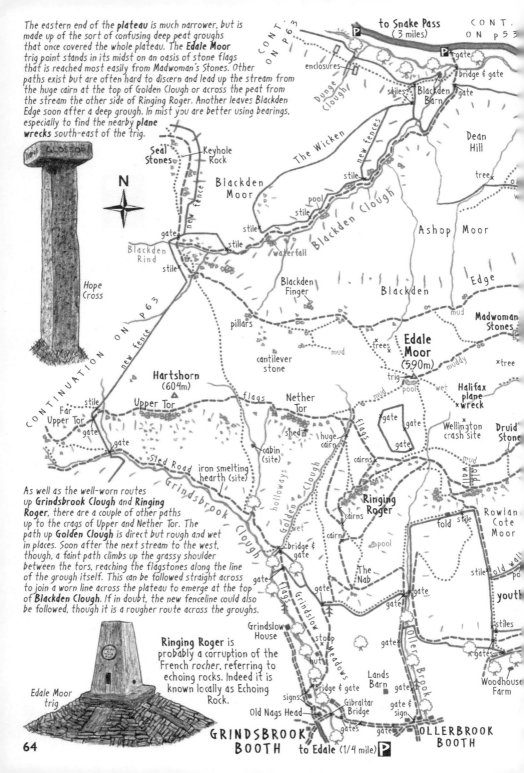

The eastern end of the **plateau** is much narrower, but is made up of the sort of confusing deep peat groughs that once covered the whole plateau. The **Edale Moor** trig point stands in its midst on an oasis of stone flags that is reached most easily from Madwoman's Stones. Other paths exist but are often hard to discern and lead up the stream from the huge cairn at the top of Golden Clough or across the peat from the stream the other side of Ringing Roger. Another leaves Blackden Edge soon after a deep grough. In mist you are better using bearings, especially to find the nearby **plane wrecks** south-east of the trig.

As well as the well-worn routes up **Grindsbrook Clough** and **Ringing Roger**, there are a couple of other paths up to the crags of Upper and Nether Tor. The path up **Golden Clough** is direct but rough and wet in places. Soon after the next stream to the west, though, a faint path climbs up the grassy shoulder between the tors, reaching the flagstones along the line of the grough itself. This can be followed straight across to join a worn line across the plateau to emerge at the top of **Blackden Clough**. If in doubt, the new fenceline could also be followed, though it is a rougher route across the groughs.

Ringing Roger is probably a corruption of the French *rocher*, referring to echoing rocks. Indeed it is known locally as Echoing Rock.

Edale Moor trig

64

to Snake Pass (3 miles)

CONT. ON p 53

CONTINUATION ON p 63

enclosures

Dunge Clough

stiles

Blackden Barn

bridge & gate

gate

The Wicken

new fences

Dean Hill

tree

Seal Stones

Keyhole Rock

Blackden Moor

stile

pool

stile

Blackden Clough

Ashop Moor

gate

stile

stile

Blackden Rind

waterfall

stile

Blackden Finger

Blackden

Edge

mud

Madwoman Stones

Hope Cross

GLOSSOP

new fence

pillars

cantilever stone

trees

mud

Edale Moor (590m)

muddy

tree

trig

pool

wet

Halifax plane wreck

Hartshorn (604m)

Upper Tor

flags

Nether Tor

mud

flags

gate

gate

Wellington crash site

Druid Stone

Far Upper Tor

stile

gate

gate

shed

cabin (site)

huge cairn

flags

cairns

gate

gate

mud

Sled Road

iron smelting hearth (site)

Grindsbrook Clough

holloways

Golden Clough

wet

cairns

Ringing Roger

cairns

fold

stile

Rowland Cote Moor

cairn

pool

The Nab

stile

old wall

youth

bridge & gate

gate

flags

Grindslow

gate

gate

stiles

Grindslow House

stoop

hut

gate

Ollerbrook

gate

gates

signs

Grindslow Meadows

Lands Barn

gate

gate & sign

Woodhouse Farm

Old Nags Head

Gibraltar Bridge

Bridge & gate

gates

gate

GRINDSBROOK BOOTH

to Edale (1/4 mile)

OLLERBROOK BOOTH

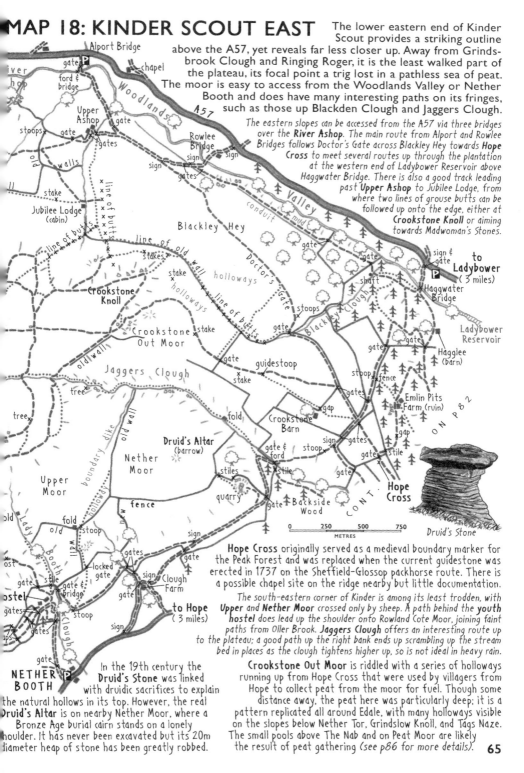

MAP 18: KINDER SCOUT EAST

The lower eastern end of Kinder Scout provides a striking outline above the A57, yet reveals far less closer up. Away from Grindsbrook Clough and Ringing Roger, it is the least walked part of the plateau, its focal point a trig lost in a pathless sea of peat. The moor is easy to access from the Woodlands Valley or Nether Booth and does have many interesting paths on its fringes, such as those up Blackden Clough and Jaggers Clough.

The eastern slopes can be accessed from the A57 via three bridges over the River Ashop. The main route from Alport and Rowlee Bridges follows Doctor's Gate across Blackley Hey towards Hope Cross to meet several routes up through the plantation at the western end of Ladybower Reservoir above Haggwater Bridge. There is also a good track leading past Upper Ashop to Jubilee Lodge, from where two lines of grouse butts can be followed up onto the edge, either at Crookstone Knoll or aiming towards Madwoman's Stones.

Druid's Stone

Hope Cross originally served as a medieval boundary marker for the Peak Forest and was replaced when the current guidestone was erected in 1737 on the Sheffield-Glossop packhorse route. There is a possible chapel site on the ridge nearby but little documentation.

The south-eastern corner of Kinder is among its least trodden, with Upper and Nether Moor crossed only by sheep. A path behind the youth hostel does lead up the shoulder onto Rowland Cote Moor, joining faint paths from Oller Brook. Jaggers Clough offers an interesting route up to the plateau; a good path up the right bank ends up scrambling up the stream bed in places as the clough tightens higher up, so is not ideal in heavy rain.

In the 19th century the **Druid's Stone** was linked with druidic sacrifices to explain the natural hollows in its top. However, the real **Druid's Altar** is on nearby Nether Moor, where a Bronze Age burial cairn stands on a lonely shoulder. It has never been excavated but its 20m diameter heap of stone has been greatly robbed.

Crookstone Out Moor is riddled with a series of holloways running up from Hope Cross that were used by villagers from Hope to collect peat from the moor for fuel. Though some distance away, the peat here was particularly deep; it is a pattern replicated all around Edale, with many holloways visible on the slopes below Nether Tor, Grindslow Knoll, and Tags Naze. The small pools above The Nab and on Peat Moor are likely the result of peat gathering (see p86 for more details).

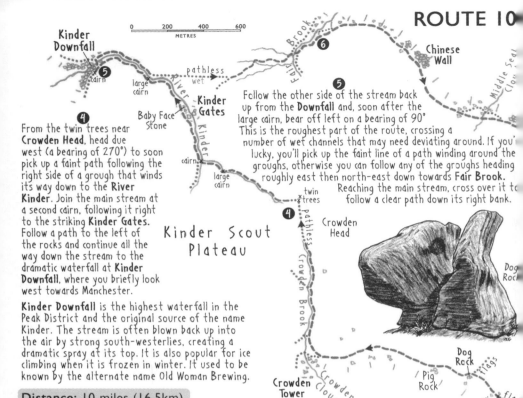

Kinder Downfall

Kinder Gates

cairn

large cairn

River Kinder

Baby Face Stone

pathless wet

Fair Brook

6

Chinese Wall

Middle Seal Clough

5

5

Follow the other side of the stream back up from the **Downfall** and, soon after the large cairn, bear off left on a bearing of 90°. This is the roughest part of the route, crossing a number of wet channels that may need deviating around. If you're lucky, you'll pick up the faint line of a path winding around the groughs, otherwise you can follow any of the groughs heading roughly east then north-east down towards **Fair Brook**. Reaching the main stream, cross over it to follow a clear path down its right bank.

4

From the twin trees near **Crowden Head**, head due west (a bearing of 270°) to soon pick up a faint path following the right side of a grough that winds its way down to the **River Kinder**. Join the main stream at a second cairn, following it right to the striking **Kinder Gates**. Follow a path to the left of the rocks and continue all the way down the stream to the dramatic waterfall at **Kinder Downfall**, where you briefly look west towards Manchester.

cairn

large cairn

Kinder Scout Plateau

twin trees

4

pathless

Crowden Brook

Crowden Head

Dog Rock

Kinder Downfall is the highest waterfall in the Peak District and the original source of the name Kinder. The stream is often blown back up into the air by strong south-westerlies, creating a dramatic spray at its top. It is also popular for ice climbing when it is frozen in winter. It used to be known by the alternate name Old Woman Brewing.

Crowden Tower

Crowden Clough

Dog Rock

Pig Rock

flags

cairn

flag

Distance: 10 miles (16.5km)

Ascent: 540m

Difficulty: Strenuous

Parking: Large pay-and-display car park by the main road in Edale.

Public Transport: Edale is on the Hope Valley railway line between Sheffield and Manchester.

Character: A wide-ranging tour of the different faces of Kinder Scout, including Grindslow Knoll, Kinder Downfall, Edale Moor trig and Ringing Roger. The route crosses the plateau three times and reveals views to the north, south and west. It is necessarily pathless in places on the rough plateau and navigation requires the use of a compass, particularly when the clouds are down.

3

Turn hard left before the summit cairn of **Grindslow Knoll** and follow a flagged path across the southern edge of the moor. At **Dog Rock**, you join another large path and continue left towards **Crowden Clough**. Nearing the clough, bear right onto a smaller path up the right-hand side of the stream. This winds its way onto the plateau and appears to cross the stream, but stay on the right bank on a fainter line. Eventually this peters out with the stream, but as you emerge onto the barren heart of **Kinder Scout** continuing north leads to a pair of striking conifers (the twin trees).

Peat Moor was first recorded in 1699, a local name for an extensive area of moor that provided peat fuel for those in Upper Booth, Barber Booth and Grindsbrook Booth. Peat Moor is likely to have been dug from the medieval period until the late 19th century, its slopes scored by countless holloways – the direct ones were sledways, while the zigzag routes were used by packhorses and carts. The peat, once a few metres thick, has been entirely stripped from the surface as far as Grindslow Knoll, leaving pools standing in the former peat pits and a narrow ridge (known as a baulk) that marked the boundary between the different hamlets' peat grounds.

the twin trees on Kinder Scout plateau

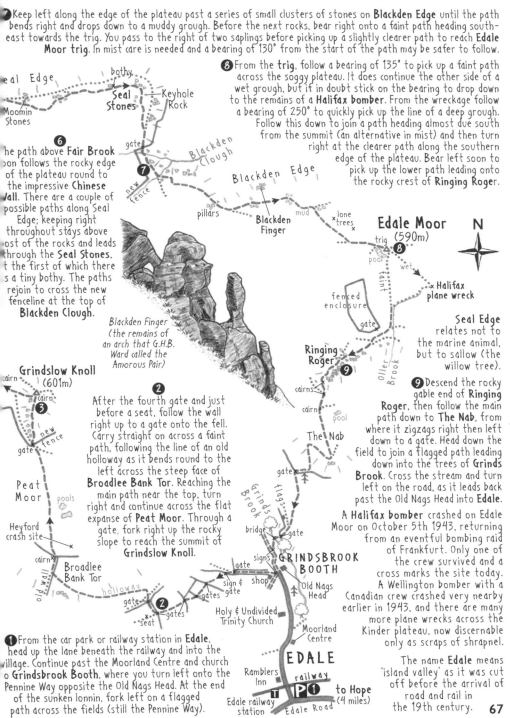

7 Keep left along the edge of the plateau past a series of small clusters of stones on **Blackden Edge** until the path bends right and drops down to a muddy grough. Before the next rocks, bear right onto a faint path heading south-east towards the trig. You pass to the right of two saplings before picking up a slightly clearer path to reach **Edale Moor trig**. In mist care is needed and a bearing of 130° from the start of the path may be safer to follow.

8 From the **trig**, follow a bearing of 135° to pick up a faint path across the soggy plateau. It does continue the other side of a wet grough, but if in doubt stick on the bearing to drop down to the remains of a **Halifax bomber**. From the wreckage follow a bearing of 250° to quickly pick up the line of a deep grough. Follow this down to join a path heading almost due south from the summit (an alternative in mist) and then turn right at the clearer path along the southern edge of the plateau. Bear left soon to pick up the lower path leading onto the rocky crest of **Ringing Roger**.

6 The path above **Fair Brook** on follows the rocky edge of the plateau round to the impressive **Chinese Wall**. There are a couple of possible paths along Seal Edge; keeping right throughout stays above most of the rocks and leads through the **Seal Stones**, at the first of which there is a tiny bothy. The paths rejoin to cross the new fenceline at the top of **Blackden Clough**.

Blackden Finger (the remains of an arch that G.H.B. Ward called the Amorous Pair)

Edale Moor (590m)

Seal Edge relates not to the marine animal, but to sallow (the willow tree).

9 Descend the rocky gable end of **Ringing Roger**, then follow the main path down to **The Nab**, from where it zigzags right then left down to a gate. Head down the field to join a flagged path leading down into the trees of **Grinds Brook**. Cross the stream and turn left on the road, as it leads back past the Old Nags Head into **Edale**.

2 After the fourth gate and just before a seat, follow the wall right up to a gate onto the fell. Carry straight on across a faint path, following the line of an old holloway as it bends round to the left across the steep face of **Broadlee Bank Tor**. Reaching the main path near the top, turn right and continue across the flat expanse of **Peat Moor**. Through a gate, fork right up the rocky slope to reach the summit of **Grindslow Knoll**.

A **Halifax bomber** crashed on Edale Moor on October 5th 1943, returning from an eventful bombing raid of Frankfurt. Only one of the crew survived and a cross marks the site today. A Wellington bomber with a Canadian crew crashed very nearby earlier in 1943, and there are many more plane wrecks across the Kinder plateau, now discernable only as scraps of shrapnel.

The name **Edale** means 'island valley' as it was cut off before the arrival of road and rail in the 19th century.

1 From the car park or railway station in **Edale**, head up the lane beneath the railway and into the village. Continue past the Moorland Centre and church to **Grindsbrook Booth**, where you turn left onto the Pennine Way opposite the Old Nags Head. At the end of the sunken lonnin, fork left on a flagged path across the fields (still the Pennine Way).

67

MAP 19: KINDER SCOUT SOUTH (Brown Knoll)

Brown Knoll and Colborne Moor stand at the head of Edale and blend seamlessly into both Kinder Scout and Rushup Edge. However, their peaty wastes have far more in common with Kinder than the Great Ridge. Though it can be reached from the Chapel-en-le-Frith road to the south, the moor is most easily accessed from Upper Booth and Barber Booth. Its steep ramparts, with Tags Naze in particular towering over the head of the valley, appear somewhat impenetrable, but a series of old holloways give access to these fascinating slopes. Most will simply trudge past on the flagged path over Brown Knoll, but there is plenty more to be discovered here.

Jacob's Ladder is a shortcut on the Pennine Way forged by Jacob Marshall of Edale Head in the 17th century. Driving his packhorse train between Edale and Hayfield, he sent the packhorses round the track while he cut up the steep bank. Eventually he dug steps, some of which can still be made out to the right of the new surface. Edale Head, often called Youngit House after the nearby bridge, was said to be haunted and was last lived in around 1894.

Edale Cross stands at the top of the ancient packhorse route between Hayfield and Edale. It was probably erected around the 12th century as a boundary cross to mark the limits of Glossop parish (then owned by the monks of Basingwerk Abbey in North Wales), but also served as a guidestone. It fell into disrepair before being re-erected in 1810 by John Gee (whose name it bears), since when the enclosure wall has been built, squeezing it in rather unceremoniously. It was previously taller but a section of the shaft has broken off. It is sometimes also known as Champion Cross, champion referring to good land within the Royal Forest of the Peak, at the heart of which it stands.

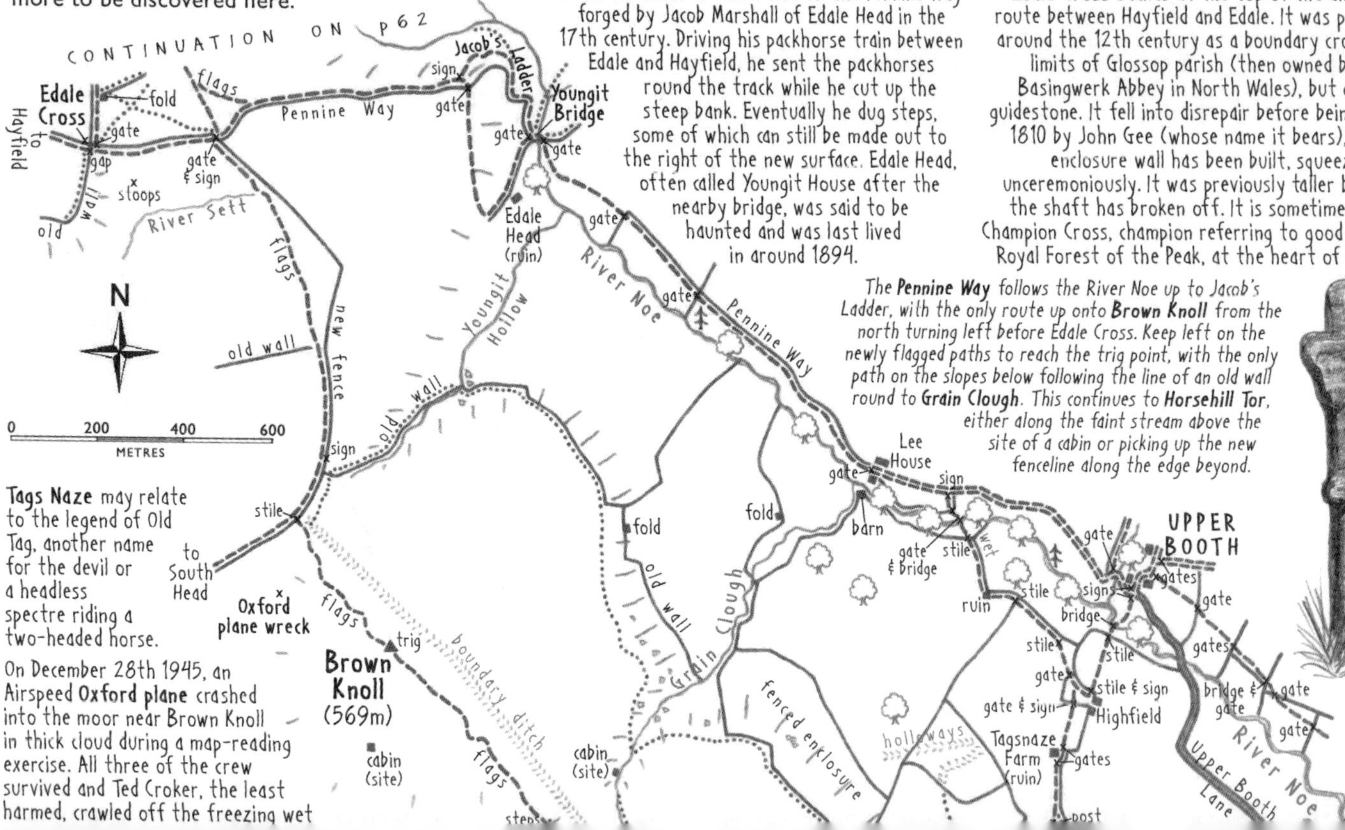

The **Pennine Way** follows the River Noe up to Jacob's Ladder, with the only route up onto **Brown Knoll** from the north turning left before Edale Cross. Keep left on the newly flagged paths to reach the trig point, with the only path on the slopes below following the line of an old wall round to **Grain Clough**. This continues to **Horsehill Tor**, either along the faint stream above the site of a cabin or picking up the new fenceline along the edge beyond.

Tags Naze may relate to the legend of Old Tag, another name for the devil or a headless spectre riding a two-headed horse.

On December 28th 1945, an Airspeed **Oxford plane** crashed into the moor near Brown Knoll in thick cloud during a map-reading exercise. All three of the crew survived and Ted Croker, the least harmed, crawled off the freezing wet

Eddle Cross

Barber Booth Tips

River Noe

Upper Booth Lane

UPPER BOOTH

Highfield

stile & sign

gate & sign

Tagsnaze Farm (ruin)

post

Lee House

barn

holloways

fenced enclosure

Grain Clough

old wall

fold

sign

boundary ditch

flags

cabin (site)

Brown Knoll (569m)

trig

cabin (site)

stile

Oxford plane wreck

to South Head

new fence

old wall

River Sett

sloops

Edale Cross

to Hayfield

fold

gate & sign

CONTINUATION ON P 62

Pennine Way

flags

Jacob's Ladder

sign

gate

Youngit Bridge

Edale Head (ruin)

River Noe

Youngit Hollow

old pit

L D M

N

0 200 400 600
METRES

The main paths lead up from the bunk-house at Dalehead lead south across Whitemoor Clough to join Chapel Gate. However, a series of fine holloways provide more direct routes onto the moor. Heading straight on at the end of the track by Dalehead leads to a gate on the edge of Colborne Moor and a faint path bears left to join the line of a holloway up the shoulder. Forking left leads along the edge above the top of Whitemoor Clough to reach Chapel Gate. The right fork joins the top of the slope leading round to a memorial cairn and then up on to Horsehill Tor. Another holloway leads up Tags Naze from The Orchard; follow the left side of the fence up from the farm to a stile then zigzag up the slope. Keep right to reach the new fence-line at the top. Other deeply carved holloways above Tagsnaze Farm are harder to reach.

Chapel Gate is a medieval packhorse route from Edale to Chapel-en-le-Frith, a chapel in the Peak Forest first recorded in 1219. It has recently been closed to off-road traffic and its surface, though improved, is still rough in places.

memorial cairn on Colborne Moor to John (Charles Gilligan)

moor with badly injured ankles. He reached the hostel at Lee House after three hours and a rescue party found the others the following morning. Ted Croker went on to play for Charlton Athletic and was Chief Executive of the FA until his death in 1992.

There are three paths leading north-west across Colborne Moor from the top of Chapel Gate. The most obvious is the flagged path that meanders all the way over Brown Knoll to the Pennine Way. To the east, a clear path follows the edge before forking left across Colborne Moor. Soon after passing the site of a sheepfold it peters out somewhat; though it can be picked up again in places, it no longer offers the simple alternative to the main route that it appears to on the OS map. The third path is fainter, following the line of an old wall to the south-west of the flags. It aims directly towards a couple of striking features on the back shoulder of the moor, the first revealing itself to be an igloo-style shelter built from the ruins of an old shooting cabin. The wall ends here but continue along the drain and gully ahead. Before bearing right across the moor towards the crenellated air shaft for the Cowburn Tunnel. You can join the main path by picking up a faint line heading northeast past a lone tree.

Built in 1891, the Cowburn Tunnel carries the Hope Valley Line between Sheffield and Manchester beneath the hills. Though only two miles long it is the deepest land tunnel in the UK, thus its not only having the one air shaft sunk on Colborne Moor for ventilation (though there is a lower one near Dalehead). Its construction doubled the population in the valley and the arrival of the station in Edale changed life here greatly. Cowburn and Colborne have the same root; cald-burn refers to a cold stream.

The Vale of Edale is made up of a series of hamlets arranged around the sites of booths, which were the summer grazing grounds of medieval vaccaries. Upper Booth (or Crowdenlee Booth), Barber Booth (or Whitemoor Lee Booth), Grindsbrook Booth, Ollerbrook Booth and Nether Booth (originally Lady Booth) all began as simple dwellings for the boothmen looking after the cows in the early cattle ranches. There were also studs for rearing horses for the royal hunt of the Peak Forest, a particular favourite of King John. The settlements and their enclosures developed from the 16th century onwards.

69

Distance: 8 miles (13km)

Ascent: 460m

Difficulty: Moderate

Parking: Free parking at car park near Barber Booth and below nearby railway viaduct.

Public Transport: Edale railway station is a further mile down the valley from Barber Booth, with trains running regularly between Sheffield and Manchester.

Character: A fine circuit around the head of Edale, taking in the summit of Brown Knoll and the true high point of Kinder Scout, as well as the interesting features of Colborne Moor and the rock playground of the Woolpacks. Many of the paths are faint, requiring careful navigation, particularly to reach the top of Kinder Scout. Extra care is needed in bad weather.

5 From the summit **cairn**, head south across the pathless plateau towards Pym Chair (the closest and most prominent of several rocks visible along the edge of the plateau) or follow a bearing of 170°. You should pass to the left of a large cluster of flat rocks. Soon after **Pym Chair**, turn left along the eroded path that leads through the wonderful natural sculpture park of the **Woolpacks**. The main path keeps left to emerge on the top of **Crowden Tower**, overlooking the head of Crowden Clough.

Barber Booth was named after the Barber family around the 15th century, before which it was Whitemoor Lee Booth.

6 At **Crowden Tower**, turn right just before the rocks and fork left as you descend to head down onto a lower nameless edge. A good path continues along the edge as it bends round to the right. The second time it does this, fork left down the grassy shoulder and descend to a stile in the new fenceline. The path continues, bearing round to the right to cross the line of an old wall and reach the edge of the moor.

Follow the wall left even as it descends steeply into **Crowden Clough** and cross the stream to join the lovely path leading down the valley into the hamlet of **Upper Booth**.

The earthworks of the only World War II **searchlight battery** in the Peak District can be seen in the field opposite Barber Booth Tips. Nicknamed Cotton East, it was used by the RAF to illuminate enemy planes during night-time raids and help

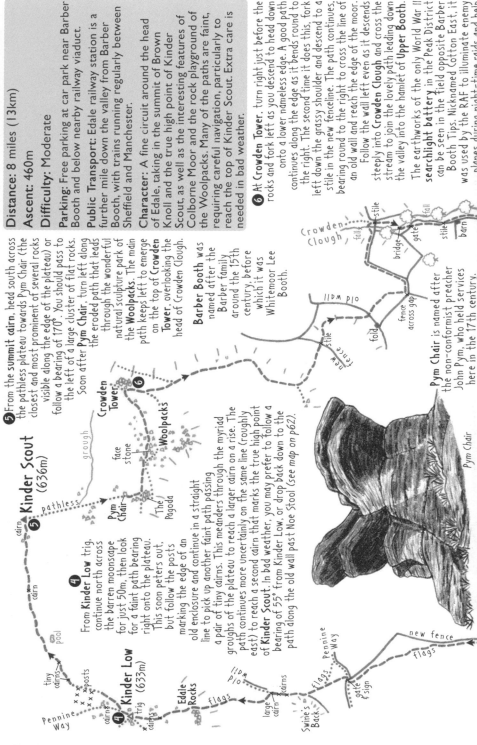

From **Kinder Low** trig, continue north across the barren moonscape for just 50m, then look for a faint path bearing right onto the plateau. This soon peters out, but follow the posts marking the edge of an old enclosure and continue in a straight line to pick up another faint path passing a pair of tiny cairns. This meanders through the myriad groughs of the plateau to reach a larger cairn on a rise. The path continues more uncertainly on the same line (roughly east) to reach a second cairn that marks the true high point of **Kinder Scout**. In bad weather, you may prefer to follow a bearing of 55° from Kinder Low, or drop back down to the path along the old wall past Noe Stool (see map on p62).

Pym Chair is named after the non-conformist preacher John Pym, who held services here in the 17th century.

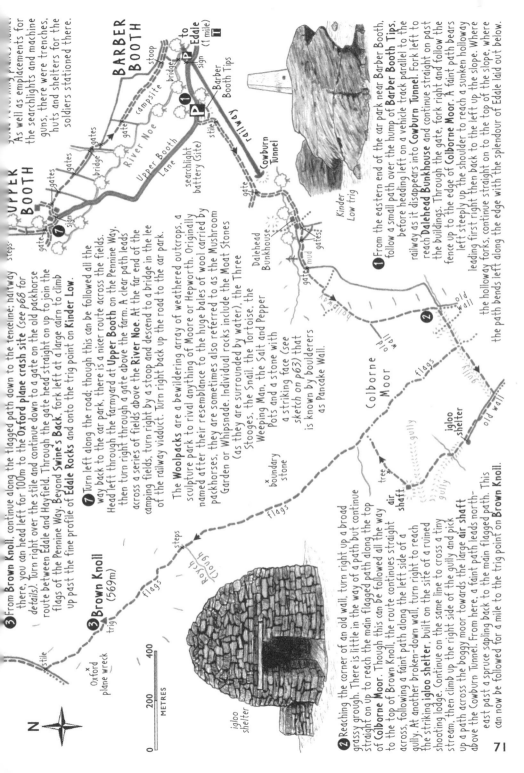

...As well as emplacements for the searchlights and machine guns, there were trenches, huts and shelters for the soldiers stationed there.

BARBER BOOTH

UPPER BOOTH

to Edale (1 mile)

stoop · bridge · sign · campsite · Barber Booth Tips · gate · gates · River Noe · bridge · sign · gates · railway · stile · Upper Booth Lane · searchlight battery (site) · Cowburn Tunnel · gate

1 From the eastern end of the car park near Barber Booth, follow a small path over the hump of **Barber Booth Tips**, before heading left on a vehicle track parallel to the railway as it disappears into **Cowburn Tunnel**. Fork left to reach **Dalehead Bunkhouse** and continue straight on past the buildings. Through the gate, fork right and follow the fence up to the edge of **Colborne Moor**. A faint path bears left steeply up the shoulder to reach a sunken holloway leading first right then back to the left up the slope. Where the holloway forks, continue straight on to the top of the slope, where the path bends left along the edge with the splendour of Edale laid out below.

Dalehead Bunkhouse · Kinder Low trig · pond · gates

2 Reaching the corner of an old wall, turn right up a broad grassy grough. There is little in the way of a path but continue straight on up to reach the main flagged path along the top of **Colborne Moor**. Though this can be followed all the way to the top of Brown Knoll, the route continues straight across, following a faint path along the left side of a gully. At another broken-down wall, turn right to reach the striking **igloo shelter**, built on the site of a ruined shooting lodge. Continue on the same line to cross a tiny stream, then climb up the right side of the gully and pick up a path across the boggy moor towards the large **air shaft** above the Cowburn Tunnel. From here, a faint path leads north-east past a spruce sapling back to the main flagged path. This can now be followed for a mile to the trig point on **Brown Knoll**.

old wall · holloway · Colborne Moor · flags · gully · igloo shelter · tree · air shaft · gully · boundary stone · flags · steps · Rough Clough

3 From **Brown Knoll**, continue along the flagged path down to the fenceline; halfway there, you can head left for 100m to the **Oxford plane crash site** (see p68 for details). Turn right over the stile and continue down to a gate on the old packhorse route between Edale and Hayfield. Through the gate head straight on up to join the flags of the Pennine Way. Beyond **Swine's Back**, fork left at a large cairn to climb up past the fine profile of **Edale Rocks** and onto the trig point on **Kinder Low**.

3 Brown Knoll (569m) trig · Oxford plane wreck · stile · igloo shelter

7 Turn left along the road; though this can be followed all the way back to the car park, there is a nicer route across the fields. Head left through the farmyard at **Upper Booth** on the Pennine Way, then turn right through a gate above the **River Noe**. At the far end of the camping fields, turn right by a stoop and descend to a bridge in the lee of the railway viaduct. Turn right back up the road to the car park.

The **Woolpacks** are a bewildering array of weathered outcrops, a sculpture park to rival anything of Moore or Hepworth. Originally named after their resemblance to the huge bales of wool carried by packhorses, they are sometimes also referred to as the Mushroom Garden or Whipsnade. Individual rocks include the Moat Stones (as they are surrounded by water), the Three Stooges, the Snail, the Tortoise, the Weeping Man, the Salt and Pepper Pots and a stone with a striking face (see sketch on p63) that is known by boulderers as Pancake Wall.

N

0   200   400
METRES

71

THE KINDER SCOUT MASS TRESPASS

More than anything else, Kinder Scout is most closely associated with this single much-debated event in 1932, a coordinated trespass arranged by groups from both Sheffield and Manchester. The better-known Manchester side of the mass trespass was organised by the Lancashire branch of the British Workers' Sports Federation, a working-class movement linked to the Communist Party. A group from the movement had been turned back from a walk on Bleaklow a month earlier, so a showdown with the landowners was called for. Flyers were distributed and adverts printed so that, when the crowd gathered in Hayfield on 24th April 1932, a large police contingent was waiting for them. Despite reports in the Manchester papers of as many as five hundred people taking part, the number was probably closer to two hundred. Before heading up the hill, the group was famously addressed in Bowden Quarry by Benny Rothman, the Lancashire branch's secretary; however, he was never meant to speak, but the organised speaker hadn't turned up.

The trespass began near the bottom of William Clough, when they branched off the public Snake Path and were quickly met by a group of gamekeepers, who brandished sticks and tried to deter the group who had spread out across the hillside. There were minor skirmishes and a keeper was injured falling over. The trespassers were beaten back to the path and continued up the clough to Ashop Head, where they met further contingents from Sheffield; one group had walked up the Snake Path while another had crossed the Kinder plateau from Jacob's Ladder unchallenged. After a victory rally, they returned their respective ways, this modest attempt at trespassing only becoming a big deal with what happened subsequently. While the Manchester crowd took the headlines, it was ironic that the only real trespassers that day were their brethren from Sheffield.

When they returned to Hayfield, the police and gamekeepers were waiting and arrested six of those involved, one of whom had gone to aid the stricken keeper. The initial charges of unlawful assembly and breach of the peace were later increased to incitement to riotous assembly, and Benny Rothman was among five imprisoned for four to six months. The unfair nature of the trial and the draconian punishment handed out became a beacon of injustice that is often hailed as changing public sentiment towards the access movement.

However, the mass trespass was never supported by the Ramblers' Federations of either Sheffield and Manchester, nor other established rambling groups like the Sheffield Clarion Ramblers (Bert Ward was leading a walk the other side of the Peak District that day). Though they had been trespassing across the moors for years, they had little interest in this event, feeling it would only hinder their ongoing discussions with landowners over public access. There are those who think it put the access movement back twenty years and the British Workers' Sports Federation was condemned as having no real interest in access rights. Yet many of these groups were almost part of the establishment, benefiting from informal permits where working class groups could not. For Benny Rothman and his cohorts, it was very much a class issue and a fight these barely twenty-year olds were willing to go to prison for.

With the benefit of hindsight, the Kinder Trespass was a poor attempt at trespassing but a significant moment nonetheless. There were further trespasses and clashes with gamekeepers and police that year at Abbey Brook and Stanage, and five thousand attended that year's annual gathering at Winnats Pass. Though there would be no further trespasses for 50 years, the myth of the Kinder Trespass grew as the years passed and spurred many others into action. It was an inspirational event which indirectly set in motion the formation of the first national park and the many access agreements we benefit from to this day.

Benny Rothman speaking at Bowden Quarry

CHAPTER 7 – THE GREAT RIDGE

High Point: Lord's Seat, 550m

Grid Ref: SK112834

Map Sheet: OL1 (Dark Peak)

Access: No restrictions.

Public Transport: Edale and Hope are on the Hope Valley railway line and Castleton is served by the 271,272, 273 & 274 bus routes from Sheffield.

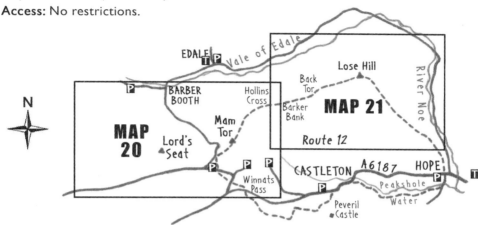

The Great Ridge is that rare thing in the Peak District; a peak or, in fact, a series of them. Local geology throws up a quirk here so that, between the gritstone tors and peat plateaus of the Dark Park, and the limestone caves and dry valleys of the White Peak, there is a single shale and sandstone ridge between Edale and Castleton. From the conical Lose Hill via Mam Tor's shattered face to the narrow twisting arête of Rushop Edge that leads up to Lord's Seat, the Great Ridge stands alone. Only beyond Lord's Seat does the ridge blends seamlessly into the southern extension of Kinder Scout's peat wastes.

The Great Ridge's name was first coined by W.A. Poucher in his book *The Peak and Pennines*, but I have heard it also referred to as the Peakland Ridge and the Mam Tor Ridge. Despite Lord's Seat being higher, Mam Tor is the central and focal point of the ridge. Its loose, craggy south-east face overlooks Castleton and forms the only break in an Iron Age fortification that once defended the summit. It has long been an important regional site, with a Neolithic burial chamber on the top, as there is at Lord's Seat.

The character of the ridge means there is little open moorland to explore, just lots of different ways up and down either side and a motorway of a path along the crest that is far removed from the seemingly empty swathes of moorland so far described in the book. It is a fine introduction to the area, though, and one that should not be overlooked.

the Great Ridge from Win Hill – Mam Tor, Lord's Seat, Barker Bank, Back Tor and Lose Hill

Though not its highest point, Mam Tor is the obvious focal point of the Great Ridge, its loose fac
towering over Castleton and the Hope Valley. Mam Tor may be the most popular peak in the
book and the whole area is riddled with paths and parking. Head west for quieter slopes,
particularly on the north side of Lord's Seat. This higher peak has as much in common with the
peat wastes of Kinder Scout, though a fine crest heads east to Mam Nick.

A number of shafts were sunk at **Black Sough Lead Mine** from 1824 in an
attempt to access the Odin lead vein successfully excavated at Odin Mine. It
followed unsuccessful attempts at Peakshill the other side of Rushup Edge
in the 18th century, but it is unclear if any lead was retrieved here.

There are a number of enticing land-slipp
knolls on the north side of **Lord's Sea**
These can be reached by dropping down
holloway from the ridge between the tw
stiles east of the summit; a rou
path then leads across the slop
This can also be picked up k
heading up the hill from a coup
of gates off the road up to **Ma
Nick**, or the stile near the top.
avoid walking on the road, th
foot of the moor can largely k
followed from Chapel Gate to Mc
Nick with only the fence abo
Upper Holt to be contended wit

The byway of **Chapel Gate** is the most obvious way up onto
Lord's Seat. The main path follows the wall along the ridge,
but another path crosses Chapel Gate at the top of the edge
overlooking Edale; follow this east along the edge to a stile
before bearing right to the main path. A more interesting if
steeper route follows a zigzagging holloway straight up the
face. Though it may be tempting to head straight up the
fenceline from the gate at the bottom of Chapel Gate, you
are better contouring across the slope to pick up the holloway
shortly before a small stream. Just before it
steps over a fence near the top, turn
left up the bank and follow a clear
path along
the edge to
the summit.

BARBER BOOTH

Manor
House

to Upper Booth

Black Sough
Lead Mine
(shaft sites)

Upper Holt

rifle
range
(site)

gate &
sign

gap

Lord's
Seat
(550m)

holloway

step over
fence

bridge

Whitemoor

Chapel Gate

sign

stakes

cairn

fold
(site)

stake

old wall

sign

gate

unmarked
summit

barrow

stakes

stile

gate

Edge

Rushup

gate &
post

gap

fence
across

wet

Sheffield Road

to Chapel-en-
le-Frith
(3 miles)

crushing circle
Odin Mine

to Pennine
Bridleway

Lord's Seat is a fine vantage point over Edale and takes
its name from William Peveril, the Lord of the Manor,
who often watched over the Peak Forest chase from
this lofty perch. The well-preserved **bowl barrow**
adjacent to the unmarked summit is a burial chamber
dating from the late Neolithic/early Bronze Age.
Despite a slight indentation in its top, it is not
thought to have been excavated. A warning flag stood
here from the 1920s to 1940s, when there was a **rifle
range** on the slope below. The high concrete wall
here held the targets at the end of the range.

Windy Knoll Cave was excavated in the 1870s and the
largest collection of bones ever unearthed in England were
found here. These included those of both arctic reindeer an
tropical bison, demonstrating the great climatic variations
when Britain was still part of the continent. The cave
entrance reminds me of the Cave of Caerbannog in *Monty
Python & the Holy Grail*. The remains of Neolithic burials
have also been found in a now-collapsed cave on **Treak Cliff**

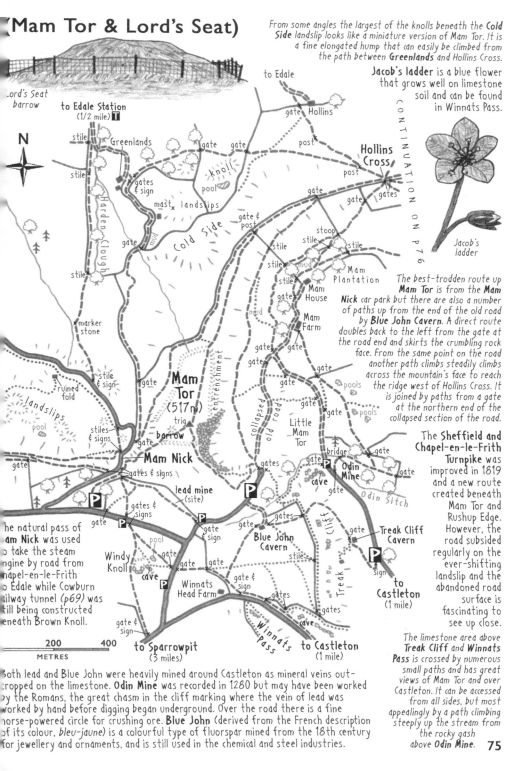

(Mam Tor & Lord's Seat)

From some angles the largest of the knolls beneath the **Cold Side** landslip looks like a miniature version of Mam Tor. It is a fine elongated hump that can easily be climbed from the path between **Greenlands** and **Hollins Cross**.

Jacob's ladder is a blue flower that grows well on limestone soil and can be found in Winnats Pass.

Jacob's ladder

CONTINUATION ON P 76

The best-trodden route up **Mam Tor** is from the **Mam Nick** car park but there are also a number of paths up from the end of the old road by **Blue John Cavern**. A direct route doubles back to the left from the gate at the road end and skirts the crumbling rock face. From the same point on the road another path climbs steadily climbs across the mountain's face to reach the ridge west of Hollins Cross. It is joined by paths from a gate at the northern end of the collapsed section of the road.

The **Sheffield and Chapel-en-le-Frith Turnpike** was improved in 1819 and a new route created beneath Mam Tor and Rushup Edge. However, the road subsided regularly on the ever-shifting landslip and the abandoned road surface is fascinating to see up close.

The limestone area above **Treak Cliff** and **Winnats Pass** is crossed by numerous small paths and has great views of Mam Tor and over Castleton. It can be accessed from all sides, but most appealingly by a path climbing steeply up the stream from the rocky gash above **Odin Mine**.

he natural pass of am Nick was used o take the steam ngine by road from hapel-en-le-Frith o Edale while Cowburn ailway tunnel (p69) was till being constructed eneath Brown Knoll.

oth lead and Blue John were heavily mined around Castleton as mineral veins out-cropped on the limestone. **Odin Mine** was recorded in 1280 but may have been worked by the Romans, the great chasm in the cliff marking where the vein of lead was worked by hand before digging began underground. Over the road there is a fine horse-powered circle for crushing ore. **Blue John** (derived from the French description of its colour, *bleu-jaune*) is a colourful type of fluorspar mined from the 18th century for jewellery and ornaments, and is still used in the chemical and steel industries.

75

The Great Ridge's lower eastern end leads steadily up to Lose Hill's shapely point, a steep but grassy eminence guarding the entrance to Edale. However, from many angles it is overshadowed by the rocky face of Back Tor that appears to defy the shale landslips from which it is formed. Accessible from Hope, Castleton and Edale, this is a popular and almost too-well-worn area, yet there are still little-explored corners to be found on the north side of the ridge.

Hollins Cross was a resting point on the coffin route between Edale and the church in Castleton. The first chapel in Edale was not built until 1633 and the current church dates from 1885.

Backtor Wood is an intriguing area to explore, sparse covering of stunted alders and birch cling to the jumble of landslipped hummocks beneath Back Tor's daunting facade. It can be reached by following any of the paths down from **Backtor Nook**, or via a couple of paths or holloways heading across the slope below Lose Hill.

memorial at Hollins Cross

Barker Bank is the largely ignored fourth summit on the ridge, an unmarked grassy dome that is overshadowed by neighbouring **Back Tor**. Back Tor's rock face - said to look like the outline of an old woman baking bread in an oven - rises precipitously above Edale and gives the short path up it a genuine mountain-like air. I am particularly taken by the lone pine that has escaped the plantation on its lee side. Its stunted form looks like a figure struggling up the slope and is a distinctive feature in most photos of Back Tor.

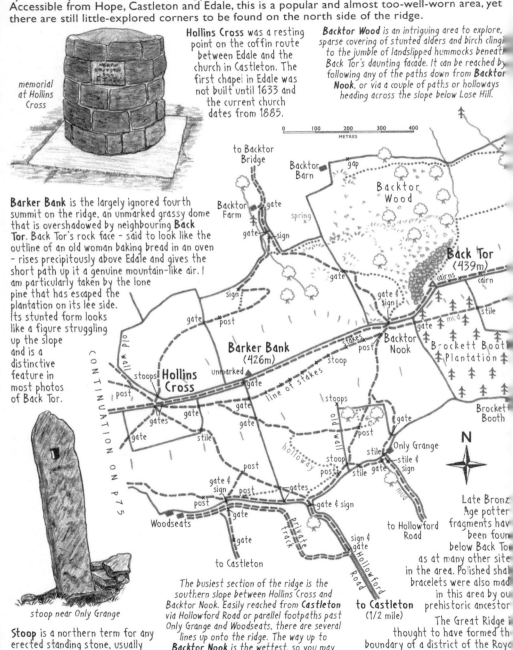

stoop near Only Grange

Stoop is a northern term for any erected standing stone, usually used either as a gatepost or a waymarking guide.

76

The busiest section of the ridge is the southern slope between Hollins Cross and Backtor Nook. Easily reached from **Castleton** via Hollowford Road or parallel footpaths past Only Grange and Woodseats, there are several lines up onto the ridge. The way up to **Backtor Nook** is the wettest, so you may be better off following one of the obvious paths or holloways up to **Hollins Cross**.

Late Bronze Age potter fragments hav been foun below Back To as at many other site in the area. Polished shal bracelets were also mad in this area by ou prehistoric ancestor

The Great Ridge i thought to have formed th boundary of a district of the Roya Forest of the Peak and may ha an early boundary wall along its crest

& Back Tor)

The northern and eastern flanks of **Lose Hill** are largely ignored as no footpaths here lead down to the road and the open access area stops some way short of it. However, it is an interesting area crossed by numerous sheeptracks and holloways. A path follows the old wall-line steeply down the north ridge from the summit to a stake. The wall then forks, with faint paths continuing left across the slope towards the foot of **Back Tor**, or right down the grassy shoulder. Following the latter, a great sheeptrack heads left from a gate near its foot and meanders around the tiny cloughs at the foot of the slope. Where it peters out, head up the slope slightly and cross the fence to pick up another faint line that continues along the boundary into **Backtor Wood**. A fine holloway also skirts around the eastern side of Ward's Piece and can be picked up by heading east from the large cairn at the major junction south of Lose Hill, or a direct grassy line heading east just a few yards south of the summit.

The route along the Great Ridge was long used by packhorse jags (lines of packhorses led by a **jagger**, named after the German jaeger ponies that were used). The sandy soil meant the going was much easier than in the wetter valleys. Coal, wool, lead and salt were brought this way to Hope, and milk was still transported to Sheffield via this route until the late 19th century. Another important jaggers' route led out of Edale via Hope Cross, crossing **Jaggers Clough** with lead bound for the market in Penistone.

Ward's Piece is named after the great G.H.B. Ward, a local walking activist who was central to achieving public access to the moors of the Peak District. He was given part of Lose Hill by the Ramblers' Association in 1945 before handing it straight to the National Trust (see p137 for more information on G.H.B. Ward).

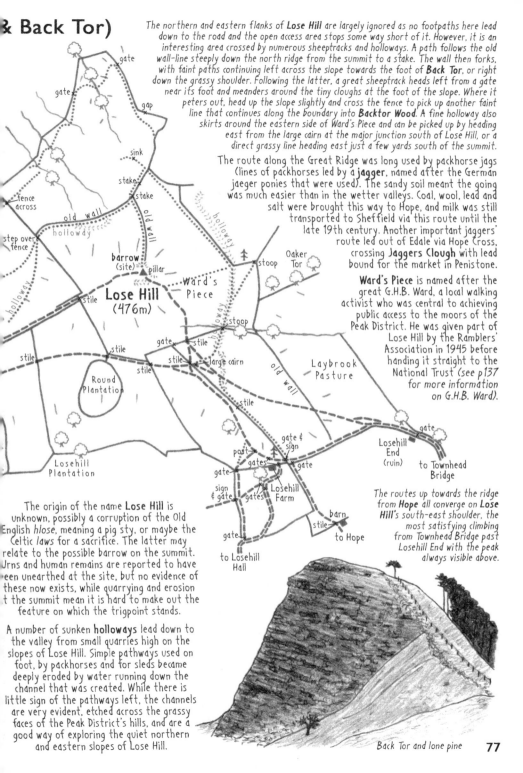

Map labels

gate, gate, gap, sink, stake, stake, fence across, old wall, step over fence, holloway, holloway, holloway, barrow (site), pillar, Ward's Piece, stoop, Oaker Tor, **Lose Hill** (476m), stile, holloway, stile, gate, stile, stile, stile, large cairn, old wall, Laybrook Pasture, Round Plantation, gate & sign, post, gates, gate, Losehill End (ruin), gate, to Townhead Bridge, Losehill Plantation, gate, sign & gate, gates, Losehill Farm, barn, stile, gate, to Hope, to Losehill Hall

The origin of the name **Lose Hill** is unknown, possibly a corruption of the Old English *hlose*, meaning a pig sty, or maybe the Celtic *laws* for a sacrifice. The latter may relate to the possible barrow on the summit. Urns and human remains are reported to have been unearthed at the site, but no evidence of these now exists, while quarrying and erosion at the summit mean it is hard to make out the feature on which the trigpoint stands.

A number of sunken **holloways** lead down to the valley from small quarries high on the slopes of Lose Hill. Simple pathways used on foot, by packhorses and tor sleds became deeply eroded by water running down the channel that was created. While there is little sign of the pathways left, the channels are very evident, etched across the grassy faces of the Peak District's hills, and are a good way of exploring the quiet northern and eastern slopes of Lose Hill.

The routes up towards the ridge from **Hope** all converge on **Lose Hill**'s south-east shoulder, the most satisfying climbing from Townhead Bridge past Losehill End with the peak always visible above.

Back Tor and lone pine

Distance: 8 miles (12.6km)

Ascent: 470m

Difficulty: Moderate (Easy if scramble avoided)

Parking: Pay car parks in Castleton, Hope and at Mam Nick. Free lay-by parking near Windy Knoll or by Hope church.

Public Transport: Hope is on the Hope Valley railway line, though this adds a mile to the route. Castleton & Hope are both served by the 271/272/273/274 buses from Sheffield.

Character: Though hardly original, this is a classic Peakland walk that is deservedly popular. I have added a twist by following the top of Winnats Pass out of Castleton. The scramble up the limestone gully here may not be for everyone, so an alternative is provided and the rest of the walking is very straightforward. The only complaint is that it can be too well trodden and consequently muddy in places.

Speedwell Cavern was the site of a failed enterprise by investors searchi for minerals like Blue John (see p75). which was discovered at another cave nearby. It ends at the Bottomless Pit a 500ft high cavern and is now home to a boat tour.

Back Tor
(439m)

Backtor Nook

cairn   cairns

gate

Barker Bank
(426m)

unmarked top

gate

memorial

Hollins Cross

gate

Windy Knoll Cave
(or the Cave of Caerbannog
– see p78 for explanation)

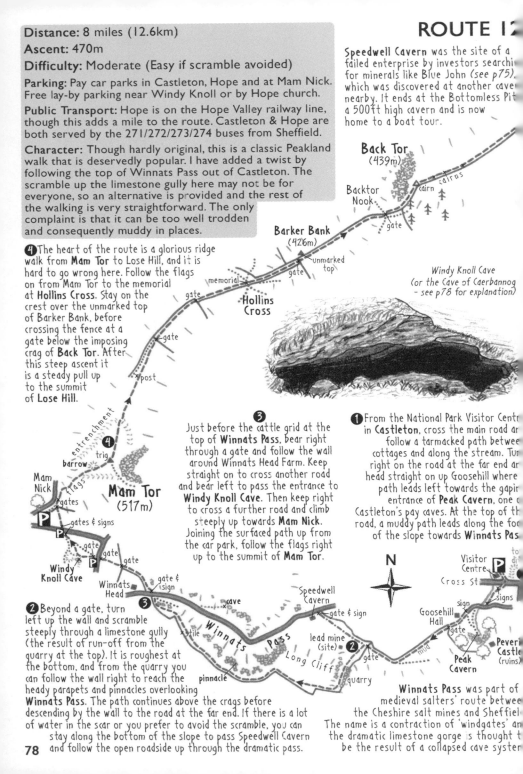

❹ The heart of the route is a glorious ridge walk from **Mam Tor** to Lose Hill, and it is hard to go wrong here. Follow the flags on from Mam Tor to the memorial at **Hollins Cross**. Stay on the crest over the unmarked top of Barker Bank, before crossing the fence at a gate below the imposing crag of **Back Tor**. After this steep ascent it is a steady pull up to the summit of **Lose Hill**.

post

entrenchment

barrow   trig   ❹

Mam Nick

flags

gates

Mam Tor
(517m)

gates & signs

gate

gate   gate

Windy Knoll Cave

Winnats Head   ❸

gate & sign

❸ Just before the cattle grid at the top of **Winnats Pass**, bear right through a gate and follow the wall around Winnats Head Farm. Keep straight on to cross another road and bear left to pass the entrance to **Windy Knoll Cave**. Then keep right to cross a further road and climb steeply up towards **Mam Nick**. Joining the surfaced path up from the car park, follow the flags right up to the summit of **Mam Tor**.

cave

stile

Winnats Pass

pinnacle

Long Cliff

Speedwell Cavern

gate & sign

lead mine (site)

gate

❷

quarry

❶ From the National Park Visitor Centre in **Castleton**, cross the main road an follow a tarmacked path between cottages and along the stream. Tur right on the road at the far end an head straight on up Goosehill where path leads left towards the gaping entrance of **Peak Cavern**, one of Castleton's pay caves. At the top of the road, a muddy path leads along the foot of the slope towards **Winnats Pass**

N

Visitor Centre

Cross St

sign   signs

Goosehill Hall

gate

mud

Peak Cavern

Peveri Castle (ruins)

❷ Beyond a gate, turn left up the wall and scramble steeply through a limestone gully (the result of run-off from the quarry at the top). It is roughest at the bottom, and from the quarry you can follow the wall right to reach the heady parapets and pinnacles overlooking **Winnats Pass**. The path continues above the crags before descending by the wall to the road at the far end. If there is a lot of water in the scar or you prefer to avoid the scramble, you can stay along the bottom of the slope to pass Speedwell Cavern and follow the open roadside up through the dramatic pass.

Winnats Pass was part of medieval salters' route betwee the Cheshire salt mines and Sheffiel The name is a contraction of 'windgates' an the dramatic limestone gorge is thought t be the result of a collapsed cave system

THE GREAT RIDGE FROM CASTLETON & HOPE

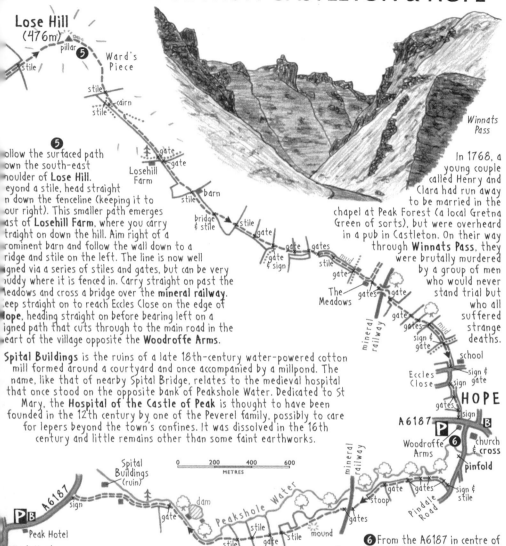

Lose Hill
(476m)
pillar ❺
Ward's Piece
stile
stile
cairn
stile

Winnats Pass

❺
ollow the surfaced path
own the south-east
houlder of **Lose Hill**.
eyond a stile, head straight
n down the fenceline (keeping it to
our right). This smaller path emerges
ast of Losehill Farm, where you carry
traight on down the hill. Aim right of a
rominent barn and follow the wall down to a
ridge and stile on the left. The line is now well
igned via a series of stiles and gates, but can be very
nuddy where it is fenced in. Carry straight on past the
Meadows and cross a bridge over the **mineral railway**.
eep straight on to reach Eccles Close on the edge of
lope, heading straight on before bearing left on a
igned path that cuts through to the main road in the
eart of the village opposite the **Woodroffe Arms**.

In 1768, a
young couple
called Henry and
Clara had run away
to be married in the
chapel at Peak Forest (a local Gretna
Green of sorts), but were overheard
in a pub in Castleton. On their way
through **Winnats Pass**, they
were brutally murdered
by a group of men
who would never
stand trial but
who all
suffered
strange
deaths.

gate
gate
Losehill
Farm
stile
barn
bridge & stile
stile
gate
gate
gate & sign
gate gates
stile
gate
The Meadows
gates
gate
gate
sign & gate
mud
mud
school
sign & sign gate
Eccles Close
gates
sign

HOPE

Spital Buildings is the ruins of a late 18th-century water-powered cotton
mill formed around a courtyard and once accompanied by a millpond. The
name, like that of nearby Spital Bridge, relates to the medieval hospital
that once stood on the opposite bank of Peakshole Water. Dedicated to St
Mary, the **Hospital of the Castle of Peak** is thought to have been
founded in the 12th century by one of the Peverel family, possibly to care
for lepers beyond the town's confines. It was dissolved in the 16th
century and little remains other than some faint earthworks.

A6187
Woodroffe Arms
❻
church & cross
pinfold

Spital Buildings (ruin)
A6187
sign
gate
dam
Peakshole Water
mineral railway
stile
gate
stile
mound
gate
gates
stoop
gates
Pindale Road
sign & stile

0   200   400   600
METRES

P B
Peak Hotel
Nag's Head

CASTLETON

astleton was created as a 12th-century new town for commercial
urposes. A grid of streets was laid out below Peveril Castle's lofty
erch and surrounded by a substantial earthwork that can still be
een near the Visitor Centre and elsewhere. It was originally
ecorded in the Domesday Book as Peak's Arse, which was the name
iven to **Peak Cavern** and evidently the small settlement in its lee
ntil the name was sanitised by the Victorians. This gaping hole
ominates the village to this day and is likely to have been inhabited
or centuries, with people living in its entrance as late as 1901 and
vorking as rope-spinners and cave guides. It was one of the **Seven
Vonders of the Peak** popularised by Thomas Hobbes in the 1600s.

❻ From the A6187 in centre of
Hope, turn right beside the Woodroffe
Arms down Pindale Road. Cross the river
and turn right 200m beyond onto a path
that joins the line of the meandering
Peakshole Water. It re-crosses the
mineral railway and aims to the right of a
curious mound in the otherwise flat
fields. A line of stiles and gates beyond
leads back towards the river, which is
then followed to pick up a vehicle track
past the ruined watermill at **Spital
Buildings**. Turn left on the main road
at the end into **Castleton** village and
follow it round the bends to reach
the Visitor Centre on Cross Street. **79**

MAM TOR

Mam Tor is one of the Peak District's most familiar landmarks, a striking dome rising above Castleton and the Hope Valley. It was the furthest north of Thomas Hobbes' Seven Wonders of the Peak in the 17th century and the only mountain on this list. Though referred to by Hobbes as Sandy Hill, the name Mam Tor is likely Celtic, meaning 'mother mountain' for its breast-like shape. Indeed it would have been a far more rounded bosom before the landslips that gives the hill its rocky south-eastern face today and its modern nickname of the Shivering Mountain.

Mam Tor's face started to slip around 3,600 years ago, caused by sandstone rocks (the Mam Tor Beds) being layered on top of unstable shales. Shale is impervious to water, which instead becomes trapped in cracks in the rock and weakens its structure so that it is unable to support the weight of rock above. The result is a slow but steady landslipping of the sort that can be seen all around Edale and the Woodlands and Derwent Valleys. The road immediately beneath its face was laid in 1819 as part of the Sheffield and Chapel-en-le-Frith Turnpike, by-passing the steep and narrow ancient route up through Winnats Pass. It was an ill-advised route; as the weight of traffic increased, so too did the landslips, and repairs had to be carried out in 1912, 1933, 1946, 1952 and 1966, before the road was finally abandoned in 1979. Looking at its contorted surface today, it seems remarkable that it could have carried traffic for so long.

Mam Tor's summit is encircled by a striking defensive rampart and covered in the flattened platforms of prehistoric buildings, but its history has several distinct phases. A short distance from the trig point is the site of a heavily eroded late Neolithic/early Bronze Age burial mound, highlighting the early significance of this site. As well as a lofty eminence, Mam Tor stands astride the boundary between the gritstone and limestone parts of the Peak, providing valuable resources from both areas for those who lived there.

Around the barrow, mostly on the north side of the hill, are the hut circles and platforms of a very large, late Bronze Age settlement. Usually these settlements were small family-based hamlets, but it is thought Mam Tor was used as a meeting place and summer shieling. The sixteen-acre enclosure was originally surrounded by only a wooden palisade, though this was later reinforced with a stone bank, perhaps reflecting a period of uncertainty and the need for more of a defensive stronghold. The presence of a spring on the north side of Mam Tor was important for the location of this early settlement, which may have predated the main landslip on the south-east face.

Though there is plenty of debate, it seems likely that the great ditch ramparts we see today date from the Iron Age, when the ditch was dug out and the banks revetted with stone. It became a very important regional site that would have been home to the local tribal rulers. After it was abandoned, possibly around 400BC, it was left to grazing sheep until tourists inspired by Hobbes' work started arriving in the late 17th century.

Mam Tor's fractured south-east face from Castleton

CHAPTER 8 – WIN HILL

High Point: Win Hill Pike, 463m

Grid Ref: SK187851

Map Sheet: OL1 (Dark Peak)

Access: No restrictions.

Public Transport: Hope and Bamford are on the Hope Valley railway line. Yorkshire Bridge and Bamford are also served by the 273/274/275 bus routes from Sheffield.

'King of the Peak! Win Hill! thou throned and crowned,
That reign'st o'er many a stream, and many a vale!'
(Ebenezer Elliott, *Win Hill*, 1835)

Small but perfectly formed, Win Hill stands at the crossroads of the northern Peak District. Its iconic nipple stands above Ladybower, the Hope Valley and Edale, and provides one of the finest viewpoints in the area. Though little more than a long limb of Kinder Scout, to which it is connected by the pass at Hope Cross, Win Hill's setting and its rocky summit warrant a separate entry in the book. G.H.B. Ward called it the Lady of the Peak and its summit on Win Hill Pike is often known as The Pimple, or sometimes Old Witches Knoll.

According to legend, a 7th-century battle took place on Win Hill to settle a boundary dispute between the Northumbrians under Edwin of Deira and King Cynegils of Wessex. The Northumbrians were stationed on Win Hill, the Saxons on Lose Hill opposite; outnumbering their enemy, the Saxons charged, only to be defeated by the Northumbrians rolling boulders down on them from a wall high up on Win Hill. Thus, it is said, the names Win and Lose Hill were enshrined forever. However, there is little historical evidence for this, not least any remains of a wall or earthwork on Win Hill. In fact Win Hill was originally Withy Hill (written as Wythinehull in the late 13th century), relating to the willow.

As a relatively modest eminence, Win Hill is easily climbed from Yorkshire Bridge, Bamford or Hope, though it may take longer to explore the forestry plantations that cloak its north side along the shore of Ladybower Reservoir.

Win Hill from Bamford Edge

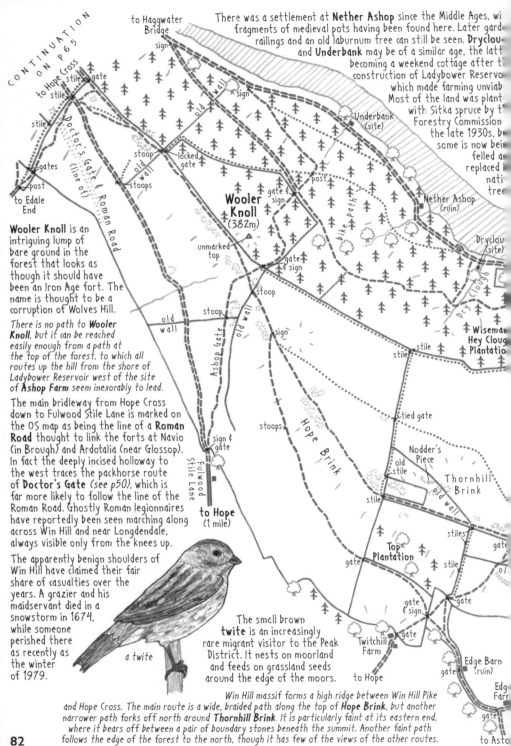

CONTINUATION ON P65

to Haggwater Bridge

to Hope Cross

sign

sign

sign

old wall

old wall

to Hope Cross

stile
stile
gate
stile

stile

Doctor's Gate & Roman Road (line of)

gates

post

to Edale End

stoop
locked gate

old wall

stoops

Underbank (site)

post

bike path

gate & sign

Wooler Knoll (382m)

Nether Ashop (ruin)

Dryclou (site)

unmarked top

gate & sign

stoop

Wiseman Hey Cloug Plantatio

Dry Clough

old wall

stoop

old wall

sign

stile

stile

Ashop Gate

sign

stile

tied gate

stoops

Hope Brink

Nodder's Piece

old stile

Thornhill Brink

old wall

stile

sign & gate

Fulwood Stile Lane

stiles

to Hope (1 mile)

gate

Top Plantation

stile

gate

ol

gate & sign

gate

Twitchill Farm

gate

to Hope

Edge Barn (ruin)

gate

Edg Far

gate

to Asto

There was a settlement at **Nether Ashop** since the Middle Ages, wi fragments of medieval pots having been found here. Later gard railings and an old laburnum tree can still be seen. **Dryclou** and **Underbank** may be of a similar age, the latt becoming a weekend cottage after t construction of Ladybower Reservo which made farming unviab Most of the land was plant with Sitka spruce by t Forestry Commission the late 1930s, b some is now bei felled a replaced nati tree

Wooler Knoll is an intriguing lump of bare ground in the forest that looks as though it should have been an Iron Age fort. The name is thought to be a corruption of Wolves Hill.

There is no path to **Wooler Knoll***, but it can be reached easily enough from a path at the top of the forest, to which all routes up the hill from the shore of Ladybower Reservoir west of the site of* **Ashop Farm** *seem inexorably to lead.*

The main bridleway from Hope Cross down to Fulwood Stile Lane is marked on the OS map as being the line of a **Roman Road** thought to link the forts at Navio (in Brough) and Ardotalia (near Glossop). In fact the deeply incised holloway to the west traces the packhorse route of **Doctor's Gate** *(see p50)*, which is far more likely to follow the line of the Roman Road. Ghostly Roman legionnaires have reportedly been seen marching along across Win Hill and near Longdendale, always visible only from the knees up.

The apparently benign shoulders of Win Hill have claimed their fair share of casualties over the years. A grazier and his maidservant died in a snowstorm in 1674, while someone perished there as recently as the winter of 1979.

a twite

The small brown **twite** is an increasingly rare migrant visitor to the Peak District. It nests on moorland and feeds on grassland seeds around the edge of the moors.

Win Hill massif forms a high ridge between Win Hill Pike and Hope Cross. The main route is a wide, braided path along the top of **Hope Brink***, but another narrower path forks off north around* **Thornhill Brink***. It is particularly faint at its eastern end, where it bears off between a pair of boundary stones beneath the summit. Another faint path follows the edge of the forest to the north, though it has few of the views of the other routes.*

MAP 22: WIN HILL

Win Hill forms a natural objective from Ladybower Reservoir or the Hope Valley, its rocky summit pimple visible from all directions and thus providing one of the finest vantage points in the whole Peak. Though Ladybower's long arms prevent ready access from the A57, it is easily climbed from Yorkshire Bridge, Thornhill and Hope, to which it presents its softer grassy side. Its dark northern face is cloaked in dense forest, but should not be ignored, for there is a warren of paths to be found here.

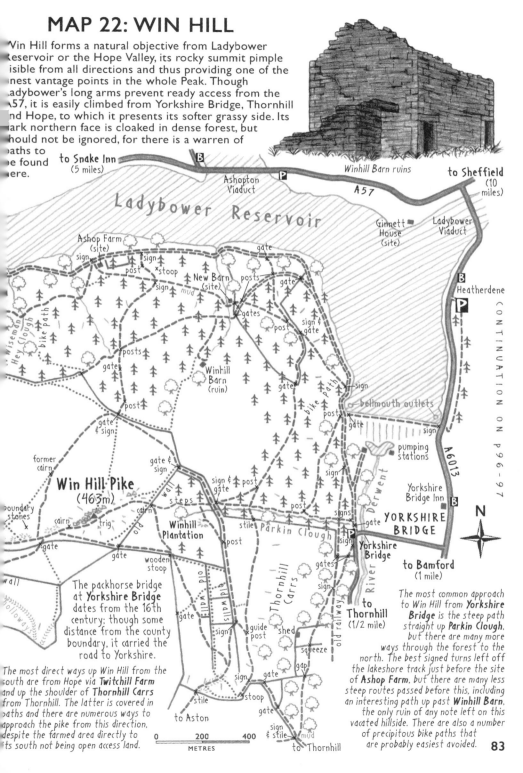

Winhill Barn ruins

to Snake Inn
(5 miles)

to Sheffield
(10 miles)

Ashopton Viaduct

A57

Ladybower Reservoir

Ginnett House (site)

Ladybower Viaduct

Ashop Farm (site)

sign

gate

New Barn (site)

posts

gate

post

Heatherdene

stoop

sign

mud

gates

sign & gate

CONTINUATION ON p96-97

Wiseman Hey Clough

bike path

posts

gate

Winhill Barn (ruin)

post

gate & sign

gate

bike path

sign

bellmouth outlets

post

gate

sign

former cairn

gate & sign

sign & gate

post

pumping stations

A6013

River Derwent

Yorkshire Bridge Inn

Win Hill Pike
(463m)

steps

cairn

sign & gate

post

signs

gate

YORKSHIRE BRIDGE

boundary stones

cairn

trig

Winhill Plantation

stile

Parkin Clough

sign

Yorkshire Bridge

N

gate

wooden stoop

post

gates

to Bamford
(1 mile)

wall

holloway

gate

wall

walls

Thornhill Carrs

sign

to Thornhill
(1/2 mile)

old railway

gate

guide post

shed

squeeze

gap

The packhorse bridge at **Yorkshire Bridge** dates from the 16th century; though some distance from the county boundary, it carried the road to Yorkshire.

The most direct ways up Win Hill from the south are from Hope via **Twitchill Farm** and up the shoulder of **Thornhill Carrs** from Thornhill. The latter is covered in paths and there are numerous ways to approach the pike from this direction, despite the farmed area directly to its south not being open access land.

sign

stile

stoop

to Aston

gate

sign & stile

mud

to Thornhill

0   200   400
METRES

The most common approach to Win Hill from **Yorkshire Bridge** is the steep path straight up **Parkin Clough**, but there are many more ways through the forest to the north. The best signed turns left off the lakeshore track just before the site of **Ashop Farm**, but there are many less steep routes passed before this, including an interesting route path up past **Winhill Barn**, the only ruin of any note left on this vacated hillside. There are also a number of precipitous bike paths that are probably easiest avoided.

83

Hope (its name simply meaning 'valley') is one of the oldest villages in Derbyshire, pre-dating the Domesday Book. It stood at a junction of ancient routes, including the Portway, the major north-south trading route, and its parish once covered two thirds of the Peak Forest.

⑥ Through a gate, turn left and follow the track in front of Upper Fulwood Farm. Just before **Bagshaw Bridge**, cut through a gate to the left and follow the river to a gate on the edge of a narrow wood. The path winds along the river bank (gorge-like in places), becoming more obvious but muddier as it nears the road and railway. Turn left on Edale Road and then right towards **Normans Farm** immediately beyond the railway. Nearing the cluster of phone boxes and interesting artefacts by the farm, bear left onto a path along a fenceline above the river bank.

Hope Churchyard Cross

St Peter's Church dates from the 14th century but was built on the site of earlier churches. On its south side is the shaft of a 9th- or 10th-century Saxon cross known as the **Hope Churchyard Cross**. The lavishly ornate stone was defaced during the Reformation, hidden in the fabric of the school during the Civil War, and only discovered when it was pulled down in 1858. Alongside is an old marked cross and, on the other side of the church, stands the **Eccles Cross**, which marked a place of worship on Eccles Hill to the south of the village.

❶ From the centre of **Hope**, turn into Edale Road opposite St Peter's Church. After 1/4 mile fork right down Bowden Lane (signed towards Hope Cemetery), then turn right again immediately beyond Killhill Bridge. The track reaches the **Old Mill** (formerly a flour mill), beyond which the path is signed up some steps and along the edge of the field. After the metal gate, turn left to pass under the railway, then head diagonally up the field beyond towards **Farfield Farm**.

⑤ The path continues along the broad ridge, soon joining the edge of the large plantation. The fort-like summit of **Wooler Knoll** stands just in the trees and can be detoured to by turning first right to a gate and then cutting left through the thin plantation. After half a mile along the forest edge, fork left and descend to a large track. Bear left down the wall, crossing a deep holloway that may be that of the **Roman Road**, and descend off the moor via a gate at the bottom, joining another path to reach **Upper Fulwood Farm**.

The tiny beauty salon on Edale Road in Hope is housed in one of the metal shacks rescued from **Tin Town** at Birchinlee, where navvies lived during the construction of the Derwent Valley reservoirs.

❼ Beyond a stile the path along the river opens out, but is not always obvious as it does not trace every meander in the stream. Avoid bearing down the bank to the left but keep straight on along the line of an old hedgerow. After crossing a shallow ford, you soon reach the first of a series of stiles and gates that lead you past the elegant spa at **Losehill House**. Carry on across the grassy meadows close to the stream to eventually join Townhead Lane. Follow this down to Edale Road, which leads right back into **Hope**, handily passing the Cheshire Cheese Inn on the way.

trough by Normans Farm

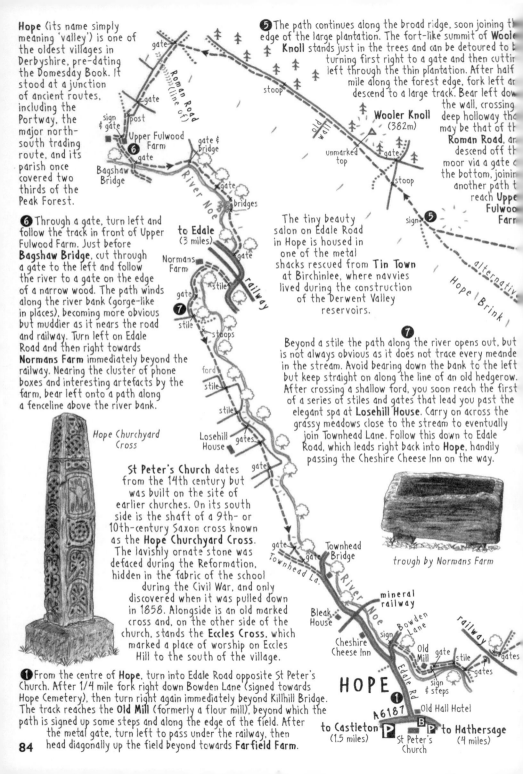

84

ROUTE 13: WIN HILL FROM HOPE

❹ Descend steeply off **Win Hill Pike** along the ridge. Soon after another large path crosses, bear right on a faint path that passes between a pair of small boundary stones. The narrow path arcs around **Thornhill Brink** with good views over Ladybower Reservoir. Beyond a tied gate, it aims left of a low nameless knoll to rejoin the main path.

Alternative Route: If it is wet and you don't want to push through soggy heather, or you don't wish to climb over the gate in the middle, the obvious main path to the south can be followed all the way instead, but I think the described route is slightly more interesting.

Distance: 7 miles (11.5km)

Ascent: 300m

Difficulty: Easy

Parking: Pay & display village car park in Hope, free parking by St Peter's Church and along Edale Road.

Public Transport: Hope is on the Hope Valley railway line between Sheffield and Manchester (the station is less than half a mile from the route), and is served by the regular 271/272/273/274 buses from Sheffield.

Character: A simple loop up onto Win Hill from the villages of Hope and Aston and back along the delightful River Noe. There are wonderful views from the top, and this is a very tame and well-trodden moor so the paths are relatively straightforward to follow throughout.

❸ Reaching a stile onto the edge of the moor, continue straight on up the bank. Keep left at an obvious fork and follow a lovely grassy path up to a wooden stoop above **Winhill Plantation**. Carry straight on here towards the right-hand side of the rocky summit of **Win Hill Pike**. It is a simple climb up the main path to the trig and one of the finest vantage points in the Peak District.

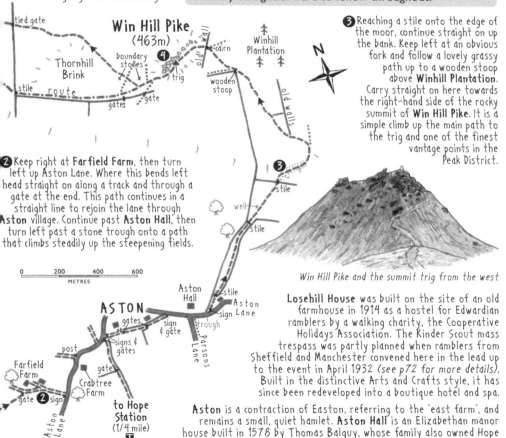

Win Hill Pike and the summit trig from the west

❷ Keep right at **Farfield Farm**, then turn left up Aston Lane. Where this bends left head straight on along a track and through a gate at the end. This path continues in a straight line to rejoin the lane through **Aston** village. Continue past **Aston Hall**, then turn left past a stone trough onto a path that climbs steadily up the steepening fields.

If starting the route at **Hope Station** (not on map), it is over half a mile along the main road to reach Hope village. It is easier to cross the footbridge by the station and follow a path along the edge of the fields. This climbs steadily to join the route on Aston Lane after a little over 1/4 mile.

Losehill House was built on the site of an old farmhouse in 1914 as a hostel for Edwardian ramblers by a walking charity, the Cooperative Holidays Association. The Kinder Scout mass trespass was partly planned when ramblers from Sheffield and Manchester convened here in the lead up to the event in April 1932 (see p72 for more details). Built in the distinctive Arts and Crafts style, it has since been redeveloped into a boutique hotel and spa.

Aston is a contraction of Easton, referring to the 'east farm', and remains a small, quiet hamlet. **Aston Hall** is an Elizabethan manor house built in 1578 by Thomas Balguy, whose family also owned Hope Hall and Derwent Hall. **Hope Hall** is now the Old Hall Hotel, which became an inn in 1730, and a weekly cattle market was held in what is now the car park from 1715 until the Foot and Mouth outbreak in 2001. **Derwent Hall**, now drowned beneath Ladybower Reservoir, was built in 1672 by Henry Balguy, who it is said hid his gold hoard here when Charles II declared the nation bankrupt.

85

PEAT GETTING

The word peat is derived from the Middle English word *pete*, referring to a cut piece of peat. Organised peat cutting for fuel is likely to have taken place since the Iron Age, but peat may have been used as early as the Neolithic era for creating the large peat barrow on Margery Hill. As fuel, peat from the base of the peat deposits burns almost as well as coal and far better than wood, the limited supplies of which were therefore reserved for industry and construction. Peat could also be made into peat charcoal for use in lime kilns and the lead and iron smelting industries, as well as used for medieval buildings, insulating roofs, cattle bedding and ash-based fertiliser. Hence it represented one of most important resources in the poor rural areas in which it was usually found.

The peat-cutting process was laborious work and usually undertaken during the summer months. First the growing turf (or top sod) was cut away in rectangular blocks and laid carefully so that it could be replaced to maintain grazing land. The peat turfs themselves were then cut in regular blocks, originally with wooden spades and later metal ones, then laid on end to dry, before being stacked carefully to finish the drying process. Once dried, they were carted or taken by sled to the adjacent settlements. In some cases the family pulled the cart themselves, but these were generally horse-drawn, making use of deep holloways cut through the moor edge. The paths down from turbary grounds were known as turf gates; the zigzag routes were used by carts while the steeper direct lines were sledways. Sometimes these are named on maps; Peat Lane runs down from Peat Moor near Grindslow Knoll, Dry Gully descends from Ringing Roger and the route down Grindsbrook Clough into Edale is known as Sled Road.

Each village had their own legally defined peat pits or turbary grounds where any commoner could cut peat – turbary was the traditional legal right to gather peat. Hope's peat pits were at Crookstone Out Moor, while those on Win Hill were used by Aston, Thornhill and the Woodlands Valley. As it is surrounded by so many settlements, it is thought the peat on Win Hill was among the earliest to be exploited, possibly even by the Romans stationed at the fort near Brough, hence its rather denuded appearance today. There are well-defined holloways leading up to the turbary grounds on the ridge from all sides, and these can be seen on Thornhill Carrs, Hope Brink and in the forest to the north.

Sometimes peat areas were closely controlled with defined turbary areas for each individual, in other places it would have been more of a free-for-all, with fights over particular sites. Some cuttings were in large-scale open-cast workings and others were linear, like those along Black Dike and several other long boundary ditches that are particularly well seen across Bleaklow. Peat Moor above Broadlee Bank Tor was one of Edale's most exploited peat grounds, with the peat almost entirely dug out. It was divided into three turbaries for the surrounding booths, from which deep holloways scale the hill's flank on all sides.

Peat cutting continued until the late 19th century and, even when cheap coal could be easily imported by rail and turnpike roads, poor households relied on it for their fuel. Large parts of the Peak District have seen almost complete removal of the peat layer down to the mineral soil, resulting in defined banks at the edges of these areas. The untouched peat remains covered in heather, while those exploited areas are characterised by grasses like molinia (purple moor grass) and nardus (matgrass). It is estimated that well over 50 million cubic metres of peat have been removed from the Peak District's moors, most of it during the medieval period. Large-scale peat removal has shaped the landscape of a great proportion of the moors up to 500m, causing great deterioration of the peat and limiting the continued growth of peat-forming sphagnum.

peat stacked for drying

CHAPTER 9 – ABNEY, OFFERTON & EYAM MOORS

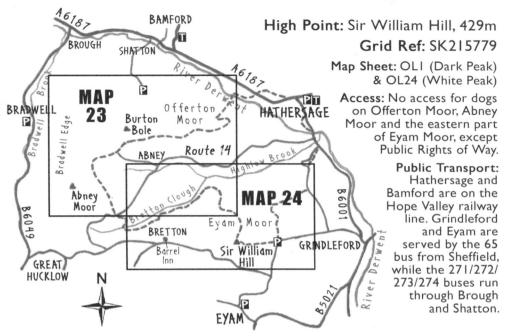

High Point: Sir William Hill, 429m

Grid Ref: SK215779

Map Sheet: OL1 (Dark Peak) & OL24 (White Peak)

Access: No access for dogs on Offerton Moor, Abney Moor and the eastern part of Eyam Moor, except Public Rights of Way.

Public Transport: Hathersage and Bamford are on the Hope Valley railway line. Grindleford and Eyam are served by the 65 bus from Sheffield, while the 271/272/273/274 buses run through Brough and Shatton.

This piecemeal collection of moors forms a natural lump of high ground separated from the Eastern Moors by the River Derwent and from Win Hill by the Hope Valley. It is the last hurrah of the gritstone moors, for its steep western and southern flanks look across the great limestone tableland of the White Peak. The three moors of Abney, Offerton and Eyam are connected by an arc of high ground around the head of beautiful Bretton Clough, but the gliding club at Camphill on Durham Edge and other large enclosed areas mean that much of it is not publicly accessible. My maps focus on those areas that are accessible, including the access land along Bretton Clough itself.

The highest point is at Sir William Hill, sometimes referred to as the Parnassus of the Peak because Eyam (its name relating to a 'water place') was known as the Athens of the Peak. Tragic but unspoilt, Eyam can be considered the last gritstone village, while nearby Great Hucklow and Bradwell are built from limestone. Different corners of the moor are most easily accessed from Hathersage, Bradwell and Eyam, but the path network is less helpful from Grindleford, Shatton and Great Hucklow.

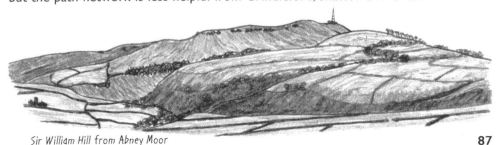

Sir William Hill from Abney Moor

MAP 23: ABNEY & OFFERTON MOORS

Abney, Offerton and Shatton Moors form a series of moorland parcels overlooking the Hope Valley that just about connect together. Though the high points at Abney Moor and Burton Bole are either inaccessible or incidental, it is an area readily accessible from Hathersage, Shatton, Bradwell and Abney, giving easy walking and some grand views towards the Dark Peak.

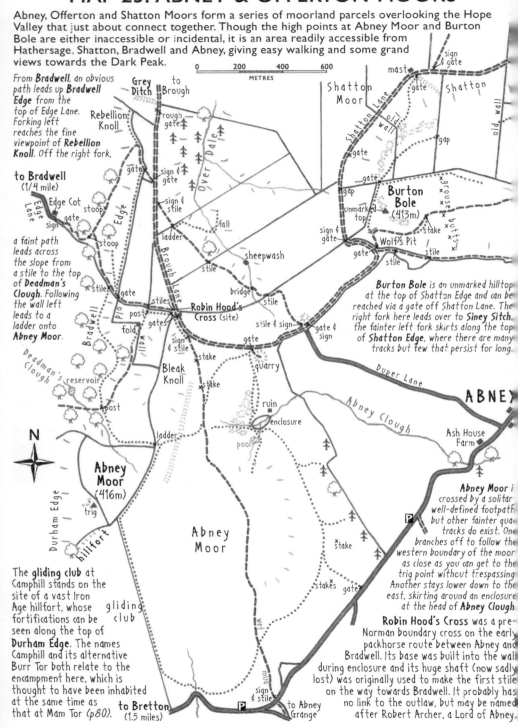

From **Bradwell**, an obvious path leads up **Bradwell Edge** from the top of Edge Lane. Forking left reaches the fine viewpoint of **Rebellion Knoll**. Off the right fork,

a faint path leads across the slope from a stile to the top of **Deadman's Clough**. Following the wall left leads to a ladder onto **Abney Moor**.

The **gliding club** at Camphill stands on the site of a vast Iron Age hillfort, whose fortifications can be seen along the top of **Durham Edge**. The names Camphill and its alternative Burr Tor both relate to the encampment here, which is thought to have been inhabited at the same time as that at Mam Tor (p80).

Burton Bole is an unmarked hilltop at the top of Shatton Edge and can be reached via a gate off Shatton Lane. The right fork here leads over to **Siney Sitch**, the fainter left fork skirts along the top of **Shatton Edge**, where there are many tracks but few that persist for long.

Abney Moor i crossed by a solitar well-defined footpath but other fainter qua tracks do exist. One branches off to follow the western boundary of the moor as close as you can get to the trig point without trespassing Another stays lower down to the east, skirting around an enclosure at the head of **Abney Clough**

Robin Hood's Cross was a pre-Norman boundary cross on the early packhorse route between Abney and Bradwell. Its base was built into the wall during enclosure and its huge shaft (now sadly lost) was originally used to make the first stile on the way towards Bradwell. It probably has no link to the outlaw, but may be named after Robert Archer, a Lord of Abney.

Map labels:
Grey Ditch — to Brough — Rebellion Knoll — rough gate — Over Dale — Shatton Moor — Shatton Lane — old wall — mast — sign & gate — gate — gap — Shatton — old wall — to Bradwell (1/4 mile) — Edge Cot — Edge Lane — stoop — gate — sign — sign & gate — sign & stile — Edge — ladder — Brough Lane — fall — sheepwash — bridge — stile — gate — gate — Burton Bole (413m) — unmarked top — sign & gate — Wolf's Pit — gate — stile — stile — grouse butts — stake — Deadman's Clough — reservoir — stoop — gate — post — fold — gates — stiles — Bradwell Pig Hill — Robin Hood's Cross (site) — sign & stile — stake — Bleak Knoll — stake — stile & sign — gate & sign — quarry — Duper Lane — ladder — post — ladder — ruin — enclosure — pool — Abney Clough — ABNEY — Ash House Farm — N — Abney Moor (416m) — trig — hillfort — Durham Edge — gliding club — Abney Moor — stake — stakes — gate — wet — mud — sign & stile — P — to Bretton (1.5 miles) — to Abney Grange

Scale: 0 200 400 600 METRES

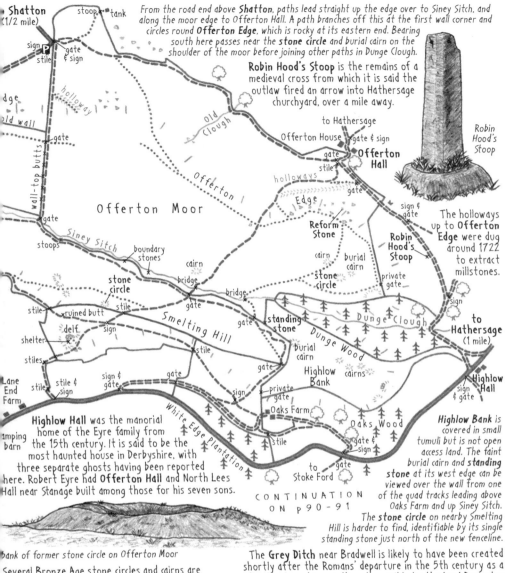

From the road end above **Shatton**, paths lead straight up the edge over to Siney Sitch, and along the moor edge to Offerton Hall. A path branches off this at the first wall corner and circles round **Offerton Edge**, which is rocky at its eastern end. Bearing south here passes near the **stone circle** and burial cairn on the shoulder of the moor before joining other paths in Dunge Clough.

Shatton
(1/2 mile)

stoop · tank

sign
P
gate
& sign
stile

ge
old wall

gate

holloway

wall-top butts

gate

Old Clough

Offerton Edge

Offerton Moor

Siney Sitch

stoops

boundary stones

cairn

bridge

stone circle

bridge

stile · ruined butt · stile

delf
sign
shelter
stiles
stile & sign

Lane End Farm

mping barn

White Edge Plantation

Smelting Hill

gate

gate

Reform Stone

cairn

burial cairn

stone circle

standing stone

burial cairn

Dunge Clough

Dunge Wood

Highlow Bank

cairns

private gate

Oaks Farm

gate
sign

stile

to Stoke Ford

gate

Oaks Wood

gate & sign

sign & gate

Highlow Hall

Robin Hood's Stoop is the remains of a medieval cross from which it is said the outlaw fired an arrow into Hathersage churchyard, over a mile away.

to Hathersage

Offerton House

gate & sign

Offerton Hall

gate
stile

holloways

gate

sign & gate

Robin Hood's Stoop

private gate

sign

to **Hathersage** (1 mile)

Robin Hood's Stoop

The holloways up to **Offerton Edge** were dug around 1722 to extract millstones.

Highlow Bank is covered in small tumuli but is not open access land. The faint burial cairn and **standing stone** at its west edge can be viewed over the wall from one of the quad tracks leading above Oaks Farm and up Siney Sitch. The **stone circle** on nearby Smelting Hill is harder to find, identifiable by its single standing stone just north of the new fenceline.

Highlow Hall was the manorial home of the Eyre family from the 15th century. It is said to be the most haunted house in Derbyshire, with three separate ghosts having been reported here. Robert Eyre had **Offerton Hall** and North Lees Hall near Stanage built among those for his seven sons.

CONTINUATION ON p90-91

bank of former stone circle on Offerton Moor

Several Bronze Age stone circles and cairns are scattered across **Offerton Moor**, though none are particularly clear. The stone circle above Dunge Clough had its stones removed some time since the 18th century, leaving a 25m diameter oval bank. 50m away is a robbed burial cairn, into whose side a shooting butt has been dug. **Abney Moor** seems surprisingly empty in comparison, though there are a couple of barrows on the grounds of the adjacent gliding club. It also once boasted a remarkable barrow surrounded by upright stones, in which were discovered cremated human bones, jet beads and an arrowhead. Unfortunately this is said to have been destroyed for the construction of walls during the scourge of Parliamentary enclosure.

The **Grey Ditch** near Bradwell is likely to have been created shortly after the Romans' departure in the 5th century as a frontier boundary earthwork, possibly by the local Pecsaetan tribe. It was probably only a temporary boundary between the Britons and the advancing Angles, and may later have served as part of the boundary between Northumbria and Mercia. It runs for a mile across Bradwell Brook and defended approaches to the Hope Valley. Grey in this case may be a corruption of *har*, relating to a boundary. **Rebellion Knoll** and **Deadman's Clough** are other curious names on Bradwell Edge that may be related to a 7th-century battle which is usually said to have been fought on the slopes of Win Hill but makes more sense here.

boundary stone, Siney Sitch

89

MAP 24: EYAM MOOR & BRETTON CLOUGH

Eyam Moor is a small but intriguing area of moorland on the northern flank of Sir William Hill. It is home to a wonderful array of prehistoric sites, but is loath to reveal its secrets amid its thick heather and bracken. Bretton Clough, while not strictly moorland, is mostly designated open access land and lies along the foot of Eyam Moor. It is a beautiful wooded valley beneath a series of steep knolls and, at its western end, possesses a series of magnificent landslip features rising like volcanic cones from the valley floor. Both areas are easily accessed from Sir William Hill Road to the south or the road through Abney to the north, though Bretton Clough has more in the way of clear paths.

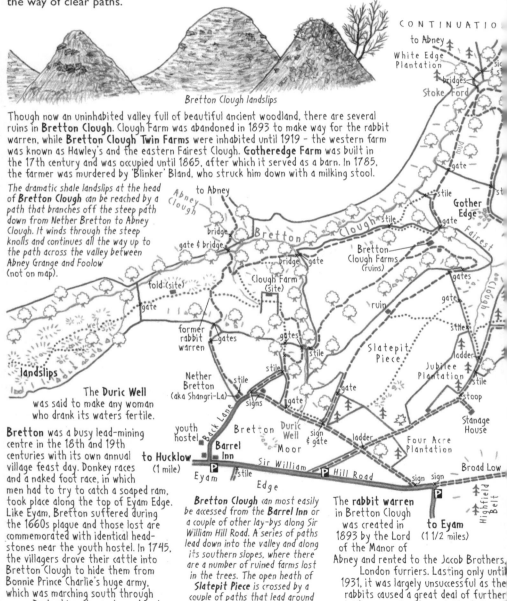

Bretton Clough landslips

Though now an uninhabited valley full of beautiful ancient woodland, there are several ruins in **Bretton Clough**. Clough Farm was abandoned in 1893 to make way for the rabbit warren, while **Bretton Clough Twin Farms** were inhabited until 1919 - the western farm was known as Hawley's and the eastern Fairest Clough. **Gotheredge Farm** was built in the 17th century and was occupied until 1865, after which it served as a barn. In 1785, the farmer was murdered by 'Blinker' Bland, who struck him down with a milking stool.

*The dramatic shale landslips at the head of **Bretton Clough** can be reached by a path that branches off the steep path down from Nether Bretton to Abney Clough. It winds through the steep knolls and continues all the way up to the path across the valley between Abney Grange and Foolow (not on map).*

The Duric Well
was said to make any woman
who drank its waters fertile.

Bretton was a busy lead-mining centre in the 18th and 19th centuries with its own annual village feast day. Donkey races and a naked foot race, in which men had to try to catch a soaped ram, took place along the top of Eyam Edge. Like Eyam, Bretton suffered during the 1660s plague and those lost are commemorated with identical headstones near the youth hostel. In 1745, the villagers drove their cattle into Bretton Clough to hide them from Bonnie Prince Charlie's huge army, which was marching south through Derbyshire. It was turned back just a few days later in Derby.

*Bretton Clough can most easily be accessed from the **Barrel Inn** or a couple of other lay-bys along Sir William Hill Road. A series of paths lead down into the valley and along its southern slopes, where there are a number of ruined farms lost in the trees. The open heath of **Slatepit Piece** is crossed by a couple of paths that lead around the head of **Fairest Clough** and onto the edge of Eyam Moor.*

The **rabbit warren** in Bretton Clough was created in 1893 by the Lord of the Manor of Abney and rented to the Jacob Brothers, London furriers. Lasting only until 1931, it was largely unsuccessful as the rabbits caused a great deal of further subsidence on already unstable shale and killed the valley's hazel and rowan trees.

90

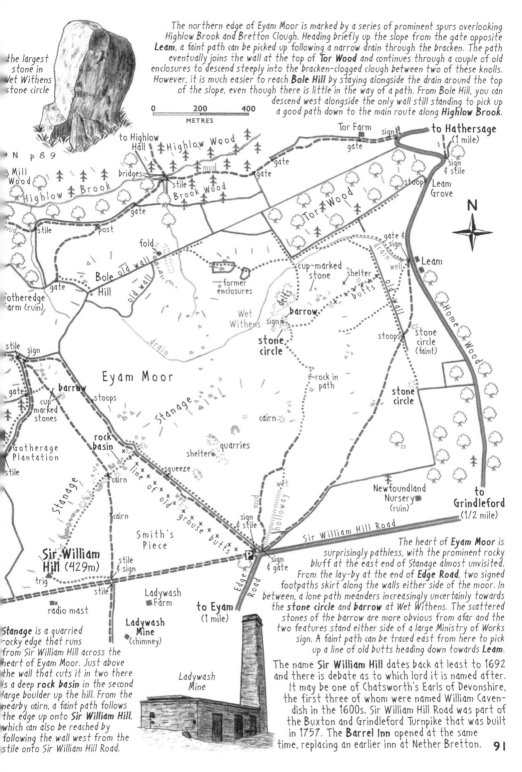

the largest stone in Wet Withens stone circle

The northern edge of Eyam Moor is marked by a series of prominent spurs overlooking Highlow Brook and Bretton Clough. Heading briefly up the slope from the gate opposite **Leam**, a faint path can be picked up following a narrow drain through the bracken. The path eventually joins the wall at the top of **Tor Wood** and continues through a couple of old enclosures to descend steeply into the bracken-clogged clough between two of these knolls. However, it is much easier to reach **Bole Hill** by staying alongside the drain around the top of the slope, even though there is little in the way of a path. From Bole Hill, you can descend west alongside the only wall still standing to pick up a good path down to the main route along **Highlow Brook**.

0   200   400
METRES

N p 89

to Highlow Hall

Highlow Wood

Mill Wood

Highlow Brook

bridges

mud

stile

Brook Wood

gate

gate

Tor Farm

sign

to Hathersage
(1 mile)

gate

sign & stile

stoops

Leam Grove

Tor Wood

N

gate

post

stile

mud

fold

old wall

former enclosures

cup-marked stone

shelter

butts

gate & sign

drain

well

Leam

Bole Hill

old wall

Fotheredge Farm (ruin)

gate

dels

Wet Withens

sign

barrow

stone circle

old wall

Home Wood

stoops

stone circle (faint)

stile

sign

Eyam Moor

barrow

cup-marked stones

stoops

Stanage

rock in path

cairn

stone circle

Gotherage Plantation

stile

rock basin

cairn

squeeze

shelter

quarries

line of old

wet

grouse butts

mud

holloway

Newfoundland Nursery (ruin)

to Grindleford
(1/2 mile)

Stanage

cairn

Smith's Piece

sign & stile

P

sign & gate

Sir William Hill Road

Sir William Hill (429m)

stile & sign

trig

stile

radio mast

Ladywash Farm

Edge Road

to Eyam
(1 mile)

Stanage is a quarried rocky edge that runs from Sir William Hill across the heart of Eyam Moor. Just above the wall that cuts it in two there is a deep **rock basin** in the second large boulder up the hill. From the nearby **cairn**, a faint path follows the edge up onto **Sir William Hill**, which can also be reached by following the wall west from the stile onto Sir William Hill Road.

Ladywash Mine (chimney)

Ladywash Mine

The heart of **Eyam Moor** is surprisingly pathless, with the prominent rocky bluff at the east end of Stanage almost unvisited. From the lay-by at the end of **Edge Road**, two signed footpaths skirt along the walls either side of the moor. In between, a lone path meanders increasingly uncertainly towards the **stone circle** and **barrow** at Wet Withens. The scattered stones of the barrow are more obvious from afar and the two features stand either side of a large Ministry of Works sign. A faint path can be traced east from here to pick up a line of old butts heading down towards **Leam**.

The name **Sir William Hill** dates back at least to 1692 and there is debate as to which lord it is named after. It may be one of Chatsworth's Earls of Devonshire, the first three of whom were named William Cavendish in the 1600s. Sir William Hill Road was part of the Buxton and Grindleford Turnpike that was built in 1757. The **Barrel Inn** opened at the same time, replacing an earlier inn at Nether Bretton.

91

ROUTE 14: OFFERTON, ABNEY & EYAM MOOR

Distance: 11½ miles (18.5km)

Ascent: 580m

Difficulty: Moderate

Parking: Pay car parks in Hathersage. Free parking at Hathersage railway station and along Jaggers Lane, as well as lay-bys on Sir William Hill Road and near Abney village.

Public Transport: Hathersage is on the Hope Valley railway line between Sheffield & Manchester.

Character: A fine walk that combines the three moors of this massif with the charming woods and landslips of Bretton Clough. The route takes in most of the stone circles and other prehistoric features that characterise these moors, as well as the high point of Sir William Hill.

Note: Dogs are allowed only on Public Rights of Way on these moors, but can be taken if the alternative route is followed across Eyam Moor.

❷ Across the **stepping stones**, head straight on u the hill towards **Offerton Hall** on a clear path acro the fields. Join the track to pass between Offerto House and Hall, then turn right at the second of tw paths on the bend (at the stile not the gate). Follo the line steeply up onto **Offerton Edge**, forking let to join a path along its crest. By a rock near the fo end, turn right on a grassy quad track - where there the small mound of a tumulus on the right (you can head left for 100m to the clear earth ring (not th closer heap of stones) of a **stone circle** and a ring cairn alongside. The grass track continues across Sin Sitch to a gate, just to the left of which a cross-marked **standing stone** is embedded in the wall corn

rock basin on Eyam Moor

The name **Wolf's Pit** is intriguing, possibly relating to a place where wolves were trapped prior to or during their extermination by Edward I in the 13th century.

❸ Turn right along the wall as far as the next gate, then head le across **Offerton Moor**. Just before the crest, bear right on a faint pa that winds up the gentle shoulder, passing near another stone circle (identified by i solitary remaining stone). The path joins the main path along the edge of the moor a passes below the unmarked high point of **Burton Bole** to reach a vehicle track. Follow th left, passing the junction with Duper Lane, then turn left through a gate onto **Abney Moo** Keep right to head up the slope and join the main route heading left across the moor. the gate is locked you can continue to the next stile and follow this path instea

❹ The path descends to the road at the far side of **Abney Moor** Head straight across and join the lane leading down to **Abney Grange**. Just before the building turn right at a stile and follow the path down the wall into **Bretton Clough**. Across the leaning bridge (hang on!), bear left up to a gate and join a lovely pat winding through the dramatic **landslips** above the clough. Finally reaching a path junction, turn left down towards the stream and after 150m double back right to cross a side stream. Keep left on this path through the trees to drop down to a gate. The path continues along the fenceline before bearing left over a stile to pick its way across a steep bank and descend to **Fairest Clough**. Over the stream bear right up to a stile and, soon after, join a larger path continuing down the clough.

Sir William Hill mast

The ancient **landslips in Bretton Clough** are some of the most spectacular in the Peak, forming a series of steep sugarloaf hills rising uncannily from the valley floor. It would be easy to assume this was the rabbit warren, but that **92** was located further east.

cup and ring marked stone on Eyam Moor

FROM HATHERSAGE

The stepping stones across the River Derwent were laid in 1509 on an important trading route to Sheffield, but are far more liable to be inundated now than ever before. This was the inadvertent result of efforts by the council to realign the stones and make passage across them safer.

1 There are alternative routes out of **Hathersage** to start the walk, depending on whether you think the stepping stones will be passable. Assuming dry summer weather, follow the B6001 right into town from the station and main car park. Turn left onto the main road by the **George Hotel**, then fork right up Jaggers Lane (unsigned). At the end of the houses, turn left on a footpath across the railway. Head straight across the main road beyond and drop down the slope to follow the **River Derwent** for a quarter of a mile to the stepping stones.

Alternative Route: If it is or has been wet, play it safe and head left out of town on the B6001 for half a mile. Across **Leadmill Bridge**, turn right and follow the path alongside the River Derwent. Keep right by the river, passing through **Goose Nest Wood** and joining a fenced path all the way to the side of the stepping stones.

5 Follow the muddy path down through the trees and take the first path right, pulling steeply up onto a shoulder and doubling back to **Gother Edge** with fine views back over Bretton Clough. After the second stile, take the middle of three paths heading up onto **Eyam Moor** past a striking **ring cairn** and cup-marked stone. At a cairn on the crest, turn right and follow a faint path along the edge towards the trig point on **Sir William Hill**. Head left down towards the track, following the wall until a stile allows access to it. Follow the track left to reach the junction with **Sir William Hill Road**.

Abney Grange was granted to the Cistercian monks of Rufford Abbey in Nottinghamshire, but the name Abney relates to 'Abba's land'.

Wet Withens stone circle is over 30m in diameter with a low ring around it. 10 stones remain of what was once around 18. The barrow alongside was once vast, but like any of its stones were robbed in the 18th century.

7 Follow the road left from **Leam**, heading straight on at the sharp bend to drop down the bank and rejoin the road by **Hazelford Hall**. A path runs down the field alongside the lane; at the bottom, turn left along the B6001 back into **Hathersage**.

6 At the junction, turn left through the gate and follow a path to the left of an obvious groove across **Eyam Moor**. This becomes steadily fainter and jags left just after a boulder in the path, heading towards the vast ring of **Wet Withens stone circle** (the sign and a small mound just beyond it are more identifiable from a distance). There is no simple route off the moor from here, but a very faint line can be picked up in an east-north-east direction from the circle's most prominent stone. It soon bends left and joins a faint path along a line of old stone butts down to an old wall. Continue descending straight on through the rough bracken to reach the gate by **Leam**. If you don't wish to visit the stone circle, a simpler **alternative route** follows the more obvious path along the edge of the moor from Sir William Hill Road.

Map labels

to Bamford (2 miles)
stepping stones
Jaggers Lane
railway
ladders
stile
sign & gate
Coggers Lane
George Hotel
YHA
A6187
Little John
HATHERSAGE
railway
railway station
N
bridge
sign & gate
gate
River Derwent
alternative route
Offerton House
sign & gate
Offerton Hall
gate
stile
Offerton Edge
tumulus
cairn
stone circle
standing stone
gate
Nether Hall
gate & sign
gate
gate & sign
Leadmill Bridge
Goose Nest Wood
gate
barn
sign & gate
Plough Inn
sign & stile
gate
mud
to Grindleford (1.5 miles)
Hazelford Hall
stiles & signs
Tor Wood
stile & sign
Leam Farm
sign & gate
Leam
old wall
butts
stoops
alternative route
Stoke Ford
pond
stile
Gotheredge Farm (ruin)
stile
Gother Edge
sign
stile
ring cairn (& cup-marked stone)
Fairest Clough
barrow
sign
faint line
Wet Withens stone circle
rock in path
cairn
rock basin
cairn
Eyam Moor
groove
alternative route
Standage
Sir William Hill (429m)
trig
x mast
sign & stile
Sir William Hill Road
sign & gate
to Eyam (1 mile)

93

THE EYAM PLAGUE

'Struck by turns, in solitary pangs, They fell, unblest, unturned, and unmourned'
(James Thomson, *The Seasons*, 1730)

The village of Eyam is most closely associated with the plague which visited it in the 17th century and its inhabitants' selfless actions. The Black Death, transmitted to people from rats via fleas, had wiped out populations across Europe from the 14th century, but lesser plagues continued through the subsequent centuries. In 1632 Curbar, among several other places in Yorkshire and Derbyshire, was visited by a plague, but in 1664-65 a sixth of London's population died from a particularly virulent outbreak of the plague and it was this that arrived in Eyam towards the end of 1665.

In September 1665, Eyam was a busy village of around three hundred and fifty inhabitants. A few days after the local celebrations of Wakes Week, a box of old clothes arrived from London at Mrs Cooper's, a cottage near the church since known as the Plague House. When her lodger, George Viccars, opened the box, he thought the clothes damp and hung them by the fire to dry. He was a travelling tailor who had been making clothes for wakes week and the bundle was possibly sent by a relative who had picked the cloth up cheaply. He died within four days and other members of the household quickly followed. Several more died over the coming weeks and it was soon realised that this was the dreaded plague.

The plague largely abated during the winter months, though a few villagers were still struck down by it, so virulent was this strain. But by the following summer the disease reawakened with its full might. Many wanted to flee the village, but were persuaded by Revd William Mompesson to quarantine themselves, staying within the confines of the village, an area defined by certain wells, hills and streams. He had been in Eyam only for a short time when the plague arrived, so he relied on an appearance by the previous vicar, Revd Stanley, to gain the trust of the locals. The Earl of Devonshire at Chatsworth provided the villagers with food and other necessities as long as they stayed. Articles were left on the edge of the village, with coins left in disinfected water mixed with vinegar in troughs and wells. Most people knew to avoid the village, cutting it off as if it didn't exist, but a woodsman from Bubnell passed through. He happened to catch a cold that day and his neighbours, thinking it was the plague, threatened to shoot him until the Earl of Derbyshire's doctor arrived to save him.

After much pleading from his wife, Mompesson did send his own children away, as did some of the more wealthy inhabitants. Others hid in neighbouring hills and valleys, sitting out the summer isolated in makeshift huts. A Mr Merril lived for several weeks in a hut near the top of Sir William Hill with only a cockerel for company. When the cock returned home one day, it was a sign that the plague had run its course. However Bretton itself was also affected, with several families succumbing here and being buried in Bretton Clough.

Church assemblies were held outside in the Cucklet Delf to prevent further contagion, with Mompesson preaching from a natural arch there. The churchyard had

closed its gates by the end of June, so families had to bury their own dead in the fields. When the last fell or there was no-one fit for the task, a man named Marshall Howe undertook the duty (he remarkably lived until 1698). By October 1666, 85% of Eyam's population had been wiped out, but the plague never spread beyond the village. The last victim, Abraham Morton, died on 1st November, after which the village was overrun with hares, rabbits and game as there were so few people left. Revd Mompesson survived but, having buried his wife and infant, soon left for a post in Eakring, Nottinghamshire. His name lives on in the local placenames of Mompesson's Brook and Well, and a memorial is held every August at the Cucklet Church.

a gravestone in Eyam

CHAPTER 10 – STANAGE

High Point:
High Neb, 458m

Grid Ref: SK228853

Map Sheet: OL1 (Dark Peak)

Access: No access for dogs on northern sections (Maps 25 & 26), other than Public Rights of Way.

Public Transport: Hathersage and Bamford are on the Hope Valley railway line. Bus 51 runs from Sheffield to Lodge Moor, and buses 273 & 274 to Ladybower and Bamford.

Stanage has long been Sheffield's playground and is considered the birthplace of modern rock climbing, with the first climbs made here in the late 19th century. Despite the cliffs only being 25m high at their highest point near High Neb, they stretch almost unbroken for four miles with hundreds of technically challenging routes. Stanage (never Stanedge locally) simply means 'stone edge'.

Though Stanage Edge (and the shorter but equally dramatic Bamford Edge) are the defining features of this moor, they are surrounded by some fascinating areas of moorland. Hallam Moors previously formed part of Rivelin Chase and slope down to Wyming Brook and the Rivelin Dams, while Bamford Moor is covered in prehistoric circles, cairns and stones. It is easily explored from Lodge Moor, Ladybower, Bamford or Hathersage.

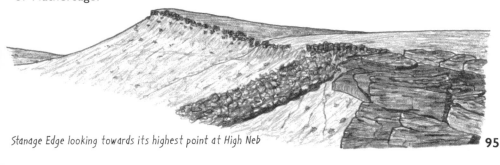

Stanage Edge looking towards its highest point at High Neb

MAP 25: STANAGE WEST (Bamford & Moscar Moors)

The northern end of Stanage Edge, crowned by its highest point on High Neb, looks out over a great plateau of moorland that ends overlooking Ladybower at the sudden rock faces of Bamford Edge. It is an intriguing area that appears so unassuming on the OS map, yet is littered with stone circles and other ancient sites and is surprisingly well trodden. Access is easy from all sides and it is an area well worth exploring.

The **7 Stones of Hordron** is an unusual freestanding stone circle (most in the area have a bank around them), though its stones number at least a dozen. The largest is known as the Fairy Stone and the site is associated with strange lights. Towards the south side of the moor there is another smaller circle with a raised bank. Nearby, the **Old Woman** is a beautifully fluted stone that once stood 8ft high, its hunched back thought to resemble an old woman. It now lies flat, having been tragically broken in the 1930s to prevent its use as a guide by ramblers. The **Moscar Stone** (also used as a way-marker) is marked CP as a civil parish boundary marker.

Bamford Edge can be accessed from the Heatherdene car park by a path straight up through the plantation. Beyond a stile at the top, bend left up the clough to emerge near a pair of sighting pillars (see p102). Another path climbs through the other end of **Woodlane Plantation** and ascends the edge through some beautiful old oaks.

Moscar Moor can most easily be accessed from the A57 via a good track by **Cutthroat Bridge** that leads below Hordron Edge to a series of grouse butts in **Jarvis Clough**. Another path follows Hordron Edge from a locked gate near Strines Lane End and joins it after passing the **7 Stones of Hordron** stone circle. Good paths continue across the clough and round to the tors of Bamford Edge, or along the line of butts heading left up towards **Stanage End** and joining the path below the edge.

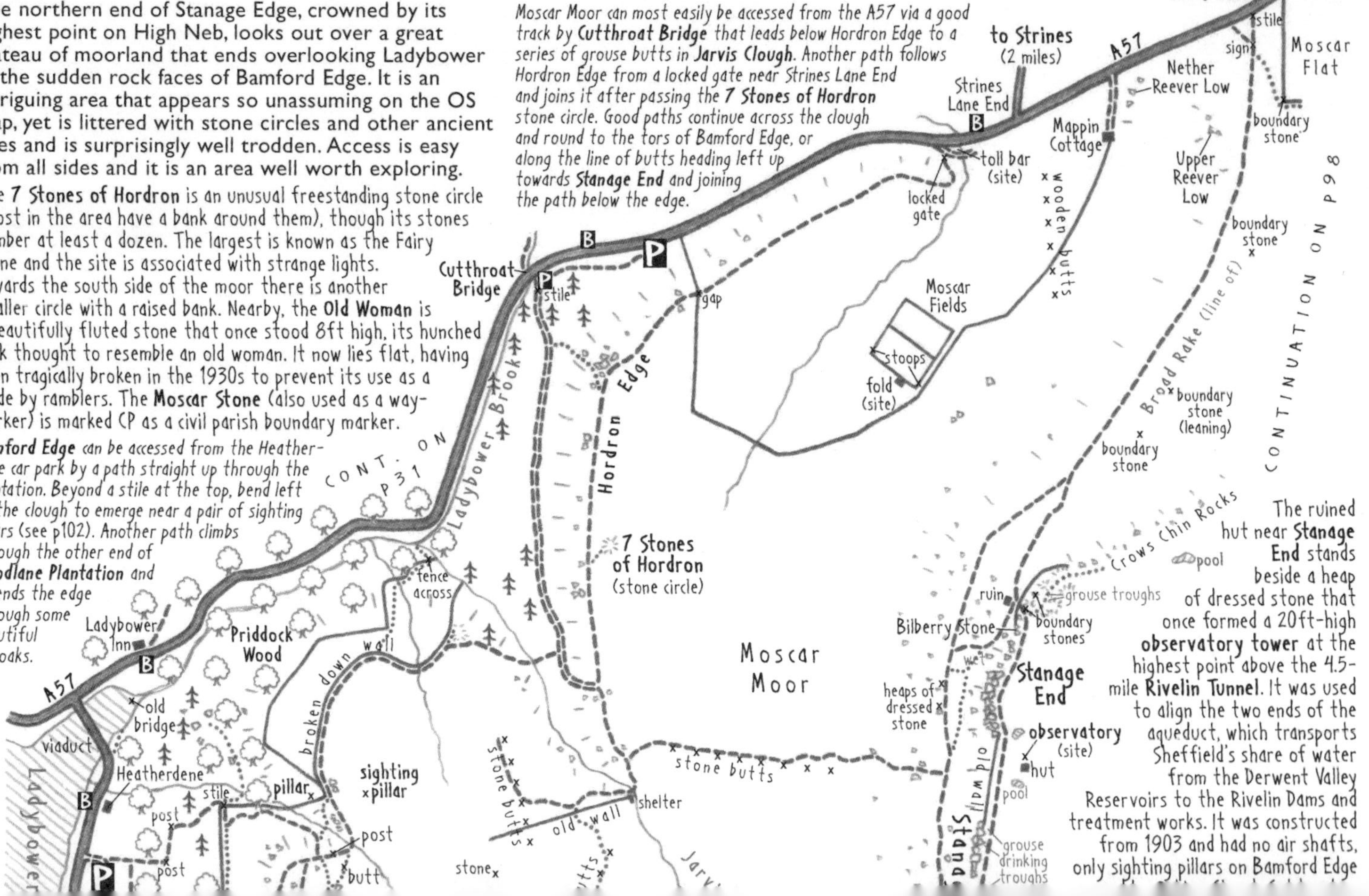

The ruined **Stanage End** stands beside a heap of dressed stone that once formed a 20ft-high **observatory tower** at the 4.5-highest point above the 4.5-mile **Rivelin Tunnel**. It was used to align the two ends of the aqueduct, which transports Sheffield's share of water from the Derwent Valley Reservoirs to the Rivelin Dams and treatment works. It was constructed from 1903 and had no air shafts, only sighting pillars on Bamford Edge.

Map labels:

to Crosspool (6 miles)
Moscar Flat
MOSCAR
to Moscar (6 miles)
CONTINUATION ON p98
stile
sign
boundary stone
Nether Reever Low
Upper Reever Low
A57
boundary stone
boundary stone (line of)
Broad Rake (line of)
boundary stone
boundary stone (leaning)
Cow's Chin Rocks
pool
grouse troughs
grouse troughs
observatory (site)
hut
grouse drinking troughs
old wall
Stanage End
Bilberry Stone
Boundary stones
heaps of dressed stone
ruin
Stana...
to Strines (2 miles)
Mappin Cottage
Strines Lane End
toll bar (site)
wooden butts
locked gate
Moscar Fields
stoops
fold (site)
Moscar Moor
stone butts
shelter
Jarv...
old wall
stone butts
stone
CONTINUATION
Hordron Edge
7 Stones of Hordron (stone circle)
gap
Cutthroat Bridge
Ladybower Brook
fence across
broken down wall
Priddock Wood
sighting pillar
pillar
post
butt
stile
Heatherdene
post
post
old bridge
Ladybower Inn
viaduct
A57
Ladybower

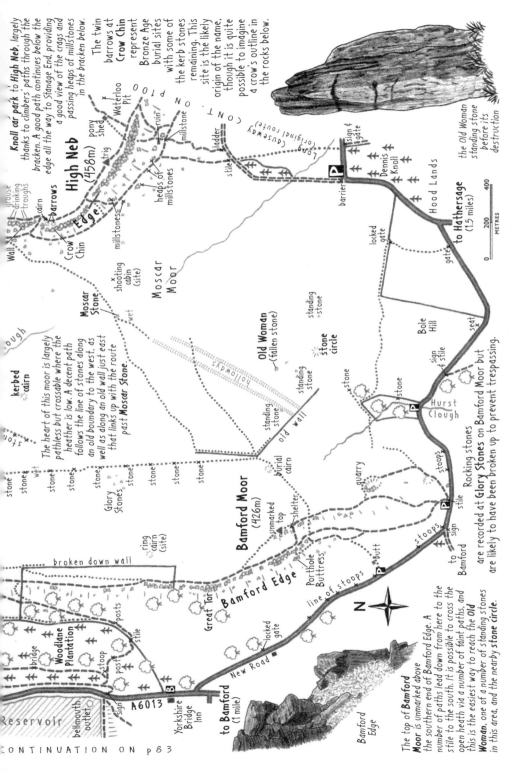

Knoll car park to High Neb, largely thanks to climbers' paths through the bracken. A good path continues below the edge all the way to Stanage End, providing a good view of the crags and passing heaps of millstones in the bracken below.

The twin barrows at **Crow Chin** represent Bronze Age burial sites with some of the kerb stones remaining. This site is the likely origin of the name, though it is quite possible to imagine a crow's outline in the rocks below.

the Old Woman standing stone before its destruction

Waterloo Pit

pony shed

ruin

millstone

ladder

stile

High Neb (458m)

trig

O P 1 0 0

L O N G

(C O N T . O N

Long (causeway) (original route)

grouse drinking troughs

Wall

cairn

barrows

Crow Chin

E d g e

heaps of millstones

millstones

millstones

P

barrier

sign & gate

sign & gate

Dennis Knoll

Hood Lands

to Hathersage
(1.5 miles)

locked gate

gate

0   200   400
METRES

Mosscar Moor

shooting cabin (site)

Mosscar Stone

wet

The heart of this moor is largely pathless but crossable where the heather is low. A decent path follows the line of stones along an old boundary to the west, as well as along an old wall just east that links up with the route past *Mosscar Stone.*

ough

kerbed cairn

stone

Old Woman (fallen stone)

hollows

standing stone

Stone circle

standing stone

Bole Hill

seat

stone

stone

x stone

Hurst Clough

standing stone

old wall

stoop x

stone

stone

stone x

stone x

stone

stone

stone

stone x

stone x

stone x

Glory Stones

wet

stone

stone

ring cairn (site)

broken down wall

Bamford Moor (426m)

unmarked top

burial cairn

shelter

quarry

stoops

P

stile

Rocking stones are recorded at **Glory Stones** on Bamford Moor but are likely to have been broken up to prevent trespassing.

P

sign

to Bamford

stoops

butt

posts

Great Tor

Bamford Edge

line of stoops

P

Woodlane Plantation

stile

stoop

posts

locked gate

New Road

N

Porthole Buttress

Bridge

Bridge

stoop

sign

A6013

Yorkshire Bridge Inn

bellmouth outlet

Reservoir

to Bamford (1 mile)

The top of **Bamford Moor** is unmarked above the southern end of Bamford Edge. A number of paths lead down from here to the stile to the south. It is possible to cross the open heath via a number of faint paths, and this is the easiest way to reach the **Old Woman**, one of a number of standing stones in this area, and the nearby **stone circle.**

Bamford Edge

CONTINUATION ON p 83

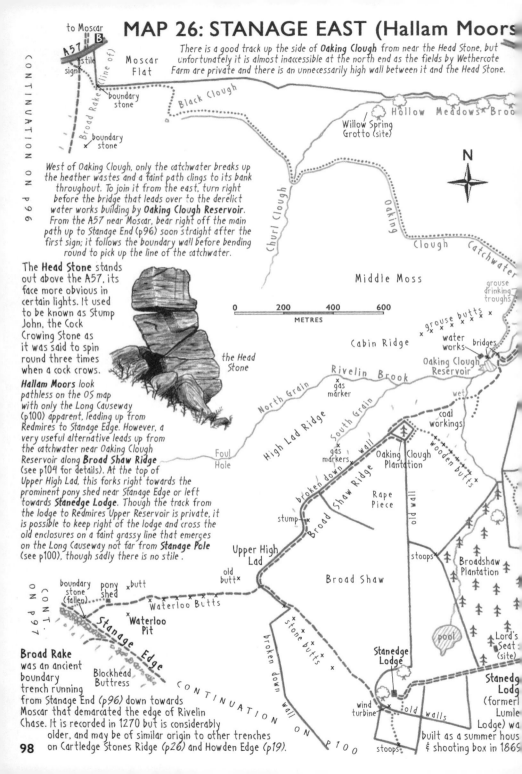

to Moscar

to Moscar

A57 B

stile

sign

Moscar
Flat

boundary
stone

Black Clough

Hollow Meadows Broo

Willow Spring
Grotto (site)

boundary
stone

N

There is a good track up the side of **Oaking Clough** from near the Head Stone, but unfortunately it is almost inaccessible at the north end as the fields by Wethercote Farm are private and there is an unnecessarily high wall between it and the Head Stone.

West of Oaking Clough, only the catchwater breaks up the heather wastes and a faint path clings to its bank throughout. To join it from the east, turn right before the bridge that leads over to the derelict water works building by **Oaking Clough Reservoir**. From the A57 near Moscar, bear right off the main path up to Stanage End (p96) soon straight after the first sign; it follows the boundary wall before bending round to pick up the line of the catchwater.

Churl Clough

Oaking Clough

Catchwater

Middle Moss

grouse drinking troughs

0   200   400   600
METRES

grouse butts

Cabin Ridge

water works

bridges

Oaking Clough Reservoir

The **Head Stone** stands out above the A57, its face more obvious in certain lights. It used to be known as Stump John, the Cock Crowing Stone as it was said to spin round three times when a cock crows.

the Head Stone

Rivelin Brook

gas marker

wet

coal workings

Hallam Moors look pathless on the OS map with only the Long Causeway (p100) apparent, leading up from Redmires to Stanage Edge. However, a very useful alternative leads up from the catchwater near Oaking Clough Reservoir along **Broad Shaw Ridge** (see p104 for details). At the top of Upper High Lad, this forks right towards the prominent pony shed near Stanage Edge or left towards **Stanedge Lodge**. Though the track from the lodge to Redmires Upper Reservoir is private, it is possible to keep right of the lodge and cross the old enclosures on a faint grassy line that emerges on the Long Causeway not far from **Stanage Pole** (see p100), though sadly there is no stile.

North Grain

High Lad Ridge

South Grain

gas markers

wall

Oaking Clough Plantation

wooden butts

broken down

Broad Shaw Ridge

Rape Piece

old wall

Foul Hole

stump

stoops

Broadshaw Plantation

Upper High Lad

old butt

Broad Shaw

boundary stone (fallen)

pony shed

butt

Waterloo Butts

pool

Lord's Seat (site)

Waterloo Pit

Stanage Edge

stone butts

Stanedge Lodge

Stanedge Lodge (formerl Lumle Lodge) wa

Broad Rake was an ancient boundary trench running from Stanage End (p96) down towards Moscar that demarcated the edge of Rivelin Chase. It is recorded in 1270 but is considerably older, and may be of similar origin to other trenches on Cartledge Stones Ridge (p26) and Howden Edge (p19).

Blockhead Buttress

CONTINUATION

broken down wall on

P100

wind turbine

old walls

stoops

built as a summer hous & shooting box in 186

CONTINUATION ON p96

CONTINUATION ON p97

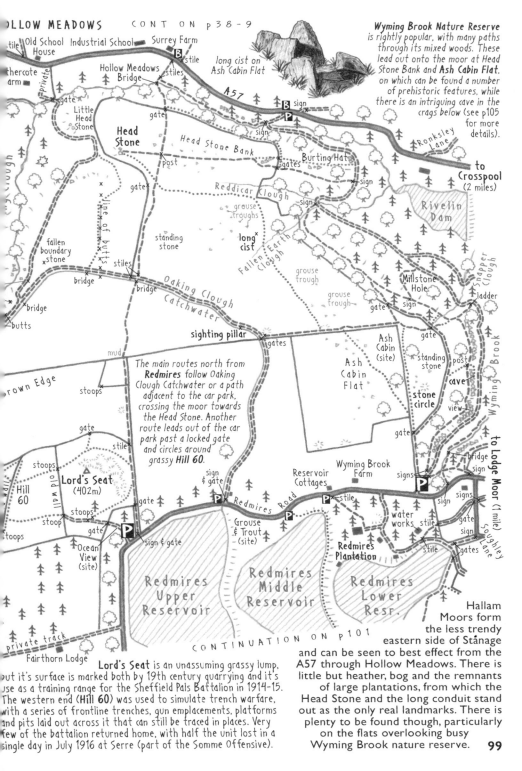

CONT ON p38-9

Old School House
Industrial School
Surrey Farm
stile
B
stile
stiles
long cist on Ash Cabin Flat

Hollow Meadows Bridge
A57
thercote arm
private
gate
Little Head Stone
gate
Head Stone
post
Head Stone Bank
gate
B sign
P
sign
Burting Hat
gates
sign
Ronksley Lane

to Crosspool (2 miles)

Reddicar Clough
grouse troughs
sign
sign
Rivelin Dam

line of butts
standing stone
long cist
Fallen Earth Clough
grouse trough
Millstone Hole
ladder
gate
sign

fallen boundary stone
stiles
bridge
bridge
Oaking Clough Catchwater
grouse trough
gate
sign
Ash Cabin (site)
standing stone
post
gate

bridge
butts
sighting pillar
gates
Ash Cabin Flat
cave
view
stone circle

rown Edge
mud
stoops
The main routes north from **Redmires** follow Oaking Clough Catchwater or a path adjacent to the car park, crossing the moor towards the Head Stone. Another route leads out of the car park past a locked gate and circles around grassy **Hill 60**.
gate
bridge
sign

gate
stile
sign & gate
Wyming Brook Farm
signs
P
signs
sign
gate

stoops
Lord's Seat (402m)
stoops
stoop
stoops
Hill 60
old mill
gate
gate
P
Ocean View (site)
sign & gate
gate
P
P
Redmires Road
Grouse & Trout (site)
Reservoir Cottages
P
stile
water works
sign
signs
stile
gate
sign
stile
gates
Soughley Lane

to Lodge Moor (1 mile)

Redmires Plantation

private track
Fairthorn Lodge
Redmires Upper Reservoir
Redmires Middle Reservoir
Redmires Lower Resr.

CONTINUATION ON P101

Wyming Brook Nature Reserve is rightly popular, with many paths through its mixed woods. These lead out onto the moor at Head Stone Bank and **Ash Cabin Flat**, on which can be found a number of prehistoric features, while there is an intriguing cave in the crags below (see p105 for more details).

Lord's Seat is an unassuming grassy lump, but it's surface is marked both by 19th century quarrying and it's use as a training range for the Sheffield Pals Battalion in 1914-15. The western end (**Hill 60**) was used to simulate trench warfare, with a series of frontline trenches, gun emplacements, platforms and pits laid out across it that can still be traced in places. Very few of the battalion returned home, with half the unit lost in a single day in July 1916 at Serre (part of the Somme Offensive).

Hallam Moors form the less trendy eastern side of Stanage and can be seen to best effect from the A57 through Hollow Meadows. There is little but heather, bog and the remnants of large plantations, from which the Head Stone and the long conduit stand out as the only real landmarks. There is plenty to be found though, particularly on the flats overlooking busy Wyming Brook nature reserve. **99**

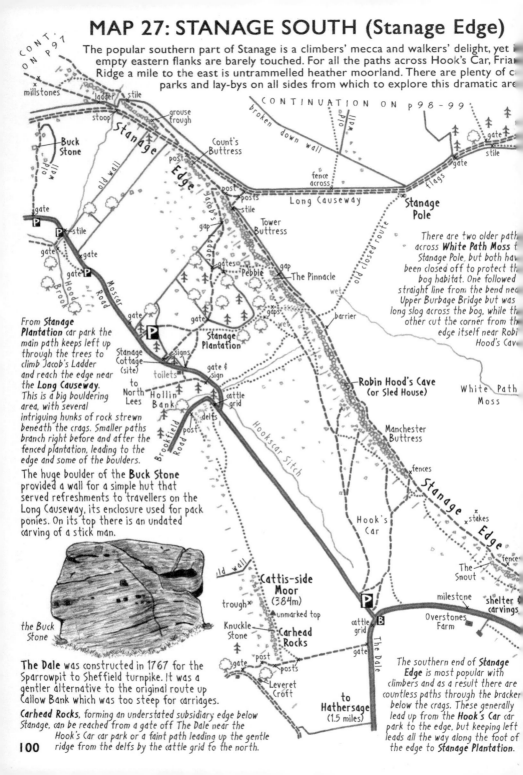

MAP 27: STANAGE SOUTH (Stanage Edge)

The popular southern part of Stanage is a climbers' mecca and walkers' delight, yet i
empty eastern flanks are barely touched. For all the paths across Hook's Car, Fria
Ridge a mile to the east is untrammelled heather moorland. There are plenty of c
parks and lay-bys on all sides from which to explore this dramatic are

CONTINUATION ON p98-99

millstones

ladder   stile

stoop

grouse
trough

Stanage Edge

Buck
Stone

Count's
Buttress

broken down wall

mast pipe

old wall

post

gate

stile

gate

stile

gate

flags

P   P stile

gate

gate P

Brook

Hood Road

Moscar Road

post

posts

stile

Jacob's Ladder

gap

gates

Tower
Buttress

Pebble

The Pinnacle

gap

gaps

wet

barrier

fence
across

Long Causeway

Stanage
Pole

There are two older path
across **White Path Moss** t
Stanage Pole, but both hav
been closed off to protect th
bog habitat. One followed
straight line from the bend nea
Upper Burbage Bridge but was
long slog across the bog, while th
other cut the corner from th
edge itself near Robi
Hood's Cav

old closed route

wet

White Path
Moss

gate

P

Stanage
Plantation

signs

Stanage
Cottage
(site)

toilets

to
North
Lees

Hollin
Bank

Brookfield Road

post

delfs

gate &
sign

cattle
grid

Robin Hood's Cave
(or Sled House)

Manchester
Buttress

fences

Stanage Edge

stakes

From **Stanage
Plantation** car park the
main path keeps left up
through the trees to climb
Jacob's Ladder
and reach the edge near
the **Long Causeway**.
This is a big bouldering
area, with several
intriguing hunks of rock strewn
beneath the crags. Smaller paths
branch right before and after the
fenced plantation, leading to the
edge and some of the boulders.

The huge boulder of the **Buck Stone**
provided a wall for a simple hut that
served refreshments to travellers on the
Long Causeway, its enclosure used for pack
ponies. On its top there is an undated
carving of a stick man.

the Buck
Stone

The Dale was constructed in 1767 for the
Sparrowpit to Sheffield turnpike. It was a
gentler alternative to the original route up
Callow Bank which was too steep for carriages.

Carhead Rocks, forming an understated subsidiary edge below
Stanage, can be reached from a gate off The Dale near the
Hook's Car car park or a faint path leading up the gentle
ridge from the delfs by the cattle grid to the north.

Hookscar Sitch

old wall

Cattis-side
Moor
(384m)
unmarked top

trough

Knuckle
Stone

Carhead
Rocks

Hook's
Car

The
Snout

fence

milestone

shelter &
carvings

Overstones
Farm

cattle
grid

P

B

gate

The Dale

gate posts

post

Leveret
Croft

to
Hathersage
(1.5 miles)

The southern end of **Stanage
Edge** is most popular with
climbers and as a result there are
countless paths through the bracker
below the crags. These generally
lead up from the **Hook's Car** car
park to the edge, but keeping left
leads all the way along the foot of
the edge to **Stanage Plantation**.

100

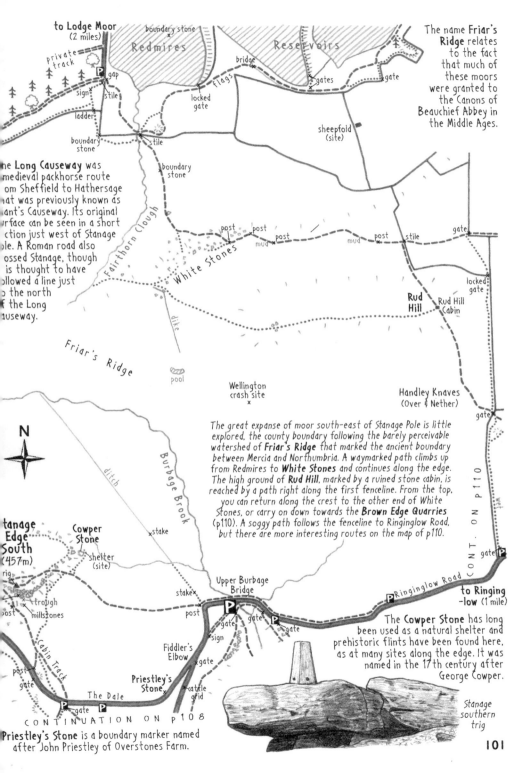

to Lodge Moor (2 miles)

boundary stone ×

Redmires   Reservoirs

private track

gap

P

sign

stile

ladder

boundary stone

bridge

flags

locked gate

gates

gate

The name **Friar's Ridge** relates to the fact that much of these moors were granted to the Canons of Beauchief Abbey in the Middle Ages.

stile

boundary stone

sheepfold (site)

...he **Long Causeway** was ...medieval packhorse route ...om Sheffield to Hathersage ...at was previously known as ...ant's Causeway. Its original ...urface can be seen in a short ...ction just west of Stanage ...le. A Roman road also ...ossed Stanage, though ...is thought to have ...llowed a line just ...o the north ...f the Long ...auseway.

Fairthorn Clough

White Stones

post post post   post   stile   gate

mud   mud

dike

locked gate

Rud Hill ×   Rud Hill Cabin

Friar's Ridge

pool

Wellington crash site ×

Handley Knaves (Over & Nether)

gate

N

ditch

Burbage Brook

The great expanse of moor south-east of Stanage Pole is little explored, the county boundary following the barely perceivable watershed of **Friar's Ridge** that marked the ancient boundary between Mercia and Northumbria. A waymarked path climbs up from Redmires to **White Stones** and continues along the edge. The high ground of **Rud Hill**, marked by a ruined stone cabin, is reached by a path right along the first fenceline. From the top, you can return along the crest to the other end of White Stones, or carry on down towards the **Brown Edge Quarries** (p110). A soggy path follows the fenceline to Ringinglow Road, but there are more interesting routes on the map of p110.

CONT. ON p110

wet

...tanage Edge South (457m)

...rig

...ost × trough

millstones

Cowper Stone ×

shelter (site)

stake

stake ×

post

Upper Burbage Bridge

P

gate

sign

gate

P

gate

Ringinglow Road

P

to Ringing -low (1 mile)

gate P

The **Cowper Stone** has long been used as a natural shelter and prehistoric flints have been found here, as at many sites along the edge. It was named in the 17th century after George Cowper.

Cabin Track

post

gate

Fiddler's Elbow

gate

Priestley's Stone ×

cattle grid

The Dale

P gate P

CONTINUATION ON p108

Priestley's Stone is a boundary marker named after John Priestley of Overstones Farm.

Stanage southern trig

101

ROUTE 15: STANAGE & BAMFORD EDGES FROM HATHERSAGE

Distance: 11½ miles (18.5km)

Ascent: 580m

Difficulty: Moderate

Parking: Pay car park on Oddfellows Road in Hathersage. Free parking in lay-bys on the moor edge at New Road & The Dale.

Public Transport: Hathersage is on the Hope Valley railway line and 271/272 bus route from Sheffield. The 271, 273 & 274 buses also run from Sheffield to Bamford.

Character: A fine tour along the whole length of Stanage Edge, also taking in Bamford Edge, Callow Neb and the 7 Stones of Hordron. The route can be started in either Hathersage or Bamford, and is on good paths throughout.

Note: no access for dogs on Bamford & Moscar Moors.

4 Follow the clear path along the top of **Bamford Edge** past Great Tor and fork left to stay along the line of the crags. Continue across the top of a small clough and pass a pair of stone sighting pillars before joining the line of an old wall. Stay on the main path as it angles down into **Jarvis Clough** and joins a vehicle track on the other side. At the top of the track, detour about 300m left along the top of Hordron Edge to reach the impressive **7 Stones of Hordron** stone circle.

5 Retrace your steps along **Hordron Edge** and continue straight on, before turning left up towards Stanage shortly before the track crosses Jarvis Clough. Follow a line of grouse butts and then a meandering path through the bracken to reach the main path running below **Stanage Edge**. Follow this right and keep left at the first fork. Soon after, the most obvious line continues up a gully onto the trig point on **High Neb** at its highest point. I recommend staying below the edge for a bit longer, though, so fork right, picking your way through the boulders to round **Crow Chin** and pass through the remarkable array of abandoned millstones below High Neb. Several other paths lead up the edge but you can carry on to join the **Long Causeway** as it angles up to the top of the slope.

6 Fork right off the **Long Causeway** at a post to join the obvious path along the top of the most popular part of Stanage Edge. Some way beyond the plantation, look out for **Robin Hood's Cave**, reached by cutting down onto a broad rocky platform and ducking through a wet tunnel to emerge on its dramatic parapet (see p.106 for more details). Continue to the second trigpoint

3 Turn right at the crossroads by the school in Bamford, then follow the track steeply up **Bamford Clough**, which is still open to pedestrians. Emerging on New Road, go right as far as a stile leading out onto the moor. Take the left path, then keep straight on up the slope onto **Bamford Moor**. The unmarked summit can be reached by heading straight on near a small shelter, but the route bears left down to the first real crags of **Bamford Edge**.

The pillars on Bamford Edge were used as sighting markers for the Rivelin Tunnel that carries ten million gallons of water a day from Derwent Reservoir to the Rivelin Dams.

102

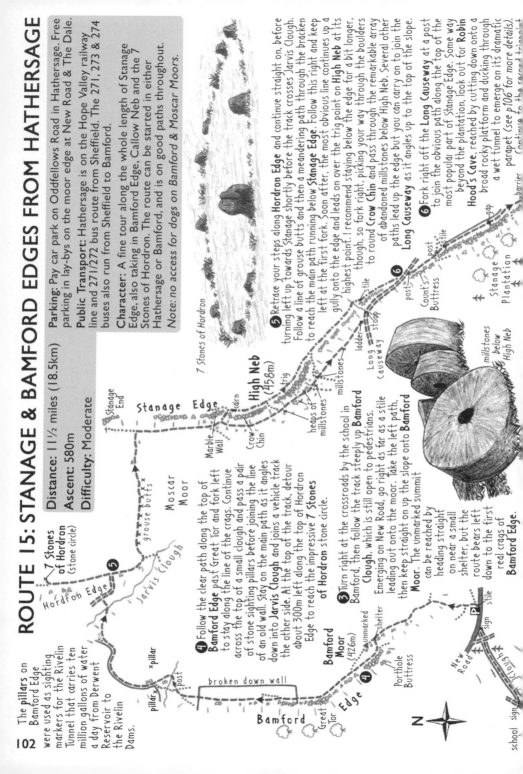

7 Stones of Hordron

7 Stones of Hordron (stone circle)

Hordron Edge

Jarvis Clough

grouse butts

Moscar Moor

Stanage End

Stanage Edge

High Neb (458m)

cairn

Crow Chin

Marble Wall

heaps of millstones

trig

millstones

millstones below High Neb

ladder stile

Long Causeway

stoop

post

stile

Count's Buttress

post

stile

Stanage Plantation

gap

barrier

×pillar

pillars

post

broken down wall

Bamford Moor (426m)

unmarked

shelter

Bamford Edge

Great Tor

Porthole Buttress

Bamford

New Road

P

sign

stile

Clough

school

sign

N

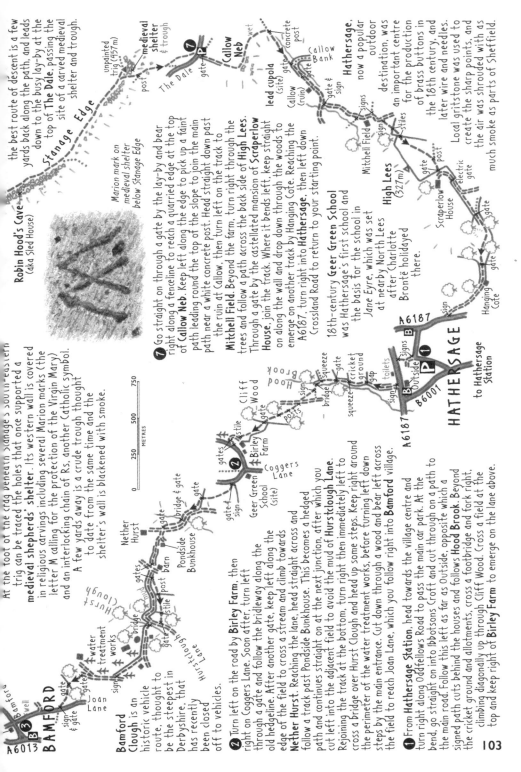

the best route of descent is a few yards back along the path, and leads down to the busy lay-by at the top of **The Dale**, passing the site of a carved medieval shelter and trough.

Stanage Edge

unpainted trig (457m)

post

The Dale

medieval shelter & trough

7 **P** gate **Callow Neb**

Callow Bank

wet

concrete post

Hathersage

Callow gate

At the foot of the crag beneath Stanage's south-eastern trig can be traced the holes that once supported a **medieval shepherds' shelter.** Its western wall is covered in religious carvings including several Marion marks (the letter M calling for the protection of the Virgin Mary) and an interlocking chain of Rs, another Catholic symbol. A few yards away is a crude trough thought to date from the same time and the shelter's wall is blackened with smoke.

Robin Hood's Cave (aka Sled House)

Marion mark on medieval shelter below Stanage Edge

7 Go straight on through a gate by the lay-by and bear right along a fenceline to reach a quarried edge at the top of **Callow Neb.** Keep left along the edge to pick up a faint path leading round the top of the slope to join the main path near a white concrete post. Head straight down past the ruin at Callow, then turn left on the track to **Mitchell Field.** Beyond the farm, turn right through the trees and follow a path across the back side of **High Lees.** Through a gate by the castellated mansion of **Scraperlow House,** join the track. Where it bends left, keep straight on along the wall and drop down through the woods to emerge on another track by Hanging Cote. Reaching the A6187, turn right into **Hathersage,** then left down Crossland Road to return to your starting point.

lead cupola (site)

Callow (ruin)

gate & sign

signs

Mitchell Field

sign

Stiles

High Lees (327m)

Scraperlow House

electric gate

gate

post

gate

Hanging Cote

sign

Hathersage, now a popular outdoor destination, was an important centre for the production of brass buttons in the 18th century, and later wire and needles. Local gritstone was used to create the sharp points, and the air was shrouded with as much smoke as parts of Sheffield.

18th-century **Geer Green School** was Hathersage's first school and the basis for the school in Jane Eyre, which was set at nearby North Lees after Charlotte Brontë holidayed there.

A6187 B

HATHERSAGE

Signs **P** **1**

B6001

to Hathersage Station

A6187 B

toilets

signs

cricket ground

gap

squeeze gate

squeeze

bridge

sign

Hood Brook

Cliff Wood

gate

stile

posts

Birley Farm

gates

2

Geer Green School (site)

gate & sign

Coggers Lane

2 Turn left on the road by **Birley Farm,** then right on Coggers Lane. Soon after, turn left through a gate and follow the bridleway along the old hedgeline. After another gate, keep left along the edge of the field to cross a stream and climb towards **Nether Hurst.** Reaching the lane, head straight across and follow a track past Pondside Bunkhouse. This becomes a hedged path and continues straight on at the next junction, after which you cut left into the adjacent field to avoid the mud of **Hurstclough Lane.** Rejoining the track at the bottom, turn right then immediately left to cross a bridge over Hurst Clough and head up some steps, before turning left down steps by the main entrance. Cut down through a wood and bear left across the field to reach Joan Lane, which you follow right into **Bamford** village.

Nether Hurst

gates

bridge & gate

stile post barn

gate

Hurst (Clough)

Pondside Bunkhouse

Hurstclough Lane

gate

bridge

gate

water treatment works

signs

gate

BAMFORD

Bamford well

sign & gate

gate

Joan Lane

A6013 B **3**

Bamford Clough is an historic vehicle route, thought to be the steepest in Derbyshire, that has recently been closed off to vehicles.

0 250 500 750
METRES

1 From **Hathersage Station,** head towards the village centre and turn right along Oddfellows Road to pass the main car park. At the bend, go straight on into Ibbotsons Croft and cut through on a path to the main road. Follow this left as far as Outside, opposite which a signed path cuts behind the houses and follows **Hood Brook.** Beyond the cricket ground and allotments, cross a footbridge and fork right, climbing diagonally up through Cliff Wood. Cross a field at the top and keep right of **Birley Farm** to emerge on the lane above.

ROUTE 16: HIGH NEB FROM LODGE MOOR

Distance: 9½ miles (15.5km)

Ascent: 270m

Difficulty: Moderate

Parking: Free car park at Wyming Brook and small lay-by beside Lodge Moor Road. People also park at the end of Redmires Road, but be aware there are yellow lines here.

Public Transport: The route starts at the Lodge Moor bus terminus for the 51 bus, which runs regularly from Sheffield centre seven days a week.

Character: A very satisfying circuit of Hallam Moors, taking in Wyming Brook and Redmires Reservoirs, as well as the highest section of Stanage Edge. Providing an interesting alternative to the well-worn route past Stanage Pole, the paths are largely easy to follow and relatively dry.

Note: No access for dogs on sections 3 and 4 of this route.

There is a faint Bronze Age stone circle on **Ash Cabin Flat** that is best made out by its oval bank and a striking cist near **Fallen Earth Clough** *(see map on p99)*. Many of the heaps of rocks seen near here are prehistoric clearance cairns as the area was farmed by small family groups, whose settlements and hut circles are found scattered across the moorland fringe between Head Stone Bank and Ash Cabin Flat.

❹ Keep right of the plantation and cross the broken down wall above to pick up a path following it steadily up **Broad Shaw Edge**. This was once a plantation but only an occasional stump remains. Where the path bends round towards **Stanage Lodge**, turn right and pass a line of grouse butts on the way up to the pony shed, which makes a good lunch shelter. It is only a few yards beyond to **Stanage Edge**, where the view over the Derwent and Hope Valleys suddenly opens out. Head right for 200m to reach the trig on **High Neb**, the highest point on the edge.

High Neb
(458m)

❺ Turn back at **High Neb** and head south-east along Stanage Edge, continuing down the crags as far as the **Long Causeway**, a wide ancient track. Follow this left up to **Stanage Pole** and on to the more modern plantations beyond. You can follow the track all the way down to Redmires and turn right on a path by the upper reservoir, but I find it less tedious to bear right at a stile soon after reaching the plantation. A narrower path follows the fence to a ladder stile and continues through the bracken the other side to a second stream, beyond which a stile leads **104** back over to the main route.

❸ Turn right alongside the conduit and follow it to its end by **Oaking Clough Reservoir**. Turn left by the dam on a path up the bank and along the clough. Where this reaches a grassy area, bear right to cross the reedy stream and pick up a path up through the bracken toward the tiny plantation above.

Gin Piece relates to the use of a horse gin working a trial hole here, while rape was the first crop grown on nearby **Rape Piece**.

Stanage Pole (previously known as Thurstone Pole) may have been first erected by monks to guide travellers on the Long Causeway as early as the 16th century, or it may principally have been a boundary marker - this has been a frontier since Northumbria and Mercia were divided here. It has been felled and reinstated many times over the years, including in 1879, 1915 and as recently as 2016. Among the carvings around its foot are various dates and initials of surveyors who have beaten the bounds since 1550.

Lord Furnival had a 14-th-century hunting lodge at **Lord's Seat** in what is now the plantations by Redmires. An outbuilding here was used as a chapel by dissenters after the 1662 Uniformity Act, and a Bible chained to a stone table remained here until the 1900s.

a grouse drinking trough near High Neb

2 From **Wyming Brook** car park, follow the broad track very briefly, before bearing left at a sign just beyond the vehicle barrier. The path winds along the top of the crags to reach a post beneath a striking pine tree. (To reach the intriguing **cave**, turn right here on a rough path steeply down the slope and bend round to the right to a cluster of rocks, at the far end of which is the entrance to the cave.) Continue along the top of the woods to a small stream, where you turn left up the far side to reach a gate onto the moor. Cross **Ash Cabin Flat** and bear left up the wall to reach the conduit near the sighting pillar.

water works cabin in Oaking Clough

The **cave** above Wyming Brook is said to have been the hiding place for a couple of German prisoners of war who had escaped the camp at Redmires. They saw out the rest of World War II here and there is a carving by the entrance dated 1944 that may be theirs.

1 From the bus terminus by the former **Lodge Moor Hospital**, follow Redmires Road briefly left away from town, before taking the first path on the right down to **Fox Hagg**. Keep left along the wall at the top of these woods, birch turning to oak then pine as you eventually near **Wyming Brook**. Bear right here to cross the stepping stones and reach the car park, an alternative starting point.

Redmires Reservoirs were built following the cholera epidemic that devastated Sheffield in 1832. Water from across Hallam Moors flows into it via Oaking Clough Catchwater, while Rivelin Reservoirs below get their water directly from Derwent Reservoir through the Rivelin Tunnel.

7
Follow the clear path along the old line of **Redmires Conduit** all the way to Lodge Moor Road - it may be preferable to follow a nice path along the edge of the adjacent plantation for a section in the middle. At the road, turn immediately left on another path and keep left around the houses on the site of **Lodge Moor Hospital**. You soon reach the road right by the bus terminus.

In 1875, a **racecourse** was laid out on Lodge Moor with a grandstand, but the enterprise folded after only two years. It then became **Redmires Camp**, an army base that served in World War I for training the Sheffield Pals Battalion and later as a prisoner of war camp. A larger camp a quarter of a mile away housed up to 5,300 prisoners of war during World War II and the whole site was subsequently planted with trees between Redmires Road and Conduit.

6 A clear path runs along the south side of **Redmires Reservoirs**, staying close to their shores. At a gate beyond the lower reservoir, turn left and descend towards **Redmires Plantation**. Halfway down, turn right over a basic stone stile and pick up a walled route across the fields near **Wyming Brook Farm** that follows the underground line of Redmires Conduit. At Soughley Lane the route continues straight on along the conduit, though a shortcut returns directly to Wyming Brook car park by turning left and keeping left again at the end.

The **grouse drinking troughs** along Stanage Edge and across Hallam Moors were carved in the early 20th century for estate owner William Wilson. There are 108 in total, numbered in separate sequences with one sequence starting at 1 near the Long Causeway and continuing to 35 at Stanage End. As well as many boundary stones marked 'WW', Wilson also built an iron fence alongside the Long Causeway to keep sheep out after losing a case with a farmer over stray sheep. It became known by ramblers as the Iron Curtain. He also bought the **Grouse & Trout Inn**, one of two pubs (along with Ocean View on p99) by Redmires Reservoirs, just to close it, as it was too close to his estate.

Stanage Pole

ROBIN HOOD'S CAVE (or SLED HOUSE)

The most famous feature on Stanage Edge is Robin Hood's Cave, which according to legend was a hideout of Robin Hood and Little John. The cave is right on the county boundary and would be a great place for an outlaw to hide, able to disappear into whichever county they were not being sought. It also has two entrances, so it is possible to imagine them escaping out of its chimney at the top.

South Yorkshire and Derbyshire have very strong connections with Robin Hood. His birthplace was said to be at Little Matlock in the Loxley Valley on the edge of Sheffield, where there used to be a Robin Hood Inn. The stream that flows down from Dennis Knoll to Hathersage below Stanage is also Hood Brook and the adjacent site of the Raddle Inn (at the junction of three ancient roads) was known as Hood Lands. However, these landmarks may originally have referred to the devil rather than Robin Hood, *hud* being the Gaelic word for devil. Little John is famously said to have been buried in Hathersage, where a grave of a huge man (Little John was Robin's ironic nickname for him) in St Michael's Churchyard is marked with his name. Yet it seems more likely these stones marked out the village perch, a distance of 13½ feet used for medieval land measurement and often laid out at the parish church.

Robin Hood's Cave is marked on 17th-century maps and as late as 1822 as Sled House. The name refers to its use for storing the sleds with which villagers transported peat and stone collected on the moor down to the valley. These routes can still be seen scored into the moor beneath the eastern end of Stanage and cutting across the south-eastern corner of Cattis-side Moor. The association with Robin Hood is likely to have been invented in the Victorian era and is first referred to by this name in 1868. This would not be the only time this happened, but it is particularly ironic here as the area does have genuine earlier connections with Robin Hood.

looking out of Robin Hood's Cave

Though Robin Hood may never have set foot in it, the cave has been used as a shelter and dwelling on many occasions. Palaeolithic artefacts were discovered in it, including a rib incised with a carving of a horse, dating from around the same time as people were living in caves at Creswell Crags and other sites across Derbyshire. Climbers call the cave the Grand Hotel, referring to its use as a great bivvy for generations of climbers. The sandy floor is very welcoming when it is not flooded with water, but the cave suffered partial collapse from a roof-fall in 1953 which blocked part of the recess behind its entrance and means the hotel is now rather less grand. There are many classic climbs close to the cave, including Inverted V, Hargreaves Original Route (on which many have died) and Christmas Crack (a route traditionally done on Christmas Day).

CHAPTER 11 – BURBAGE

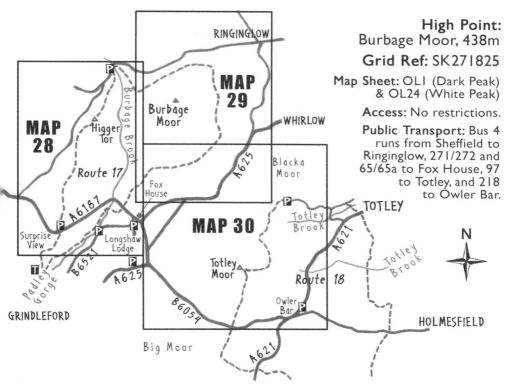

High Point:
Burbage Moor, 438m

Grid Ref: SK271825

Map Sheet: OL1 (Dark Peak)
& OL24 (White Peak)

Access: No restrictions.

Public Transport: Bus 4
runs from Sheffield to
Ringinglow, 271/272 and
65/65a to Fox House, 97
to Totley, and 218
to Owler Bar.

Burbage is a popular and dramatic moorland area centred around Burbage Brook before it drops down into the beautiful woods of Padley Gorge. On one side are the Burbage Edges (a relatively modern appellation for a number of separate edges), and on the other the rocky ramparts of Carl Wark, Higger Tor and Over Owler Tor, while the highest point of Burbage Moor stands on a heathery waste towards Houndkirk Moor. I have appended to this Totley Moor and Blacka Moor, which are often included in the Eastern Moors, but the moors here all blend seamlessly into each other.

The name Burbage, originally that of the stream, pre-dates the 13th century. Some suggest it is a corruption of 'barber', a term used to refer to a Celtic foreigner (as was the word 'welsh'). However, it probably relates to a fortification (*bur*) and a tract of land (*bage*). The fortification is likely to be that at Carl Wark, just one of many remarkable sites, including Millstone Edge, Mother Cap, Longshaw Lodge, Houndkirk Hill and Padley Gorge. There is more to see each time you return to this remarkable moorland, which is readily accessed from the edge of Sheffield above Ringinglow, Whirlow and Totley, as well as Grindleford Station and Hathersage.

Burbage Moor and Higger Tor from Carl Wark

MAP 28: BURBAGE WEST (Burbage Brook)

This is one of the most popular and well-trodden moors in the Peak District, frequented by climbers and day-trippers alike. As well as the long crags of Burbage Rocks, Wild Moor Stones Edge and Millstone Edge, the unique ramparts of Carl Wark, Higger Tor and the Owler Tors make this area instantly recognisable. It houses a warren of paths that I have done my best to convey. Focused around Burbage Brook, it can be explored easily from the car parks at Longshaw, Surprise View or Upper Burbage Bridge.

The **lead cupola** at Callow Fields was a coal-fired furnace used for smelting lead from the 1740s and its slag heaps are still visible beneath **Callow Neb**. It was more efficient than a traditional smelting mill and required no water, but the Derbyshire lead industry rapidly collapsed after 1820.

Burbage Plantation (planted in the 1960s in the shape of Great Britain) is one of the few parts of this moor not covered in paths. Though the brook can be followed all the way, there are few paths out of the valley until the **packhorse bridge** is reached. Rough lines can also be traced down either side of the old plantation climbing up towards *Higger Tor*.

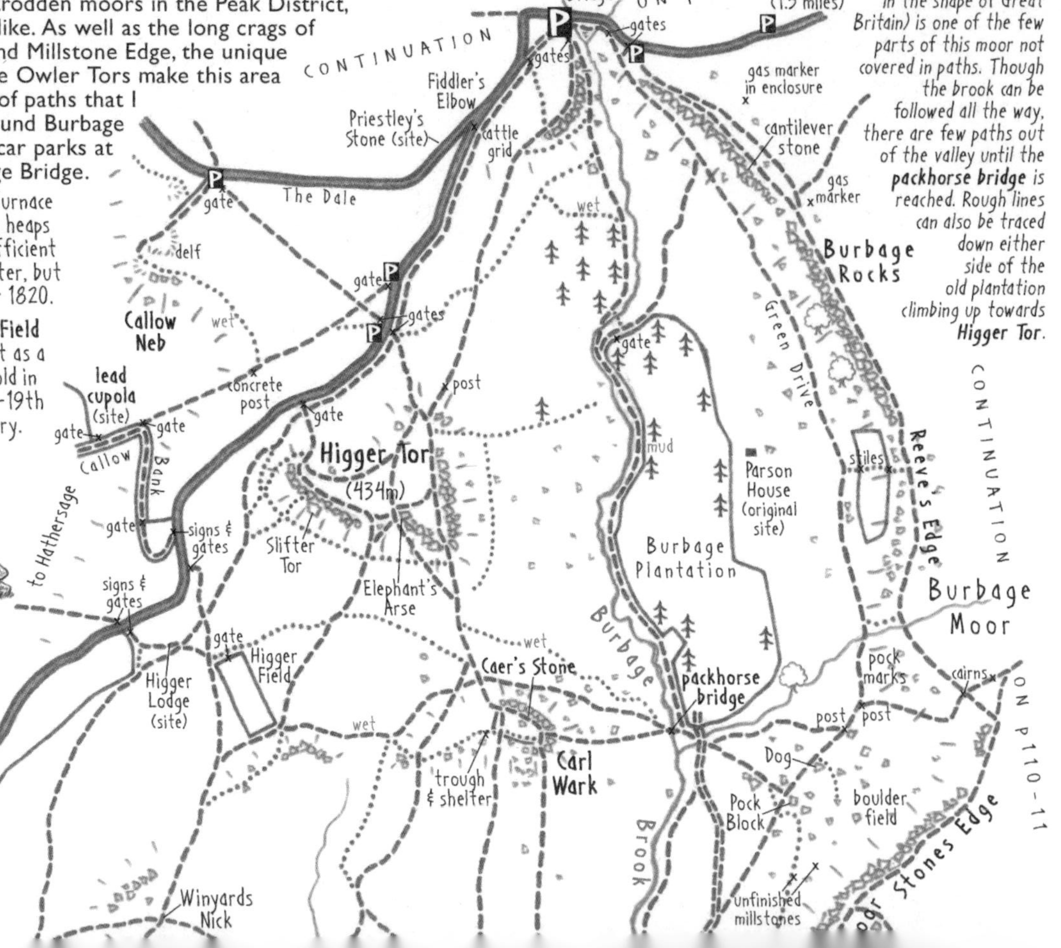

Higger Field was built as a sheepfold in the mid-19th century.

Mother Cap (a striking beacon across Burbage that may have been lit by a fire at night during prehistoric rituals)

The wet hollow in the middle of **Hathersage Moor** can make it tricky to get across from Carl Wark towards Mother Cap. The paths down the hill from Carl Wark all tend to lead back towards **Toad's Mouth** and the one heading west towards some jagged rocks by Higger Field is disappointingly wet. You are better dropping down to the slight stream, then keeping right by a seat to climb back up to **Winyards Nick**. There are also a couple of paths towards the birch-shrouded Secret Garden, though these can be hard to pick up in this direction.

CONTINUATION ON P110-11

Burbage Moor

Reeve's Edge

Burbage Rocks

Green Drive

gas marker in enclosure

cantilever stone

gas marker
gas x marker

Parson House (original site)

Burbage Plantation

Packhorse bridge

Burbage Brook

Pock marks
post
post

boulder field

Dog

Pock Block

unfinished millstones

Over Stones Edge

cairns

Carl Wark

Caer's Stone

trough & shelter

to Ringinglow (1.5 miles)

Upper Burbage Bridge ON P 101

gates
gates
gates

cattle grid

Fiddler's Elbow

Priestley's Stone (site)

The Dale

CONTINUATION

gate
wet
gate
gates
mud

x post

Higger Tor (434m)

Elephant's Arse

Slitter Tor

wet

wet

Higger Field

gate

Higger Lodge (site)

Winyards Nick

concrete post

Callow Neb

delf

wet

lead cupola (site)

gate

gate

Callow Bank

signs & gates

signs & gates

gate

gate

to Hathersage

stiles

to Scraperlow

stile & sign

Whim Road

Brook

stiles

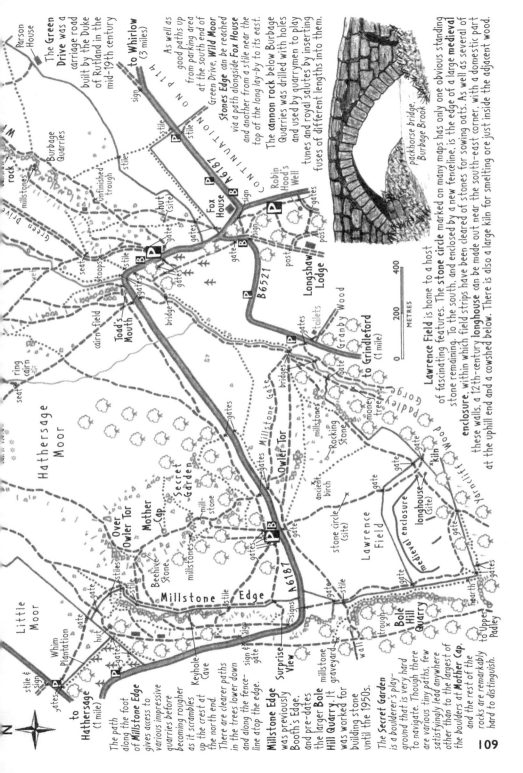

Lawrence Field is home to a host of fascinating features. The stone circle marked on many maps has only one obvious standing stone remaining. To the south, and enclosed by a new fenceline, is the edge of a large medieval enclosure, within which field strips have been cleared of stones for sowing oats. As well as several of these walls, a 12th-century longhouse can be made out near the south-east corner, with a domestic part at the uphill end and a cowshed below. There is also a large kiln for smelting ore just inside the adjacent wood.

The Green Drive was a carriage road built by the Duke of Rutland in the mid-19th century

As well as good paths up from parking area at the south end of Green Drive, Wild Moor Stones Edge can be reached via a path alongside Fox House and another from a stile near the top of the long lay-by to its east.
The cannon rock below Burbage Quarries was drilled with holes and used by quarrymen to play tunes and royal salutes by inserting fuses of different lengths into them.

packhorse bridge, Burbage Brook

The path along the foot of Millstone Edge gives access to various impressive quarries before becoming rougher as it scrambles up the crest at the north end. There are clearer paths in the trees lower down and along the fence-line atop the edge.

Millstone Edge was previously Booth's Edge, and pre-dates the larger Bole Hill Quarry. It was worked for building stone until the 1950s.

The Secret Garden is a boulderer's playground that is very hard to navigate. Though there are various tiny paths, few satisfyingly lead anywhere other than to the largest of the boulders at Mother Cap, and the rest of the rocks are remarkably hard to distinguish.

0   200   400
METRES

109

MAP 29: BURBAGE EAST (Houndkirk Moor)

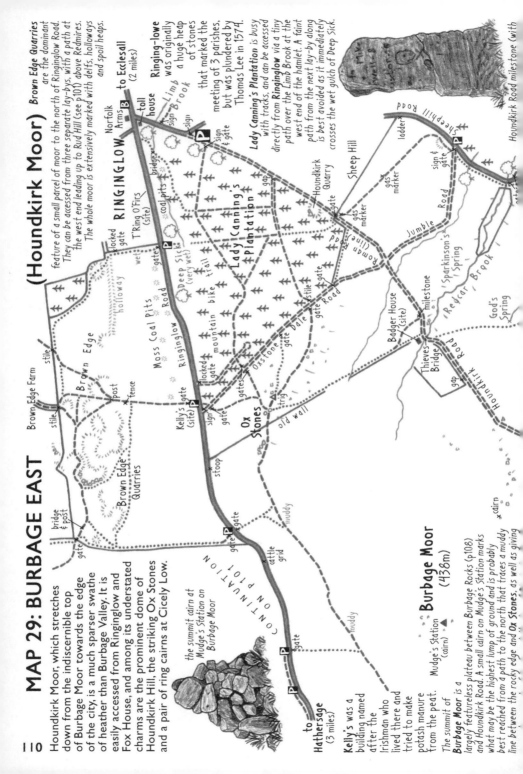

Houndkirk Moor, which stretches down from the indiscernible top of Burbage Moor towards the edge of the city, is a much sparser swathe of heather than Burbage Valley. It is easily accessed from Ringinglow and Fox House, and among its understated charms are the prominent dome of Houndkirk Hill, the striking Ox Stones and a pair of ring cairns at Cicely Low.

Brown Edge Quarries are the dominant feature of a small parcel of moor to the north of Ringinglow Road. They can be accessed from three separate lay-bys, with a path at the west end leading up to Rud Hill (see p101) above Redmires. The whole moor is extensively marked with delfs, holloways and spoil heaps.

Ringing-lowe was originally a huge heap of stones that marked the meeting of 3 parishes, but was plundered by Thomas Lee in 1574.

Lady Canning's Plantation is busy with tracks, and can be accessed directly from Ringinglow via a tiny path over the Limb Brook at the west end of the hamlet. A faint path from the next lay-by along crosses the wet gulch of Deep Sick.

Kelly's was a building named after the Irishman who lived there and tried to make potash manure from the peat. The summit of *Burbage Moor* is a largely featureless plateau between Burbage Rocks (p108) and Houndkirk Road. A small cairn on Mudge's Station marks what may be the highest lump of ground and is probably best reached from a path to the north that traces a muddy line between the rocky edge and Ox Stones, as well as giving

Houndkirk Road milestone (with

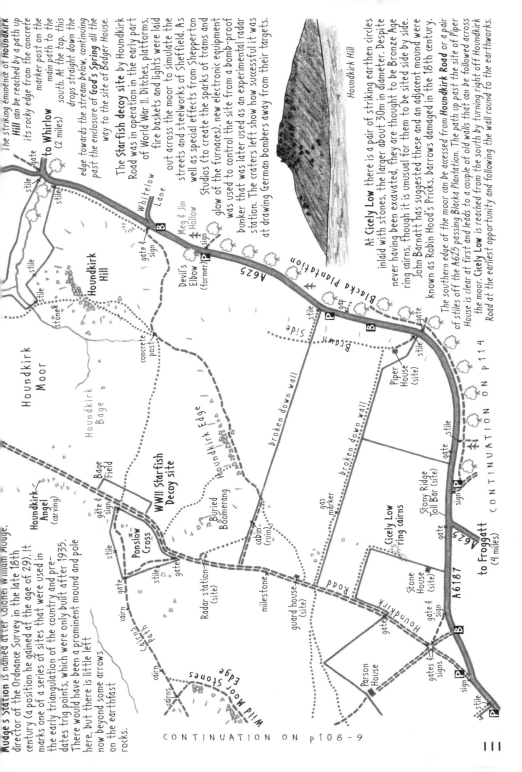

The striking eminence of **Houndkirk Hill** can be reached by a path up its rocky edge from the concrete marker post on the main path to the south. At the top, this drops straight down the edge towards the stream below, continuing past the enclosure of **God's Spring** all the way to the site of Badger House.

The **Starfish decoy site** by Houndkirk Road was in operation in the early part of World War II. Ditches, platforms, fire baskets and lights were laid out across the moor to simulate the streets and steelworks of Sheffield. As well as special effects from Shepperton Studios (to create the sparks of trams and glow of the furnaces), new electronic equipment was used to control the site from a bomb-proof bunker that was later used as an experimental radar station. The craters left show how successful it was at drawing German bombers away from their targets.

Houndkirk Hill

At **Cicely Low** there is a pair of striking earthen circles inlaid with stones, the larger about 30m in diameter. Despite never having been excavated, they are thought to be Bronze Age ring cairns, though it is unusual for them to be sited side by side. John Barnatt has suggested these and an adjacent mound were known as Robin Hood's Pricks, barrows damaged in the 18th century.

The southern edge of the moor can be accessed from **Houndkirk Road** or a pair of stiles off the A625 passing Blacka Plantation. The path up past the site of Piper House is clear at first and leads to a couple of old walls that can be followed across the moor. Cicely Low is reached from the south by turning right off Houndkirk Road at the earliest opportunity and following the wall round to the earthworks.

Mudge's Station is named after Colonel William Mudge, director of the Ordnance Survey in the late 18th century (a position he gained at the age of 29). It marks one of a series of sites that were used in the early triangulation of the country and pre-dates trig points, which were only built after 1935. There would have been a prominent mound and pole here, but there is little left now beyond some arrows on the earthfast rocks.

to Whitlow (2 miles)

Whitelow Lane

Houndkirk Hill

Meg & Jin Hollow

Devil's Elbow

(former) P sign

A625

Blacka Plantation

Houndkirk Moor

Houndkirk Bage

Houndkirk Edge

concrete post

Brown Side

Piper House (site)

broken down wall

gas marker

Bage Field

Houndkirk Angel (carving)

WWII Starfish Decoy site

Buried Boomerang

cabin (ruin)

Ponslow Cross

Radar station (site)

milestone

Cicely Low ring cairns

Cairns Path

guard house (site)

Houndkirk Road

Stone House (site)

Stony Ridge Toll Bar (site)

A6187

to Froggatt (4 miles)

Wild Moor Stones

Wild Moor Edge

Parson House

CONTINUATION ON p114

CONTINUATION ON p108-9

ROUTE 17: BURBAGE & PADLEY GORGE FROM GRINDLEFORD STATION

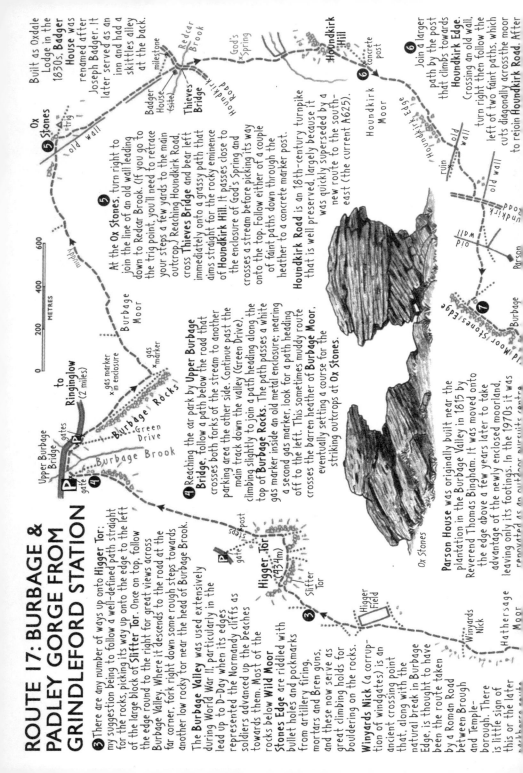

3 There are any number of ways up onto **Higger Tor**: my suggestion being to follow a well-defined path straight for the rocks, picking its way up onto the edge to the left of the large block of **Slipper Tor**. Once on top, follow the edge round to the right for great views across Burbage Valley. Where it descends to the road at the far corner, fork right down some rough steps towards another low rocky tor near the head of Burbage Brook.

The **Burbage Valley** was used extensively during World War II, particularly in the lead up to D-Day when its edges represented the Normandy cliffs as soldiers advanced up the beaches towards them. Most of the rocks below **Wild Moor Stones Edge** are riddled with bullet holes and pockmarks from artillery firing, mortars and Bren guns, and these now serve as great climbing holds for bouldering on the rocks.

Winyards Nick (a corruption of windgates) is an ancient crossing point that, along with the natural break in Burbage Edge, is thought to have been the route taken by a Roman Road between Brough and Templeborough. There is little sign of this or the later

4 Reaching the car park by **Upper Burbage Bridge**, follow a path below the road that crosses both forks of the stream to another parking area the other side. Continue past the main track down the valley (Green Drive), climbing slightly to join a path heading along the top of **Burbage Rocks**. The path passes a white gas marker inside an old metal enclosure; nearing a second gas marker, look for a path heading off to the left. This sometimes muddy route crosses the barren heather of **Burbage Moor**, eventually setting a course for the striking outrops at **Ox Stones**.

At the **Ox Stones**, turn right to join the line of an old wall leading down to Redar Brook. (If you go to the trig point, you'll need to retrace your steps a few yards to the main outcrop.) Reaching Houndkirk Road, cross **Thieves Bridge** and bear left immediately onto a grassy path that aims straight for the rocky eminence of **Houndkirk Hill**. It passes close to the enclosure of God's Spring and crosses a stream before picking its way onto the top. Follow either of a couple of faint paths down through the heather to a concrete marker post.

Houndkirk Road is an 18th-century turnpike that is well preserved, largely because it was quickly superseded by a new route to the south-east (the current A625).

Parson House was originally built near the plantation in the Burbage Valley in 1815 by Reverend Thomas Bingham. It was moved onto the edge above a few years later to take advantage of the newly enclosed moorland, leaving only its footings. In the 1970s it was renovated as an outdoor pursuits centre

5 Built as Oxdale Lodge in the 1830s, **Badger House** was renamed after Joseph Badger. It later served as an inn and had a skittles alley at the back.

6 Join a larger path by the post that climbs towards **Houndkirk Edge**. Crossing an old wall, turn right then follow the left of two faint paths, which cuts diagonally across the moor to rejoin **Houndkirk Road**. After

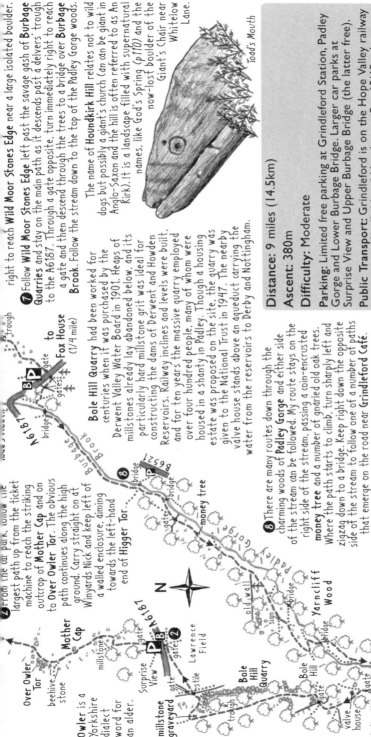

right to reach **Wild Moor Stones Edge** near a large isolated boulder.

⑦ Follow **Wild Moor Stones Edge** left past the savage gash of **Burbage Quarries** and stay on the main path as it descends past a delvers' trough to the A6187. Through a gate opposite, turn immediately right to reach a gate and then descend through the trees to a bridge over **Burbage Brook**. Follow the stream down to the top of the **Padley Gorge** woods.

The name of **Houndkirk Hill** relates not to wild dogs but possibly a giant's church (an can be giant in Anglo-Saxon and the hill is often referred to as An Kirk). It is a landscape filled with supernatural names, like God's Spring (p110) and the now-lost boulder of the Giant's Chair near Whitelow Lane.

Todd's Mouth

Distance: 9 miles (14.5km)
Ascent: 380m
Difficulty: Moderate

Parking: Limited free parking at Grindleford Station, Padley Gorge and Lower Burbage Bridge. Larger car parks at Surprise View and Upper Burbage Bridge (the latter free).

Public Transport: Grindleford is on the Hope Valley railway line between Sheffield and Manchester. Bus 65/65a also stops at Nether Padley every two hours.

Character: A wonderfully varied walk, mixing Burbage's rocky tors with the sylvan delights of Padley Gorge and the broad heathery sweep of Houndkirk Moor. The popular Burbage Valley circuit is extended here to include a loop around Ox Stones and Houndkirk Hill, with extensive views over both Sheffield and the Hope Valley. The paths are largely well trodden, the only problem with route-finding being the sheer number of paths that complicate the picture.

Bole Hill Quarry had been worked for centuries when it was purchased by the Derwent Valley Water Board in 1901. Heaps of millstones already lay abandoned below, and its particularly hard millstone grit was ideal for constructing the dams of Derwent and Howden Reservoirs. Railway inclines and levels were built, and for ten years the massive quarry employed over four hundred people, many of whom were housed in a shanty in Padley. Though a housing estate was proposed on the site, the quarry was given to the National Trust in 1947. The nearby valve house stands above an aqueduct carrying the water from the reservoirs to Derby and Nottingham.

⑧ There are many routes down through the charming woods of **Padley Gorge** and either side of the stream can be followed. My route stays on the right side of the stream, passing a coin-encrusted **money tree** and a number of gnarled old oak trees. Where the path starts to climb, turn sharply left and zigzag down to a bridge. Keep right down the opposite side of the stream to follow one of a number of paths that emerge on the road near **Grindleford Café**.

① From the famous **Grindleford Café**, follow the road over the railway and past Padley Mill. Turn right up a track to reach a gate into the woods, soon after which you fork left past a water works valve house. Climb steadily up the quarried slopes of Bole Hill, keeping right to reach a gate then turning left up the next slope. Follow the main path all the way past **Bole Hill Quarry** to reach a huge graveyard of discarded millstones. Immediately beyond, follow a small path back to the right, climbing to a stile above the quarry. Head straight on across Lawrence Field to reach the main road opposite the **Surprise View** car park.

...from the car park, follow the largest path up from the ticket machine to reach the striking outcrop of **Mother Cap** and on to **Over Owler Tor**. The obvious path continues along the high ground. Carry straight on at Winyards Nick and keep left of a walled enclosure, aiming towards the left-hand end of **Higger Tor**.

Over Owler Tor
beehive stone
Mother Cap
millstone

Owler is a Yorkshire dialect word for an alder.

millstone graveyard

gate to Fox House (1/4 mile)

A6187
Burbage Brook
bridge

B6521
bridge
money tree
gate
Padley Gorge
old wall
Yarncliff Wood
sign
bridge

N

Surprise View
A6187
gate
gate
stile
Lawrence Field
trough

Bole Hill Quarry
Bole Hill
valve house
trough

Padley Mill
railway
Totley Tunnel
sign
sign
Grindleford Café
Grindleford railway station
NETHER PADLEY
B6521
The Maynard

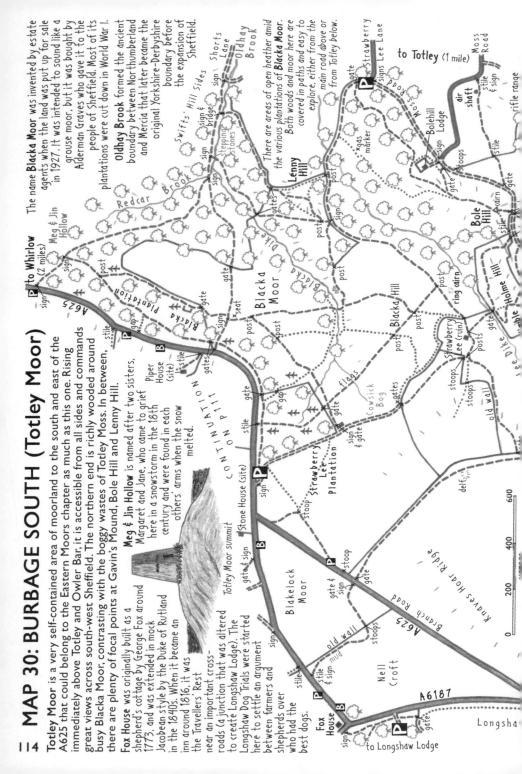

MAP 30: BURBAGE SOUTH (Totley Moor)

Totley Moor is a very self-contained area of moorland to the south and east of the A625 that could belong to the Eastern Moors chapter as much as this one. Rising immediately above Totley and Owler Bar, it is accessible from all sides and commands great views across south-west Sheffield. The northern end is richly wooded around busy Blacka Moor, contrasting with the boggy wastes of Totley Moss. In between, there are plenty of focal points at Gavin's Mound, Bole Hill and Lenny Hill.

Fox House was originally built as a shepherd's cottage by George Fox around 1773, and was extended in mock Jacobean style by the Duke of Rutland in the 1840s. When it became an inn around 1816, it was near an important cross-roads (a junction that was altered to create Longshaw Lodge). The Longshaw Dog Trials were started here to settle an argument between farmers and shepherds over who had the best dogs.

Meg & Jin Hollow is named after two sisters, Margaret and Jane, who came to grief here in a snowstorm in the 18th century and were found in each others' arms when the snow melted.

The name Blacka Moor was invented by estate agents when the land was put up for sale in 1927. It was intended to sound like a grouse moor, but it was bought by Alderman Graves who gave it to the people of Sheffield. Most of its plantations were cut down in World War I.

Oldhay Brook formed the ancient boundary between Northumberland and Mercia that later became the original Yorkshire-Derbyshire boundary before the expansion of Sheffield.

There are areas of open heather amid the various plantations of Blacka Moor. Both woods and moor here are covered in paths and easy to explore, either from the main road above or from Totley below.

to Totley (1 mile)

to Whirlow (2 miles)

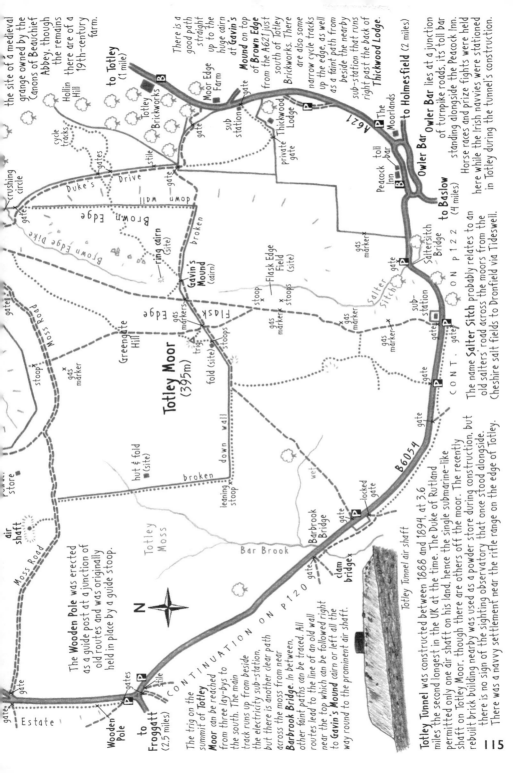

ROUTE 18: TOTLEY MOOR FROM TOTLEY

Distance: 7½ miles (12.3km)

Ascent: 380m

Difficulty: Easy

Parking: Free parking in Totley at the end of Strawberry Lee Lane and along Totley Hall Lane. Lay-by on B6054 between Owler Bar and Fox House.

Public Transport: Totley (opposite the Cross Scythes) is on the regular 97 & 218 bus routes from Sheffield.

Character: A short climb over Bole Hill to the summit of Totley Moor, before returning via the pleasant wooded valleys of Millthorpe and Totley Brooks. Good paths and great views throughout.

1 Turn right off the A621 onto Hillfoot Road shortly after the Cross Scythes at the top end of **Totley** (or continue straight on if coming from Totley Hall Lane). After the school, bear left down Chapel Lane, which quickly becomes a footpath leading down across **Needham's Dike**. Turn left along Penny Lane, passing the **Cricket Inn**, and at the junction head straight on up Strawberry Lee Lane. Follow this quiet road all the way to the car park by the bottom of Moss Road.

Totley Hall was built in 1623, probably by George Newbould whose initials adorn its doorway. It was bought by the City Council in 1944 and run as a College of Housecraft for many years, but has recently been converted into luxury apartments.

2 Go through the small car park and turn left immediately beyond the gate. A small path winds steadily up through the trees past Bolehill Lodge to the small hillock of **Bole Hill**. Follow the main path down to Moss Road, going right through the gate at the top of the lane, then forking immediately left. Keep left across **Brown Edge Dike** then, where a fence joins from the left, head right up the bank to join a path along the line of an old wall along **Brown Edge** with great views over Totley. Turn right up one of a couple of paths that lead up to the huge cairn of **Gavin's Mound**. Continue straight on towards the higher ground of Flask Edge, at the top of which you bear right to reach the trig point on top of **Totley Moor**.

Gavin's Mound is named after Gavin Hodgkinson, the Sheffield Polytechnic student who began building the modern cairn from the stones of an old shepherds' meeting cairn in 1982 so he could see it from his tower block in Totley. About 50-80m north are the very faint remains of a **ring cairn**, from which **Bronze Age urns**, cremation remains and a pygmy incense cup have been recovered. It is about 7m in diameter with a small cairn at its centre and a wide bank around it, discernable by a few fallen kerb stones.

Spoil and debris from lead smelting is strewn across **Bole Hill**, a common name across Derbyshire. A bole was a primitive hearth generally found on west-facing hillsides which provided good ventilation. Coal was extracted from a site below nearby Duke's Drive, as well as from charcoal; the circular hearths of which can be seen in Bole Hill Wood.

7 Across Totley Brook, fork left up through **Gillfield Wood** and head straight across the main track to reach a narrow gate out into the fields. Follow the edge of the field to a vehicle track, which can be followed all the way back into **Totley**. It joins the end of Totley Hall Lane, which leads up past **Totley Hall** to the main road.

Totley, thought to mean 'Tota's clearing', appeared in the Domesday Book as Totinglei. Totley Hall Lane follows an important ancient route that ran the length of Derbyshire until the county boundary was

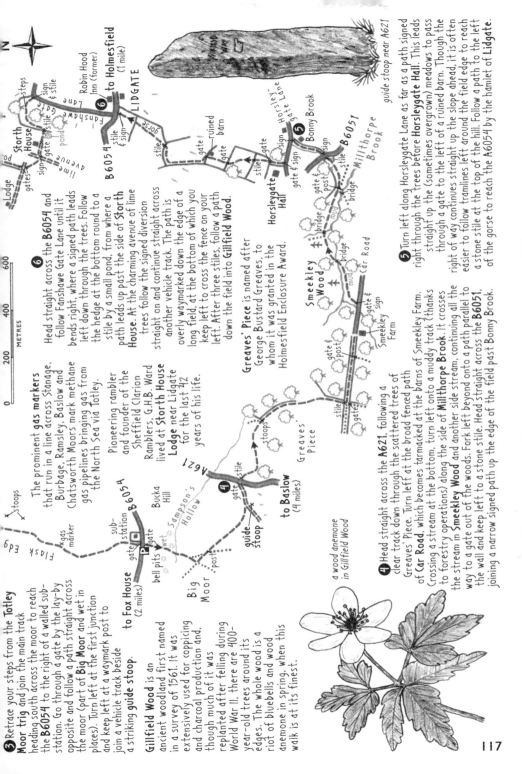

3 Retrace your steps from the **Totley Moor** trig and join the main track heading south across the moor to reach the **B6054** to the right of a walled sub-station. Go through a gate by the lay-by opposite and follow a path straight across the moor (part of **Big Moor** and wet in places). Turn left at the first junction and keep left at a waymark post to join a vehicle track beside a striking **guide stoop**.

Gillfield Wood is an ancient woodland first named in a survey of 1561. It was extensively used for coppicing and charcoal production and, though much of it was replanted after felling during World War II, there are 400-year-old trees around its edges. The whole wood is a riot of bluebells and wood anemone in spring, when this walk is at its finest.

The prominent **gas markers** that run in a line across Stanage, Burbage, Ramsley, Baslow and Chatsworth Moors mark methane gas pipelines bringing gas from the North Sea via Totley.

Pioneering rambler and founder of the Sheffield Clarion Ramblers, G.H.B. Ward lived at **Storth House Lodge** near Lidgate for the last 42 years of his life.

6 Head straight across the **B6054** and follow Fanshawe Gate Lane until it bends right, where a signed path leads left down through the trees. Follow the hedge at the bottom round to a stile by a small pond, from where a path leads up past the side of **Storth House**. At the charming avenue of lime trees follow the signed diversion straight on and continue straight across another vehicle track. The path is overly waymarked down the edge of a long field, at the bottom of which you keep left to cross the fence on your left. After three stiles, follow a path down the field into **Gillfield Wood**.

Greaves' Piece is named after George Bustard Greaves, to whom it was granted in the Holmesfield Enclosure Award.

4 Head straight across the **A621**, following a clear track down through the scattered trees of Greaves' Piece. Turn left at the broad fenced path of **Car Road**, which becomes tarmacked at the barns of Smeekley Farm. Turn left onto a muddy track (thanks to forestry operations) along the side of **Millthorpe Brook**. It crosses the stream in **Smeekley Wood** and another side stream, continuing all the way to a gate out of the woods. Fork left beyond onto a path parallel to the wall and keep left to a stone stile. Head straight across the **B6051**. Joining a narrow signed path up the edge of the field past Bonny Brook.

5 Turn left along Horsleygate Lane as far as a path signed right through the trees before **Horsleygate Hall**. This leads straight up the (sometimes overgrown) meadows to pass through a gate to the left of a ruined barn. Though the right of way continues straight up the slope ahead, it is often easier to follow tramlines left around the field edge to reach a stone stile at the top of the hill. Follow a path to the left of the gorse to reach the A6054 by the hamlet of **Lidgate**.

a wood anemone in Gillfield Wood

guide stoop near A621

CARL WARK

'And here, on this ledge,
Of stone, thrown together
by uplift and ice-scour,
they danced and sang, gave gifts.'
(Melanie Giles, *Carl Wark*)

Carl Wark rises above the Burbage Brook like a brooding volcanic eminence, presenting an intimidating rocky face on all sides that 19th-century antiquarian Sidney Addy likened to 'an immense blackened altar'. The rocky plateau is 230m long with a reinforced natural edge and two defined entrances, as well as a narrow gap between the boulders on its eastern side. The main feature though is a great dry stone rampart along the western edge, a construction unique in northern England. An outer stone wall overlays a high earthen rampart on the side of the tor that is most vulnerable to attack and is often seen as evidence of its use as an Iron Age hillfort.

However, Carl Wark's true use remains a mystery. It is overshadowed by a slightly higher natural fortress at Higger Tor and there is no access to water within the fortification, so it is of limited use defensively. There is also no evidence of any settlement within the rampart's rough rocky interior, whose jumble of boulders seem to prevent any practical development. The only excavation at the site took place in 1950, but was unable to date the man-made wall and its results were never published, so many of the findings have been lost.

The name itself is equally mysterious. Carl Wark may relate to Caer, or possibly Caels (referring to the Gaels), both suggesting a Celtic origin. Caer's Chair is a large rock with a large hollow in it on the north side of Carl Wark where a British chieftain is said to have sat when serving out justice. It is often referred to locally as Charles Work, a corruption of *churls*, a reference to the better-off peasants. Karl was also the name given in Norse to the god Odin, who was often cast as the devil in the Middle Ages; thus it may have been a way of referring to this pagan structure as the 'devil's work'.

There are those who have suggested Carl Wark was constructed in the 5th or 6th centuries, due to its similarity to Dark Age forts in Scotland. Others suggest it is even earlier than the Iron Age, representing the earliest stone wall discovered in Britain. Rather than dig the usual earthen ditch and rampart on the impossibly rocky ground, the amount of stone available meant it was far easier to build a vast wall. Indeed it is most similar in construction to the enclosure of Meg's Wall on Gardom's Edge *(see p124)*, which has been dated to the late Bronze Age (1300-900BC). This was used for ceremonial rather than defensive purposes and Carl Wark may have been similar, as Melanie Giles suggests in her poem. Carl Wark makes more sense in this context. It is more sheltered than Higger Tor and possesses a more pleasing symmetry. It may have been used by those whose settlements, burial cairns, clearance cairns and field systems have been found across the moor to the south-west in two separate family groups, one near Winyards Nick and one near Toad's Mouth. These have been dated from the early Bronze Age right through to the Iron Age and are likely to have been used and reused during this period, as probably was Carl Wark itself. It may even have been used a defensive site in Dark Age struggles between Celtic tribes or Saxon kingdoms, and has been suggested as the true site of the Battle of Win Hill. Until further excavation, though, Carl Wark is keeping a hold of its secrets.

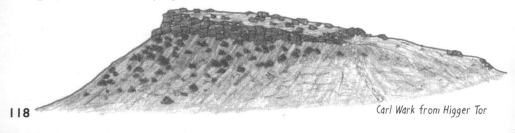

Carl Wark from Higger Tor

N

High Point:
Windlow Hill (aka
White Edge Moor),
388m

Grid Ref: SK266783

Map Sheet:
OL24 (White Peak)

Access:
No restrictions.

Public Transport:
Bus 218 runs from
Sheffield to Owler
Bar and Baslow,
and bus 65/65a from
Sheffield to Calver.

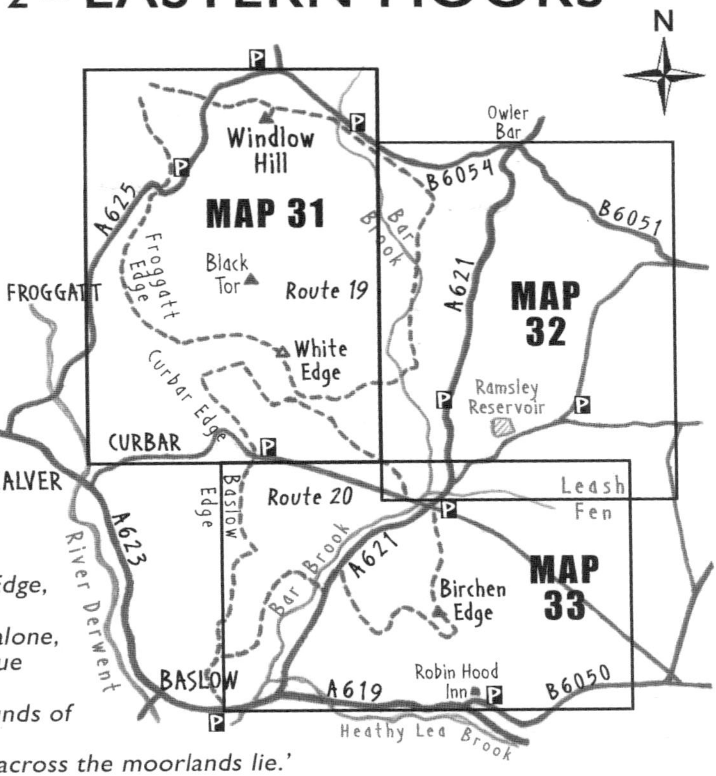

*'Froggatt Edge, Curbar Edge,
   and Baslow Edge,
I will go up, I will go all alone,
Up to the moors, the blue
   and cloudy sky;
Even to those fierce rounds of
   blackened stone
Whose ramparts sharp across the moorlands lie.'*
(Ethel Gallimore, *Pride of the Peak*)

The Eastern Moors is a modern name for a long southward limb of the Pennine moorlands, reaching from Burbage down to Chatsworth. This chapter is focused on its heartland, a series of connected moors and heaths centred on Bar Brook and the Big Moor, another modern name that links the medieval commons of Froggatt, Curbar and Bubnell. The moor's high point at the northern end of White Edge is Windlow Hill, an old name I have reinstated over the rather prosaic White Edge Moor. Unlike White's Moor lower down the moor, which is named after the White family of Tedgness Farm in Grindleford, White Edge relates to the whitey bent grass that grows there.

   The western side of the moor is defined by a series of fine rocky edges overlooking the Derwent Valley, but there is far more to this area. Bar Brook is home to the finest array of prehistoric sites covered in this book; Leash Fen is one of three rare raised mires; and Ramsley Moor and Big Moor are great places to see migrating birds as well as the large population of red deer. The Eastern Moors were threatened with large-scale aforestation in the early 1980s when the reservoirs there were abandoned by Severn Trent Water Authority. This led to its inclusion in the national park in 1984, when it was bought by the National Park; it is now managed by the Eastern Moors Partnership, a collaboration between the National Trust and RSPB.

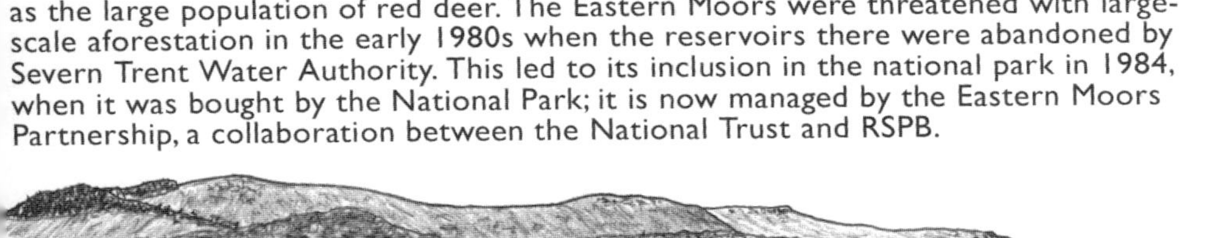

Windlow Hill, White Edge, Froggatt Edge and Curbar Edge from Eyam Moor

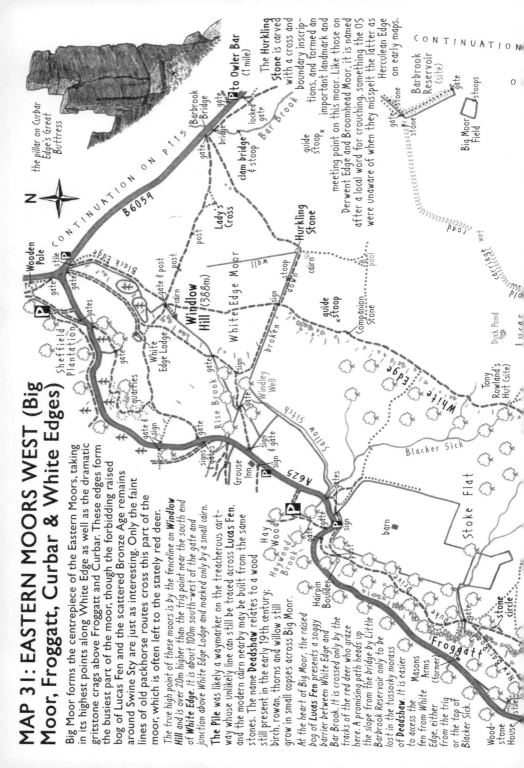

MAP 31: EASTERN MOORS WEST (Big Moor, Froggatt, Curbar & White Edges)

Big Moor forms the centrepiece of the Eastern Moors, taking in its highest points along White Edge as well as the dramatic gritstone crags above Froggatt and Curbar. These edges form the busiest part of the moor, though the forbidding raised bog of Lucas Fen and the scattered Bronze Age remains around Swine Sty are just as interesting. Only the faint lines of old packhorse routes cross this part of the moor, which is often left to the stately red deer.

The true high point of these moors is by the fenceline on **Windlow Hill** *and is over 20m higher than the trig point near the south end of* **White Edge.** *It is about 100m south-west of the gate and junction above White Edge Lodge and marked only by a small cairn.*

The Pile was likely a waymarker on the treacherous cart-way whose unlikely line can still be traced across **Lucas Fen,** and the modern cairn nearby may be built from the same stones. The name **Deadshaw** relates to a wood

still present in the early 19th century; birch, rowan, thorns and willow still grow in small copses across Big Moor.

At the heart of Big Moor, the raised bog of **Lucas Fen** presents a soggy barrier between White Edge and Bar Brook. It is crossed only by the tracks of the red deer who graze here. A promising path heads up the slope from the bridge by Little Barbrook Reservoir only to be lost in the tussocky morass of **Deadshaw.** It is easier to access the fen from White Edge, either from the trig or the top of Blacker Sick.

The **Hurkling Stone** is carved with a cross and boundary inscrip-tions, and formed an important landmark and meeting point on this moor. Like those on Derwent Edge and Broomhead Moor, it is named after a local word for crouching, something the OS were unaware of when they misspelt the latter as **Herculean Edge** on early maps.

the pillar on Curbar Edge's Great Buttress

CONTINUATION

Barbrook Reservoir (site)

Big Moor Field

gate
stoop
stoops

gate
stone
gatestone

carriage road
wet

Pto Owler Bar
(1 mile)

Barbrook Bridge
gate
bridge
locked gate
gate

clam bridge
& stoop

Barbrook

guide stoop ×

guide stoop

CONTINUATION ON P115

B6054

Black Edge

Lady's Cross

post

post

Hurkling Stone
cairn

Windlow Hill (568m)
cairn

White Edge Moor
110m

wall

stoop
down

sign

cairn

guide stoop ×

Companion Stone

pool

Duck Pond

Lucas

Wooden Pole
N
stile
gate
gates
gates

Sheffield Plantation

quarries

White Edge Lodge

gate & post

gate
sign
P

gate & post

gate

sign

gate & sign

gates
tracks
signs

Rise Brook

Windley Well
gate
sign

White Edge

Tony Rowland's Hut (site)

Blacker Sick

Sallow Sitch

Grouse Inn

A625

sign & gate
sign
gates

sign
post

P

A
gate
sign

barn

Stoke Flat

stone circle

Hay Wood

Haywood Brook

Hairpin Boulder
post

Masons Arms (former)

Wood-stone House
stile

Duke's Drive

New Road

Froggatt

gate

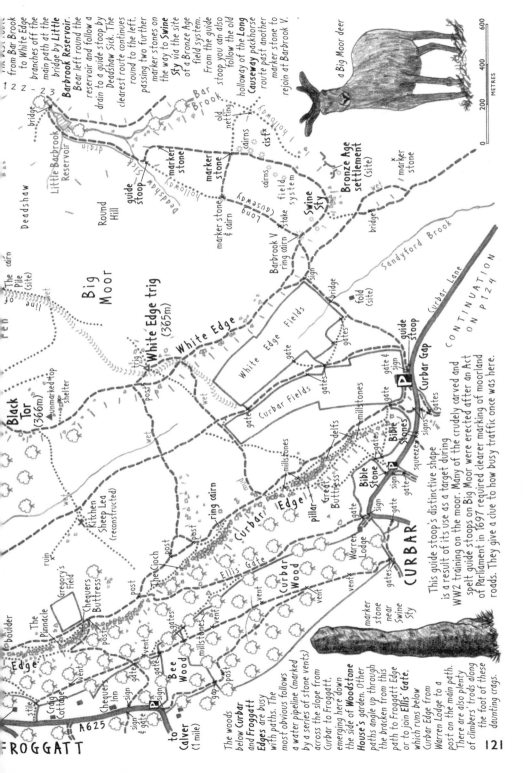

122 - 3

from Bar Brook to White Edge branches off the main path at the old bridge by **Little Barbrook Reservoir**. Bear left round the reservoir and follow a drain to a guide stoop by **Deadshaw Sick**. The clearest route continues round to the left, passing two further marker stones on the way to **Swine Sty** via the site of a Bronze Age field system. From the guide stoop you can also follow the old holloway of the **Long Causeway** packhorse route past another marker stone to rejoin at Barbrook V.

a Big Moor deer

This guide stoop's distinctive shape is a result of its use as a target during WW2 training on the moor. Many of the crudely carved and spelt guide stoops on Big Moor were erected after an Act of Parliament in 1697 required clearer marking of moorland roads. They give a clue to how busy traffic once was here.

The woods below **Curbar** and **Froggatt Edges** are busy with paths. The most obvious follows a water pipeline (marked by a series of stone vents) across the slope from Curbar to Froggatt, emerging here below the side of **Woodstone House's** garden. Other paths angle up through the bracken from this path to Froggatt Edge or to join **Ellis' Gate**, which runs below Curbar Edge from Warren Lodge to a post on the main path. There are also plenty of climbers' trods along the foot of these daunting crags.

marker stone near Swine Sty

MAP 32: EASTERN MOORS EAST (Ramsley Moor & Bar Brook)

The bell pits scattered across **Bucka Hill** are the remains of **Saltersitch Colliery**, where coal was extracted in the 17th and 18th centuries. The shallow hollows were once simple shafts that were filled in after excavation and have since sunk a little. 'Bucka' is a dialect word for a thick piece of bread on which butter was spread with one's thumb.

To the east of Bar Brook, Ramsley Moor and Leash Fen are more popular with birdwatchers than walkers. The boggy moorland here is home to short-eared owls, redpolls and many birds of prey, particularly on the raised bog of Leash Fen. The prevalence of wet carr woodland means that good paths are hard to come by, but the valleys on either side are well trodden, with Bar Brook in particular home to an impressive array of Bronze Age stone circles and cairns.

The **Companion Stones** are part of an Arts in the Peak project, each paired with an historic guide stoop.

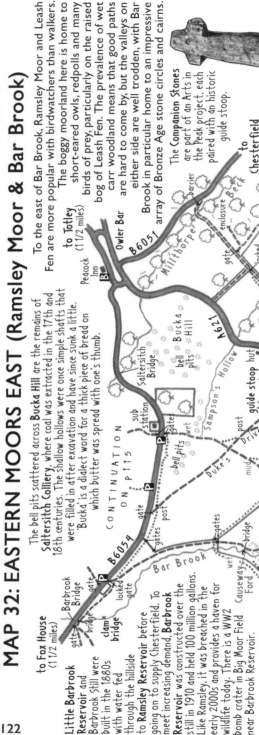

Shillito Cross, once known as Shepherd's Cross

Car Road and the path across **Greaves' Piece** offer the obvious links from Ramsley Moor to Barbrook Reservoir, but there are a couple of fainter paths to the south. One follows the edge of the trees beside Car Road up to a gate leading straight across the main road. The other follows the north side of the nearby clough up to a lay-by; a path on the south side of this loses

to Fox House (1½ miles)

Little Barbrook Reservoir and **Barbrook Still** were built in the 1880s with water fed through the hillside to **Ramsley Reservoir** before going on to supply Chesterfield. To meet increasing demand, **Barbrook Reservoir** was constructed over the still in 1910 and held 100 million gallons. Like Ramsley, it was breached in the early 2000s and provides a haven for wildlife today. There is a WW2 bomb crater in Big Moor Field near Barbrook Reservoir.

*It is possible but not straightforward to walk around the site of **Barbrook Reservoir**. There are paths on three sides but to the northwest it is rough going along either side of the fence.*

Godfrey's Cross (often called Fox Lane Cross) is a medieval boundary cross originally erected by the monks of Barlow Grange. In 1893, it was carved 'Here lies Godfrey' by Godfrey Silcock before he emigrated to New Zealand. **Shillito Cross** has similar origins and was named after Jonathan Shillito.

to Totley (1½ miles)

to Chesterfield (6 miles)

Owler Bar

Peacock Inn

B6051

B6054

A621

Bucka Hill

bell pits

Saltersitch Bridge

sub station

Millthorpe Brook

barrier

enclosure

locked gates

Smeekley Wood (private)

Smeekley Farm

Greaves Piece

Car Road

gas markers

Sampson's Hollow

guide stoop hut

Companion Stone

gas marker

Car Top

Duke's Drive

Barbrook III stone circle

Salter's Ford

pools

Long Causeway

Barbrook Cottage

Barbrook Reservoir (site)

Causeway Ford

Stoops

Big Moor Field

Big Moor

Little Barbrook Reservoir

Bar Brook

Barbrook Bridge

dam bridge

locked gate

Wetts Bank

CONTINUATION ON P115

CONTINUATION ON p120

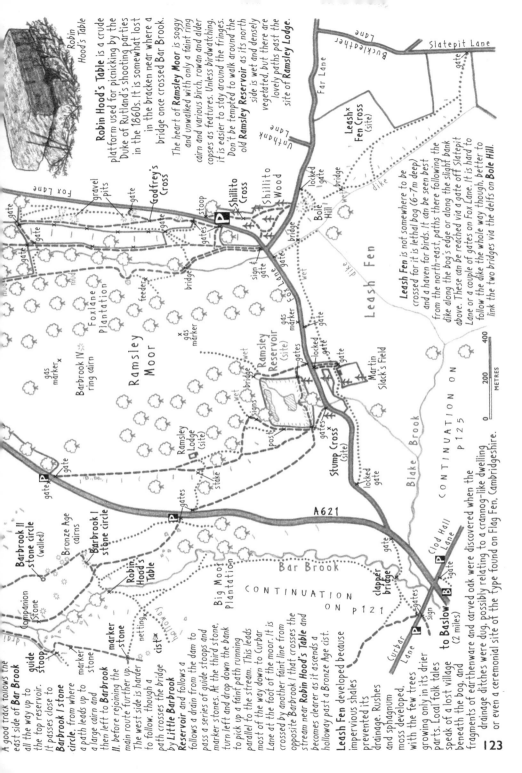

Robin Hood's Table

Robin Hood's Table is a crude platform used for picnicking by the Duke of Rutland's shooting parties in the 1860s. It is somewhat lost in the bracken near where a bridge once crossed Bar Brook.

The heart of **Ramsley Moor** is soggy and unwalked with only a faint ring cairn and various birch, rowan and alder copses as features. Unless birdwatching, it is easier to stay around the fringes. Don't be tempted to walk around the old **Ramsley Reservoir** as its north side is wet and densely vegetated, but there are lovely paths past the site of **Ramsley Lodge**.

Leash Fen is not somewhere to be crossed for it is lethal bog (6–7m deep) and a haven for birds. It can be seen best from the north-east, paths there following the dike along the bog's edge or along the slight bank above. These can be reached via a gate off Slatepit Lane or a couple of gates on Fox Lane. It is hard to follow the dike the whole way though, better to link the two bridges via on **Bole Hill**.

Slatepit Lane

Buckleather Lane

Far Lane

Unthank Lane

Leash× Fen Cross (site)

Fox Lane

gravel pits

gate

Godfrey's Cross

stoop

Shillito Cross

Shillito Wood

locked gate

bridge

Bole Hill

dike

bridge

gate

gates

sign

Fox Lane

wet

gas marker

Leash Fen

dike

Foxlane Plantation

feeder

mud

Barbrook IV ring cairn

gas marker×

Ramsley Moor

gas marker

gates

locked gate

gate

wet

bridge

wet

signs

Ramsley Reservoir (site)

gates

locked gate

Martin Slack's Field

Ramsley Lodge (site)

post

gates

stake

Stump Cross× (site)

Blake Brook

locked gate

0   200   400
METRES

CONTINUATION ON p125

gate

Barbrook II stone circle (walled)

Companion stone

guide stoop

Barbrook I stone circle

marker stone

marker stone

Bronze Age cairns

Barbrook

Robin Hood's Table

netting

cist (hollow)

gates

A621

Bar Brook

Big Moot Plantation

CONTINUATION ON p121

Clod Hall Lane

clapper bridge

gate

gate

gates

sign

Curbar Lane

to Baslow (2 miles)

A good track follows the east side of **Bar Brook** all the way up to the top reservoir. It passes close to **Barbrook I stone circle**, from where a path leads up to a large cairn and then left to **Barbrook II** before rejoining the main route further up. The west side is harder to follow, though a path crosses the bridge by **Little Barbrook Reservoir** and follows a drain from the dam to pass a series of guide stoops and marker stones. At the third stone, turn left and drop down the bank to pick up a faint path running parallel to the stream. This leads most of the way down to Curbar Lane at the foot of the moor. It is crossed by another faint line from opposite Barbrook I that crosses the stream near **Robin Hood's Table** and becomes clearer as it ascends a holloway past a Bronze Age cist.

Leash Fen developed because impervious shales prevented its drainage. Rushes and sphagnum moss developed, with the few trees growing only in its drier parts. Local folk tales speak of a lost village beneath the bog, and fragments of earthenware and carved oak were discovered when the drainage ditches were dug, possibly relating to a crannog-like dwelling, or even a ceremonial site of the type found on Flag Fen, Cambridgeshire.

123

The **Bible Stones** are a series of four roadside stones between Curbar Gap
Curbar that were engraved with Bible verses by Edwin Gregory in the 1
century. He was one of the Duke of Rutland's mole-catchers and had rece
recovered from a serious illness, so he did this to show
gratitude to God. Today's readings are Hebrews 7:25, Isa
1:18, John 5:24 (next to a trough) and Matthew 16:

The five **Cundy Graves** can be found in t
bracken below Baslow Edge and mark t
burial site of the Cundy family of near
Grislow Field, who fell victim to t
plague thirty years befo
it famou
reach
Ey

Warren
Lodge
gate
sign
**Bible
Stone**
& trough
**Bible
Stones**
gate
sign &
squeeze
gates
sign
CURBAR
stiles
gate
squeezes
sign
sign &
gate
**Curbar
Gap** guide
stoop
gates
viewpoint

CONTINUATION ON
Curbar Lane
P121
locked
gate

Square
Stone
millstones
**Cundy
Graves**
vent

WWII Starfish
decoy site

Sandyford Brook

guide stoop &
companion stone

Barbrook
Mill (site)

Baslow Edge
Gun
Buttress
old wall

Eaglestone
Flat
pile of
stones

**smelting
mill** (ruin)
ruin
gate
**Rock
End**
stile
bri

gates
vent
sign
gate
**Eagle
Stone**
post
**Wellington's
Monument**
Bar Brook

Blackstone Edge

Gardom's Edge
gate
**standing
stone**
cairn
aligned
pits

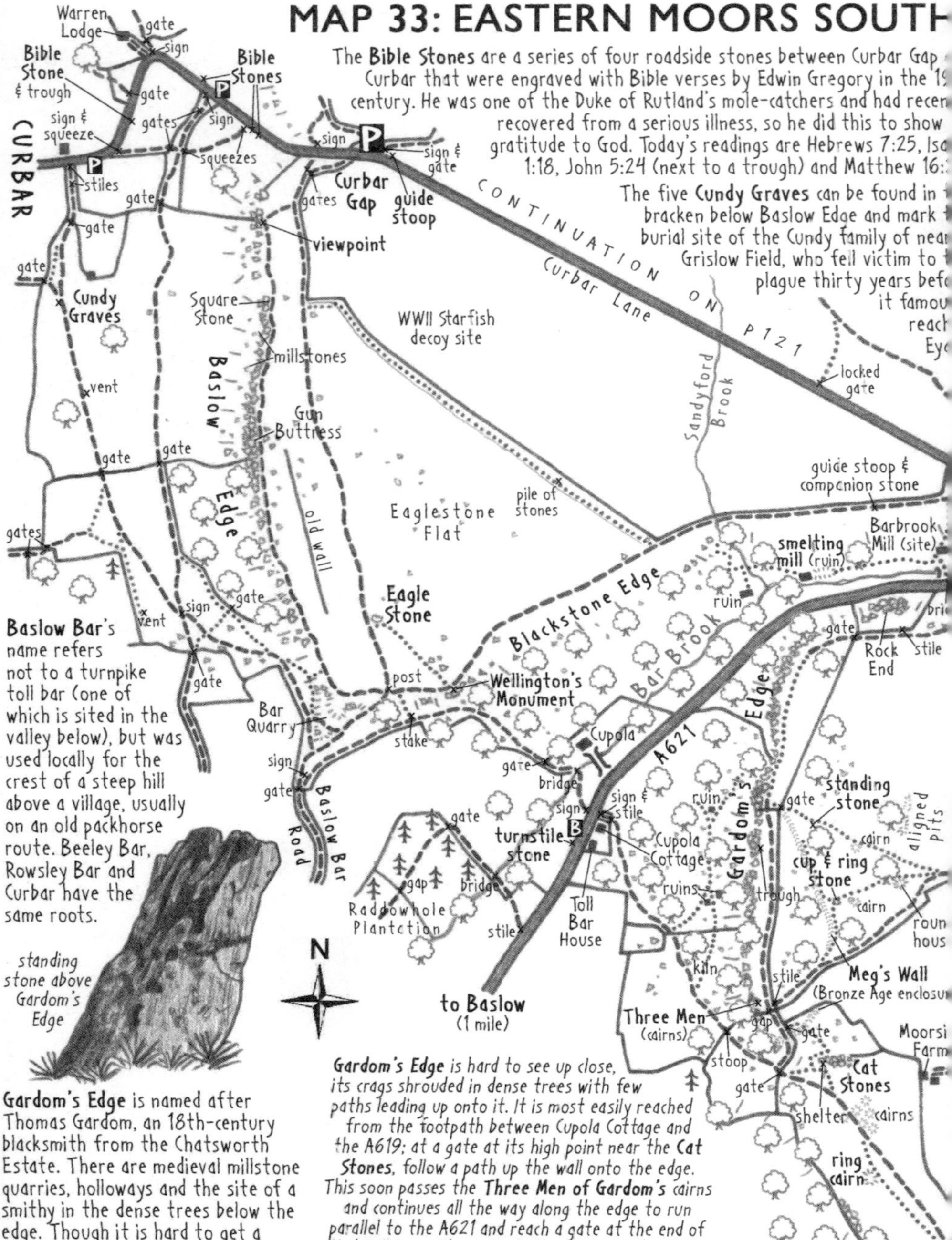

Baslow Bar's
name refers
not to a turnpike
toll bar (one of
which is sited in the
valley below), but was
used locally for the
crest of a steep hill
above a village, usually
on an old packhorse
route. Beeley Bar,
Rowsley Bar and
Curbar have the
same roots.

Bar
Quarry
sign
gate
stake
Cupola
A621
ruin
**cup & ring
stone**
cairn
roun
hous

*standing
stone above
Gardom's
Edge*

Baslow Bar Road
gap
bridge
gate
bridge
Raddowhole
Plantction
stile
**turnstile
stone**
B
sign &
stile
**Cupola
Cottage**
ruins
trough
**Toll
Bar
House**
kiln
stile
cairn
Meg's Wall
(Bronze Age enclosu
Moorsi
Farm

N

to Baslow
(1 mile)

Three Men
(cairns)
stoop
gate
gap
gate
**Cat
Stones**
shelter
cairns

Gardom's Edge is named after
Thomas Gardom, an 18th-century
blacksmith from the Chatsworth
Estate. There are medieval millstone
quarries, holloways and the site of a
smithy in the dense trees below the
edge. Though it is hard to get a
close-up view of the edge, it is a
good climbing area. The prominent
Apple Buttress was named by Eric
Byne after he found an apple in the
crack there in the 1930s. It turned
out to have been left there
by a woman he later married.

124

Gardom's Edge is hard to see up close,
its crags shrouded in dense trees with few
paths leading up onto it. It is most easily reached
from the footpath between Cupola Cottage and
the A619; at a gate at its high point near the **Cat
Stones**, follow a path up the wall onto the edge.
This soon passes the **Three Men of Gardom's** cairns
and continues all the way along the edge to run
parallel to the A621 and reach a gate at the end of
Clod Hall Lane. The ancient sites all lie on the birch-
scattered moor to the east of the edge. A path from
the gate by the Three Men follows the wall to
Birchen Edge, but bearing left onto a faint path
at the first bend brings you upon the remarkable
cup & ring-marked stone and subsequently a
Bronze Age round house. A path from the next
gate north leads past the striking **standing stone**.

ring
cairn
A619
to
Baslow
(1 mile)
Heath

CONTINUATION

Baslow, Gardom's & Birchen Edges)

The southern end of the Eastern Moors is lower but forms a continuation of the rocky Eastern Edges, most of them here densely cloaked in trees. There are many fascinating prehistoric sites to be found, particularly on Gardom's Edge, where the finest carved stone in the Peak District lies beneath the bracken and birch. The area is most easily explored from Curbar, Curbar Gap or lay-bys along the surprisingly busy rat run of Clod Hall Lane.

the Three Ships on Birchen Edge

The **Three Ships** are striking boulders shaped like the prows of ships and carved with the names of three of Nelson's ships at the Battle of Trafalgar; Victory, Defiance and Royal Sovereign (misspelt Soverin).

Nelson's Monument was put up and carved by local stonemason Samson Savage shortly after Nelson's death at the Battle of Trafalgar. A pilgrimage was organised by Dr E.H. Wrench in 1905, when this date was carved into it. The vulgar stone cross of **Wellington's Monument** faces it on Blackstone Edge and was put up by Dr Wrench to commemorate the Duke's visit to the moor as a quest of the Duke of Rutland in 1866.

Leash Fen is particularly hard to explore from Clod Hall Lane as there are no paths out into the wilderness. A locked gate opposite Clod Hall Farm leads to a rough drain heading north, which can be followed up to **Whibbersley Cross**, but by then you will have probably had enough of the coarse tussocks.

Clod Hall was the site of a squatters' house built of clods of peat.

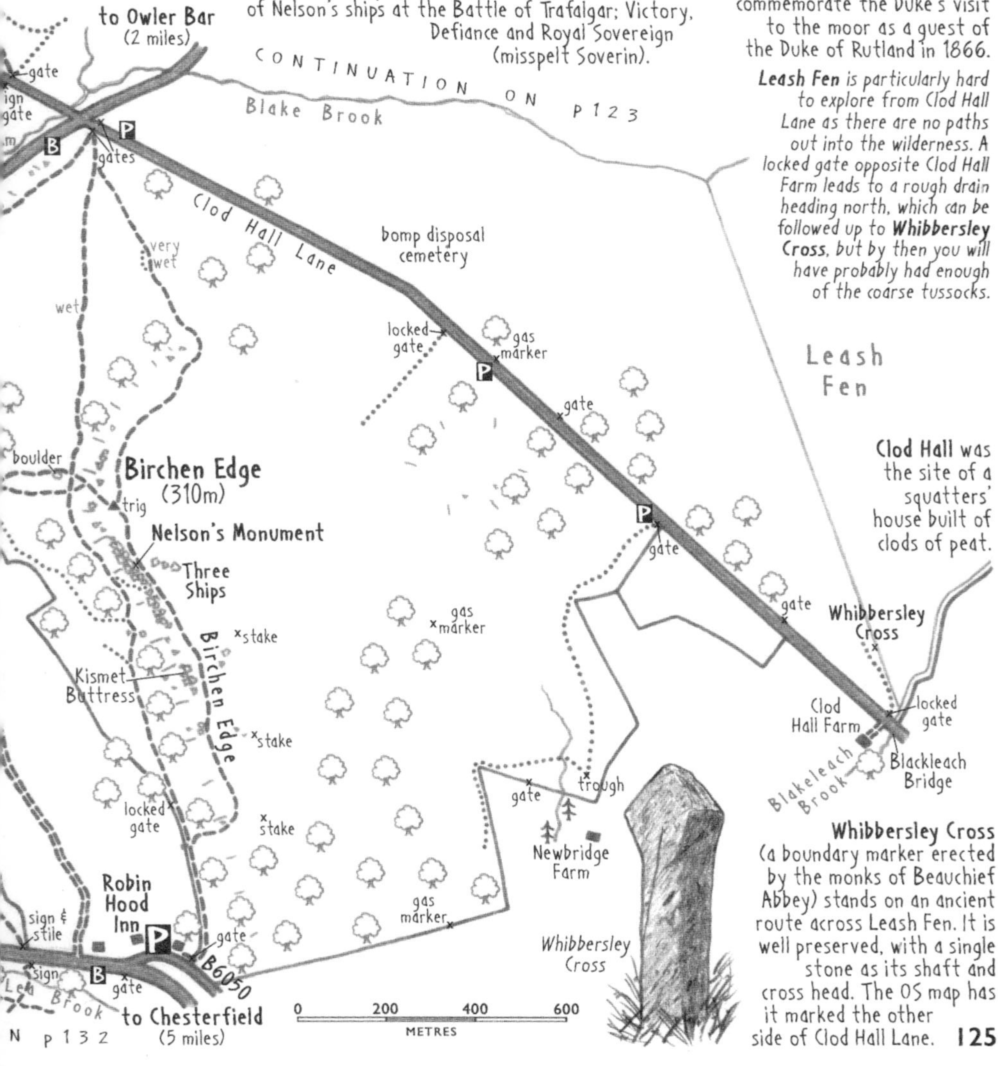

Whibbersley Cross (a boundary marker erected by the monks of Beauchief Abbey) stands on an ancient route across Leash Fen. It is well preserved, with a single stone as its shaft and cross head. The OS map has it marked the other side of Clod Hall Lane.

Map labels:
- to Owler Bar (2 miles)
- sign gate
- sign gate
- B
- P gates
- CONTINUATION ON p123
- Blake Brook
- Clod Hall Lane
- very wet
- wet
- bomp disposal cemetery
- locked gate
- gas marker
- P
- gate
- boulder
- Birchen Edge (310m)
- trig
- Nelson's Monument
- Three Ships
- Birchen Edge
- Kismet Buttress
- x stake
- gas marker
- x stake
- Leash Fen
- P
- gate
- gate
- Whibbersley Cross
- Clod Hall Farm
- locked gate
- Blakeleach Brook
- Blackleach Bridge
- locked gate
- x stake
- gate
- trough
- Newbridge Farm
- Whibbersley Cross
- Robin Hood Inn
- sign & stile
- P
- gate
- gas marker
- B6050
- Sign
- B
- gate
- Lea Brook
- N p132
- to Chesterfield (5 miles)

Scale: 0 200 400 600 METRES

125

1 From **Grindleford station**, follow a path up the hill to the immediate right of the café building. Head straight across the main road and fork right at the top of the rough steps to follow **Rise Brook** up through **Oak's Wood**. Carry straight on until it opens out, then go right across the stream before heading left up the other side on a grassy line across White's Moor.

The **Barbrook stone circles** are thought to be the early Bronze Age monuments of small family groups. There are also over 67 barrows and cairns on this holy ground to the east of the stream, one of which has been restored near Barbrook I. **Barbrook II** has also been restored to its original appearance with standing stones incorporated into a walled bank and a central cist in which a cremation urn was found. **Barbrook I** possesses the most striking standing stones but would have originally had a similar walled bank. **Barbrook III**, though faint, has one of the largest diameters in the Peak District. **Stoke Flat stone circle** has several missing stones and would also have been embanked.

7 Rejoin the main path after the **stone circle** and continue through the trees, forking left to reach the A625. A few yards to the right, turn left through a gate and cross Haywood Brook. Fork left below the car park to descend past an old quarry into **Hay Wood**. Now fork right twice to maintain your height along the slopes of Tumbling Hill, before eventually dropping down to the edge of **Grindleford**. Reaching the road, bear immediately right back up into the woods, then fork left on a path down to the rocky stream you followed up from **Grindleford station** earlier.

White Edge Lodge, one of three identical Jacobean-style shooting lodges built by the Duke of Rutland in the 1830s, stands out prominently on the skyline. The others were Ramsley Lodge (now ruined) and Thickwoods Lodge (by Owler Bar).

The **Bronze Age settlement** near **Swine Sty** is identifiable by the footings of its huts (islands of short grass amid the bracken and coarser grass) and the remains of its walled enclosures below the shallow edge. Flint artefacts suggest the area may have been occupied even earlier. The area above is covered with clearance cairns, barrows and a field system, where the ground was cleared for cultivation. There is also evidence of a workshop where shale was worked to produce polished buttons, rings and bracelets, and a stone cist in the lee of a small rocky outcrop.

126

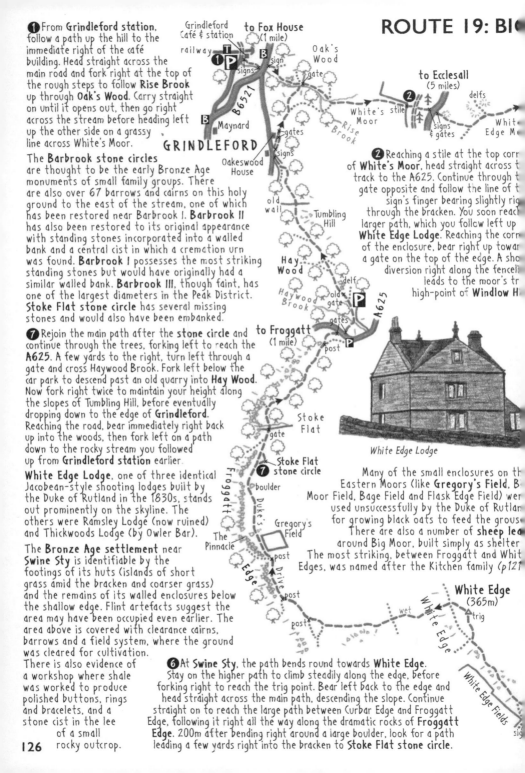

White Edge Lodge

2 Reaching a stile at the top corn of **White's Moor**, head straight across t track to the A625. Continue through t gate opposite and follow the line of t sign's finger bearing slightly rig through the bracken. You soon reach larger path, which you follow left up **White Edge Lodge**. Reaching the corn of the enclosure, bear right up towar a gate on the top of the edge. A sho diversion right along the fencel leads to the moor's tr high-point of **Windlow H**

Many of the small enclosures on th Eastern Moors (like **Gregory's Field**, B Moor Field, Bage Field and Flask Edge Field) wer used unsuccessfully by the Duke of Rutlan for growing black oats to feed the grous There are also a number of **sheep lea** around Big Moor, built simply as shelter The most striking, between Froggatt and Whit Edges, was named after the Kitchen family (p121

6 At **Swine Sty**, the path bends round towards **White Edge**. Stay on the higher path to climb steadily along the edge, before forking right to reach the trig point. Bear left back to the edge and head straight across the main path, descending the slope. Continue straight on to reach the large path between Curbar Edge and Froggatt Edge, following it right all the way along the dramatic rocks of **Froggatt Edge**. 200m after bending right around a large boulder, look for a path leading a few yards right into the bracken to **Stoke Flat stone circle**.

Distance: 8½ miles (13.5km)
Ascent: 360m
Difficulty: Moderate

Parking: Free car park by Grindleford Station or pay car park at Hay Wood on A625. Also lay-bys along the B6054 and A625.

Public Transport: Grindleford is on the Hope Valley railway line between Sheffield and Manchester and bus 65/65a from Sheffield.

Character: A varied circuit of the Eastern Moors, combining the woods of Grindleford, the high points of White Edge and Windlow Hill and the prehistoric sites of Big Moor. The route passes four stone circles as well as taking in Lady's Cross and Froggatt Edge. Mostly straightforward walking, with an alternative route offered around the rough bracken-clogged section between Barbrook I and Swine Sty.

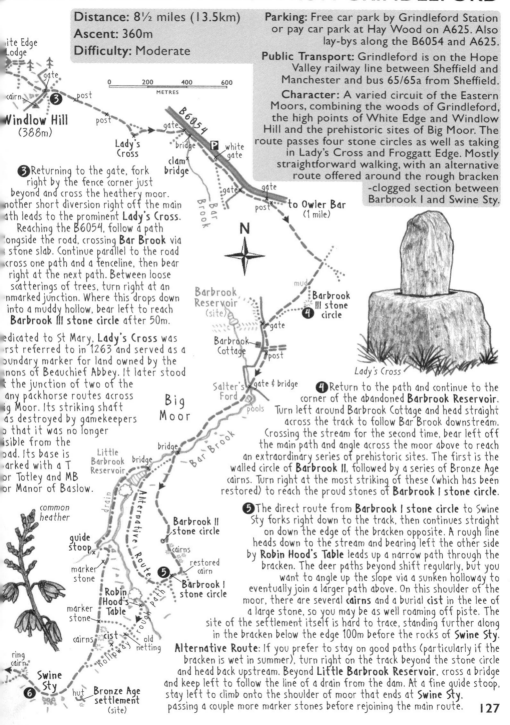

ite Edge Lodge

gate

cairn ❸ post

Windlow Hill (388m)

post

Lady's Cross

B6054

gate

bridge

P white gate

clam bridge

0 200 400 600
METRES

N

gate

gate post **to Owler Bar** (1 mile)

mud

Barbrook Reservoir (site)

Barbrook III stone circle ❹

Bar Brook

gate

Barbrook Cottage

post

Salter's Ford

gate & bridge

pools

Big Moor

Little Barbrook Reservoir

bridge

Bar Brook

drain

common heather

guide stoop

marker stone

Robin Hood's Table

marker stone

cairns cist

ring cairn

Swine Sty ❻

hut **Bronze Age settlement** (site)

Alternative Route

rough path

holloway old netting

Barbrook II stone circle

cairns

restored cairn

❺ **Barbrook I stone circle**

Lady's Cross

❸ Returning to the gate, fork right by the fence corner just beyond and cross the heathery moor. nother short diversion right off the main ath leads to the prominent **Lady's Cross**.
Reaching the B6054, follow a path ongside the road, crossing **Bar Brook** via stone slab. Continue parallel to the road cross one path and a fenceline, then bear right at the next path. Between loose scatterings of trees, turn right at an nmarked junction. Where this drops down into a muddy hollow, bear left to reach **Barbrook III stone circle** after 50m.

edicated to St Mary, **Lady's Cross** was rst referred to in 1263 and served as a oundary marker for land owned by the anons of Beauchief Abbey. It later stood t the junction of two of the any packhorse routes across ig Moor. Its striking shaft as destroyed by gamekeepers o that it was no longer isible from the oad. Its base is arked with a T or Totley and MB or Manor of Baslow.

❹ Return to the path and continue to the corner of the abandoned **Barbrook Reservoir**. Turn left around Barbrook Cottage and head straight across the track to follow Bar Brook downstream. Crossing the stream for the second time, bear left off the main path and angle across the moor above to reach an extraordinary series of prehistoric sites. The first is the walled circle of **Barbrook II**, followed by a series of Bronze Age cairns. Turn right at the most striking of these (which has been restored) to reach the proud stones of **Barbrook I stone circle**.

❺ The direct route from **Barbrook I stone circle** to Swine Sty forks right down to the track, then continues straight on down the edge of the bracken opposite. A rough line heads down to the stream and bearing left the other side by **Robin Hood's Table** leads up a narrow path through the bracken. The deer paths beyond shift regularly, but you want to angle up the slope via a sunken holloway to eventually join a larger path above. On this shoulder of the moor, there are several cairns and a burial cist in the lee of a large stone, so you may be as well roaming off piste. The site of the settlement itself is hard to trace, standing further along in the bracken below the edge 100m before the rocks of **Swine Sty**.

Alternative Route: If you prefer to stay on good paths (particularly if the bracken is wet in summer), turn right on the track beyond the stone circle and head back upstream. Beyond **Little Barbrook Reservoir**, cross a bridge and keep left to follow the line of a drain from the dam. At a fine guide stoop, stay left to climb onto the shoulder of moor that ends at **Swine Sty**, passing a couple more marker stones before rejoining the main route.

ROUTE 20: THE EASTERN EDGES FROM BASLOW

Distance: 8½ miles (13.8km)

Ascent: 370m

Difficulty: Easy

Parking: Pay car parks in Baslow and at Curbar Gap. Small lay-bys on Clod Hall Lane and Curbar Lane.

Public Transport: Bus 218 (towards Bakewell) runs regularly from Sheffield to Baslow, stopping near the Devonshire Arms.

Character: Explore the four edges of Gardom's, Birchen, Curbar and Baslow from Baslow village, taking in both Nelson's and Wellington's Monuments as well as a series of fine prehistoric sites above Gardom's Edge. Mostly straightforward walking on good paths with a short scramble up Birchen Edge that can easily be avoided.

Curbar Gap was the route of Rumbling Street, a Roman Road which ran from the lead mining areas of the Peak to Chesterfield and the port at Bawtry, and later part of a turnpike between Chesterfield and Sparrowpit.

The **Eagle Stone** is the largest gritstone boulder in the Peak District. Its name is a corruption of Aigle Stone, possibly after a deity who hurled the stone here, or possibly from haggle (as somewhere packmen met and exchanged goods). The stone is one of many said to spin round when a cock crows, and Baslow girls once demanded their men climb the stone before accepting a marriage proposal. There are also tales of **Gabriel's Hounds** (or the Gabble Ratchets) being heard on Eaglestone Flat – they are said to be evil spirits hunting the souls of the dead and anyone that hears them is doomed to die.

6 Head straight across the road at **Curbar Gap** and fork right away from the wall to reach the viewpoint at the end of **Baslow Edge**. Follow the edge all the way along until the path bends round to a junction above Blackstone Edge. It is a short diversion left to the huge **Eagle Stone**, from where a small path doubles back right to nearby **Wellington's Monument**. Follow the main path right to return to the junction and bear left down the hill. This lane track is the

5 Turn left at the sign and descend across **Sandyford Brook**. At the wall corner beyond, fork right to join a path between the walled enclosures of White Edge and Curbar Fields. At the far edge of the enclosure, turn left along the wall, then continue straight on at the next corner to reach the dramatic face of **Curbar Edge**. A surfaced path leads left down to Curbar Gap, but it is more interesting to follow the edge – the faint path here curves back to join the main path at a gate above **Curbar Lane**.

4 From the **Birchen Edge** trig point, continue along the top of the slope until the path bends down to cross the soggy grassland below. There is one particularly wet section, which is best circumnavigated to the left, but you soon reach a gate onto **Clod Hall Lane**. Turn left and, after heading straight across the A621, turn right through a gate on the right. Fork left and follow the clear path across the hillside. Go right up the bank where it forks, though the paths soon rejoin to reach a sign at the foot of **White Edge**.

---

to Totley (4 miles)

Clod Hall Lane

gate

Curbar Lane

Brook

0 200 400 600
METRES

Swine Sty

marker stone ×

White Edge

wet

bridge

5 sign

bridge

Sandyford Brook

White Edge Fields

pool

gate

Curbar Fields

gate

Curbar Gap

P Curbar Lane

gate

6 Signs

gate

Square Stone

viewpoint

Curbar Edge

millstones ×

pillar ×

millstones ×

to Curbar (½ mile)

P

Baslow Edge

Eaglestone

the Eagle Stone

128

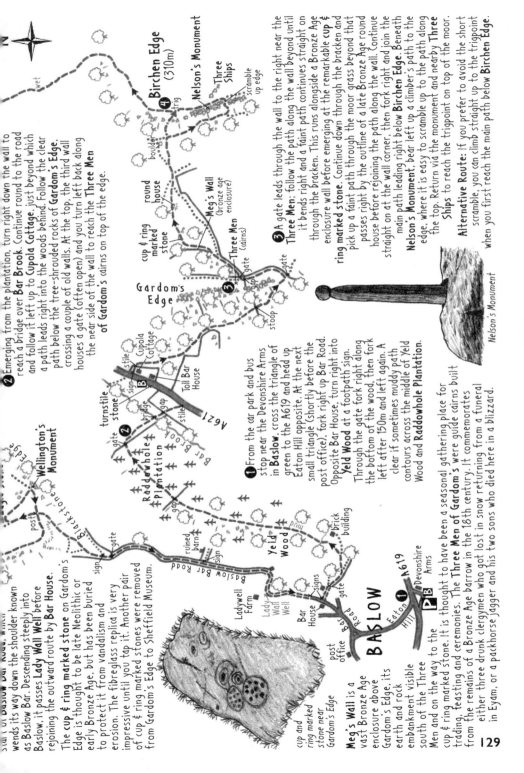

2 Emerging from the plantation, turn right down the wall to reach a bridge over **Bar Brook**. Continue round to the road and follow it left up to **Cupola Cottage**, just beyond which a path leads right into the woods behind. Follow the clear path below the tree-shrouded rocks of **Gardom's Edge**, crossing a couple of old walls. At the top, the third wall houses a gate (often open) and you turn left back along the near side of the wall to reach the **Three Men of Gardom's** cairns on top of the edge.

Birchen Edge (310m)

Nelson's Monument

Three Ships

ring

boulder

scramble up edge

cup & ring marked stone

round house

Meg's Wall (bronze age enclosure?)

Gardom's Edge

Three Men (cairns)

3 A gate leads through the wall to the right near the **Three Men**: follow the path along the wall beyond until it bends right and a faint path continues straight on through the bracken. This runs alongside a Bronze Age enclosure wall before emerging at the remarkable **cup & ring marked stone**. Continue down through the bracken and pick up a faint path through the moor grass beyond that passes right by the outline of a late Bronze Age round house before rejoining the path along the wall. Continue straight on at the wall corner, then fork right and join the main path leading right below **Birchen Edge**. Beneath **Nelson's Monument**, bear left up a climber's path to the edge, where it is easy to scramble up to the path along the top. Return via the monument and nearby **Three Ships** to reach the trigpoint on top of the moor.

Alternative Route: If you prefer to avoid the short scramble, you can climb straight up to the trigpoint when you first reach the main path below **Birchen Edge**.

Nelson's Monument

stoop

gate

gate

turnstile stone

gate sign

gap

stile

sign

Cupola Cottage

Toll Bar House

A621

bridge

Bar Brook

2

Raddewhole Plantation

gap

Wellington's Monument

...Edge

Blackstone...

post

sign

gate

sign

ruined barn

Baslow Bar Road

mud

brick building

Yeld Wood

Ladywell Farm

Lady Wolf Well

Bar House

post office

1 From the car park and bus stop near the Devonshire Arms in **Baslow**, cross the triangle of green to the A619 and head up Eaton Hill opposite. At the next small triangle (shortly before the post office), fork right up Bar Road. Opposite Bar House, turn right into **Yeld Wood** at a footpath sign. Through the gate fork right along the bottom of the wood, then fork left after 150m and left again. A clear if sometimes muddy path contours across the middle of Yeld Wood and **Raddwhole Plantation**.

BASLOW

Eaton Hill

A619

Devonshire Arms

signs

gate

1

P B

cup and ring marked stone near Gardom's Edge

Meg's Wall is a vast Bronze Age enclosure above Gardom's Edge, its earth and rock embankment visible south of the Three Men and on the way to the cup & ring marked stone. It is thought to have been a seasonal gathering place for trading, feasting and ceremonies. The **Three Men of Gardom's** were guide cairns built from the remains of a Bronze Age barrow in the 18th century. It commemorates either three drunk clergymen who got lost in snow returning from a funeral in Eyam, or a packhorse jagger and his two sons who died here in a blizzard.

...of Baslow Bar Road, which wends its way down the shoulder known as Baslow Bar. Descending steeply into Baslow, it passes **Lady Wall Well** before rejoining the outward route by **Bar House**.

The **cup & ring marked stone** on Gardom's Edge is thought to be late Neolithic or early Bronze Age, but has been buried to protect it from vandalism and erosion. The fibreglass replica is very impressive until you tap it. Another pair of cup & ring marked stones were removed from Gardom's Edge to Sheffield Museum.

MILLSTONE QUARRYING

Quarrying has been an important industry in the Peak District for centuries, both in the gritstone and limestone areas, leaving its mark on many of the moorland landscapes. From the monstrous Hope Cement Works, the largest in the UK and sited on the boundary between the limestone and shale that provide the main ingredients of cement, to the hundreds of small quarries that were cut into the natural edges of Stanage, Burbage, and Froggatt on the opposite side of the Derwent Valley.

As well as building stone, millstones were hewn in situ here from the 15th century. Derbyshire millstones were generally used for milling oats and corn rather than wheat, which they tended to discolour during milling, a particular problem with the popularisation of white bread from the 18th century. However, not all of the circular stones were millstones; grindstones were used for sharpening blades and tools (although the coarse stone was unfortunately unsuitable for grinding the fine knives produced in Sheffield); and crushing stones were used for pulping wood, crushing lead ore, and making paint. These were generally larger (weighing several tonnes) and identifiable by having square holes than round holes at their centre. Troughs, lintels and gate stoops were also hewn in these quarries.

Early millstone workers were independent, often seasonal and could sell directly to merchants or agents at ports like that at Bawtry, to which a lot of the stones were transported before the Chesterfield Canal was constructed. They worked in isolated places on top of the moors, cutting and dressing stones where they lay, often making would use of the best earthfast boulders, which were easier to work. The completed stones were dragged down deep holloways by horse and sled to be loaded onto drugs (or carts). Such was the weight of the stones that they paid a particularly high toll on the turnpikes. There are records of stones being carted over Redmires and Ringinglow by horse and oxen, but the main route was known as Millstone Gate and led from Millstone Edge towards Chesterfield.

The industry was at its peak in the 17th century when war in Europe restricted the import of superior stones from the Rhine and Fontainebleau. By then tenant quarry-masters were in place, paying hewers per stone. Many of the sites around Hathersage were controlled by the Rotherhams, who were able to set very low wages for stone workers. The plug-and-feather method had become widespread, producing a line of regular deep hollows in the edge of the split stone that can be seen in many left on site today. A line of kiln-dried wooden plugs with metal shields were wetted, then hammered into the rock, lifting the stone cleanly apart as the wood dried over a couple of days. Gunpowder was later used at places like Millstone Edge and Bole Hill, enabling deep quarries to be dug into the best beds of rock.

Demand for millstones declined in the late 19th century due to new milling methods and the bottom fell out of the market completely in the 1920s, leaving lines of finished millstones scattered around the eastern edges. There are also many offcuts and failures that were abandoned in situ, often propped up at an angle for dressing – millstones that split or weren't cutting right, massive troughs that split late in the process, or crude shapes that were quickly discarded. The earlier stones are domed on one side, while the more regular flat-edged ones date from the 19th century. Remote sites usually also had a blacksmith's hut, where the masons' tools were regularly sharpened, and the footings of these can often be seen, as well simple loading bays where stones were rolled onto carts. This once busy industrial landscape now lies quiet.

abandoned millstones

CHAPTER 13 – CHATSWORTH MOORS

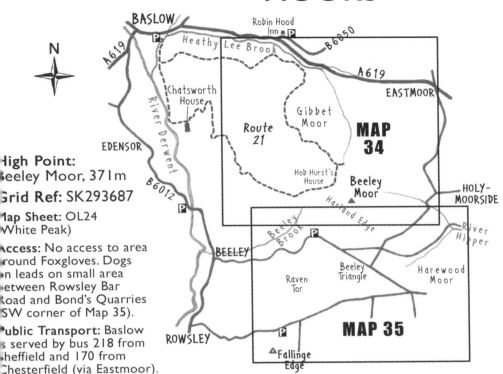

High Point:
Beeley Moor, 371m

Grid Ref: SK293687

Map Sheet: OL24
(White Peak)

Access: No access to area
around Foxgloves. Dogs
on leads on small area
between Rowsley Bar
Road and Bond's Quarries
(SW corner of Map 35).

Public Transport: Baslow
is served by bus 218 from
Sheffield and 170 from
Chesterfield (via Eastmoor).

Chatsworth Moors form the far south-eastern extension of the gritstone moors of the
Pennines. Though the gritstone continues towards Matlock and beyond, the open access
land ends at Fallinge Edge with enclosed fields and forests covering the rest of this
ridge of high ground. This was the hardest moorland area to decide on a name for; it
could equally be East Moor or Beeley Moor, but really it is a collection of separately
named moors that could usefully be grouped together under the title of the
Chatsworth Moors. These moorland parcels are separated by several busy back roads
around Beeley Triangle, some more accessible than others. Few are well walked other
than around the edge of the Chatsworth Estate itself. The high point on Beeley Moor is
undistinguished, the trig point standing unhelpfully at the other end of Harland Edge.

The name Chatsworth means 'Ceatt's enclosure', referring to a Saxon landowner, and
it is to the Cavendish's estate that the bulk of this moorland belonged. Before the 18th-
century landscaping that saw large-scale forest planting, the moor would have stretched
most of the way down to Chatsworth House, with the Stand hunting tower a striking
beacon across the wastes.

Beeley Moor and Harland Edge from Beeley Triangle

Until it was realigned in 1824, the **turnpike road** into Baslow crossed Heathy Lee Brook below the Robin Hood Inn and followed the line of the path below Under Pasture Edge to emerge at the old bridge by the Devonshire Arms.

The only car park on the north side of the moor is by the **Robin Hood Inn**. 100m down the road, a path leads down to a bridge across Heathy Lee Brook. Paths then lead straight on up onto **Under Pasture Edge**, right along the conduit at its foot into **Chatsworth Park**, or left up the stream to join the vehicle track onto **Gibbet Moor**. All the other routes leading off this track into the plantations at the top of the estate are private.

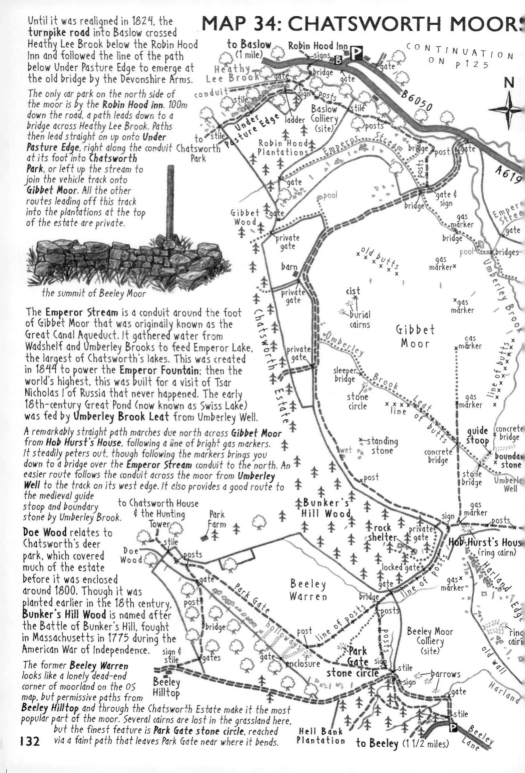

the summit of Beeley Moor

The **Emperor Stream** is a conduit around the foot of Gibbet Moor that was originally known as the Great Canal Aqueduct. It gathered water from Wadshelf and Umberley Brooks to feed Emperor Lake, the largest of Chatsworth's lakes. This was created in 1844 to power the **Emperor Fountain**; then the world's highest, that was built for a visit of Tsar Nicholas I of Russia that never happened. The early 18th-century Great Pond (now known as Swiss Lake) was fed by **Umberley Brook Leat** from Umberley Well.

A remarkably straight path marches due north across **Gibbet Moor** from **Hob Hurst's House**, following a line of bright gas markers. It steadily peters out, though following the markers brings you down to a bridge over the **Emperor Stream** conduit to the north. An easier route follows the conduit across the moor from **Umberley Well** to the track on its west edge. It also provides a good route to the medieval guide stoop and boundary stone by Umberley Brook.

Doe Wood relates to Chatsworth's deer park, which covered much of the estate before it was enclosed around 1800. Though it was planted earlier in the 18th century, **Bunker's Hill Wood** is named after the Battle of Bunker's Hill, fought in Massachusetts in 1775 during the American War of Independence.

The former **Beeley Warren** looks like a lonely dead-end corner of moorland on the OS map, but permissive paths from **Beeley Hilltop** and through the Chatsworth Estate make it the most popular part of the moor. Several cairns are lost in the grassland here, but the finest feature is **Park Gate stone circle**, reached via a faint path that leaves Park Gate near where it bends.

This large swathe of open moorland surrounds the plantations at the top of the
Chatsworth House Estate and is home to a fine array of prehistoric sites and medieval
boundary stones and guide stoops. Its true top is unmarked in the heather of Beeley
Moor, but its focal point is Hob Hurst's House, a well-preserved Bronze Age ring cairn
where the few paths across the moor all meet. It is best explored from the Robin
Hood Inn or a rough parking area on Beeley Lane at the top of Hell Bank Plantation.

The notorious **Pottery Cottage Murders** took place at Eastmoor on the A619 in January 1977, after
Billy Hughes escaped from a police car while being transported to court in Chesterfield. He took the
unsuspecting occupants hostage in terrible weather and held them in separate rooms. While sending
one of the family on errands, he killed the other four one by one. Hughes was shot in Cheshire
following a chase after police were finally informed, and subsequently there were protests
whenever attempts were made to bury or cremate him locally.

gas marker pole

Umberley Brook may be named after *umber*, a reddish-
brown earthy mineral used as a pigment and sometimes
known as raddle or reddle (hence the various Raddlepits and
Reddle, Reddale and Reddicar Cloughs found around the area).

Brampton East Moor is a lonely grassy swathe that is difficult to
access and generally left to the sheep. A rough track can be picked up by a private gate
below **Rod Knoll** (reached by following the boundary fence round from Syda Lane) and
followed to join a new fenceline leading down to Umberley Brook. The only feature here
is a vast heap of stone that comprises a **ruined sheepfold** and the remains of a
prehistoric cairn. This site can also be reached by following a faint path along the
Emperor Stream conduit from the main track up onto Gibbet Moor; crossing Umberley
Brook, the path follows the stream a short way before petering out below the fold.

Hob Hurst's House

Hob Hurst's House is a distinctive ring cairn with a rare square ditch
and embankment around it and five of what may have been thirteen
stones in place. When excavated in 1853 by Thomas Bateman, human
bones, two pieces of galena (a lead ore) and the remains of a fire
were found. Hob i'th Hurst was a mischievous wood spirit said to
inhabit ancient features such as this. Reports vary as to whether
he helped the local community, turned milk sour or made crops fail.

Beeley Moor Colliery was worked from at least
as early as the 16th century and consisted of
ten opencast pits and over twenty deeper
shafts, two of which have spoil heaps and
the obvious sites of horse-powered gins.
Further trial holes were dug in the
19th century, but little was found.

The name **Harland
Edge** relates to the
Old English word *har*
for a parish or hundred
boundary, as do nearby
Harewood Grange (p135) (a
possession of Beauchief Abbey from
the 13th century) and **Holymoorside**
(a corruption of Harley Moor Side).

The true summit of **Beeley Moor** is marked by a stake in one
of a series of ruined quarry buildings on the heather ridge above
Harland Edge, close to a small rock outcrop. Though there is a
tentative sheeptrack along the edge from **Hob Hurst's House**, it is
largely a rough tramp to it or **Harland South** trig (which itself is hard to
reach, see p135). The only path across the moor from this side is a well
waymarked old peatcutters' path from Syda Lane to Hob Hurst's House.

Map labels

Wadshelf
Top Bridge
to Chesterfield (5 miles)
Stonelow Bridge
broken down wall
B
EAST-MOOR
Brook
ruined fold
cairn
enclosure
gate
tied gate
Brampton East Moor
Rod Knoll
private gate
Umberley Sick
posts
post
post
post
wet
posts
gate
Syda Lane
old butts
clay pits
guide stoop (and companion stone)
Hipper Sick
pools
locked gate
to Holymoorside (1 1/2 miles)
gate
boundary stone
Longside Moor
ruins
stake & ruin
Beeley Moor (371m)
boundary stone
boundary stone
Harland South (367m)
trig
Harland Edge
Sick

0 200 400 600
METRES

MAP 35: CHATWORTH MOORS SOUTH (Beeley)

This feels like the last hurrah of the Pennine Moors on the east side of Derbyshire, but the rugged heathery faces of Fallinge and Harland Edges retain a wild charm. Though Beeley Moor is criss-crossed by busy back roads, it is remarkably hard to access and consequently little trodden. There are paths along neither of the edges nor to Harland South trig, so often you end up gazing over an impenetrable high estate wall or presented with a locked gate. The west end of Rowsley Bar Road offers the best point of exploration, though concocting any sort of round route is very tricky. Harewood and Longside Moors offer gentler, grassier slopes and more satisfying (if still rather limited) paths.

Fallinge Edge is a quarry-riddled edge crested by the small crag of *Raven Tor*. It is most easily accessed from Rowsley Bar Road via a couple of gates by *Bond's Quarries*. Paths from each peter out on the heather-covered edge, but other faint lines can be picked up running either above or below the quarries. The path through the bracken below is better, while the path above runs near the *triple cairns* (three interlinked barrows within a cairnfield) and top of Raven Tor. From Beeley Lane to the north there is only one stile onto this part of *Beeley Moor*, with a good track leading from it joining the line of gas markers across the heart of the moor – unfortunately there is no access point at the other end of this useful line.
The *ring cairn* on Fallinge Edge is hard to reach, but best found by following a heathery holloway from the near the junction of these paths.

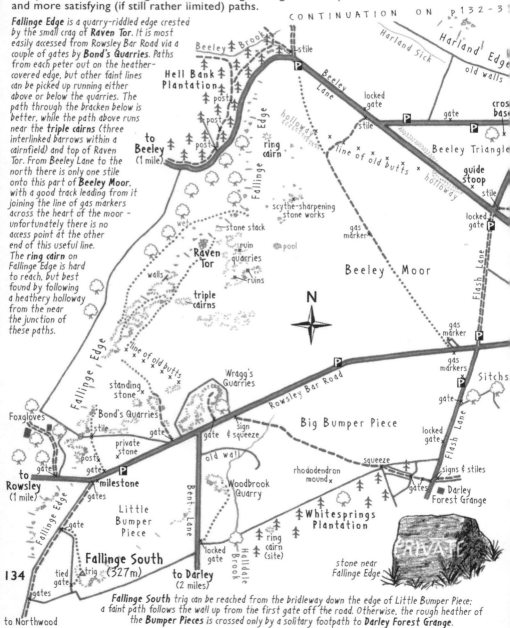

CONTINUATION ON P 132-3

134

Fallinge South trig can be reached from the bridleway down the edge of Little Bumper Piece; a faint path follows the wall up from the first gate off the road. Otherwise, the rough heather of the *Bumper Pieces* is crossed only by a solitary footpath to *Darley Forest Grange*.

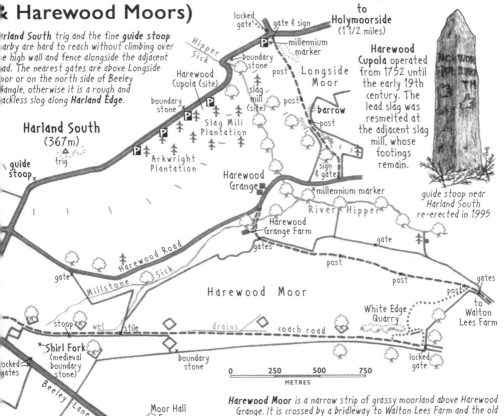

rland South trig and the fine **guide stoop**
arby are hard to reach without climbing over
e high wall and fence alongside the adjacent
ad. The nearest gates are above Longside
oor or on the north side of Beeley
iangle, otherwise it is a rough and
ackless slog along **Harland Edge**.

Harland South
(367m)

Harewood Cupola operated from 1752 until the early 19th century. The lead slag was resmelted at the adjacent slag mill, whose footings remain.

guide stoop near
Harland South
re-erected in 1995

Harewood Moor is a narrow strip of grassy moorland above Harewood Grange. It is crossed by a bridleway to Walton Lees Farm and the old **coach road** from Beeley Triangle. This is a satisfying walk between a series of diamond-shaped copses. Near the western end, you can peek over the wall to the right to see the beautifully carved medieval boundary stone at **Shirl Fork**. The coach road ends at a locked gate at its eastern end, but a path shortly before leads up past **White Edge Quarry** and down the slope to join the bridleway along the bottom edge of the moor.

Harewood Moor's most striking features are the series of regular diamond enclosures either side of the coach road. It has been suggested they were sheep shelters that became overgrown, but their layout suggests they were planted with Scots pine as part of the Devonshire's estate to add landscape interest along the coach road.

There was an 18th-century scythe-sharpening and grind-stone industry among the jumbled workings above **Fallinge Edge**, which also provided flagstones and building stone. There are dozens of quarried hollows and the remains of huts scattered all across this rough plateau, as well as earlier coalpits that were used to fuel lead smelting at Smeltingmill Wood just down the hillside. Particularly impressive is a massive stone trough abandoned where it was being worked after it cracked during carving.

During World War II, there was a firing range used by the Home Guard in **Wragg's Quarries**, which had ceased to be worked by the end of the 19th century. The Home Guard also manned a permanent roadblock by Moor Hall Farm in case of invasion via the moors.

Shirl Fork stands unassumingly in a field at the edge of Harewood Moor, but it is the oldest stoop on the moor, referred to as early as the 13th century. It is marked with a number of crosses and stands now at the junction of Beeley, Harewood, Darley and Ashover parishes, and may once have marked the line of an ancient Roman route called Hereward Street. It may also have marked the boundary of Mercia and Northumberland in the Dark Ages. Its name possibly comes from the same root as Carl Wark, an Old German word that became *churl* and was bastardised to Charles Fork in some records. George Wigglesworth has suggested it may relate to *sirle*, an Old English word for armour that died out in the 14th century, and the fork may refer to a long-lost gallows at this undoubtedly important site.

Shirl Fork

135

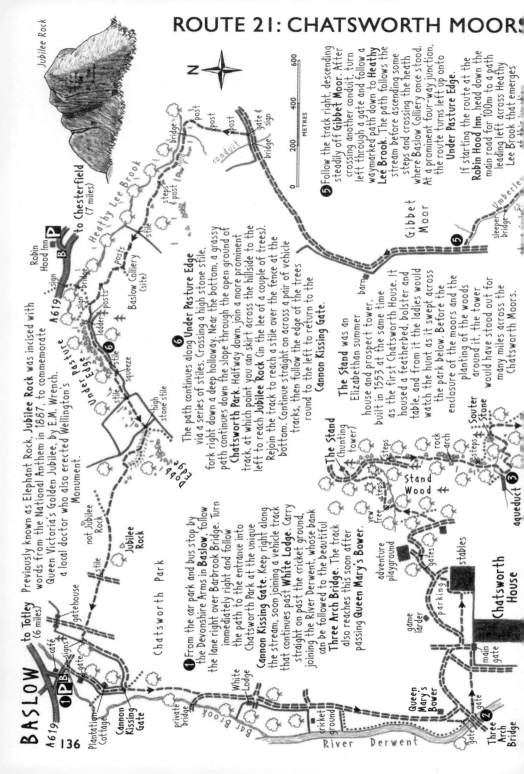

ROUTE 21: CHATSWORTH MOORS

1 From the car park and bus stop by the Devonshire Arms in **Baslow**, follow the lane right over Barbrook Bridge. Turn immediately right and follow the path to the entrance into Chatsworth Park at the unique **Cannon Kissing Gate**. Keep right along the stream, soon joining a vehicle track that continues past **White Lodge**. Carry straight on past the cricket ground, joining the River Derwent, whose bank can be followed to the beautiful **Three Arch Bridge**. The track also reaches this soon after passing **Queen Mary's Bower**.

5 Follow the track right, descending steadily off **Gibbet Moor**. After crossing another conduit, turn left through a gate and follow a waymarked path down to **Heathy Lee Brook**. The path follows the stream before ascending some steps and crossing the heath where Baslow Colliery once stood. At a prominent four-way junction, the route turns left up onto **Under Pasture Edge**.

If starting the route at the **Robin Hood Inn**, head down the main road for 100m to a path leading left across Heathy Lee Brook that emerges at this junction.

6 The path continues along **Under Pasture Edge** via a series of stiles. Crossing a high stone stile, fork right down a deep holloway. Near the bottom, a grassy path continues down the slope through the open ground of **Chatsworth Park**. Halfway down, join a more prominent track, at which point you can skirt across the hillside to the left to reach **Jubilee Rock** (in the lee of a couple of trees). Rejoin the track to reach a stile over the fence at the bottom. Continue straight on across a pair of vehicle tracks, then follow the edge of the trees round to the left to return to the **Cannon Kissing Gate**.

The Stand was an Elizabethan summer house and prospect tower, built in 1553 at the same time as the first Chatsworth House. It housed a featherbed, bolster and table, and from it the ladies would watch the hunt as it swept across the park below. Before the enclosure of the moors and the planting of the woods around it, the tower would have stood out for many miles across the Chatsworth Moors.

Previously known as Elephant Rock, **Jubilee Rock** was incised with words from the National Anthem in 1887, to commemorate Queen Victoria's Golden Jubilee, by E.M. Wrench, a local doctor who also erected Wellington's Monument.

BASLOW
A619
to Totley (6 miles)
to Chesterfield (7 miles)
Robin Hood Inn
136

& HOUSE FROM BASLOW

2 At **Three Arch Bridge**, turn left towards the left edge of **Chatsworth House**. Continue past the ornate main gate up towards the vast stables building. Skirt around its left side then head left up the track towards the adventure playground. If this route is blocked during events, the main vehicle track can be followed up from the bridge and through the parking areas. Beyond a gate, fork right on a track that leads above the adventure playground into **Stand Wood**. After 200m, double back to the left on an obvious path that ends up climbing very steeply up the side of a rocky stream. It emerges below **the Stand**, a 16th-century hunting tower and fine vantage point over the estate. Return to the track below the tower and follow it left, before bearing left up some steps onto a magical path below the crags. Beyond the rock arch, carry straight on to descend slightly to the **aqueduct**; when the stream is flowing, it is worth dropping down the hill to see the waterfall off the end of the aqueduct.

3 From the **aqueduct**, follow the zigzag path up the side of the stream to where it emerges dramatically from the pool on top of the **Souter Stone**. Turn right at the junction just beyond and carry straight on through **Stand Wood** to join a vehicle track. Follow this briefly up the hill, then bear right onto a path. Turn right at the next junction to emerge from the woods at a high stile, following Park Gate steadily up onto the moorland above. The path bends left after half a mile and, just beyond, a faint path leads left to **Park Gate stone circle**.

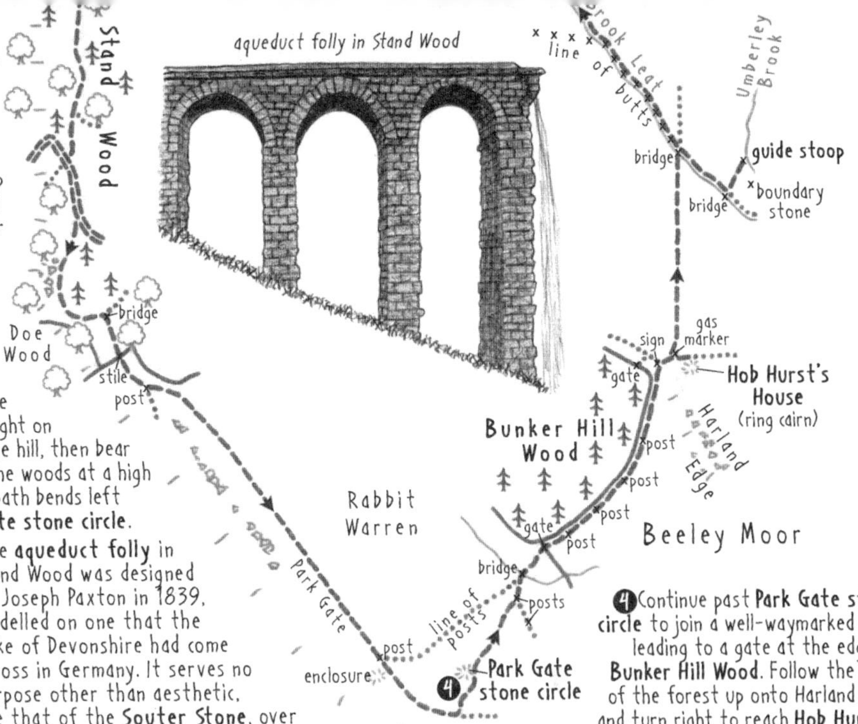

Stand Wood
Doe Wood
bridge
stile
post
Park Gate
enclosure
post
line of posts
Rabbit Warren
Park Gate stone circle
4
bridge
posts
gate
post
post
post
post
Bunker Hill Wood
gate
sign
gas marker
Hob Hurst's House (ring cairn)
Harland Edge
Beeley Moor
bridge
bridge
line of butts
Brook Leat
Umberley Brook
guide stoop
boundary stone

aqueduct folly in Stand Wood

Distance: 9 miles (14.7km)

Ascent: 280m

Difficulty: Easy

Parking: Pay car parks near Devonshire Arms in Baslow and alongside Robin Hood Inn on A619.

Public Transport: The 218 bus from Sheffield stops by the public car park near the Devonshire Arms.

Character: A grand tour of the varied landscape within the Chatsworth Estate, blending the moors with the parkland and enchanting woods lower down. As well as the ancient sites of Hob Hurst's House and Park Gate Stone Circle, the route visits the Stand, aqueduct, Jubilee Rock and of course the Devonshire's grandiose house itself.

Note: During some events, parts of Chatsworth Park may be closed, but the route up into Stand Wood should still be accessible; follow local advice.

The **aqueduct folly** in Stand Wood was designed by Joseph Paxton in 1839, modelled on one that the Duke of Devonshire had come across in Germany. It serves no purpose other than aesthetic, like that of the **Souter Stone**, over which the stream tumbles further up.

Elizabethan **Chatsworth** was very different from today. Bess of Hardwick built a beautiful and understated house, surrounded by a walled garden from the Three Arch Bridge to the cricket ground. **Queen Mary's Bower** was built within this on a former fishpond; a gazebo, then a popular garden feature, it was used by Mary Queen of Scots on her numerous visits in the 1570s when she was a prisoner in Sheffield Castle. It wasn't until the late 17th century that the house was rebuilt by the Dukes of Devonshire and the grounds subsequently remodelled in the open landscape style by Capability Brown.

4 Continue past **Park Gate stone circle** to join a well-waymarked path leading to a gate at the edge of **Bunker Hill Wood**. Follow the edge of the forest up onto Harland Edge and turn right to reach **Hob Hurst's House**, a ring cairn in a fenced enclosure. Retrace your steps to a gas marker post, turning right to head due north across the moor. Reaching **Umberley Brook Leat**, you can divert briefly right to reach a fine **guide stoop** and nearby medieval boundary stone, while the onward route follows the conduit left. You pass a large but faint stone circle before reaching the track along the edge of **Gibbet Moor**.

G.H.B. WARD

"The man who never was lost never went very far" (Bert Ward)

It is hard to go far when researching the history of South Yorkshire's moors without coming across the name and legacy of G.H.B. Ward, founder of the Sheffield Clarion Ramblers. George Herbert Bridges Ward was born in Sheffield in 1876 and worked as an engineer fitter, being involved in the trade union and serving as a Sunday school teacher before becoming interested in socialism. His parents died and left him money in 1900, so he left his job for a time and went to the Canary Islands. He subsequently became fluent in Spanish and befriended a couple of non-violent anarchist politicians in Spain. After one was executed in 1909, he wrote the impassioned book *The Truth About Spain* that had significant impact in Spain,

Working as a civil servant upon his return, he also wrote articles for the radical *Sheffield Guardian*. He was more interested in improving character than in mass organisation, though, and condemned communism. Rambling for him was about mind and body and the cover of most of the Clarion handbooks bore the slogan 'A Rambler made is a man Improved'. The first *Sheffield Clarion Ramblers' Prospectus* was published in 1902, but quickly grew from four pages to up to two hundred pages, replete with photos, poetry, quotations, lists of recommended books and Ward's own essays. Some of these were spiritual, but many were epic tomes on the history of the moors and, in particular, the ancient routes across them. They were accompanied by detailed hand-drawn maps and were the basis for many of the access wrangles that followed, as more and more routes were claimed as public paths.

A considered and respected man, as well as a Freemason, Ward managed various negotiations with landowners to allow the Clarion Ramblers access to moors that others were prohibited from. It has been suggested that he was not involved in the communist-organised Kinder Trespass of 1932 due to conflicts of interest. In addition, landowner James Watts had a writ served against Ward, threatening court action if he was caught trespassing on the west side of Kinder Scout. In the Clarion handbook, Ward did, however, condemn the punishments that were meted out to those involved.

He moved with his family to Storth House Lodge near Holmesfield, where he lived until his death in 1957. The Eastern Moors became his local stamping ground and he did much to research the ancient packhorse trails and features found there, providing many of the finer details quoted in this book. He was involved in the public purchase of much of the Longshaw Estate when it was sold by the Duke of Rutland in 1927 and was among those who convinced J.G. Graves to purchase Blacka Moor and give it to the people of Sheffield. He refused an OBE in 1945, the same year the top of Lose Hill was bought with funds collected by public appeal and given to him. He immediately handed over the land, now named Ward's Piece, to the National Trust.

Bert Ward

BIBLIOGRAPHY

Addy, Sidney Oldall – *A Glossary of Words used in the Neighbourhood of Sheffield, Including a Selection of Local Names, and Some Notices of Folklore, Games, and Customs* (London: English Dialect Society, 1888)

Ardron, Paul A. – *Peat Cutting In Upland Britain, with Special Reference to the Peak District* (Sheffield: University of Sheffield, 2014)

Baker, Ernest A. – *Moors, Crags and Caves of the High Peak and the Neighbourhood* (London: John Haywood, 1903)

Barnatt, John – *Stone Circles of the Peak* (London: Turnstone, 1978)

Barnatt, John – *The Henges, Stone Circles and Ringcairns of the Peak District* (Sheffield: University of Sheffield, 1990)

Barnatt, John, & Bannister, Nicole – *The Archaeology of a Great Estate: Chatsworth and Beyond* (Oxford: Windgather Press, 2009)

Barnatt, John, Bevan, Bill, & Edmonds, Mark – *An Upland Biography: Landscape and Prehistory on Gardom's Edge, Derbyshire* (Oxford: Windgather Press, 2017)

Barrows, John Campion – *Walks around Totley* (Sheffield: John Campion Barrows, 1995)

Bellamy, Rex – *The Peak District Companion* (London: David & Charles, 1981)

Besley, Paul – *Dark Peak Walks* (Milnthorpe: Cicerone, 2017)

Bevan, Bill – *Conservation Heritage Assessment Edale Valley: Moors for the Future Report No. 3* (Moors for the Future, 2006)

Bevan, Bill – *Sheffield's Golden Frame: The Moorland Heritage of Burbage, Houndkirk and Longshaw* (Wilmslow: Sigma Leisure, 2007)

Boulton-Smith, Anthony – *Derbyshire Place-names* (Stroud: Sutton, 2005)

Bradfield Local History Group – *Bygones of Bradfield Vols I-III* (Sheffield: Bradfield Local History Group, 1988)

Branston, Jack – *History of Langsett, and a Few More Stocksbridge Stirrings* (Sheffield: Jack Branston, 1986)

Buxton, Barbara A. – *Hathersage in the Peak: A History* (Chichester: Phillimore, 2005)

Byford, James S. – *Moorland Heritage: The Story of Derwent, Ladybower and the Woodlands Valley* (New Mills: Kinder Press, 1981)

Cameron, Kenneth – *The Place-names of Derbyshire* (Cambridge: University Press, 1959)

Cass, J.F. – *The Rivelin Tunnel 1903-1910* (Transactions of the Hunter Archaeological Society, 18)

Chandler, Chas H. – *More Rambles around Sheffield* (Sheffield Telegraph, 1915)

Claves, Peter – *Footloose in the Peak* (Leek: Churnet Valley Books, 2004)

Collier, Ron – *Dark Peak Aircraft Wrecks* (Barnsley: Wharncliffe Woodmoor, 1982)

Dalton, Roger, Fox, Howard, & Jones, Peter – *Classic Landforms of the Dark Peak* (Sheffield: Geographical Association, 1990)

Derry, John – *Across the Derbyshire Moors* (Sheffield: Sir W.C. Leng & Co, 1934)

Dransfield, John Ness – *A History of the Parish of Penistone* (Penistone: Don Press, 1906)

Eardley, Denis – *Villages of the Peak District* (Stroud: Amberley, 2009)

Edale Society, The – *The Book of Edale: Portrait of a High Peak Village* (Bath: Halsgrove, 2003)

Edgar, Jenny (ed.) – *An Accessible Wilderness: Life at Stanage and the North Lees Estate* (Wotton-under-Edge: Derbyshire County Council, 2003)

139

Evans, Seth – *Bradwell: Ancient and Modern* (London: Forgotten Books, 2017)

Firth, J.B. – *Highways and Byways in Derbyshire* (London: Macmillan & Co., 1908)

Henderson, Mark P. – *Folktales of the Peak District* (Stroud: Amberley, 2013)

Hey, David – *A History of Penistone and District* (Barnsley: Wharncliffe, 2002)

Hey, David – *A History of the Peak District Moors* (Barnsley: Pen & Sword, 2014)

Hey, David – *A History of the South Yorkshire Countryside* (Barnsley: Pen & Sword, 2015)

Hey, David – *Derbyshire: A History* (Lancaster: Carnegie, 2008)

Hey, David – *Historic Hallamshire* (Ashbourne: Landmark, 2002)

Hey, David – *Packmen, Carriers and Packhorse Roads* (Leicester: University Press, 1980)

Holland, John – *The Tour of the Don* (London: R. Groombridge, 1837)

Holmes, Chris – *The Bogtrotters' Guide: Exploring and Walking the Dark Peak* (Wilmslow: Sigma Press, 1994)

Howard, Terence M. – *A Moorland Notebook: A Personal Appraisal of the High Moors of South Yorkshire and Part of North Derbyshire* (Sheffield: Terence M. Howard, 1994)

Howitt, William – *Rural Life of England* (London: Longman, Orme, Brown, Green & Longmans, 1838)

Hutchinson, J. – *Tour through the High Peak of Derbyshire* (Macclesfield: J. Wilson, 1809)

Jennings, Louis J. – *Rambles among the Hills* (London: John Murray, 1880)

Jewitt, Llewellynn – *The Ballads and Songs of Derbyshire* (London: Bemrose, 1867)

Jones, Melvyn – *The Making of the South Yorkshire Landscape* (Barnsley: Wharncliffe, 2000)

Jones, Melvyn (ed.) – *Aspects of Sheffield: Discovering Local History: Vol 1* (Barnsley: Wharncliffe, 1997)

Kingsnorth, Paul – *Beast* (London: Faber & Faber, 2016)

Leyland, John – *The Peak of Derbyshire: Its Scenery and Antiquities* (London: Seeley & Co., 1891)

McCloy, Andrew (ed.) – *Peak District Boundary Walk* (Sheffield: Friends of the Peak District, 2017)

McMeeken, Louis – *Place Names of the Peak District* (Buxton: Louis McMeeken, 1998)

Merrill, John N. – *Dark Peak Aircraft Walks* (Darley Dale: Walk & Write, 2001)

Porteous, Crichton – *Peakland* (London: Robert Hale, 1954)

Poucher, William Arthur – *The Peak and Pennines* (London: Constable, 1966)

Price, David – *Sheffield Troublemaker: Rebels and Radicals in Sheffield History* (Chichester: Phillimore, 2008)

Redfern, Roger – *Peak District Hill Country* (Wilmslow: Sigma Leisure, 1993)

Redfern, Roger – *Peak District Memories* (Wilmslow: Sigma Leisure, 1997)

Richards, Mark – *High Peak Walks* (Milnthorpe: Cicerone, 1982)

Robinson, Brian – *Walls across the Valley: The Building of the Howden and Derwent Dams* (Cromford: Scarthin, 1993)

Robinson, Brian (ed.) – *The Seven Blunders of the Peak: Some Derbyshire Legends Reassessed* (Cromford: Scarthin, 1994)

Rotherham, Ian D., & Handley, Christine (eds) – *War and Peat* (Sheffield: Wildtrack, 2013)

Rothman, Benny – *The 1932 Kinder Trespass* (Timperley: Willow, 1982)

Sadler, Geoffrey – *Foul Deeds and Suspicious Deaths in and around Chesterfield* (Barnsley: Wharncliffe, 2013)

Savage, Mick – *The Mystery of Carl Wark: Peak District Fortress or Folly?* (Sheffield: ALD Design & Print, 1999)

Sharpe, Neville T. – *Crosses of the Peak District* (Ashbourne: Landmark, 2002)

Sheldon, John – *A Short History of Baslow and Bubnell* (Baslow: S.M. Evans, 1975)

Sissons, Dave, & Smith, Roly (eds) – *Right to Roam: A Celebration of the Sheffield Campaign for Access to Moorland* (Sheffield: SCAM, 2005)

Sissons, David (ed.) – *The Best of the Sheffield Clarion Ramblers' Handbooks* (Tiverton: Halsgrove, 2002)

Sissons, David, Howard, Terry, & Smith, Roly – *Clarion Call: Sheffield's Access Pioneers* (Sheffield: Northern Creative Print Solutions, 2017)

Smith, Albert Hugh – *The Place-names of the West Riding of Yorkshire* (Cambridge: University Press, 1963)

Smith, Howard – *The Guide Stoops of the Peak District* (Ashbourne: Landmark, 2009)

Smith, Howard – *The Long Causeway* (Howard Smith, 2017)

Smith, Howard with Pyatt, Angie & , Beedham, Ann – *The Story of the Snake Road and Sheffield to Glossop Turnpike Trail* (Hunstanton: Witley Press, 2014)

Smith, Roly – *Peak District: Eastern Moors and the South* (London: Frances Lincoln, 2005)

Smith, Roly – *Peak District: Northern and Western Moors* (London: Frances Lincoln, 2005)

Smith, Roly (ed.) – *A Peak District Anthology* (London: Frances Lincoln, 2012)

Smith, Roly (ed.) – *Kinder Scout: Portrait of a Mountain* (Leicester: De Montfort Press, 2002)

Stephenson, Tom – *Forbidden Land: The Struggle for Access to Mountains and Moorland* (Manchester: University Press, 1989)

Stroud, Gill & Barrett, Dave – *Extensive Urban Survey – Derbyshire* (Swindon: English Heritage, 2009)

Taylor, Alan Faulkner – *Peakland Rockscapes* (Derby: Higham Press, 1992)

Thompson, Francis – *Chatsworth: A Short History* (London: Country Life, 1951)

Tomlinson, Tom – *Ye Ancient Parish of Habenai* (Hathersage: Valley Printers)

Toulson, Shirley – *Derbyshire: Exploring the Ancient Tracks and Mysteries of Mercia* (London: Wildwood House, 1980)

Webb, Simon – *The Suffragette Bombers* (Barnsley: Pen & Sword, 2014)

Whittow, J.B. – *Landscapes of Stone* (Bath: Bath Press, 1986)

Wigglesworth, George – *Asker Lane from Hassuk Kjarr* (Matlock: George Wigglesworth, 2011)

Wilks, John – *Walks through History: Derbyshire* (Derby: Breedon, 1999)

Wood, William – *Tales and Traditions of the High Peak* (London: Bell & Daldy, 1862)

Wood, William – *The History and Antiquities of Eyam* (Derby: Richard Keene, 1865)

Websites and Blogs

www.everythingoutdoors.co.uk
www.grough.co.uk
www.markavery.info
www.paulbesley.blog
www.stevemoxon.co.uk
www.totleyhistorygroup.org.uk
easternmoorshistoryandarchaeology.wordpress.com

INDEX / GAZETTEER

144

THE WEST YORKSHIRE WOODS

Part 1: The Calder Valley

a hand-drawn guide to walking and exploring
the woodlands in the borough of Calderdale

Christopher Goddard

THE WEST YORKSHIRE MOORS

a hand-drawn guide to walking and exploring all of the county of West Yorkshire's open access moorland

Brand new second edition with new and updated routes

Christopher Goddard

All books, as well as maps, prints and posters, are available from my website. I would also welcome your feedback, queries and any suggestions or corrections you may have.

www.christophergoddard.net